D0910962

官僚軍閥大番附

	軍閥ノ方	官僚ノ方
大關	寺内正毅	清浦奎吾
關脇	山本權兵衛	牧野伸顯
小結	田中義一	後藤新平
前頭	長谷川好道	仲小路廉
前頭	上原勇作	小松原英太郎
前頭	明石元二郎	田健二郎
前頭	島村速雄	横田國臣
前頭	加藤友三郎	安廣伴一郎
前頭	東郷平八郎	一木喜德郎
前頭	上泉德彌	山縣伊三郎

前頭	軍閥ノ方	官僚ノ方
前頭	堀内文次郎	石黒忠悳
同	井山貴	穗積陳重
同	川上景明	田中光顯
同	松村景衞	松室致
同	中村雄二	平沼騏一郎
同	由比光衛	目賀田種太郎
同	長岡外史	波多野敬直
同	財部彪	有松英義
同	奥保鞏	水野錬太郎
同	伊集院五郎	岡喜七郎
同	齋藤實	林權助
同		内田康哉

行司
三浦梧樓　伊藤巳代治　平田東助

前頭	軍閥ノ方	官僚ノ方
前頭	大谷喜久藏	古賀廉造
同	佐藤鋼次郎	金子堅太郎
同	佐藤鐵太郎	都筑馨六
同	安東貞美	末松謙澄
同	神尾光臣	柴田家門
同	秋山好古	阪谷芳郎
同	山下源太	下村宏
同	中村覺	岡田良平
同	加藤定吉	兒玉秀雄
同	入代六郎	内田嘉吉
同	村上格一	江木千之
同		勝田主計

勸進元
山縣有朋　松方正義　芳川顯正

前頭　同同（軍閥ノ方）
大島健一　柴山矢吾　楠山遜良　一戸兵衞

呼出　奴（軍閥ノ方）
肥田理吉　小松樣剛　中野清次　川島遙郎　大内富一　建部遯吾　德富蘇峰　杉山茂丸

前頭　同同（官僚ノ方）
平山成信　阿部浩　安樂兼道　圓城班

呼出　奴（官僚ノ方）
吉田奈良九　惠美臺吉　兒中籠前　杉室吉平　山岡良助　留岡幸介　松村喝　加藤勝賞　桑田熊　上杉慎吉　清愛　成信浩

新舊思想家競

<table>
<tr><th>新ノ方（進步過激家）</th><th></th><th>舊ノ方（保守穩健家）</th></tr>
<tr><td>大關　河上肇</td><td></td><td>大關　井上哲次郎</td></tr>
<tr><td>關脇　福田德三</td><td></td><td>關脇　德富蘇峰</td></tr>
<tr><td>小結　吉野作造</td><td></td><td>小結　上杉愼吉</td></tr>
<tr><td>前頭　堺利彦</td><td></td><td>前頭　筧克彦</td></tr>
<tr><td>前頭　堀江歸一</td><td></td><td>前頭　建部遯吉</td></tr>
<tr><td>前頭　谷本富</td><td></td><td>前頭　松崎藏之助</td></tr>
<tr><td>前頭　牧野英一</td><td></td><td>前頭　遠藤隆吉</td></tr>
<tr><td>前頭　美濃部達吉</td><td></td><td>前頭　戸水寛人</td></tr>
<tr><td>前頭　今井嘉幸</td><td></td><td>前頭　田中穗積</td></tr>
</table>

前頭

新ノ方		舊ノ方
市村光惠		澤柳政太郎
安部磯雄		丘淺次郎
河田嗣郎		長瀨鳳輔
田川大吉郎		姉崎正治
長谷川如是閑		小林丑三郎
大庭柯公		阪谷芳郎
山川均		三井甲之
山川菊榮		田中萃一郎
大杉榮		佐藤綱次郎
荒畑寒村		

前頭

新ノ方		舊ノ方
高畠素之		佐藤鐵太郎
細井和喜藏		福本日南
室伏高信		内田良平
木村久一		西村天囚
大山郁夫		黑岩周六
石田友治		末永節
田阪貞雄		杉中有美
布施辰治		靑柳有美
山崎今朝彌		惠美光山
吉田三市郎		

前頭

新ノ方		舊ノ方
三浦鐵太郎		中島氣鈴
向井軍治		矢島楫子
生田長江		棚島絢子
馬場孤蝶		嘉悅孝子
大場米蜂		右島一泡
高島米峰		岩崎吉平
與謝野晶子		飯島和三郎
山田わか		田中守一
丸山侃堂		淺野破凡
生方敏郎		森田俊一
久津見蕨村		江間俊三郎
鈴木文治		森田義郎

行司　三宅雪嶺　新渡戸稲造　田中王堂

勸進元　大隈重信　尾崎行雄　江木衷

War and National Reinvention

Japan in the Great War, 1914–1919

Harvard East Asian Monographs, 177

War and National Reinvention

Japan in the Great War, 1914–1919

Frederick R. Dickinson

Published by the Harvard University Asia Center
and distributed by Harvard University Press
Cambridge (Massachusetts) and London, 1999

Printed in the United States of America

The Harvard University Asia Center publishes a monograph series and, in coordination with the Fairbank Center for East Asian Research, the Korea Institute, the Reischauer Institute of Japanese Studies, and other faculties and institutes, administers research projects designed to further scholarly understanding of China, Japan, Vietnam, Korea, and other Asian countries. The Center also sponsors projects addressing multidisciplinary and regional issues in Asia.

Library of Congress Cataloging-in-Publication Data
Dickinson, Frederick R., 1961–
    War and national reinvention : Japan in the Great War,
1914–1919 / Frederick R. Dickinson.
      p. cm. -- (Harvard East Asian monographs ; 177)
    Includes bibliographical references and index.
    ISBN 0-674-94655-3 (cloth : alk. paper)
    1. World War, 1914–1918--Diplomatic history.   2. World War,
1914–1918--Japan.   3. Japan--Foreign relations--1912–1945.   I. Title.
II. Series.
     D621.J3 D53 1999
     940.3'2252--dc21   99-23508
                                        CIP
Index by the author

    ♾ Printed on acid-free paper

Last figure below indicates year of this printing
09 08 07 06 05 04 03 02 01 00

Endpaper illustrations: (*left*) "Ranking of bureaucrats and the military clique," *Aka*, August 1, 1919. On the model of broadsides announcing the ranks of wrestlers for an upcoming sumō tournament, this handbill ranks prominent Japanese bureaucrats on the right, important members of the "military clique" on the left, based on their relative influence. (*right*) "Battle of the old and new thinkers," *Aka*, July 1, 1919. Similarly, this handbill lists practitioners of the "old thought" on the left, "new thought" on the right. Reproduced courtesy of Meiji shinbun zasshi bunko, Faculty of Law, Tokyo University.

To Mary E. Hildebrand and Richard F. Dickinson

for untold sacrifices on a mission to Japan,

from which this book ultimately emanates

(not to mention its author)

Contents

Illustrations   xi

Preface   xv

Note on Japanese and Chinese Names   xix

Introduction   1

1   Imperialism in the Context of National Renovation   7

   *Japanese Diplomacy in Isolation 8/   The Primacy of Nation-
   Building 10/   Korea and Conscription in the Context of National
   Renovation 13/   Empire and Arms in the Context of National
   Renovation 14/   Oligarchic Politics in the Context of National
   Renovation 17/   Renovation on the Model of Imperial
   Germany 21/   War and the Consolidation of Empire, Arms, and
   Oligarchic Rule 24/   Peace and the Dissolution of Empire, Arms,
   and Oligarchic Rule 26/   The Taishō Contest over the Meiji
   Legacy 28/   Visions of a Taishō Renovation 31*

2   "Divine Aid" and the "Destiny of Japan":
   The Great War as Opportunity   33

   *World War I and the Quest for Empire 34/   Empire in the
   Service of Domestic Politics 58/   The Genrō Versus Prime
   Minister Ōkuma, September 1914 77/   Synopsis 80*

3   Imperialism in the Service of Democracy: Katō
    Takaaki and the Twenty-One Demands   84
    The Twenty-One Demands in International Context 85/
    The Politics of the Twenty-One Demands 93/ Synopsis 114

4   Anticipating a New Order in Asia: Yamagata Aritomo,
    Tanaka Giichi, and an Autonomous Foreign Policy   117
    The Lingering Influence of Katō Takaaki 119/ The Troublesome
    Politics of Japan's China Policy 123/ Tanaka Giichi and the Plot
    for Civil War in China 126/ Yamagata Aritomo and the Quest
    to Contain the United States 138/ The Politics of the 1916 Russo-
    Japanese Convention 148/ Synopsis 151

5   Last Chance of an Opportune War: Preempting
    Woodrow Wilson in Asia   154
    General Terauchi Masatake's Quest for National Unity 156/
    An Expansive Definition of Japanese Rights in Asia: The Nishihara
    Loans 159/ The Politics of the Nishihara Loans 164/ America
    Enters the War 175/ Revolution in Russia 179/ The Opportunity
    of Intervention in Siberia 180/ The Political Push for a
    Siberian Expedition 190/ Synopsis 200

6   Versailles in the Context of National Renovation:
    Wilson Arrives in Japan   204
    Versailles and the Challenge of a New World Order 205/ Hara
    Takashi as Symbol of Political Reform 211/ Hara Takashi as
    Conservative Reaction to Woodrow Wilson 217/ Hara Takashi,
    Yamagata Aritomo, and Defensive Preparations for Peace 223/
    The Social and Political Effects of Wilson in Japan 229/ The
    Conservative Battle to Retain the Old Order 232/ Synopsis 235

7 Conclusion   239

   *Restoring Agency to Japanese Leadership 241/ The Politics of
   National Reinvention 242/ The Great War in the Context of National Reinvention 245/ The Manchurian Incident in the Context of
   National Reinvention 247/ Reconceptualizing Japanese Leadership
   in the Twentieth Century 256*

8 Epilogue   259

Reference Matter

   Notes   263

   Bibliography   325

   Index   345

Illustrations

1   "The Yamato Princess [i.e., Japan], presiding resolutely over Asia." *Jiji shinpō*, June 13, 1914.   6

2   "European war and Japan. A windfall by the European storm! Take it Pa Okuma by all means!" (translated in original). *Tokyo Puck*, August 10, 1914. Courtesy of Shimizu Isao. The two likenesses of Premier Ōkuma and Foreign Minister Katō stand out here in the appeal to grab the fortuitous bean of the "European disturbance" and the "Far Eastern problem."   34

3   Katō Takaaki. *Jiji shinpō*, January 17, 1917.   36

4   Prince Yamagata Aritomo. "Joy—No others to divide power and glory with him since Prince Ito's death" (translated in original). *Tokyo Puck*, July 8, 1911.   40

5   Marquis Inoue Kaoru. *Tokyo Puck*, October 10, 1908.   48

6   Major General Tanaka Giichi. *Tokyo Nichinichi shinbun*, October 8, 1918.   51

7   Count Terauchi Masatake. *Jiji shinpō*, January 11, 1917.   54

8   Baron Gotō Shinpei. *Jiji shinpō*, January 14, 1917.   56

9   "A fine big game this! The bagging of it will recover popularity at home" (translated in original). *Tokyo Puck*, October 10, 1914. Foreign Minster Katō uses the spear of diplomacy to bag the World War I tiger for political purposes. Standing by are three members of his political

party, the Dōshikai, and a representative of the elder
statesmen.   58

10   "It's a game that has cost much labor. The cook should
      be careful to dress it nicely" (translated in original). *Tokyo
      Puck*, November 20, 1914. The army presents Katō with
      the fish of Qingdao, and all are eager to see what the
      foreign minister will do with it.   85

11   "The reasons why Foreign Minister [Katō] is disliked:
      because of continuing diplomatic failures? No. Because,
      with the huge pipe of war, he doesn't kowtow to the *genrō*."
      Tokyo Puck, July 1, 1915. Courtesy of Shimizu Isao.   93

12   "Now it is the time to stop the mad horse, or it may
      cause further nuisance to the neighbors" (translated in
      original). *Ōsaka Puck*, May 1, 1916, cover. Courtesy of
      Shimizu Isao. Japan in kimono tries to restrain the wild
      horse of China.   123

13   "The keystone of Asia." *Jiji shinpō*, July 2, 1916. Russia
      and Japan pound the keystone into the troublesome
      catfish below.   138

14   "After the windbag, the saber." *Ōsaka Puck*, November 1,
      1916. The transfer of power from Count Ōkuma to
      General Terauchi.   156

15   "Wilson whoipping [*sic*] Kaiser" (translated in original).
      Ōsaka Puck, June 15, 1918. Japanese caption reads, in
      part, "The American president proclaims that he must
      fight until he transforms the enemy into a genuine
      human being."   175

16   "In the Paris conference, everything looks as if to belong
      to Wilson. What will he achieve for us after all" (translated
      in original). *Ōsaka Puck*, February 15, 1919. Wilson, in
      multiple incarnations, is riding, grooming, and tending
      the League of Nations horse.   205

17   "The universal suffrage and the Minister. Hara is a fogy
      behind the time after all" (translated in original). *Ōsaka*

Puck, March 1, 1919. Courtesy of Shimizu Isao. Dressed as
a Shintō priest, Hara is reluctant to give his blessing to
the propertyless class (i.e, to give them voting rights).   217

18 "The artificial bank is leaking. The tide of the thought
washes everything before it" (translated in original). *Ōsaka
Puck*, April 1, 1919. Courtesy of Shimizu Isao. Workers
attempt to maintain the dike to keep out democracy,
national self-determination, radicalism, and socialism.   229

19 "She had been hungry, until her stomach was fill [*sic*] with
such nurishing [*sic*] stuff as the Peace Treaty, the League
of Nations, etc. She has now over eaten. Doctors, called
Japan, England, America, France and other [*sic*] seem
to be satisfied that their Goddess of Peace is well fed.
But will she ever be able to digest what she has take in?"
(translated in original). *Tokyo Puck*, October 1, 1919.
Courtesy of Shimizu Isao.   238

20 "In Germany, as the military clique loses weight through
continuing military losses, various champions of peace raise
their heads and threaten to overturn the State." *Jiji shinpō*,
September 4, 1918.   245

21 "Do the armies have to hold up by the command of Wilson?"
(translated in original). *Ōsaka Puck*, April 1, 1919. Courtesy
of Shimizu Isao. The Japanese soldier joins the defeated
German soldier here in surrendering his military hardware
to Woodrow Wilson.   247

Preface

This study sprang from an interest in U.S.-Japanese relations, which I pursued while a graduate student in the Law Faculty of Kyōto University in 1983. Seeking an understanding of the present alliance, I proposed to study its origins in the 1950s. A Japanese friend would later describe my master's thesis on the Mutual Defense Assistance Agreement of 1954 as equivalent to traditional Japanese comedy, or *rakugō*. I began with the question of why the United States and Japan agreed to establish the foundations for Japanese rearmament in 1954. And while I attempted to explain motivations in Tokyo as well as Washington, I was ultimately unable, given the paucity of resources on the Japanese side, to dispel the notion that the security relationship was simply a one-sided affair. The question of why in 1954, my friend exclaimed, was moot. The United States placed Japan at the center of its containment strategy in East Asia and the recently vanquished Japan was compelled to comply.

My attempt to create a more dynamic picture of Japanese decision making subsequently led me at Yale University to examine Japanese history and diplomacy before 1945. In particular, I decided that an exploration of the World War I period offered the best glimpse of subsequent developments in Japanese history and foreign policy. European and American scholars had, after all, long identified the Great War as the departure point for the principal political, diplomatic, social, economic, and ideological developments of the twentieth century.

My choice of the Great War turned out to be fortuitous. For no sooner had I begun my research for the present project in Tokyo in the fall of 1989 than news of the collapse of the Berlin Wall seized the headlines. As I began examining the origins of the twentieth century in Japan, I found myself living what would likely be regarded as the departure point for the twenty-first century. As I read in the archives the excitement of Japanese bureaucrats, generals, politicians, and opinion leaders at the transformation of the international order in 1919, I lived the fervor of speculation from 1989 to 1991 over the probable shape of a new post–Cold War world.

Since 1989, speculation in the United States of the likely direction of Japan, the linchpin of U.S. Cold War strategy in Asia, in the post–Cold War era has produced a cottage industry of books on the future of the alliance. As with my original project on U.S.-Japanese relations, however, the majority of these English-language studies seem to founder on their analysis of Japanese policy. Rather than capture the complexity of the debate in Tokyo over political and diplomatic change, they tend to reduce Japanese policymaking to a simple formula. Prejudiced by the record of U.S.-Japanese relations after 1945, many of these works, in particular, take for granted the willingness of Japanese statesmen to follow a U.S. lead. After all, one study argues, Japanese leaders have always been "determined to follow" the rules of the international game.[1] Meanwhile, the enduring power of memories of the Pacific War has guaranteed a starkly divergent vision of Japanese leadership and behavior in Marxist analyses in Japan and in the popular literature in the United States. Far from "followers," Japanese elites and soldiers emerge in this literature as men of enormous ambition capable of perpetrating the most heinous crimes against peace and humanity.[2]

The present study focuses upon Japan's experience in the Great War in an effort to move beyond this bifurcated vision of Japanese leadership and behavior. It also aims to identify the 1914 to 1919 years as one of three critical watersheds in the history of modern Japan. Political scientists and historians alike frequently cite the "Meiji restoration" of 1868 and the Allied occupation of Japan following the Second World War as the two great formative events in the development of modern Japan. Commentators looking to predict the direction of Japan after the end of the Cold War often seek guidance in these two periods of dramatic change. But the displacement of the feudal for a modern regime in 1868 and the experiment in social revolution through foreign occupation after the Second World War were extraordinary events that will never be duplicated. More germane to Japan's future national trajectory is an analysis of an era of momentous change sans revolution, when the Japanese debated among themselves, without the burden of an occupying force, the relative merits of a new world order.[3] Indeed, as in 1919, Japan in the post-Cold War era faces a transformation of the international arena that raises serious questions about the established national trajectory. And just as the evolution of the world order after World War I presaged the true start of the twentieth century, the end of the Cold War paves the way for the next. An examination of the war that laid the foundation for the present century, in other words, will likely yield instructive lessons for Japan in the twenty-first century.

I am indebted to several individuals and institutions for making this study possible. I am particularly grateful to James Crowley, who guided this project in its infancy and who has profoundly affected the way I view modern Japanese history. In addition to Professor Crowley, Mikiso Hane, David Titus, Mark Peattie, Walter McDougall, Christopher Szpilman, and Robert Kane read the entire manuscript at various stages of production and offered invaluable criticisms and suggestions for revision. A generous grant from the Japan–United States Educational Commission (Fulbright) greatly facilitated my research in Japan. In the United States, liberal support from the Reischauer Institute of Japanese Studies at Harvard enabled me to rework the study into its present form. At Harvard, I owe a particular debt of gratitude to Akira Iriye and Albert Craig for creating a vibrant and nurturing environment for the study of modern Japanese history and diplomacy.

I would like to extend my deep gratitude to the many people who have facilitated my research in Japan. Thanks first go to the late Kōsaka Masataka, who initially sparked my interest in history during my tour as a masters student at Kyōto University and who provided invaluable moral and intellectual support until his untimely death in 1996. Since his initial assignment as my tutor at Kyōdai in 1983, Professor Kōsaka's foremost disciple, Sako Susumu, has continued to answer my most cryptic queries about Japanese history and life. As a Fulbright scholar, I had the pleasure of working with Mitani Taichirō, who continues to share his boundless knowledge and most penetrating insights into Taishō era political and intellectual history. Itō Takashi generously donated the unpublished papers of Yamagata Aritomo and introduced me to an exciting group of young Japanese historians attending his modern Japanese history seminar at Tokyo University. Among these scholars, I owe special thanks to Suetake Yoshiya and Koike Seiichi for their help with the archival resources of the National Diet Library and Japanese Foreign Ministry, respectively. Sakai Yūkichi guided me through collections at the Center for Modern Japanese Legal and Political Documents at Tokyo University, and Shōji Jun'ichirō through the Office of War History, Japan Defense Agency. Kobayashi Michihiko became the trusted intellectual companion whose meticulous research and perceptive analysis of Japanese military strategy and diplomacy before World War I kept my enthusiasm for my own research alive. Karube Tadashi and Nakashizuka Michi donated their time and considerable skills for private instruction in the arcane language and tortuous script of Taishō era letters. Kitaoka Shin'ichi, Banno Junji, Baba Akira, Hatano Sumio, and Asada Sadao all contributed invaluable insights and sound advice on archival sources and on the problem of analyzing the interrelationship of foreign policy and domestic politics. Hatano Masaru shared his expertise on World War I era politics and diplomacy and graciously donated copies of unpublished army and navy documents in the possession of the Nihon seiji gaikōshi kenkyūkai. Itō Yukio showed genuine appreciation for my work and patiently instructed me on the complexities of Japanese political history. And Shimizu Isao proved ever willing to discuss the captivating world of Japanese political cartoons and to lend his rare personal copies of *Tokyo Puck* and *Ōsaka Puck*.

Finally, I would like to express my deep gratitude for the patience and support of my wife, Béatrice, and children, Alyssa and Ian, who had to wait much too long for Papa to come out and play. I am, of course, solely responsible for the substance and conclusions of this study.

Note on Japanese and Chinese Names

I have followed the practice of rendering Japanese and Chinese names according to local custom, surname first. All Chinese personal and place names are romanized according to the *pinyin* system.

War and National Reinvention

Japan in the Great War, 1914–1919

Introduction

... frankness as never before,
disillusions as never told in the old days,
hysterias, trench confessions,
laughter out of dead bellies.

There died a myriad,
And of the best, among them.
For an old bitch gone in the teeth,
For a botched civilization.

> —Ezra Pound, "Hugh Selwyn
> Mauberly (Life and Contacts)," 1920

The tidal wave of [democratic] world thought may destroy all order and
damage the essence of our National Polity.

> —Prime Minister General Terauchi Masatake, April 1917

The death of over nine million combatants had predictable effects on the
main protagonists of the Great War. French critic Camille Mauclair
noted that the war had "figuratively but powerfully dug a trench between
yesterday's ideas and those of today."[1] German architect Walter Gropius
lamented a world that had "come to an end."[2] And when American
doughboys began dying in the fields of Lorraine, the Yanks, as well,
grieved the abrupt end of an age of innocence, "grinding the American
Beauty roses to dust in that whore's bed," as John Dos Passos put it.[3]
U.S. participation confirmed the global reach of this principally European struggle for power. But the repercussions of this colossal conflict
spread even farther afield than the Americas. This is a study of the war in
one of those distant places: East Asia.

Imperial Japan followed her British allies into war in August 1914 by expelling German troops and warships from Asia and the Pacific. In 1917, Japanese destroyers steamed to the Mediterranean to join the hunt for German submarines. These operations were sideshows compared to the carnage of the Marne, Verdun, or the Somme. But Japan was not as invisible to the main belligerents as most major surveys of the Great War suggest.[4] Ever conscious of Japan's war potential, both sides worked to procure Japanese arms and men. And questions about Japanese war aims kept statesmen in Allied capitals ever vigilant against a separate peace between Japan and Germany. In the United States, it spurred a second wave of hysteria over a possible U.S.-Japanese war.[5]

Japan was to remain faithful to the Allies in the battle against Germany. But while French and British troops waged a desperate struggle for survival in Europe, the Japanese relished the opportunity to consolidate and expand established interests on the Asian continent. In fact, granted a free hand by the distraction of great power attention to Europe to pursue those interests at will, many Japanese statesmen operated well outside the accepted parameter of great power relations in China and anticipated the unbridled expansionism of a subsequent age. Students of the Second World War in Asia, in other words, may find some of the events described in this volume familiar. Japan did not, during the Great War, threaten to conquer all of Asia or the Western Pacific. But her armed forces did seize China's Shandong province, establish a long-term presence in the South Pacific, and most spectacularly, overrun Manchuria and Siberia. Nor was this the extent of her ambition. While the great powers were preoccupied with war on a distant continent, Japanese policymakers tried to destroy the central authority in Beijing, invade China's vital centers, and create an independent state in the Russian Far East. They pondered annexing the Chinese Republic, occupying Singapore, and waging war against the United States.

Specialists on both sides of the Pacific have highlighted many of Japan's diplomatic initiatives during the war individually in meticulously researched monographs and essays. But few authors have focused on the years 1914 to 1919 to assess the impact of the war upon Japan. Nor have Japanese historians followed their European and American counterparts in viewing the First World War as a major watershed in the twentieth century. "Japan," according to one authority, "did not really experience World War I." She did not, therefore, join the twentieth century until 1945.[6]

The Japanese did, of course, escape the human, financial, and physical costs accompanying the war in Europe. By the armistice of November 1918, Japanese war dead numbered less than two thousand, not even one percent of British fatalities at the battle of the Somme alone. Japanese reserves were not depleted but augmented during the war by the creation of new markets for Japanese arms, shipping, and textiles. And Japanese soil remained uncluttered by trenches, broken rifles, or rotting corpses. Japanese towns lack the monument to casualties in the Great War that occupies a central place in small towns in all the major belligerents. Nor has Japan ever followed its former European and American allies in designating armistice day on November 11 a national holiday.

But if Japan was spared the ravages of the Great War, she confronted, nonetheless, the same disturbing truth that faced the main belligerents: evidence that something had gone terribly wrong with the old order, that what in the nineteenth century had been viewed as progress might only have represented a "botched civilization." In 1917, President Woodrow Wilson deftly placed the United States on the winning side of momentous world change. Drawing upon America's distinction as a nation born free of old world tyranny, Wilson defined humanity's first total war as a product of that tyranny, particularly, of German militarism and imperialism. The United States, in this schema, stood for progress. It entered the war to "end all wars" to make the world "safe for democracy."

The Japanese, on the other hand, suddenly found themselves on the wrong side of global change. This was a sober moment. For Japan had been hailed in the latter part of the nineteenth century as the "pioneer of progress in the Orient" for her successful adoption of the trappings of Western civilization. By contrast, after the Allied defeat of Imperial Germany in 1918, Japanese elites discovered that they had, perhaps, followed the wrong national model. They had looked to Imperial Germany as the vanguard of modernity and had forged a state on the foundation of empire, arms, and authoritarian rule in imitation of Kaiser Wilhelm. Many of them had, in fact, viewed the outbreak of war in 1914 as an opportunity to fortify oligarchic rule against the growing momentum for democratic reform within Japan. As devastating as evidence of a failed civilization was to Allied leaders and publicists, the military defeat of the nation that had guided Japanese national development marked for many in Japan a calamity of equal magnitude. Woodrow Wilson's redefinition of the world order threatened to "destroy all order" and damage the essence of Japan's "National Polity."[7]

While this is a study of Japanese aims during the First World War, then, its implications reach beyond the specific issue of war aims. It views the impact of the war in Japan not as a simple foreign policy event but as a watershed in the much more portentous question of national identity. It seeks, therefore, not merely to elucidate patterns of Japanese foreign policy or foreign policy decision making in the twentieth century. It hopes, rather, to contribute to the study of nations and nationalism in the modern era. Since the early 1980s, this literature has stressed the "invented" or "imagined" character of national identity in the modern age. And it has unveiled a pattern of invention in such diverse realms as language, culture, and the writing of history.[8]

In the past decade, the number of studies attempting to incorporate Japan into this international dialogue on inventing traditions has grown substantially.[9] None of these analyses, however, has included foreign policy among the tools employed by modern Japan's founders and their successors in forging a modern national identity. This mirrors the general neglect of foreign policy in recent studies of nations and nationalism. But if we increasingly recognize the willful "invention" of the supposedly "traditional" symbol of the emperor in the nineteenth century, of Japanese historical analyses of neighboring China in the early twentieth century, or of images in the troubled 1930s of a pristine, communal, agricultural Japan, we must also view foreign policy goals as something more than a strategic response to external events. In fact, we may understand that Japanese elites forged a diplomatic posture largely in deference to the domestic requirements of nation-building.

Viewed as a vital component in the construction of a national identity, foreign policy becomes less the story of diplomatic negotiations than of a heated domestic debate over the national essence. I have in this study, then, relied less upon diplomatic correspondence than upon documents best suited to capture the domestic discussion: the personal papers of Japan's most powerful elites, parliamentary records, and the Japanese media. My aim is to view Japanese foreign policy as one component of the much larger enterprise preoccupying her leaders since the 1860s, the quest for national "renovation." That quest lay at the heart of the increasing volatility of domestic politics throughout the 1920s. It would, as well, be central to Japan's renewed drive for national power in the 1930s.

Fig. 1   The Yamato Princess

1 Imperialism in the Context of National Renovation

Thus, in the future, in name and in fact our country can begin to take its place among the nations of the world.

—Kido Takayoshi, 1868

Modern Japan used to begin on a hazy day in July 1853, when a commodore in the U.S. Navy, drawn to a political, economic, and social "vacuum," anchored his two steam frigates and two sloops in Uraga Bay to demand an opening to foreign intercourse.[1] Historians no longer speak of a "vacuum" in mid-nineteenth-century Japan but recognize Japanese antecedents to modern development that long predate the arrival of Commodore Perry. Some even consider the American intrusion secondary. Indigenous movements for reform, one scholar has argued, had greater "intrinsic significance" in altering the Japanese political landscape than did Perry.[2]

But Perry's "black ships" remain the predominant symbol of Japan's entrance into the modern world. And as a symbol of unsolicited violence, they sustain the image of a trying debut for modern Japan. In its most extreme form, America's intrusion justifies Japan's later history of aggression. "Haven't you ever heard of Perry?" Ishiwara Kanji challenged the American prosecutor at the International Military Tribunal for the Far East in 1946. "For its own defense (Japan) took your country as its teacher and set about learning to be aggressive. . . . Why don't you subpoena Perry from the other world and try *him* as a war criminal?"[3]

The isolation of diplomatic decision making from other concerns of state has reinforced this image of a difficult entrance into the modern world. While Marxist historians in Japan long anchored their critique of Japanese imperialism in a detailed analysis of political and economic developments within Japan, diplomatic historians, in Japan as well as the United States, have generally described Japanese diplomacy as a strategic calculation in response to external events. The consequence has been a familiar story of a Japan forever disadvantaged on the world stage.[4]

JAPANESE DIPLOMACY IN ISOLATION

The story begins with Japan's forced incorporation into the "treaty port imperialism" introduced by the great powers originally in China. Just as the British and French had compelled Beijing at gunpoint to liberalize commerce with the outer world, Perry and the first U.S. consul-general to Japan, Townsend Harris, coerced the military overlord of the Tokugawa regime (1600–1867), the shōgun, to open Japanese ports to foreign residence and commerce on disadvantageous terms. Nineteenth-century treaty port imperialism deprived both Japan and China of the basic rights of sovereignty: the ability to set one's own tariffs and to try foreign nationals in domestic courts. Most diplomatic histories and many general studies of modern Japan highlight the efforts of modern Japan's founders to rectify these "unequal" treaties as desperate attempts to remove the humiliating status thrust upon their nation.

Japan, of course, would succeed long before China in rectifying her inferior international status. In fact, not only were the unequal treaties abrogated by 1911, Japan became an imperial power in her own right. Only thirteen years after Perry compelled the shōgun at gunpoint to begin friendly intercourse, three Japanese warships sailed to Kanghwa Island to duplicate this act of extortion upon Korea.[5] Less than twenty years later, Japan defeated China and acquired an empire in Taiwan and the Pescadores Islands and preponderant influence in Korea. In 1902, Japan allied with the greatest naval power on earth, Britain, to protect her growing continental interests. The alliance enabled Japan to defeat Russia in war and to add southern Sakhalin and South Manchuria to the formal empire in 1905. Korea became a protectorate in the same year and was formally annexed in 1910. By 1919, slightly over sixty years after submitting to the unequal treaties, Japanese delegates were sitting at an international negotiating table, the Versailles Peace Conference, as one of the Big Five victors of World War I.

Overshadowing this story of Japanese achievement, however, is often a subplot of diplomatic crisis. For every account of Japanese success on the international stage, there is evidence of troubling failure. Japan may have defeated the former political, military, and cultural hegemon in Asia in 1895. But she was compelled to relinquish a portion of her spoils, Liaodong peninsula (Manchuria), by a tripartite intervention of the great powers.[6] The Japanese navy annihilated the Russian Baltic Fleet in 1905. But the Japanese public bemoaned their delegates' inability to obtain either all of Sakhalin Island or a promise of reparations from the tsar at the Portsmouth Peace Conference. Japan joined the councils of the great powers at Versailles. But she remained conspicuously silent during much of the deliberations and failed to obtain inclusion in the Covenant of the League of Nations of a "racial equality" clause that would have conferred official recognition of Japanese equality with the Western world.

In the subplot of Japanese diplomatic troubles in the twentieth century, U.S.-Japanese relations hold center stage. With the acquisition of the Philippines in the Spanish-American War in 1898, the United States, like Japan, became a major player in the great power scramble for influence in East Asia at the turn of the century. Much of the diplomatic activity in Asia from this time, then, revolved around the effort by these two budding empires to work out their respective positions in Asia. They were able to do so with some success thanks to the *realpolitik* of the Roosevelt administration.[7] But in 1909 President Taft abandoned Roosevelt's recognition of Japanese special interests in South Manchuria and hoped to "smoke Japan out" of northeast Asia.[8] President Wilson continued the confrontational posture at Versailles by challenging Japan over her principal wartime acquisition, Shandong province in China. Perhaps the most recounted story of U.S. pressure on Japan is the record of American attitudes toward Japanese immigration in the first quarter of the twentieth century. From 1906 to 1924, those attitudes spawned increasingly exclusionist measures, from enforced segregation of Japanese public school children in San Francisco to a complete ban on Japanese immigration to American shores.[9]

In the history of European imperialism, international conflict and checks upon expansionary drives are recognized as part and parcel of the imperialist game. Germany failed to take sole possession of Samoa in 1885 and 1894 because of British and U.S. resistance.[10] Superior British firepower forced French explorer Captain Marchand to withdraw from Fashoda on the Nile in 1899. Historians do not conclude by such failures that Germany and France were persecuted on the international stage. Japanese contemporaries, however, cited the Triple Intervention and the Portsmouth peace as proof of Japan's maltreatment at the hands of the great powers. And American racial politics suggest to many that the great Western powers never genuinely accepted Japan as an equal on the world stage.[11] But neither contemporary slogans nor ex post facto American guilt over the politics of race in the United States should color our understanding of the preoccupations of Japanese policymakers at the turn of the century. While Japanese statesmen kept a close watch on the volatile international arena, they were neither overwhelmed nor necessarily principally concerned by the force of external events.

THE PRIMACY OF NATION-BUILDING

Historians have attributed Japan's swift response to the Western challenge relative to the Chinese example to a superior Japanese capacity to adapt to nineteenth-century geopolitics. The classic survey of East Asia's "modern transformation" finds "predisposing factors" to "Japanese responsiveness" in the history of Japan's borrowings from the continent, its strong sense of separate identity from China, and the centripetal political tendencies of the hierarchical, feudal Japanese society.[12] But the ultimate divergence of Japanese and Chinese history in the modern age should not obscure genuine similarities in the preceding period. Among the important parallels was the place of "foreign affairs" in the larger discourse on national policy.

Studies of diplomacy in seventeenth-century China and Japan have distinguished the worldview of early modern elites in both countries by their adoption of the symbols of "the Chinese world order."[13] "Foreign policy" as described by specialists of international affairs presumes a modern conception of the state, with a clear distinction between a "domestic" and "foreign" realm. But policymakers in Qing China (1644–1911) and Tokugawa (Edo) Japan conceived of their world not in terms of "domestic" and "foreign," but as one great core of civilization. At the original home of this worldview, China, the Chinese emperor stood at the apex of an elaborate administrative hierarchy supported by Neo-Confucian ideology. Although the emperor and his advisers maintained contact with peoples living beyond their administrative control, they did not conceive of them as "foreign." They were, rather, "barbarian," simply unschooled in worldly (civilized) ways, unfamiliar, that is, with the symbols and manners of the Neo-Confucian hierarchy of the center. Intercourse with these barbarians was thought of not as negotiating with a foreign power but as part of organizing the realm.

During the Muromachi period (1338–1573), the Japanese accepted the Chinese concept of civilization by paying tribute to the Chinese emperor. But the rulers of the Tokugawa dynasty stood the Chinese world order on its head. Like the Chinese, they created a hierarchical world clothed in Neo-Confucian ideology. At the center of that world, however, stood not the Chinese emperor but the Japanese shōgun. Some historians have argued that this conscious transformation of the Chinese world order facilitated Japan's rapid metamorphosis, relative to her Asian neighbors, into a modern nation-state.[14] But despite the relocation of the center, the worldview of early modern Japanese elites remained remarkably similar to that of their Chinese counterparts. In particular, like the Qing, the Tokugawa conceived of "foreign affairs" as one aspect of organizing the realm.

Thus, the founder of the Tokugawa dynasty, Ieyasu, and his immediate successors painstakingly ordered relations with Japan's neighbors primarily to stabilize the realm in the wake of their ascension to power. As Ronald Toby has shown, tribute missions from Korea and the Ryūkyūs were a powerful means of legitimizing shōgunal authority in the first half of the seventeenth century.[15] And the ultimate political sanction that the emperor bestowed upon the shōgun was recognition of his ability to manage what the modern world would consider foreign affairs. He was granted the title of *seii tai shōgun* (barbarian-subduing generalissimo) for pacifying peoples on the periphery of the realm.

Nor were Japanese leaders in the early nineteenth century inherently more forward-looking than their Chinese counterparts. They saw

China's defeat in the Opium War, for example, not as proof of the superiority of Western organization and firepower, but rather as evidence of Chinese internal decay. Like the Manchu rulers, the Japanese perceived human civilization in organic terms, in cycles of growth and decline. Vulnerability to external attack offered the most powerful proof of internal decay. The Opium War taught modern Japan's early political activists (the so-called *shishi*, forerunners of the 1930s ultranationalists) not that they should emulate the West but that they should rejuvenate the internal order.[16]

The same can be said of Commodore Perry's sudden appearance in Uraga Bay in 1853. Perry's intrusion has led some to identify fear of foreign intrusion as the principal motive of the Satsuma and Chōshū samurai who were to topple the shōgun.[17] But to attribute the actions of these men to the threat of invasion and to characterize modern Japanese history as a "confrontation with the West" fundamentally misconstrues the relationship between domestic and foreign affairs in the history of modern Japan.[18] As they would regard the Sino- and Russo-Japanese Wars and their successors would view the First World War, these men saw in Perry not a threat, but an opportunity.[19] Satsuma and Chōshū had been enemies of the Tokugawa before the latter established political hegemony in 1600. They were two of only three large *tozama* domains that had fought on the losing side in the decisive battle of Sekigahara.[20] The inability of the shōgun in the 1850s to accomplish the primary duty of his political legitimization, to subdue the barbarians, provided ready grounds to resume the battle that had been suspended with the Tokugawa victory in 1600.[21]

By the same token, the principal concern of these men in founding a new regime was not, despite the rhetoric of *sonnō jōi* (revere the Emperor, expel the barbarian), to repel a foreign invasion.[22] It was to effect internal rejuvenation, or renovation. They dubbed their enterprise, in fact, the Meiji Renovation (*Meiji ishin*).[23] In this context, foreign relations were significant first and foremost for the bearing that they had on the primary enterprise of internal rejuvenation. In the immediate aftermath of the fall of the shōgunate, "renovation" meant consolidating a new and highly tenuous hold upon political power. In the first two decades of the Meiji era (1868–1912), modern Japan's founders formulated all policy, domestic and foreign, with a view to legitimizing their new regime. Recognizing the unifying power of the mechanisms of the modern nation-state, they proposed to do so through the modern enterprise of nation-building.

KOREA AND CONSCRIPTION IN THE CONTEXT OF NATIONAL RENOVATION

Considered in this light, key events in the history of Japanese imperialism assume a new character. The 1873 debate over a proposed invasion of Korea (*seikan ron*), for example, has long received attention as the principal point of departure for over three quarters of a century of Japanese imperialist expansion.[24] But the true significance of the controversy lies not in its relationship with later continental ventures. It deserves, rather, a prominent place in the history of Japanese nation-building.[25] Just as Tokugawa Ieyasu had looked to relations with the outer world, particularly Korea, to bestow legitimacy upon his fledgling regime, the early Meiji leadership hoped to obtain external confirmation of their new polity through a renewal of contacts with Korea.[26] The Korean king's refusal to respond to Japanese overtures represented something much more serious than the loss of potentially lucrative trade or of a national security guarantee. It marked a direct repudiation of the new regime in Tokyo. The proposed military expedition to Korea in 1873 was intended primarily, then, to avenge the national insult symbolized by Korean recalcitrance.[27]

The proposed campaign had an even more explicit internal function critical to the political legitimacy of the new regime: in the words of one of its main proponents, it was to "divert abroad the attention of those who desire civil strife."[28] Indeed, initial attempts to consolidate political control had dramatically depressed the social status of Japan's former elite, the samurai. Having lost their pensions, and their exclusive rights to possess a family name, travel on horseback, and, most important, to bear arms, many of Japan's warriors were bristling with discontent. A foreign expedition, it was hoped, would help channel this negative energy abroad. Although Japan's new leaders ultimately decided against a military venture in Korea in 1873, they did send 3,600 samurai to Taiwan the following year in the name of punishing Taiwanese aborigines for the slaughter of fifty-four Ryūkyūan fisherman.

A vital component of the early attempt to consolidate control was the creation of a conscript army. The army did, of course, ultimately become the principal arm of Japanese imperial expansion. But, just like Japanese plans for a foreign expedition, designs for a national ground force were originally formulated with the aim of building not an empire but a nation. The army's principal object at its inception was not national defense, but the cultivation and preservation of national unity.[29] It promised to serve that aim in two ways. First, it would mobilize at the behest of the central government to quash internal rebellion. This the new 46,000–man force did in the first decade of the new regime, crushing several major samurai uprisings, including the most serious threat to the new regime, the revolt of Saigō Takamori in 1877. Just as significant, from their study of the role of conscription in the unification of Prussia, the architects of national conscription in Japan viewed the creation of a conscript force as a valuable means of shattering feudal class barriers and fostering a sense of nation.[30]

EMPIRE AND ARMS IN THE CONTEXT OF NATIONAL RENOVATION

Japan's early expeditions abroad and military reforms at home were, thus, essential tools in consolidating the new regime. That process of consolidation took two decades and, by the mid-1880s, had erected the basic infrastructure of a modern nation-state: a central government, a national system of taxation, national education, universal conscription, and a nationwide network of railroads and telegraphs. Having successfully transformed a fractured feudal polity into a unified nation-state, modern Japan's founders turned in the last decade of the nineteenth century to an even greater enterprise: positioning Japan among the most advanced countries on earth. Based upon extensive travel and investigation of Europe and the United States, they identified three basic criteria of a great power: constitutional government, empire, and a strong military. From the mid-1880s to the Russo-Japanese War, then, these men transformed Japan into a constitutional monarchy and empire supported by a robust military. They did so primarily to count their new nation-state among the great powers on earth.

Constitutional monarchy had become the standard political blueprint in nineteenth-century Europe. Ironically, while it had originated as a check on arbitrary power, modern Japan's founders adopted the legal basis for monarchic rule in an effort to strengthen, not weaken, central authority. Unlike the great European nation-states, after all, Japanese feudalism was now attempting to leap into the modern era without having passed through an age of absolutism. The father of the Meiji constitution, Count Itō Hirobumi, then, spoke in the 1880s of a mission to "strengthen the authority of the ruler and make it weightier."[31]

Like her fundamental political choice, Japan's drive for empire originated in the 1880s as an essential component of the project of national self-definition. Like constitutional government, empire had become in the "age of imperialism" a critical gauge of a civilized state. Great nations vied for power based upon the size of their armies, the range of their fleets, and the sweep of their territories. Granted by the great powers the relative freedom to construct their own empire at will, modern Japan's founders looked to imperial expansion as a principal element of their quest for international power and respect.[32]

Analyses of the "age of imperialism" have long identified Social Darwinism as a driving force behind the expansionary fervor of the age. In the case of Japan, discussions of a "struggle for survival of the fittest" have convinced some that Japanese statesmen genuinely considered the Western powers "ravenous wolves" who posed an imminent threat to national security.[33] One scholar finds in Meiji foreign policy a "paranoid style" of perpetual "anxiety about Western imperialism."[34] On a more sober note, the same specialist appropriately observes that, while Japanese leaders no longer feared direct Western aggression after the 1850s, they worried about denying imperial territory in East Asia to the great Western powers. If Korea or China were to fall under Western dominion, after all, Japan would be increasingly vulnerable to Western pressure.[35]

But one should not exaggerate the concern of Japanese leaders with the strategic map of Asia in the 1880s. The Social Darwinist fervor of the latter half of the nineteenth century, in fact, spoke principally to the question of internal health, not external security. Like Charles Darwin's celebrated flora and fauna, states in late nineteenth-century international politics assumed the properties of organic matter, living cycles of growth and decay. Victory in war and imperial expansion became *the* symbols of national vigor and a guarantee for a robust future. Failure to expand, by contrast, signified national decline. Internal decay could ultimately invite foreign pressure or invasion. But Japanese statesmen in the age of imperialism, like many of their powerful Western counterparts, worried first about the nation's internal health. Failure to seize territory in Asia was worrisome not because it meant an imminent threat of Japanese international isolation but because it was evidence of a Japanese lack of vigor. Just as Theodore Roosevelt would call for annexation of the Philippines to count Americans among the "bolder and stronger" peoples on earth, leading Christian and advocate of representative government Ukita Kazutami would hail imperialism at the turn of the century as a superior path toward national strength.[36]

As in many of her Western counterparts, then, imperialism in Japan in the nineteenth century was more proactive than suggestions of a "paranoid style" indicate. The lesson of Perry was not that Japan was vulnerable to imminent destruction from without but that she was hopelessly inadequate for the modern world within. From an early stage, Japanese leaders worked actively to reconstruct their nation to compete with the great powers in the scramble for overseas territories. They brooded less about the passive enterprise of protecting the homeland than about the active bid to project Japanese power abroad. Only two years after Perry's arrival, in fact, the inspiration for many future national leaders from the Chōshū domain, Yoshida Shōin, proposed that Japan "foster national strength and conquer Manchuland, Korea, and China."[37] Japanese educator and purveyor of things Western Fukuzawa Yukichi spoke in 1882 of Japan becoming the "leader of the Asia" (*Tōyō no meishu*).[38] And Count Itō Hirobumi described Japan's principal foreign policy goal in 1889 as "manifesting abroad the dignity and power of Japan."[39] The Japanese leadership declared war against China in 1894, then, not in the name of self-defense but as an active attempt to guarantee Japan's international standing. Japanese troops occupied the Korean royal palace in July 1894 to validate Japan as the principal proponent of "world civilization" in Asia.[40]

If possession of an empire was in the latter half of the nineteenth century an essential criterion of a great power, so too was the principal tool in establishing such dominion, large ground and naval forces. Empire-building in Europe was facilitated by a revolution in military organization in the mid-nineteenth century. Railroads, compulsory military service, regionally based methods of mobilization, and a new means of command under a General Staff Office had all facilitated a transition from the relatively small-scale, static accumulation of troops that typified French military organization (the garrison) to large-scale, mobile, self-sufficient operational units combining infantry, cavalry, artillery, engineers, and supply troops perfected by Prussia (the division). After the defeat of France in the 1870 Franco-Prussian War, every state in continental Europe rushed to adopt the institutions that had facilitated the Prussian victory.[41]

Japan was no exception. Dazzled by the spectacular success of a nation even younger than their own, modern Japan's founders immediately turned from France to Germany for military advice and converted the small garrison troops of Japan's first conscript army into a large offensive force capable of projecting power beyond Japanese shores. As with their adoption of constitutional government and pursuit of empire, then, the architects of Meiji Japan created a powerful military establishment in the 1880s to seize a world trend. The Imperial Army and Navy originated not in response to an imminent threat to national security but as part of Japan's attempt to become a great power.

OLIGARCHIC POLITICS IN THE CONTEXT OF NATIONAL RENOVATION

If renovation—or to be more specific, nation-building—was the basic context within which modern Japan's founders defined their foreign policy goals, so too did it define the basic framework of politics in Imperial Japan. But whereas Japan's favorable international circumstances in the nineteenth century greatly facilitated the task of empire-building, her domestic political situation was much less advantageous. On the contrary, the attempt to forge a unified nation-state from over 270 feudal domains produced severe political tumult that would plague the new state and seriously complicate its foreign policy until its ultimate destruction in 1945. This does not conform with the usual image of Meiji era policymaking. Historians typically praise modern Japan's founders for successful accomplishments at home, while they stress the challenges faced by the same men abroad.[42] And just as scholars attribute to Meiji era statesmen a greater "responsiveness" to outside stimuli, they describe these men as much more skillful politically than their Chinese counterparts.[43]

The architects of Meiji Japan differed from Chinese statesmen in one sense. They represented a new class of leadership. While the Qing imperial line and its bureaucratic advisers continued to manage state affairs well into the twentieth century, in Japan, lower-ranking samurai from Japan's western-most domains overthrew the feudal regime (the *bakufu*) by 1868. A vigorous scholarly debate has long raged over the revolutionary nature of this political change. But the men who overthrew the Tokugawa were hardly revolutionaries. Their initial motives, in fact, represent more continuity than change. They were, as noted above, traditional enemies of the Tokugawa. And they viewed military operations against the *bakufu* as an extension of their long-time political rivalry.

Nor was the subsequent decision to create a modern nation-state entirely novel. After toppling the shōgun, these men confronted the problem of how to consolidate their own rule. They were astute enough to recognize the power of the centralizing mechanisms of a modern nation-state. But in adopting these mechanisms, the Satsuma and Chōshū samurai did not far exceed the imagination of the founders of the Tokugawa regime. Their actions were not driven by any new political philosophy or conception of the state. On the contrary, in consolidating their rule, they aimed, like their predecessors, to establish overwhelming political hegemony.

The means by which they attempted to do so, in fact, eventually proved to be much less effective than the mechanisms chosen by the Tokugawa shōguns. While both the Tokugawa and the Meiji regimes created a class system to sharpen the distinction between ruler and subject, the Tokugawa had also institutionalized an elaborate system of checks and balances to regulate competing demands within the ruling circle. Modern Japan's founders, on the other hand, failed to do so. Rather, they attempted to secure political hegemony by investing all sovereignty in the person of the emperor. The problem, as we shall see, was that the emperor did not actually rule, but was beholden to a group of advisers (initially, modern Japan's founders themselves), whose power derived largely from the informal personal relationships among themselves and the principal sovereign. The result was an endless jockeying for power among these elites. The perpetual political battles were to have a decisive effect on the diplomacy of Imperial Japan.

Contrary to the impression imparted by standard diplomatic histories of modern Japan, the principal preoccupation of Meiji Japan's founders in their first two decades of rule was not to effect a revision of the unequal treaties. Rather, they confronted a much more serious problem: how to guarantee their political hegemony over 270 some-odd feudal domains. The modern invention of the nation-state seemed to offer an attractive solution: abolish these fiefdoms. But to centralize functions that had for over 250 years been carried out by each feudal domain proved to be a formidable enterprise. Studies that stress the modernizing successes of the Meiji period generally downplay the complications that accompanied the initial effort to consolidate control.[44] But that effort took over two decades and encountered resistance in all quarters: several major samurai rebellions, hundreds of peasant uprisings, and by the 1880s, a viable political opposition movement led by samurai who were former members of the ruling circle.

Only in the late 1880s could the architects of Imperial Japan harbor any hope for their own political future. By that time they had created a regime of unprecedented centralized power guided by a new ruling class. In place of the political hegemony of the samurai under the Tokugawa, the principal prerogative of rulership went to the Japanese emperor, a handful of elder statesmen (genrō), a larger body of both hereditary and appointed peers, and a new civilian and military bureaucracy.[45]

The distinguishing feature of the new national polity created by modern Japan's founders was the centrality of the Japanese emperor. Although the imperial family had languished in relative obscurity in Kyōto for over 700 years, the samurai from Satsuma and Chōshū had deposed the shōgun in the name of a "restoration" of imperial rule. Under the Meiji constitution, all powers and prerogatives of governance—legislative, executive, and judicial—resided in the person of the emperor. While this did not mean that the emperor actually ruled, it did signify that all members of the ruling class ultimately derived their authority from their relationship to the head of state, not to any body of representative opinion. This was the principal device by which modern Japan's founders hoped to insulate themselves from the serious political turbulence that had plagued them in their first two decades of rule.

The *genrō* were the men in closest political proximity to the emperor. They had all participated in the campaign against the *bakufu* and had assumed the principal responsibility of nation-building. With only one exception, they hailed from the two domains most responsible for the fall of the feudal regime, Satsuma and Chōshū. By virtue of their status as the emperor's closest advisers, they hoped to remain the final arbiters of decision making in Imperial Japan.

Although only nine men ultimately enjoyed the appellation "elder statesman," there was a larger body of nonelected elites who derived their power from association with the *genrō* or from the possession of an imperial title. A peerage system was introduced in 1884 and over five hundred titles granted to members of the old court nobility, former heads of feudal domains (*daimyō*), and to men who had rendered meritorious service to the state. These peers wielded formal power through their influential positions in the imperial court, within the civilian bureaucracy, or through membership in the Privy Council or the Upper House of the Imperial Diet.

Since they marked the greatest proximity to the titular head of government, appointments at the imperial court went to only a handful of men most intimately connected with the inner ruling circle. The civilian bureaucracy was staffed by a small corps of professionals trained at the principal national institution of higher learning, Tokyo Imperial University, and ultimately selected through a rigorous national civil service examination. The Privy Council, originally created in 1888 to discuss Itō Hirobumi's draft constitution and composed of anywhere between twelve and twenty-four members appointed by the emperor, deliberated on foreign treaties and provided a pivotal bureaucratic check on cabinet diplomacy. Finally, the Upper House, originally convened in 1898 and consisting of 396 members, could veto any initiatives made by the elected officials in the Lower House.

Military rank was as important on the scale of political power in Imperial Japan as an imperial title or appointment. And like their titled civilian counterparts, Japan's generals and admirals wielded authority by virtue of their direct tie to the emperor. At the same time that the emperor had assumed all powers of government, he became the supreme commander of the armed forces. And legal measures instituted from 1879 to 1907 ensured service autonomy from both civilian administrators and elected officials. These included the adoption of a general staff system in 1879 and the 1907 proclamation excluding military organization, education personnel, and codes of battle from the purview of the prime minister.

The final component of the new ruling class created by modern Japan's founders was the Lower House of the Imperial Diet with 466 representatives. The considerable tax qualification for membership in this house guaranteed that Japan's first elected officials would all be local notables of conspicuous means.[46] But without the direct tie to the emperor enjoyed by their military or titled counterparts, these men, at the outset of the parliamentary system, occupied the bottom ranks of the ruling circle. Their exclusive claim to influence rested in their power of budgetary review.

RENOVATION ON THE MODEL OF IMPERIAL GERMANY

In choosing their fundamental foreign policy and domestic political institutions, then, modern Japan's founders were swayed principally by the concern for national glory and domestic political hegemony. In the name of national and personal political power, they adopted the most up-to-date conventions of nineteenth-century nation-building: empire abroad, constitutional monarchy at home. Recent studies of nation-building in modern Japan describe this incorporation of the most modern elements of nationhood as a Japanese attempt to identify with the most civilized nations on earth.[47] But if the architects of Meiji Japan aspired broadly to identify with world civilization, they recognized one nation in particular as the most appropriate model for Japan in the modern world: Imperial Germany. Just as many of their successors were to view Nazi Germany as *the* model for progressive social and political engineering in the 1930s, modern Japan's founders considered Kaiser Wilhelm's empire in the last two decades of the nineteenth century in many respects the most advanced power in the world.

The Japanese were not alone in their admiration for Imperial Germany at the close of the century. Otto von Bismarck's victory over the principal European hegemon of the age, France, in the 1870 Franco-Prussian War confirmed the Reich as the most spectacular new power on earth. Europe's great continental powers rushed to replicate German military organization and training in the wake of this success. And as many American graduate students as Japanese doctors flocked to Germany in the 1880s and 1890s to receive medical training in German universities.

But Japanese scholars and statesmen had a particular incentive to look to Berlin for inspiration. Like Japan, after all, Germany had just joined the ranks of modern nation-states, and its protectionist and state-centric policies were well-tailored for a young nation on a crash program of national unification and industrial development. While sharing the international zeal for German military organization and medical science, then, Japanese scholars and statesmen looked to Berlin, as well, for guidance in law, class (creation of a peerage), local government, police, education, philosophy, political economy, historical methodology, geology, even literature. From the mid-1880s, in particular, the nationalist, militarist, bureaucratic character of German thought and institutions replaced the more liberal tenor of British thought and practices that had defined the "civilization and enlightenment" movement of the first two decades of the Meiji era. Following the pattern of bureaucratic professionalization in Germany, Tokyo Imperial University became the official training ground for the Japanese bureaucracy in 1886, and a wave of German and German-trained professors began teaching Hegelian romanticism and Listian neo-mercantilism in place of the empiricism of John Stuart Mill and laissez faire of Adam Smith.[48]

The substitution of German for British models had the greatest repercussions in the most fundamental political and diplomatic choices made by modern Japan's founders. The resolute attempt to concentrate political power in Japan's new system of constitutional monarchy marked an explicit rejection of British parliamentarism. Councilor Ōkuma Shigenobu was ejected from the ruling circle in 1881 for advocating the immediate opening of a national assembly along British lines, and the father of the Meiji Constitution, Itō Hirobumi, spoke of the German constitutional model as an antidote to "the erroneous belief that the words of English, American, and French liberals and radicals are eternal verities."[49] In drafting the constitution, Itō followed the advice of German scholars Rudolf Gneist and Herman Roessler in defining the throne, not the parliament, as the locus of sovereignty in Imperial Japan.[50]

If the German example was uppermost in the mind of the father of the Meiji constitution, so too did it inspire the chief architect of modern Japan's imperial expansion. Meiji Japan, as we have seen, eagerly adopted the system of military organization and training that was seen to have produced the Prussian victory over France in 1871: a regionally based army corps, a General Staff Office, a General Staff College, even Prussian officers to staff the new college. In so doing, it was following a general trend in continental Europe. But it was doing much more than that. As an island nation, after all, Japan might have learned from the British promotion of naval power rather than the German emphasis on large-scale ground forces. In reorganizing Japan's small garrison troops into large-scale divisions and defining the new Imperial Army as the first line of national defense, in other words, the founder of the Imperial Japanese Army, Yamagata Aritomo, was making an explicit choice. He was rejecting the more obvious option of becoming a great maritime power on the model of Britain to become a continental empire following Imperial Germany.[51] Indeed, Prussian officers provided Japan not only with a model for military organization but, for the first time, a strategic justification for Japanese interest on the Asian continent. The Korean peninsula, Major Jacob Meckel began teaching his charges at the new Japanese War College in 1884, was a "dagger at the heart" of Japan. The control over the peninsula by a third country would threaten the security of the home islands and must, therefore, be prevented.[52]

WAR AND THE CONSOLIDATION OF EMPIRE, ARMS, AND OLIGARCHIC RULE

Imperial Japan came to resemble Imperial Germany, then, through the conscious design of her founders. And, just as the modern nation-state Germany emerged from the crucible of war, the new political and diplomatic institutions adopted by Itō Hirobumi and his associates merged into a viable national entity for the first time through military conquest. By the 1890s, as we have seen, Itō and others had created the foundations of a powerful new ruling class. They had done so largely by means of legal reform and imperial decree. But such paper proclamations did not lend automatic legitimacy to the new regime. Government appeals before 1894 for loyalty and patriotism, a prominent nationalist writer would later observe, amounted to empty theory and half-belief.[53]

Nor was the new constitutional monarchy without its structural flaws. The location of full sovereignty in the person of the emperor insulated policymakers from the popular opposition that had plagued modern Japan's founders in their first two decades of rule. But because the emperor did not actually rule, policymaking was afflicted by severe competition among those claiming to rule in the emperor's name. Disputes among the elder statesmen had plagued Meiji politics from the beginning and were resolved only by the creation of an informal balance of power, increasingly facilitated by and largely consisting in genrō alliances with other components of the ruling circle. The lack of civilian control of the armed forces guaranteed unregulated competition between the army and navy for resources. And the Diet, initially intended as a rubber stamp of official policy, wielded, from its first session, considerable influence through its command of the purse.

The steady advance of the power of the Diet was accompanied, as well, by the unexpected rise of a new force: political parties. In drafting the basic framework of government for modern Japan, the father of the Meiji constitution, Itō Hirobumi, had originally vowed that cabinets should "have no connections whatever" with any political party.[54] But from their initial creation in the 1870s by samurai excluded from the inner ruling circle, parties came to occupy a central place in the politics of Imperial Japan. By 1900, Itō recognized the importance of party organization for his own political authority and formed a political party of his own, the Rikken Seiyūkai (Constitutional Association of Political Friends).[55]

The future of the new polity created by the victors of 1868, then, was by no means certain in the early 1890s. It took an external event to deliver to the *genrō* the international respectability, national recognition, and political unity that they had craved since their initial seizure of power: war. Military victory against China in 1895 stirred the excitement of the western world. "Japan," proclaimed an American educator, "is now the most interesting country in the world. She is the pioneer of progress in the Orient."[56] The war transformed the archipelago from a chain of islands to an empire, adding Taiwan, the Pescadores Islands, and preponderant political and economic influence in Korea to the map of Imperial Japan. Military victory validated a major new investment in arms.[57] And it roused for the first time a sense of nation. The war, contemporaries observed, had changed the spirit of loyalty and patriotism from empty theory into concrete "national consciousness."[58]

The war offered, in other words, the strongest validation of the Meiji Renovation and its principal architects. As the Japanese public celebrated Japanese victories in woodblock prints and magic lantern shows, they hailed, as well, the new Japanese polity and its founders. Applause for military conquest was, by definition, applause for the new trajectory of constitutional monarchy, arms, and now, empire. And banzais for the emperor were, by definition, salvos for the new ruling class said to be acting in his behalf: the *genrō*, the armed forces, the civilian bureaucracy, and peers. Thanks to the Sino-Japanese War, Japan's founding fathers had, for the first time, forged a viable national identity clearly distinct from the two and a half centuries of Tokugawa rule. On the model of the fastest rising power in Europe, Imperial Germany, the nation had become an empire supported by a strong army and navy and directed by a hegemonic civilian and military elite.

War also had the salutary effect of containing, if only for a brief moment, the fissures that had plagued the ruling circle from the outset. In their first six parliamentary sessions, for example, Japan's new MPs contested every budget presented to them, compelling the cabinet to dissolve the Diet three times and prorogue it twice. With the outbreak of war against China, however, they rallied in enthusiastic support for the state agenda. Japan's legislators convened the Seventh Imperial Diet (October 18–22, 1894) at the embarkation point for troops poised for the continent, Hiroshima, and passed all government expenditures, including the mammoth 150 million yen war budget, without a dissenting vote.[59] War, as Robert Pollard long ago observed, bestowed immediate victory upon the oligarchy in its battle with the opposition. If, from an international perspective, the contest against China solved the question of who should rule Korea, "from the domestic point of view it decided who should rule Japan."[60]

The nationalizing and unifying effects of the Sino-Japanese War were reinforced by Japan's war against Russia in 1904. Japan's defeat this time of a Western power, and one of the world's greatest continental empires, won for her the long-coveted status of sovereign nation, equal in standing with the world's great powers. Japanese legations overseas were upgraded to embassies and, by 1911, Japan enjoyed full tariff autonomy.[61] Military operations, moreover, dramatically expanded the scope of all three components of the Meiji state: empire, arms, and oligarchic rule. Following the model of the Sino-Japanese War, the genrō directed all important operations of the war,[62] their armed forces received immediate Diet authorization for expansion, and the empire was augmented for the first time to include territory on the continent, specifically, in South Manchuria. Imperial Japan, then, was very much the product of war. The defining institutions of the Meiji state—empire, a large army and navy, and oligarchic rule—were all forged in the crucible of war and depended on international conflict for their sustenance.[63]

PEACE AND THE DISSOLUTION OF EMPIRE, ARMS, AND OLIGARCHIC RULE

If war was the principal adhesive of the Meiji state as constructed by the founding fathers, then peace was its most powerful solvent. War with China may have roused a sense of nationhood. But the subsequent peace brought renewed challenges to the genrō conception of the state. Having hoped to insulate the government from the vagaries of political parties, Itō Hirobumi was, nonetheless, compelled to allow party participation in the cabinet for the first time in 1896. The Diet authorized a doubling of the standing army and Imperial Navy immediately following the Sino-Japanese War, but the Seiyūkai and Kensei Hontō (Real Constitutional Government Party) parties resisted the increase in property taxes needed to support naval expansion. Likewise, while the public had cheered the victories against Russia, they jeered the government's inability to obtain all of Japan's demands at the peace table.[64] The jeers felled the oligarchic cabinet of General Prince Katsura Tarō and ushered in a new regime unprecedented in the relatively humble status of its members.[65] Finally, the fierce service competition from the inception of Japan's modern armed forces had been reflected even during the war in a serious lack of army-navy coordination.[66] "Wholesome thought and enterprises are fostered on the battlefield," went a contemporary saying, "while the nation's many ills are born of peace."[67]

The crisis spurred the second most influential genrō, Chōshū samurai Yamagata Aritomo, to action. Like his chief oligarchic rival, Itō Hirobumi, Yamagata had begun after the Sino-Japanese War to seek new ways of securing his political power in the face of the rapid changes in the domestic polity. But while Itō had chosen to form a political party (the Seiyūkai), Yamagata created a network of loyal supporters within the civilian and military bureaucracies. With the assassination of Itō in 1909, Yamagata became the chief power broker in Tokyo. And until the advent of the first party cabinet in 1918, the rivalry between Yamagata's faction and the Seiyūkai was a principal source of political conflict in Imperial Japan.

Following Itō's work in creating the basic foundation of the Meiji state, in 1907 Yamagata formulated a blueprint for national development that he hoped would guide national affairs for the next twenty-five years. It is symbolic of the differences in character between the two men that while Itō had authored the Meiji constitution, Yamagata's conception of the state was embodied in a Basic Plan of National Defense. Yamagata was, of course, the father of the Imperial Army. But the Basic Plan was much more than a strategic blueprint for the Imperial Japanese Army and Navy. It aimed to reinvigorate the Meiji enterprise as Yamagata envisioned it: empire, arms, and oligarchic rule, particularly, Yamagata faction supremacy. First, the plan outlined a "steady expansion" of Japan's interests in Manchuria and Korea and of the growing Japanese presence in South Asia and "the other shore of the Pacific Ocean."[68] This ongoing advance of empire was to be supported by another major augmentation of Japan's armed forces, to produce twenty-five standing divisions for the army (with a mobilization potential of twice that) and two battle fleets, each headed by eight capital warships, for the navy. Finally, the plan was to ensure the Yamagata faction political supremacy by maintaining army superiority over the navy and preventing cabinet interference in matters of national defense. Yamagata granted Japan's admirals their dream of two battle fleets but established in writing, once and for all, the army as the first line of imperial defense. And in the manner of its promulgation, the plan reinforced the Meiji legacy of steadily increasing military autonomy from civilian rule. It was drafted exclusively by the military (primarily the army establishment), presented to the emperor, and then bestowed by the emperor upon the cabinet for ratification without amendment.[69] In 1907, then, Yamagata looked ahead to a bright future of imperial expansion and military growth directed by an extra-cabinet military-bureaucratic elite loyal to himself.

The field marshal soon discovered, however, that no amount of planning for war could check the corrosive effects of peace. In the immediate aftermath of the war with Russia, the Diet approved funds for a dramatic expansion of six new army divisions and two dreadnought-class warships.[70] But following the pattern after the Sino-Japanese War, peace brought growing resistance in the Diet to unrestrained military spending. From 1908 to 1911, Japan's parliamentarians placed a cap on all such spending. And when administrative reform freed up new monies for national defense in 1911, budgetary priority shifted to the navy. Yamagata and his supporters in the army stood aghast as two successive cabinets authorized funds for naval modernization but refused to provide for the army's new peacetime target of twenty-five divisions.

THE TAISHŌ CONTEST OVER
THE MEIJI LEGACY

While a central component of Yamagata's vision for the Meiji state thus languished unfulfilled, the preeminent symbol of that state, the Meiji emperor, passed away. His death marked the end of an era, and for many subjects the advent of uncertain times. Returning from a trip to Russia, Vice Finance Minister Wakatsuki Reijirō found a Japan shrouded in black.[71] "Anxiety grew," the then minister of agriculture and commerce, Baron Makino Nobuaki, later noted, "as it hit home that a shadow was descending on an exalted age."[72] For Yamagata, whose own authority derived in part from his close relationship as personal military adviser to the deceased monarch, the blow was particularly great. The new emperor Taishō had little affection for the Chōshū elder and showed even less inclination to heed his advice.[73]

The problem of Taishō, however, transcended the particulars of human relationships. The end of Meiji amplified the battle for the era's soul. The Meiji emperor's death found Yamagata fortifying his vision of empire, arms, and oligarchic rule. Two months later, liberal journalist Ishibashi Tanzan offered a very different sense of the Meiji legacy. "A good many people may think that the defining characteristic of the Meiji period was the advance of imperialism," Ishibashi observed. "But I believe the implementation of democratic reform in all political, legal, and social systems and thought defines the greatest enterprise of that era."[74]

As if to confirm Ishibashi's sentiments, the ongoing competition between the services led to a major political crisis soon after the advent of Taishō. Appalled by two successive cabinets' challenge of the army's position as the first line of national defense, Yamagata backed a bold initiative by Minister of War Uehara Yūsaku in the fall of 1912. In response to Prime Minister Saionji's refusal to commit funds to expand the army by two divisions, Uehara tendered his resignation. When Yamagata declined to suggest a replacement, Saionji was compelled to dissolve the cabinet.

The genrō choice of a successor to Saionji expanded what had begun as an army-navy feud into a major confrontation between the genrō and the political parties. The oligarchic character of Japanese cabinets had begun to wane with Seiyūkai party president Saionji Kinmochi's assumption of the prime ministry in 1906 and 1911. But the selection to premier in 1912 of Katsura Tarō, a Yamagata protégé from Chōshū, recently appointed Lord Keeper of the Privy Seal, marked a clear reversal of the momentum toward representative government. The result was a major public uproar that, for the first time in Japanese history, brought a coalition of political parties together to destroy an oligarchic cabinet. This Taishō political crisis, as it was called, exposed the bankruptcy of the Meiji legacy of oligarchic rule less than twenty years after its formal institutionalization. The creators of that legacy and its principal political beneficiaries—the Japanese Army and civilian bureaucratic elite—would subsequently scramble, as we shall see, to restore some semblance of political power.

The Taishō political crisis was particularly disturbing in the context of dramatic political changes in China. Japanese policymakers had hoped in 1911 to mediate a settlement to the Chinese Revolution to produce in Beijing a constitutional monarchy along Japanese lines. Elder statesman Yamagata and the Imperial Army leadership attempted, as well, to use the occasion to send a fresh expedition of Japanese troops to the continent.[75] But the civilian cabinet forbade any Japanese military action in the Chinese civil war. And Tokyo lost out to the Anglo-American powers in her bid for influence over a politically transformed Beijing. Rather than heed the advice of Japan in remolding the Qing dynasty into a constitutional monarchy, Chinese general Yuan Shikai accepted the mediation of Britain and created a republic on the model of the United States. Having explicitly rejected republican rule for their own state in 1889, Japanese elites were appalled. It was, warned Terauchi Masatake, the governor general of Korea, a "serious matter for Japan's National Polity [kokutai]."[76]

Nor did the political future of the Yamagata faction or the army in the new Taishō era look bright. In response to the challenge of the parties posed by the Taishō political crisis, Yamagata and the surviving genrō chose navy admiral Yamamoto Gonnohyōe from the Satsuma domain to succeed Katsura Tarō in February 1913. But far from calming the political waters, Yamamoto stirred them to greater tumult. For he built a cabinet upon the foundation of the Seiyūkai majority in the Lower House and continued to grant budgetary priority to the navy. The admiral, moreover, pushed for civilian rule at home and in Japan's colonies.[77] And he challenged Yamagata's infusion of the civilian bureaucracy with his own followers by expanding the number of political appointees among Japan's civil servants.[78]

VISIONS OF A TAISHŌ RENOVATION

Yamamoto's challenge spurred calls for renovation, a Taishō Renovation. The Meiji Emperor was dead; Japan had entered a new age. What better chance to launch a project of internal rejuvenation on the scale of the great Meiji enterprise? In April 1914, Yamamoto was felled by a bribery scandal and a campaign by Yamagata's allies in the House of Peers against the Seiyūkai naval budget.[79] Deliberating on a successor, Yamagata urged a return to the "harmonious cooperation" that he now imagined had characterized relations within the ruling circle before the spread of "democracy" and "confusion of public sentiment" since the Taishō political crisis.[80]

More specifically, Chōshū genrō Inoue Kaoru called for a second renovation to neutralize the three principal challenges to the political supremacy of the Yamagata faction and the army: the Satsuma faction, the Seiyūkai, and the navy. To lead the charge, he nominated Count Ōkuma Shigenobu to the prime ministry. As a contemporary of the genrō from the Saga domain, Ōkuma could be expected to maintain his neutrality in the Satsuma-Chōshū feud exacerbated by Yamamoto. He had, as well, a long history of conflict with the Seiyūkai as head of the rival Kensei Hontō and had served since 1912 as chairman of the army reserves.

Ironically, however, although Yamagata and Inoue were launching a bold new bid for the Yamagata faction and army political supremacy, they could only do so in 1914 by making a tangible overture to the advocates of political reform. Ōkuma was suited to neutralize the principal political challenges to the Yamagata faction. But he also boasted impeccable credentials as an enemy of oligarchic rule. While he had participated in the toppling of the bakufu and had joined the founding members of the Meiji government, his advocacy of British parliamentarism for Japan in 1881 had led to his forced retirement from the inner ruling circle. His subsequent establishment of and long association with a political party, the Kaishintō (Reform Party, predecessor to the Kensei Hontō), had secured his reputation as a champion of representative government. Thus, while Yamagata and Inoue were urging Ōkuma to rein in the navy and diffuse the power of the Seiyūkai, the public was hailing the count's assumption of the prime ministry as a victory for "constitutional government" (*kensei*), or parliamentary politics.[81]

On the eve of war in Europe, then, Japan remained plagued by the fundamental legacy of the Meiji polity: political instability. In particular, the country was divided between two opposing political forces and their competing conceptions of the state. On the one side stood the Yamagata faction and its vision of a progressively expanding empire supported by a great investment in arms (particularly the army) and a hegemonic military and bureaucratic elite (the Yamagata faction itself). On the other side was poised a disparate group consisting of the enemies of oligarchic rule, members, particularly, of Japan's rapidly rising political parties, who pictured greater civilian uses for the national budget and envisioned an age when party cabinets would be the principal locus of decision making. Neither of these groups contested the most recent component of the Meiji state, empire. In fact, they almost universally greeted the outbreak of war in Europe in August 1914 as an opportunity to expand upon the imperial gains made by Japan in the wars against China and Russia.

There was, however, a qualitative difference in the gains sought by these men overseas. Beneath the apparent consensus on continental expansion, the heated battle for political power that had plagued Imperial Japan since its founding continued. The Great War, in other words, would amplify the fundamental foreign policy and political legacies of Meiji Japan. In foreign policy terms, it would bring dramatic new gains to the Japanese empire. In domestic politics, it would seriously exacerbate fundamental political tensions. To the great surprise of everyone, it would, as well, usher in a fundamentally new conception of domestic and foreign affairs.

2 "Divine Aid" and the "Destiny of Japan" The Great War as Opportunity

The effect of this Great War will, no doubt, surpass that of the Franco-Prussian War. Not only will it transform the map of Europe and the destiny of nations, it will decisively alter the twentieth-century stage.
— Shimazaki Tōson, August 8, 1914

Sojourning in Paris in August 1914, Japanese writer Shimazaki Tōson sensed the implications of Gavrilo Princip's assassination of Archduke Franz Ferdinand more readily, perhaps, than many of his countrymen. One week after Austria's declaration of war on Serbia, his regular source of mail over Siberia came to a halt. A day later, on August 2, Paris instituted martial law. Able-bodied men rushed to the front as civilians scrambled to secure supplies back home. Paris, Shimazaki observed, was under siege. And quite unexpectedly, he found himself reliving the experience of Emile Zola, who in *Nana* had chronicled the wild cries for a march "on to Berlin" forty-five years earlier.[1]

The outbreak of war in Europe had far less immediate effect in Tokyo than in Paris. Although stocks fell on the Tokyo exchange, and restaurants and pleasure quarters reported less than half the usual business,[2] the Japanese referred to the clash of armies in August 1914 as the "European War." Perhaps as a reflection of this relative distance, Japan's entrance into the Great War barely registers in the historiography of modern Japan. At most, diplomatic histories focus on Japan's initial bickering with her British ally on the terms of her military engagement.[3]

Often, the rancor is described as part of the decline of the Anglo-Japanese alliance.[4] More frequently, Japan's decision to enter the war is overshadowed by references to the most striking example of Japanese foreign policy at the time, Foreign Minister Katō Takaaki's 1915 negotiations with China, otherwise known as the Twenty-One Demands.[5] Rarely do scholars discuss Japanese belligerence in 1914 as part of the larger Japanese experience in World War I. Few Japanese specialists, in other words, have attempted to follow the example of students of European and American diplomacy in identifying the First World War as a major formative event in the twentieth century.[6]

But like the great powers, Japan enthusiastically entered the war expecting to attain long-established national goals. And like their European and American counterparts, Japanese leaders were surprised to find by war's end that those national goals were no longer appropriate in the drastically altered international circumstances of the postwar era. The wartime years would have a decisive impact upon Japanese politics, economy, and society. They would, as well, determine the character of the Japanese state in the twentieth century.[7]

WORLD WAR I AND THE QUEST FOR EMPIRE

Fig. 2   "European war and Japan"

Historians of modern Europe have long stressed the enthusiasm with which the major belligerents plunged into war in August 1914. At age seventy, the grandfather of the French Left, Anatole France, beseeched the French minister of war to "make me a soldier."[8] German poet Bruno Frank rejoiced: "Never was there a year like this, / . . . / It is given to us to take our stand or to strike out / Eastwards or westwards."[9] And British prime minister David Lloyd George hailed the chance to rediscover "the great peaks we had forgotten, of Honour, Duty, Patriotism, and, clad in glittering white, the great pinnacle of Sacrifice pointing like a rugged finger to Heaven."[10]

On the opposite side of the globe, Japanese leaders, men of letters, and adventurers expressed similar exhilaration. Elder statesman Marquis Inoue Kaoru hailed the "divine aid of the new Taishō era for the development of the destiny of Japan."[11] Yoshino Sakuzō, soon to gain celebrity as the preeminent champion of democracy in Japan, cheered "absolutely the most opportune moment" to advance Japan's future standing in China.[12] And continental adventurer Ioki Ryōzō praised the "awakening" of Japanese subjects from their petty political battles, worship of money, "anti-state nihilism," "naturalism," and "vulgar sensualism" and their return to "simplicity and purity."[13] Like their European counterparts, the Japanese welcomed the end of uncertainty and social conflict that had accompanied the rapid industrialization of the late nineteenth and early twentieth centuries. While the British had worried about industrial strife in Glasgow and civil war in Ireland and while French industry and agriculture had floundered in the rapidly expanding world economy, the Japanese after the Russo-Japanese War had confronted deep questions about the newly defined national essence. Military victory in 1905 had confirmed the success of the grand enterprise of nation-building embarked upon by the Satsuma and Chōshū samurai in 1868. But peace, the Chinese Revolution, and the death of the preeminent symbol of the nation-building effort, the Meiji emperor, raised serious questions about the future trajectory of the empire.

The Taishō political crisis of 1912 symbolized the growing rift in aspirations for the Japanese polity. On the one hand stood members of the established elite—elder statesmen, peers, and members of the civilian and military bureaucracies—who continued the quest for empire, arms, and oligarchic rule that had ensured them primacy of place in Japanese domestic politics. On the other hand was the most rapidly expanding chorus of voices in Imperial Japan, the party politicians, who equally valued Japanese national strength but envisioned themselves rather than their military-bureaucratic rivals as the principal guardians of the country's domestic and foreign policy aims. The Taishō political crisis marked a victory for the political parties in the ongoing battle to define the national essence. But the outbreak of war in Europe inaugurated an entirely new round of conflict. Elder statesmen, generals, and politicians alike looked to the war to validate their particular dreams for empire and national politics. First and foremost, they hoped to strengthen Japanese influence in China. Japan had, after all, catapulted to the ranks of the great powers for the first time through war and acquisition of a sphere of influence on the continent. Japanese policymakers universally greeted the outbreak of war in August 1914, then, as an opportunity to renew Japan's quest for national glory in China. The nature of that quest, however, remained open to question.

Fig. 3
Katō Takaaki

Foreign Minister Baron Katō Takaaki

The first to act upon his hopes for greater Japanese influence on the continent was Baron Katō Takaaki. Katō had assumed the head of the Ōkuma cabinet's Foreign Ministry (Kasumigaseki) after having served as Japan's minister and later ambassador to London and after three brief stints as foreign minister.[14] At the advent of the new cabinet in April 1914, he was, in other words, Japan's most experienced diplomat and a natural choice for the nation's top diplomatic post. This was particularly so since the elder statesmen had charged Ōkuma with the task of outmaneuvering the majority party in the Diet, the Seiyūkai. Katō was the president of the Seiyūkai's chief political rival, the Rikken Dōshikai (Constitutional Association of Friends; after 1916, the Kenseikai), and he could be expected to marshal his party behind the campaign to halt the momentum of the Seiyūkai.

Katō's political energy, as we shall see, would ultimately be too much for the elder statesmen, who had originally supported his candidacy. Indeed, in his capacity as foreign minister he almost single-handedly decided upon Japanese participation in the Great War. The story of the battle to define the nation in 1914, then, must begin with an analysis of the foreign policy of Katō Takaaki.

Historians have identified the distinguishing feature of Katō's diplomacy as its Anglocentrism. Indeed, Katō was Japan's preeminent Anglophile and promoter of the Anglo-Japanese alliance. He had originally traveled to Britain in 1883 at the age of twenty-two and ultimately spent twelve years in London, first as an apprentice for Mitsubishi enterprises, then as Japan's official representative to the Court of St. James. From his first visit to London, Katō marveled at the vibrancy of English society. British citizens high and low, he later reminisced, were serious and knowledgeable about public affairs, even the coachmen.[15] And he found in the British character numerous points of similarity with his own. As a youth, Katō had already demonstrated great self-confidence and a strong sense of personal responsibility. These traits were soon to distinguish him as somehow non-Japanese. En route home after his first sojourn in Britain, Katō was described by a Japanophile in Zurich as more like an "Indian prince" than a Japanese subject.[16] In his own country, Katō's outspokenness and refusal to compromise on matters of principle earned him a reputation for being "outrageously straightforward" (*baka shōjiki*) and "argumentative" (*kenka zuki*).[17] At the height of Field Marshal Yamagata's political troubles with the foreign minister, the elder statesman condemned Katō as "practically British."[18]

In the broadest sense, Yamagata was referring to Katō's proclivity to forge his own path without prior consultation with the *genrō*. More specifically, he bristled at the foreign minister's habit of briefing the *genrō* with only English-language texts of correspondence with the British in hand.[19] Critical, as well, was Katō's insistence that the diplomacy of Imperial Japan stand on the bedrock of the Anglo-Japanese alliance.

No Japanese statesman is more closely associated with the Anglo-Japanese alliance than Katō. As minister to London, he became a vocal advocate of the pact long before Japan's elder statesmen and the Foreign Ministry considered such a close relationship with the world's greatest maritime power practical.[20] And he was to insist upon the centrality of the alliance long after most decision makers in Tokyo felt the relationship had outlived its usefulness. After the Russo-Japanese War, in particular, Field Marshal Yamagata and his associates in the army had begun to look elsewhere for the best guarantor of Japan's expanding defense needs. Through the efforts of these men, Tokyo concluded three conventions with Russia between 1907 and 1912 delineating respective spheres of influence in Manchuria and Mongolia.[21] Growing frustration with British influence in central China, moreover, inspired movement toward an alliance with the power increasingly likely to challenge British hegemony in Europe, Germany.[22] In this context, Katō's swift declaration of war in August 1914 is significant not as an intensification of Anglo-Japanese tensions ultimately leading to a rupture but as a powerful reaffirmation of the alliance. At a time when Japan's most influential statesmen had begun contemplating alliances with Germany and Russia, Katō's summons for war against the kaiser "on the broad foundation of the Anglo-Japanese alliance" was remarkable.[23] At a time when sympathy for Germany and expectations of a German victory remained high in Japan, Prime Minister Ōkuma's insistence that a declaration of war was both an obligation under the Anglo-Japanese alliance and necessary "to punish German militarism" was extraordinary.[24]

If the most distinctive feature of Katō's diplomacy was its Anglocentrism, the second was its identification with the age of imperialism. In addition to being Japan's most prominent Anglophile, Katō was her consummate practitioner of imperialist diplomacy. He viewed international relations as fundamentally a clash of national interests and an international balance of power as the best guarantee of national security. The principal object of national diplomacy was the maintenance of such a balance, and Katō viewed international negotiations and alliances with states sharing similar interests as essential tools toward that end. Katō's vigorous promotion of the Anglo-Japanese alliance, then, reflected as much an attempt to affect the international balance of power as it did his reverence for the British.

For Katō and most Japanese statesmen of his generation, the critical arena of the international struggle for power was China. Since the Sino-Japanese War, the great powers had vied for special interests in China, and the principal object of Japanese diplomacy had become the acquisition and preservation of such interests for Japan. Indeed, Katō viewed the Anglo-Japanese alliance as critical primarily for its effect upon Japanese interests in China. British naval power and presence in central China offered the best guarantee against a challenge to Japan's predominant interests in the north, specifically, Manchuria.

Katō did not hesitate in this principal aim of Japanese diplomacy. Before his return from London in January 1913 to assume the Foreign

Ministry portfolio for the third time, he had discussed the importance of Japan's special interests in Manchuria with British foreign secretary Edward Grey.[25] Katō had hoped to negotiate an extension of the leases on Port Arthur (Lüshun), Dairen (Dalian), and the South Manchuria and Andong-Mukden Railways, which were to expire in ten to twenty-five years.[26] But talks had not moved beyond the conceptualization stage when new prime minister Katsura was forced to resign in February.

Katō viewed the outbreak of war in Europe, then, as an ideal opportunity to complete some unfinished business in China. And he promptly capitalized on the situation. He demanded the transfer of the German leasehold in Jiaozhou (Kiaochow) to Japan. He refused to limit the area of operation of Japanese troops to the fifty-kilometer radius around Qingdao to which German troops had been restricted. And he insisted upon Japanese occupation of the Shandong Railway. Finally, in January 1915, Katō presented Beijing with a list of items for negotiation that covered a range of interests far beyond those in Manchuria. They were to achieve notoriety as the Twenty-One Demands.

Katō's aggressive pursuit of Japanese rights has identified him with the most belligerent elements in Japanese politics.[27] And his 1915 negotiations with China regularly appear together with the Siberian Intervention of 1918 as critical steps in the eventual Japanese march to war in the 1930s.[28] But those who seek hints of Japanese behavior in the 1930s in Japanese diplomacy in 1914 and 1915 overlook the context within which the foreign minister was operating during the Great War.

Appeals for a bold initiative in China were widespread in Tokyo in August 1914. Japan's imperialist exploits in China had, after all, gained international respectability for her for the first time. But the continental momentum gained by Japan in the Sino- and Russo-Japanese Wars faltered after 1905 and even seemed on the verge of reversing. The Chinese Revolution, in particular, exposed the inferiority of Japanese influence on the continent relative to that of the grandfather of imperialist expansion in China, Britain. Like their European counterparts, then, Japanese policymakers and opinion leaders almost universally greeted the outbreak of war in Europe as an unprecedented opportunity to retrieve a sense of national glory. Those who aspired to influence diplomatic decision making showered the Ōkuma administration with proposals for a new and comprehensive relationship with Beijing.

Within this context, Katō's actions in China appear moderate. The foreign minister used all the tools of nineteenth-century imperialism at his disposal to promote Japan's standing as a great power. But, like Great Britain, which he revered as both a diplomatic and a political model, he stressed economic over territorial gain. And he consistently abided by the unwritten rules of great power competition in China. While demanding the transfer of Jiaozhou to Japan, he promised its eventual return to Beijing.[29] While refusing to confine Japanese troops to the German concession area, he sought initial permission from China to land those troops. And while he ultimately insisted upon the occupation of the entire Shandong Railway, it was not without an initial effort to restrain those troops east of Weixian.

Fig. 4
Prince
Yamagata Aritomo

Elder Statesman Prince Yamagata Aritomo

If in foreign policy terms Katō identified with Britain—remaining loyal to the Anglo-Japanese alliance and faithful to the established rules of great power competition in China since the Sino-Japanese War—few of his domestic rivals for power in 1914 were similarly inclined. In their enthusiasm for the opportunity presented by war in Europe, these men were every bit Katō's equal. But they went well beyond the foreign minister in their zeal to forge an entirely new relationship with China. If one seeks hints of Japanese behavior in the 1930s in the First World War, it is to the worldview of these men that one should turn.

Most influential among this group was Field Marshal Yamagata Aritomo. Yamagata was the most powerful of the four remaining founders of Meiji Japan who enjoyed the appellation "elder statesman" in 1914.[30] He was the father of the Imperial Japanese Army, architect of Imperial

Japan's system of local government, twice prime minister, and president of the Privy Council. After the Sino-Japanese War, he had, in opposition to rival oligarch Itō Hirobumi's creation of a political party, actively begun building an independent base of power by stacking the civilian and military bureaucracies with his supporters. With the death of Itō in 1909, this "Yamagata faction" had become the most powerful political force in Imperial Japan, giving its patriarch a decisive voice in the formation of each new government, if not in day-to-day policymaking. Having played a critical role in Japan's acquisition of an empire, the field marshal, moreover, took particular interest in the nation's foreign affairs.[31] At a time of international crisis such as war, he expected to wield a commanding voice in the formulation of Japanese war aims. He was, indeed, the first to speak in the genrō-cabinet conference convened on August 8 to deliberate on the cabinet decision for war.

Yamagata has, in recent years, become increasingly identified as a leading voice of moderation in nineteenth- and early twentieth-century Japanese politics and diplomacy.[32] According to one study, this prudence was manifest in all aspects of his life. As a youth in the Chōshū domain, he refused to join his fellow patriots in sampling the delicate meat of the poisonous blowfish, preferring, instead, to prepare the safer red snapper in a separate pot. As a leading power broker, he insisted upon dealing with the Diet with as little confrontation as possible.[33] Above all, Yamagata now embodies the faith in great power cooperation said to be shared by the architects of the Meiji state, who had been chastened by the experience of weakness vis-à-vis western imperialism.[34] In this regard, he is regularly distinguished from younger members of the army leadership, such as Tanaka Giichi and Akashi Motojirō, who appear as far more aggressive champions of army and imperial interests.[35]

The assessment is a bit surprising given that for over a quarter of a century, Yamagata, more than any other individual, was identified in both English- and Japanese-language scholarship as the "evil genius" behind Japanese militarism.[36] But it is even more astonishing given Yamagata's reputation among his contemporaries. Not only was the Chōshū genrō reviled during his lifetime by politicians and the media as the most stubborn remnant of oligarchic rule, but even his fellow elder statesmen, and policymakers such as Hara Takashi with whom he ultimately found much common ground, discovered in him a penchant for scheming. Hara described the field marshal as an "untrustworthy" man whose "words contradict his heart."[37] And fellow *genrō* Inoue Kaoru and Matsukata Masayoshi complained more than once of Yamagata's penchant for playing politics for his own personal gain.[38] Yamagata's temper was legendary. Even Emperor Meiji, with whom he had a close relationship, described the field marshal as his adviser with the shortest fuse.[39] And Chōshū subordinate Terauchi Masatake, notorious himself for his stern disposition, noted that Yamagata could not rest without giving his subordinates a good scolding at least once a day.[40] By the end of his life, Yamagata apparently came to have serious doubts about his own character. One day before his death in 1922, he warned his closest subordinate, Tanaka Giichi, that "as one gains prominence, people stop criticizing one's mistakes and flaws, and one ceases to listen to others. This is a terrible thing."[41]

Far from the scheming, hot-tempered guardian of conservatism described by contemporaries, historians now generally consider Yamagata the last even keel of the heady nation-building days of the Meiji reign. By way of demonstration, they cite his frequent appeals for cooperation with the great powers. In April 1915, for example, the elder statesman reminded Foreign Minister Katō of the "caution upon caution" exhibited vis-à-vis the great powers by his predecessors at the Foreign Ministry, Itō Hirobumi and Inoue Kaoru.[42] But such habitual pleas aside, serious attention to the substance of Yamagata's strategic thinking reveals a vision of international affairs decidedly less circumspect than that of his greatest political rival. Although Katō Takaaki placed supreme faith in the Anglo-Japanese alliance and worked well within the bounds of great power cooperation in China, Yamagata had early on lost confidence in the capacity of the alliance to protect Japanese imperial interests. Nor did he believe in any limits to those interests.

Yamagata had supported the Anglo-Japanese alliance at its outset and continued to urge positive relations with the British. In the August 8, 1914, genrō-cabinet conference to deliberate on the cabinet decision for war, he stressed continued fidelity to the alliance.[43] But it was clear at an early date that, for Yamagata, the association was merely a temporary expedient that, after the Russo-Japanese War, had largely outlived its usefulness. In the war against the tsar, formal ties with Britain had both pre-

cluded France from coming to her ally's aid and facilitated Japan's effort
to finance the war on the London market. But after Japan's defeat of
Russia, a new challenge loomed over the horizon. From 1905 to 1911,
American financial interests attempted to penetrate Japan's sphere of influence in South Manchuria.[44] Against this sally, Yamagata and his associates determined stronger ties with Russia to be the best riposte. Like
Japan, after all, Russia had a direct stake and physical presence in Manchuria. Between 1907 and 1912, then, Tokyo concluded three conventions
with St. Petersburg delineating respective spheres of influence in Manchuria and Mongolia.[45]

But relations with Britain appeared increasingly less helpful, as well, in
the context of a dramatic escalation of continental aims. Japan's stunning
victories against China and Russia not only roused a sense of nation, they
stirred in some quarters visions of an unlimited surge of Japanese power.
While Katō Takaaki hoped to maximize Japanese influence in China
within the parameters of the traditional balance of power in Asia, after
the Russo-Japanese War, Yamagata increasingly looked to Japanese continental expansion as an all-or-nothing proposition.

Nowhere is this more evident than in the field marshal's frequent references to an impending race war. Although Katō made foreign policy
decisions based upon a sober assessment of the international balance of
power, Yamagata viewed the world in the volatile terms of race. That the
field marshal's first contact with men of another race had occurred on the
battlefield might help to explain his apocalyptic vision of a future battle
between the "colored" and "white" races.[46] But, remarkably, that vision
only intensified as Japan increasingly demonstrated her fraternity with
the West by adopting the norms of Western imperialism. By 1914, Japan
had defeated China, joined the great powers to suppress the Boxer
Uprising in Beijing, and allied with the greatest naval power on earth,
Britain. Yet at the outbreak of war in Europe, while Katō spoke of eradi-
cating the German presence from Asia and strengthening the Anglo-
Japanese alliance, Yamagata described a racial conflict in which Japan
could count upon only one policy for survival: improved ties with China.

The "race war" in Europe, explained the field marshal in the August 8
genrō-cabinet conference, was a battle between the Germanic race and the
Slavs, with the "Latin race" weighing in on the side of the latter. Britain's

role in the contest, he granted, seemed anomalous. But the British openly discriminated against the Indian residents of South Africa and Canada, just as Americans increasingly persecuted Japanese on American soil. The trend would "ultimately lead to a contest between the yellow and white races."[47]

It was the Chinese, then, with whom Japan should be working to prepare for the eventual battle against the white race. Yamagata proposed approaching Chinese president Yuan Shikai directly to inform him of "the world trend of racial strife." Yuan must be convinced, he argued, that the security of Asia hinged upon the "mutual dependence and help" between Japan and China.[48] Japan and China, after all, were the only two independent countries of Asia and shared the "same color and culture" (dōshoku katsu dōbun).[49] In a memorandum presented to the foreign, finance, and prime ministers soon after the August 15 dispatch of an ultimatum to Germany, the field marshal called for a comprehensive agreement in which China would develop an "inseparable spirit [kyōdō itchi no seishin] with Japan." Specifically, she would both "trust" Japan politically and accede to "mutual reliance" in economic matters. Yamagata hoped that Beijing would consult Tokyo on all political and economic problems involving foreign countries.[50] Indeed, in the August 14 genrō-cabinet conference called to approve an ultimatum to Germany, the field marshal had urged Katō to take care of the situation "with the pretension of being the foreign minister jointly of Imperial Japan and China."[51]

By 1914, in other words, Yamagata's proclamations on China had begun to echo the language used to define Japan's relations with Korea only a decade earlier. The stipulation that the native government accede to Japanese leadership in foreign affairs, after all, had been central to the Japan-Korea Conventions of 1904 and 1905 that paved the way for a Japanese protectorate in Seoul.[52] In this context, Britain could not only not provide assistance, she stood as the principal obstacle to Japanese expansion. Britain, after all, boasted the most powerful foreign presence south of the Great Wall. Yamagata began looking beyond the alliance, then, as soon as the fertile ground of the Yangzi valley appeared within reach. It was not a long transition. Less than two years after Japan had acquired a sphere of influence in South Manchuria, the field marshal defined Japan's best military strategy on the continent as an expansion not northward in Manchuria but southward into central China.[53] At the same time, he betrayed less than full confidence in Britain in his insistence that "the empire will pursue national defense on its own strength. It is not, by any means, something that we will rely on an ally for."[54]

Identification of Britain as the main obstacle to Japanese expansion in China inspired some of Japan's most influential military-bureaucratic elites after the Russo-Japanese War to consider an alliance with London's fastest-rising enemy in Europe, Germany. Chōshū elder Katsura Tarō had, for example, traveled to Moscow in July 1912 to begin secret negotiations with German representatives on an alliance intended to "topple British (political and economic) hegemony" in Turkey, India, and China.[55] Yamagata protégé Tanaka Giichi likewise urged a political alliance with Germany in May 1914.[56] Although there is no evidence that Yamagata promoted this enterprise, his reaction to the cabinet decision for war against Germany in 1914 betrayed a clear bias for Germany at the expense of Japan's formal ally. He viewed news of the Ōkuma cabinet's decision for war, in fact, as a confusion of priorities. Although it was natural for Japan to act on behalf of her ally, Japan, he warned Kato at the August 8 genrō-cabinet meeting, "should not forget that Germany too is a friendly power."[57] Besides, the probable outcome of the war was far from certain. Although Berlin was "clearly disadvantaged" numerically, German troops were likely to advance to Paris and "capture the heart of France."[58] In that event, Yamagata later mused, "I would like to see (British Foreign Secretary Edward) Grey's face."[59] And in a prediction that proved to be wide off the mark, the field marshal proclaimed at the genrō-cabinet meeting that even if the French were victorious, "it will not bring the end of Imperial Germany." To declare war without properly manifesting Japan's faith and sincerity toward the kaiser was "absolutely inappropriate."[60]

Yamagata's inclination toward Germany over Britain continued even as Japan actively engaged in the fight against the kaiser. As 2,800 British and 29,000 Japanese troops joined hands in the siege of Qingdao, he and his fellow genrō confronted Prime Minister Ōkuma about "Britain's oppression of our interests in southern China."[61] And in July 1915, the field marshal lamented the decline of pro-Japanese attitudes in the British government and popular sentiment.[62] Nor did British military prowess impress the elder statesman. As if fighting for someone else's sake rather than for their own interests, the British Army, he observed in July 1915, "does not work enough."[63] In February 1915 he gave Japan's allies only a 40 percent chance of defeating the Central Powers.[64] And in pressing for a Russo-Japanese alliance, he echoed the connection between stronger ties with St. Petersburg and those with Berlin voiced by early promoters of a German-Japanese pact. Detecting the rise of a "pro-German faction" in Russia in the summer of 1915, he championed a Russo-Japanese alliance, in part, to pave the way for "Japanese-German friendship."[65] "It is not Britain from which we should be learning," Yamagata ultimately believed, "but, in the future, at least for the next few years, Germany."[66]

A closer inspection of the field marshal's August 8 appeal to remain "faithful" to the Anglo-Japanese alliance, then, confirms not an enduring deference to Britain but unwavering respect for London's mortal enemy, Germany. It was important to stress the Anglo-Japanese alliance, the field marshal explained to the cabinet, in order to demonstrate to "our friend Germany" that Japan was taking up arms only because of an obligation to Britain.[67] Likewise, combined operations with Britain in China were absolutely necessary "to show that [Japan] is acting reluctantly [in declaring war against the kaiser]."[68] They would, moreover, prevent Japan from being singled out for criticism "when the problem of a violation of [Chinese] neutrality arises."[69]

Nor should we be misled by Yamagata's periodic pleas for prudence in Japan's relations with the great powers. Such appeals emerge from this context of an all-or-nothing proposition in China, which, far from representing caution, as we see here, steered Yamagata and his associates into the arms of the supposed enemy, Germany. In his entreaties regarding the great powers, the field marshal may have been referring to diplomatic means, but by no means did he accurately reflect his own ends. In fact, we may interpret his call for prudence to indicate personal recognition of the drastic nature of his own aims. Well aware that his goals would raise eyebrows in the West, Yamagata urged caution in their pursuit. To think of Japan now as equivalent in international stature to Britain and thereby abandon the country's traditional circumspection vis-à-vis the great powers, he warned in April, smacked of overconfidence.[70] And zealous pronouncements of race, he had stressed in August 1914, would undoubtedly "harm the sympathies" of the great powers.[71] But the fundamental object remained. Pursue an "inseparable spirit" between Japan and China in anticipation of a future race war, the elder statesman urged. But do so quietly, without causing undue alarm in the West. That Yamagata did not sense a fundamental incompatibility in these aims places him together with Prime Minister Konoe Fumimaro, who in July 1941 would not recognize the incongruity of occupying southern Indochina while continuing peace negotiations with the United States.

Nor does the field marshal differ fundamentally from the foreign minister of the second Konoe cabinet (July 1940–July 1941), Matsuoka Yōsuke, on the principal challenge to an autonomous Japanese diplomacy. Initial dreams of expansion south of the Great Wall had identified Britain as Japan's greatest obstacle. But the recent rapid ascent of the United States to the position of a world power, with growing interests in Asia, placed Washington uppermost in the minds of many in Tokyo as the greatest potential challenge to Imperial Japan. The United States had, after all, offered the stiffest resistance to Japanese penetration of its most coveted territory in China, South Manchuria. Britain's preoccupation with Europe with the outbreak of war naturally amplified this shift of focus to the United States. American actions, Yamagata's August 1914 memorandum to the cabinet declared, were the "most important" consideration in Japan's China policy. The United States was affluent, and her trade with China had grown remarkably. As a spectator to the great European disturbance, America would not only not be adversely affected by the war, she could possibly seize a "monopoly on the prize" of China. The Chinese government had doubted Japan's real intentions and had long looked to the United States to restrain Japan. If Japan continued to inspire Chinese doubts, Yamagata warned, Beijing would turn even more to the United States. The United States, in turn, would likely take advantage of the opportunity to further expand her influence in China.[72]

Like Matsuoka Yōsuke on the eve of the Pacific War, Yamagata's ideas for an autonomous and expansive Japanese diplomacy in opposition to American power, as we shall see, materialized over the course of the Great War. Like the future foreign minister's Tripartite Pact with Germany and Italy and Neutrality Pact with the Soviet Union, Yamagata's promotion of the Fourth Russo-Japanese Convention in 1916, the Sino-Japanese Military Agreement, and an expedition of troops to Siberia in 1918 was intended, in part, to strengthen Japan's position vis-à-vis the United States.

These initiatives contrasted sharply with the Anglocentrism and limited vision of Japanese power held by Katō. But Yamagata's worldview was by no means rare among Japan's chief decision makers in 1914. Members of the military-bureaucratic elite, in particular, shared Yamagata's casual regard for the Anglo-Japanese alliance, his idea of vast Japanese power based upon a racial understanding of the world, and his fear of the United States as the main spoiler of Japanese dreams.

Fig. 5
Marquis
Inoue Kaoru

Elder Statesman Marquis Inoue Kaoru

The second most influential of the four remaining elder statesmen, Marquis Inoue Kaoru, also took an active interest in the outbreak of hostilities in Europe. Like Yamagata, Inoue hailed from the Chōshū domain and had played a critical role in shaping the new Meiji state. As a student of Western learning and with strong connections with the Mitsui family,[73] he specialized in diplomacy and financial affairs. In 1876, he acted as deputy minister extraordinary in Japan's successful attempt to "open" Korea on the model of Commodore Perry. As foreign minister from 1879 to 1887, he attempted to negotiate a revision of Japan's unequal treaties with the great powers, in the process bringing to downtown Tokyo a two-story brick Italianate mansion (the Rokumeikan), where Western banquets and balls aimed to highlight Japan's grasp of the conventions of "civilization." After his retirement from active politics in 1898, he remained an influential voice in *genrō* councils, most recently serving as the main sponsor of the Ōkuma cabinet.

Given his special interest in the nation's diplomacy, Inoue was particularly sensitive to the opportunity presented by the war in Europe. He hailed the event, as we have seen, as "divine aid" for the development of the "destiny of Japan."[74] And like many of his contemporaries, his idea for Japan's national "destiny" included both a distinct domestic political and foreign policy component. Despite his failing health, Inoue seized the opportunity of the war to promote both elements of his vision for the Japanese nation.

In foreign policy terms, Inoue joined the spirited applause for a chance to "establish Japanese interests in Asia."[75] But like Yamagata and unlike Foreign Minister Katō, he hoped to pursue those interests outside the narrow framework of the Anglo-Japanese alliance. In fact, while Yamagata had initially supported the alliance, Inoue, along with fellow *genrō* Itō Hirobumi, had counted himself among the original promoters of an alliance with Russia. From the beginning of the century, he had leaned not toward Britain, but toward Russia and France. His preference for consolidating Japanese continental interests through territorial agreements with Russia had found expression in Japan's series of conventions with the tsar after the Russo-Japanese War. And from the time of the Chinese Revolution, he had attempted to found a Franco-Japanese Bank that would use French financial resources to fund Japanese railroads in China.[76]

Inoue's diplomatic preferences did not change with the outbreak of war in Europe. Unable because of failing health to attend the August 8 *genrō*-cabinet conference convened to deliberate on the cabinet decision for war, he submitted a memorandum to the prime minister and Field Marshal Yamagata reiterating his aspirations for closer relations with Paris and St. Petersburg. Tokyo, the marquis repeated, should rely upon French financial power to expand her continental interests. And he hoped to transform the mere "paper agreement" with Russia into something more "concrete and substantial," namely, into a military alliance. Inoue's renewed affinity for France and Russia was due in part to recent invitations from these two powers for stronger ties. And the marquis continued to press for closer relations with both powers within the existing Anglo-Japanese alliance structure. But his growing exasperation with Britain was evident. He described recent British attitudes toward the Anglo-Japanese alliance as "cool" and expressed hope that the war would grant Japan the means to seek British "repentance."[77]

Like Yamagata, Inoue's diplomatic aims were informed fundamentally by a racial conception of the world order. For him, Japan entered the war to "completely eradicate the Euro-American trends that have isolated Japan in recent years."[78] His appeals for alliances with both Russia and France, then, were less positive expressions of a basic compatibility of interests with those powers than defensive formulations in anticipation of future racial conflict. An Allied victory, the marquis feared, would yield a "white alliance" in the postwar era. The Anglo-Japanese alliance would not, apparently, provide any security against Japanese isolation after the war. Rather, the more intense the conflict, the greater London's ability to "shackle" the other great powers with her own agenda. Vanquished Germany, moreover, would resent Japan and neutral America would remain suspicious of Tokyo. Closer ties with France and Russia, then, would help prevent the "natural" rise of a "white alliance" in the postwar era and guarantee an influential Japanese voice at a peace conference.[79]

Like Yamagata, however, Inoue considered the best defense against a "white alliance" to be closer relations with China. He stressed the importance of appropriate Japanese ambassadors to Britain, France, and Russia but insisted that above all, Japan's future lay with increasing solidarity with Beijing. To promote that solidarity and to win the "admiration" of Chinese president Yuan Shikai, Inoue urged Foreign Minister Katō to dispatch a high-level emissary to Beijing.[80] The special ambassador was to negotiate a comprehensive settlement of Japanese rights in China. He was also to "place Yuan in our pocket."[81]

If a "white alliance" was the greatest challenge that Japan would face with an Allied victory, American strength posed particular difficulties in the event of an Allied defeat. Because of their increasing activity in China in recent years, the United States and Germany, Inoue apprised personal secretary Mochizuki Kotarō, would undoubtedly come to a secret accord during the war. And their "surreptitious activities" in China would escalate in the future. Alliances with France and Russia also aimed, then, to prevent further expansion of German and American power in China.[82]

Fig. 6
Major General
Tanaka Giichi

Major General Tanaka Giichi

Inoue offered his policy recommendations in the summer and fall of 1914, at a time of rapidly declining health. At seventy-nine, he found it increasingly difficult to make the long trip from his home in Okitsu (Shizuoka prefecture) to Tokyo to participate in the highest councils of decision making. He was to suffer steadily decreasing influence upon national affairs, then, until his death in September 1915.

As the oldest statesman from the former Chōshū domain was forced to withdraw from public life, however, one of the former fief's most enterprising young lieutenants, the third in command in the Yamagata faction, Major General Tanaka Giichi, began a conspicuous ascent. Tanaka is best remembered in English-language scholarship as president of the Seiyūkai and prime minister in the latter half of the 1920s.[83] The International Military Tribunal for the Far East in 1948, after all, identified the assassination of Manchurian warlord Zhang Zuolin under Tanaka's watch in 1928 as the opening act in Japan's "conspiracy" to commit crimes against peace.

But Tanaka had a decidedly greater impact upon the history of modern Japan before becoming prime minister. Coming off a brilliant stint of operational planning as an army staff officer at Imperial Headquarters during the Russo-Japanese War, he authored the main draft of the 1907 Basic Plan of National Defense, which was, as we have seen, Yamagata's attempt to define the character of the state for the next twenty-five years. His subsequent service as chief of the Military Affairs Bureau of the War Ministry and vice chief of the Army General Staff catapulted him to the center of army and national policymaking. It also involved him in schemes for domestic reform and continental expansion that were, in the end, to set the standard for army behavior in the 1930s. Those who seek a link between Japanese aims in the 1910s and the 1930s should take particular interest in the policies and actions of then major general Tanaka.

In foreign policy terms, Tanaka, like Yamagata, had expressed an early interest in reorienting Japanese allegiances from Britain to Russia. In an influential memorandum on Japanese defense policy drafted soon after the end of the Russo-Japanese War, he had urged policymakers to take advantage of the "amorous glances" cast toward Tokyo by St. Petersburg since the end of the war.[84] The result, as we have seen, was a series of three conventions with the tsar concerning Japan's interests in Manchuria and Mongolia. Had Tanaka had his way, a Russo-Japanese alliance would have superseded Japan's ties with Britain soon after the 1905 war and given Japan the opportunity to divide up Britain's possessions in Asia with St. Petersburg.[85] In May 1914, he even proposed a political alliance with Britain's most troublesome rival in Europe, Germany.[86]

Japanese policymakers did not, of course, pursue either a partition of British assets or a German-Japanese alliance. Indeed, like his mentor Yamagata, Tanaka realized that the advantages in China to be derived from an agreement with a third party were necessarily limited. Like Yamagata and Inoue, he hoped to establish Japanese interests in China primarily upon a bilateral basis. Like the two elder statesmen, he held at the center of his worldview a vision of "intimate" Sino-Japanese cooperation based upon the probability of a future race war and sought extraordinary Japanese command in China.[87] And like these two men, Tanaka viewed war as an ideal opportunity to develop such a relationship. The European conflict, he informed General Terauchi on August 12, offered "a one in a million chance" to "resolve" the problem of Sino-Japanese relations.[88]

Tanaka officially unveiled the details of his solution to the "problem" in a letter to War Minister Oka Ichinosuke in the same month. Japan, he advised, should assist with Chinese military reform and commercial development and help prevent and suppress "revolutionary disturbances." For her part, China would consult with Japan on all diplomatic matters and recognize Japan's special relationship with South Manchuria and Eastern Inner Mongolia.[89] Tanaka called for a comprehensive Sino-Japanese agreement that would grant Tokyo landownership and commercial rights and preferred rights for resource and transportation development in these two areas, plus a ninety-nine-year lease on the Guandong concession. It would permit "fortifications and other defensive facilities against countries other than China" in the region and offer Japan complete management rights for all five major railways in Manchuria and Mongolia.[90]

Katō Takaaki was, as we shall see, to promote many of these items himself in his negotiations with China in 1915. But, like Yamagata and Inoue, Tanaka hoped for much more than the fortification of existing interests that Katō was to request. Tanaka, in fact, went further even than the two elder statesmen in his recommendations for action in August 1914. If Yamagata had envisioned Japanese responsibility for Chinese foreign policy and Inoue had suggested placing Yuan in Japan's "pocket," Tanaka appealed for Yuan's elimination.[91] It was Yuan's rise to power, after all, that had wrecked Japanese plans for a constitutional monarchy in China after the 1911 revolution. "We are ridiculed by Britain," Tanaka informed mentor Terauchi, "and the main instigator is Yuan Shikai. . . . We must be prepared to get rid of Yuan."[92]

Tanaka's plans for battle against Germany, then, paid little heed either to Yuan as Chinese sovereign or China as a sovereign state. "When there is a danger of procrastinating and missing a good chance," he informed War Minister Oka, "we must prepare even for a great assault."[93] The army, he advised, should mobilize two divisions and ready another to cover all contingencies in Jiaozhou, Tianjin, Hankou, and Nanjing in the battle against the kaiser.[94] The army had tried but failed at the time of the Chinese Revolution to establish a preponderant Japanese influence and military presence on the mainland. Tanaka now looked to the European War as a second chance.

Tanaka exceeded the recommendations of the two Chōshū senior statesmen, as well, in his suggestions for the greatest potential challenge to expanded Japanese activities on the continent. Like Yamagata, he identified the United States as the principal threat. But far from recoiling from that threat, Tanaka proposed to engage it head on. Two months after the outbreak of war in Europe, a Commander Mizuno Hironori of the Imperial Navy was disciplined for publishing, without authorization, a book describing Japan's defeat in a war with the United States.[95] By contrast, Tanaka viewed the outbreak of war in Europe as an ideal chance both to establish an overwhelming Japanese military presence in China and to prepare for a military confrontation against Washington. In a September 2 letter to Inoue, he argued that military aid to Russia and support for the Allied battle against Germany would give Japan the leverage needed to "take on" the United States after the war. The problem was that, regardless of the outcome of the war in Europe, Russia, Germany, Britain, and France would reach a state of exhaustion while the United States alone would augment its strength and "extend its power to China." Tanaka hoped to implement the "empire's plan" for China "even if it comes to opening hostilities with the U. S." In fact, he argued, "if we cannot avoid a collision with the United States at some point, this is the best opportunity for the empire." Japan was at its greatest advantage while the Panama Canal had not begun operations and while the United States lacked troop strength. Until Japan could throw around her financial weight like the European powers, she would have to secure influence by force.[96]

The distinction made in recent years between Tanaka and the patriarch of the army establishment, Yamagata Aritomo, then, is supported by the historical record. Indeed, Yamagata strongly objected to the campaign to depose Yuan Shikai.[97] And in the context of Tanaka's recommendation to immediately engage the United States in battle, the field marshal unquestionably emerges as a voice of caution. But in light of Yamagata's own recommendations to offer China prior advice on all political and economic matters involving third parties in anticipation of an eventual "racial war" against the United States, the distinction is hardly worth stressing. Yamagata's apocalyptic vision of the world order remains at home in the company of Tanaka or the young officers of the 1930s who were more eager to translate their dreams of great Japanese military feats into action.

Fig. 7
Count
Terauchi Masatake

General Count Terauchi Masatake

The same can be said of the governor-general of Korea, Terauchi Masatake. Having attained the rank of general in 1906 after a distinguished administrative career in the army, Terauchi counted among the army's top leadership on active duty in 1914. As second in command in the Yamagata faction, he enjoyed a particularly influential voice in army and state affairs. Since 1912, in fact, he had been the faction's great hope for a restoration of military-bureaucratic rule.[98] In September 1916, he finally headed a "transcendental" cabinet in the faction's last overt bid to stall the forces of political change.

Recent studies of army policy place Terauchi together with Yamagata as representative of the older generation of army leadership that, in stark contrast with their more brazen subordinates such as Tanaka and Akashi Motojirō, regularly counseled caution in the pursuit of Japanese continental aims.[99] Indeed, like Yamagata, Terauchi objected to Tanaka's scheme to depose Chinese president Yuan Shikai.[100] And, as we shall see, he designed his own cabinet's approach to China as a direct repudiation of Tanaka's clandestine activities on the continent.[101]

But this new reputation marks a striking revision of the long-time notoriety of his tenure as the first and most severe governor-general of Korea. For his ruthless suppression of domestic dissent, he was known in the colony as the "iron fist." Similarly, like Yamagata, Terauchi had more in common with his brash subordinates than not. As governor-general of Korea, he was, in 1914, well removed from the center of policymaking in Tokyo. But he remained in touch with political developments through an active correspondence with Tanaka.[102] And he greeted the outbreak of war with the same burst of enthusiasm as Japan's most active imperialists. Terauchi had, after all, already honed an influential voice in Japan's imperial affairs as minister of war from 1902 to 1911 and governor-general of Korea since 1911. In mid-August, then, he spoke directly to Japan's new minister to Beijing, Hioki Eki, of a plan to take advantage of the extraordinary opportunity presented by the war.[103] After the surrender of Qingdao, he proposed, Japan should persuade China to relocate her troops in Manchuria to central China. The responsibility of "public order" in Manchuria would thus devolve to Japanese soldiers. Nor was this the extent of Terauchi's ambition. After laying claim to Manchuria as the exclusive domain of the Imperial Japanese Army, the governor-general clarified Japan's title to all of Asia. Describing his proposal as an "Asian Monroe Doctrine," he, like Yamagata and Tanaka, spoke of Japan's particular racial and cultural affinity with China. The European war was a "race war." "From our perspective as Asians, it is a war between Christians and, if we borrow their words, heathen peoples. Although we will not insist upon excluding Europeans and Americans, it is proper to inform the Westerners that, up to a point, Asia should be under the control of Asians."[104] To Yamagata confidant Sugiyama Shigemaru, Terauchi described the immediate priority as informing Chinese president Yuan of "the situation in Europe and Asia" and convincing him to follow Japanese leadership. In this way, he hoped to restrain the "haughtiness" of the Europeans and establish Japanese authority. "Eventually all of Asia should be under the control of our Emperor."[105]

Fig. 8
Baron
Gotō Shinpei

Baron Gotō Shinpei

An expanded vision of Japanese interests in China was not the monopoly of the Yamagata faction and army establishment in August 1914. There were civilian interests, as well, who viewed the outbreak of war as an unprecedented opportunity for continental gain. Among those, perhaps the most interesting and relevant in terms of future influence was Gotō Shinpei. Gotō enjoys a distinct place in the narrative of modern Japanese history, primarily for his contribution to the construction of the Japanese empire. As the first civilian administrator of Taiwan, he has been praised for transforming the territory from a rural backwater into the crown jewel of the empire.[106] As the first president of the South Manchuria Railway, he played a major role in constructing what would become Japan's principal sphere of influence on the continent.[107] Gotō is also known as the influential mayor of Tokyo in the early 1920s. And he appears regularly in diplomatic histories as the man whose negotiations with the Soviet representative to China facilitated a normalization of relations with Moscow in 1923.

In recent years, Gotō has been praised for his diplomatic foresight. In 1918 he became the first non-career minister of foreign affairs, largely, it is argued, because of his novel vision of a cooperative diplomacy.[108] It is, however, worth remembering some contemporary appraisals of the aspiring foreign minister. Gotō owed much of his success to the powerful sponsorship of the most influential men from the Chōshū domain: Kodama Gentarō, Katsura Tarō, and Terauchi Masatake. But throughout his career, he consorted with a variety of political factions: the Kaishintō, the Seiyūkai, the Dōshikai, and the army, depending upon the prevailing political winds. Far from a man with a consistent political or diplomatic philosophy, Gotō was a mercurial character. His own mentor, General Katsura Tarō, once remarked that Gotō never had anything "reasonable" to say but was worth listening to because he uttered a gem of wisdom "once in a hundred times."[109] At the ascension of Gotō to the position of home minister in the fall of 1916, Yoshino Sakuzō confessed his puzzlement at what to expect. "Whether one listens to the baron's theories or reads his books, in a word, it's a mixed bag of lies and truth, truth and gossip, and historical fact and legend."[110] Even Field Marshal Yamagata considered the baron "unpredictable" and urged Terauchi upon the formation of his cabinet in 1916 to keep him away from the Foreign Ministry portfolio, where "there is no telling what he will do."[111]

Indeed, by the First World War, Gotō had already developed quite a track record as an aggressive proponent of Japan's imperial interests. As civilian administrator of Taiwan in 1900, he had enthusiastically planned a Japanese invasion of Amoy in China's Fujian province.[112] As communications minister for the second Katsura cabinet, he had promoted a policy of railroad expansion on the continent that envisioned China's full incorporation into the Japanese empire.[113] And soon after the Chinese Revolution, Gotō had become one of the most conspicuous proponents of an alliance with Germany to replace that with Britain, which he found to be marked increasingly by "decrepitude."[114]

As we shall see, Gotō's penchant for outlandish schemes did not fade during the Great War. As Sino-Japanese talks over Katō Takaaki's Twenty-One Demands reached a stalemate in early May 1915, he urged an immediate declaration of war.[115] In December 1917, he became an early advocate of an enormous investment of Japanese funds and troops to Siberia.[116] Finally, in March 1918, he outlined an ambitious program of national mobilization and martial law to combat American "moralistic aggression."[117]

On the eve of the First World War, Gotō outlined a proposal for an Asian development bank that would make Chinese economic development a matter of intimate Sino-Japanese cooperation. The bank would be headed by a Chinese chairman and Japanese vice chairman and be capitalized by a Japanese investment of 200 million yen.[118] By October 1916, when he assumed the Home Ministry portfolio, this had expanded into a vision of a Sino-Japanese economic alliance. Like the schemes hatched by the army leadership, the alliance was founded upon the notion of a world divided between the "yellow and white races."[119] While insisting upon the need for cooperation between the races, Gotō nonetheless urged the strongest solidarity between Japan and China, an "economic alliance of the people." The association would naturally stand apart from Japan's relations with the Western world. Indeed, Gotō urged that Japan withdraw from the four-power consortium that had, since 1912, cooperated in channeling funds to Beijing.[120]

Fig. 9   Foreign Minister Katō bags the World War I tiger

EMPIRE IN THE SERVICE OF DOMESTIC POLITICS

In the context of these expansive visions of Japanese power and empire, Katō's orthodox efforts to strengthen Japan's established interests in China appear modest. But Katō usually emerges in histories of this period as more, not less, inclined toward an aggressive Japanese posture. Historians often interpret objections by Japan's military-bureaucratic elite to Katō's foreign policy initiatives as evidence of the foreign minister's relative assertiveness. But one can only confuse Katō's diplomatic position through inattention to the other essential element of the vision of the national essence promoted by these men: their conception of domestic politics.

Politics, particularly oligarchic rule, was, as we have seen, the first pillar of the Meiji state exposed to direct and sustained debate in the twentieth century. No matter how great the unifying power of war, peace invariably brought the most rapidly ascending political force, the political parties, back with their most trenchant demand: elimination of the arbitrary governance of a small clique (*hanbatsu*) of samurai from the former Satsuma and Chōshū domains and the perfection of "constitutional government." The growing power of this appeal was demonstrated in the victory for the political parties in the Taishō political crisis of 1912.

As the first instance of the destruction of an oligarchic cabinet by a coalition of political parties, the Taishō political crisis has long received extensive scholarly coverage as a major watershed in the political history of modern Japan. Political historians, however, have failed to capture the full extent of the political turbulence of the Taishō era because of their exclusive focus upon distinctly political events. After the political crisis, standard accounts of the movement for political reform known as "Taishō democracy" jump to the next striking victory for party rule, the advent of Japan's first party cabinet under Hara Takashi in 1918. Aside from a discussion of economic developments facilitating the rise of the Hara cabinet, in other words, the principal years of the Great War remain outside the main narrative of Taishō political history.

But the political turbulence sparked by the Taishō political crisis did not suddenly cease with the dawn of a major diplomatic event. It is a mistake, in other words, to view the Great War as exclusively, or even primarily, a foreign policy event. For the war was more than just an opportunity to expand Japanese interests on the continent. It was a chance for Imperial Japan's preeminent political opponents to promote, as well, their most cherished dreams for Japanese politics.

Katō Takaaki

As the first to take advantage of the diplomatic opportunity of the war, Katō Takaaki was the first to champion a particular vision of domestic politics as well. The *genrō* had worried about Katō's inclusion in the Ōkuma cabinet from its inception. Like Ōkuma, after all, the new foreign minister boasted an impressive record of defiance of oligarchic rule. As Japan's official representative to London and as foreign minister, he had worked tirelessly for Foreign Ministry supremacy in the making of foreign policy. But the elder statesmen could not have imagined the damage that Katō was to inflict upon their political authority during the Great War. While they had found their contemporary and former rival Ōkuma eager to pursue their own agenda, Katō, twenty-two years Ōkuma's junior, retained the energy to continue the battle against the oligarchs that the prime minister seemed to have abdicated. Indeed, the new foreign minister was to seize the opportunity presented by the war to monopolize the foreign policy decision-making process until his resignation in August 1915.

Katō, then, must be viewed as much as a political actor as one of Japan's ablest diplomats. Given his years of experience in London and as minister of foreign affairs, Katō is studied primarily in this latter capacity. When he is treated as a politician, the story is often one of failure. The baron's penchant for alienating even members of his own party because of rigid adherence to principle has earned him a reputation of political ineptitude, especially compared to his more charismatic political rival, Hara Takashi.[121]

But Katō's significance in the history of modern Japan lies less in his capacity for foreign policy decision making than in his politics. While his diplomacy belonged squarely within the tradition of an earlier age (nineteenth-century imperialism), his politics were truly innovative. In fact, few figures in Japanese political history can rival the impact that Katō had on the politics of Imperial Japan. Although he lacked the gift for compromise that helped to propel Hara Takashi to the prime ministry by 1918, while in office, Katō succeeded beyond all measure in his principal political aim: the establishment of cabinet superiority in the making of domestic and foreign policy. Added to his contributions to party rule during his subsequent tenure as prime minister, this success should confirm Katō as a champion of representative government of equal stature to the usually more conspicuous Hara. In fact, the last guardian of democratic reform, elder statesman Saionji Kinmochi, would cite Katō, along with three eminent statesmen of an earlier generation, as the most "respectable" men that he had known. Saionji described his successor to the Seiyūkai presidency, Hara, on the other hand, as "respectable" only "to a lesser extent."[122]

Katō's politics, like his diplomacy, were colored by his admiration for Britain. He found a general concern for politics and willingness to defend one's rights to be a natural part of British life. Even women were politically engaged, making male-female relations in Britain more than just physical; they were marked by a mutual pursuit of interests. But the British never pressed their interests with abandon. They not only possessed a broad vision beyond their immediate expertise but had a strong regard for others. In Britain, men and women would champion their rights only after considering the concerns of others, and the spirit of "give and take" characterized all debate.[123] Katō envisioned Britain as the vanguard of modern society and considered the British idea of citizenship and political responsibility the model toward which to strive. To that end, he worked tirelessly, as foreign minister and then prime minister, to bring Japanese politics into conformity with British parliamentarism.

Katō's orchestration of a decision for war against Germany on August 7, then, must be evaluated as much for its domestic political as for its foreign policy implications. Politically, the most important fact of the decision was that Katō made it without prior consultation with the genrō. In fact, his initiative was so swift that it caught all parties by surprise. The British ambassador to Tokyo, Sir Coyningham Greene, had made a formal request for Japanese assistance against the German navy in Asian waters on the afternoon of August 7. Katō then convened an extraordinary cabinet session at ten o'clock that evening, which, after four hours of debate, produced a consensus on war with Germany.

Such decisive and unilateral action by a foreign minister was not unheard of in the British cabinet system. But it was unprecedented in the short history of parliamentary government in Japan. From the beginning of the Japanese cabinet system in 1885 until Katō's first stint as foreign minister in 1900, after all, the Foreign Ministry portfolio had gone either to one of the small circle of Satsuma and Chōshū elites who had come to dominate the central government or to one of their close associates. Foreign policy decision making was very much the product of close consultation among this select group of men. Even as direct intervention in policymaking by these founders of Imperial Japan declined after the Russo-Japanese War, they expected to be called upon to provide leadership in times of national crisis. Indeed, with one of their number as prime minister, chief of the Army General Staff, and commander of forces in Manchuria, the genrō had directed the most critical diplomatic and military aspects of the war with Russia.[124]

But from his first term as foreign minister in 1900, Katō had refused to follow the accepted practice of consulting with the elder statesmen.[125] Indeed, he was a natural rival of the genrō. Like the Meiji elite, he was of samurai lineage. But he hailed neither from Satsuma nor Chōshū nor was he a contemporary of the older men. Rather, his father had been a retainer of the Owari han, a fief of the Tokugawa, whom the founders of Meiji Japan had deposed in 1868. Although Owari had ultimately sided with Satsuma and Chōshū, at age eight, Katō, unlike the genrō, was too young to have participated in the revolution. Katō, like Komura Jutarō and Hara Takashi, represented the second generation of Meiji leadership: men who had risen to power by climbing the ranks of the modern bureaucracy and by befriending those who had directly participated in the overthrow of the feudal regime. While Katō had earned the powerful support of Itō Hirobumi, his political ascent, like others of his generation, ultimately meant a decline of genrō authority.

More than anything else, Foreign Minister Katō's monopolization of diplomacy rested upon his conviction that, following the practice of the British cabinet system, the Japanese Foreign Ministry should have the exclusive right to formulate and implement foreign policy. As elder statesmen, modern Japan's founders had retained a decisive voice in Japanese diplomacy, and the army had increasingly pursued its own diplomatic agenda following its victory over Russia in 1905. Three times before accepting the nation's chief diplomatic appointment, Katō had demanded a guarantee of Foreign Ministry supremacy in the making of foreign policy. "Foreign policy," he had informed Prime Minister Katsura in 1913, "must be unified according to the principles and policies of the foreign minister."[126] In August 1914, too, Katō insisted that he and the Foreign Ministry set the diplomatic agenda in the new opportunity presented by the outbreak of war in Europe.

He did so, as we have seen, by single-handedly orchestrating a decision for war. Rather than seek prior approval from the *genrō*, Kato obtained cabinet approval and informed the elder statesmen of the fait accompli in the *genrō*-cabinet conference the following day. Nor did Katō make any attempt to heed *genrō* advice in the busy month after the outbreak of war. He ignored Inoue and Yamagata's suggestion to send a special Japanese envoy to Beijing to work out a comprehensive agreement. And, as with the cabinet decision for war, he drafted the text of an ultimatum to Germany without prior consultation with the elder statesmen. Katō limited his briefings of the *genrō* to perfunctory reports of recent negotiations with Britain, made particularly exasperating by his distribution, without translation, of English-language correspondence with London.[127]

Katō also sought to maintain strict control of the definition of Japanese war aims. The general aim, as we have seen, was to enhance the empire's position in China. But Katō hoped to do so in a manner that would strengthen the hand of the Foreign Ministry. A military engagement risked elevating the political authority of the Imperial Army. Katō initially attempted, therefore, to obtain concessions from Germany without a fight. While he energetically sought cabinet approval for a declaration of war, Katō did not propose that Japan actually *go* to war. He hoped, rather, that the threat of a military engagement would compel Germany to transfer her concession in Shandong province to Japan without open hostilities. Japan would then offer to return the concession to China in exchange for favorable terms from Beijing regarding Japan's main sphere of interest in Manchuria.[128] An important part of Katō's strategy, then, was to issue an ultimatum demanding that Germany cede Jiaozhou to Japan. To give Berlin ample time to capitulate without a fight, he set an ultimatum deadline of seven days, rather than the customary forty-eight hours.[129] Katō planned, in other words, to find a negotiated solution to the empire's aims on the continent.[130] Rather than give the Imperial Army a stage on which to swagger, Katō hoped to assure Foreign Ministry supremacy by confining imperial actions to diplomacy.

Inoue Kaoru

If domestic political goals were critical to Katō's formulation and prosecution of Japanese war aims, they were equally important to his chief political rivals. While the beneficiaries of the Taishō political crisis such as Katō saw in the war a way to continue their drive to political prominence, the principal casualties of the crisis, the members of the military-bureaucratic elite, hoped that the European conflict would, like Japan's earlier engagements with China and Russia, buttress their sagging political authority by generating national unity and renewed enthusiasm for the state.

The elder statesmen had felt the greatest effects of the rise of political parties represented by the Taishō political crisis. Indeed, the toppling of the Katsura cabinet served notice that the emperor's closest advisers could no longer sponsor a cabinet isolated from political forces in the Diet. Yamagata was later to mark the crisis as the point at which the "new thought of democracy" had spread and precipitated a "confusion of public sentiment."[131] He and Marquis Inoue Kaoru would search desperately for ways to counter the effects of such confusion.

For these two remaining politically active *genrō*, then, the war in Europe offered the opportunity both to enhance Japan's position in Asia and to calm the increasing public clamor for more representative government at home. Indeed, Inoue's August 10 exaltation of "divine aid" began with an explanation of the anticipated domestic political benefits of the war. In a word, he appealed for the "solidarity of national unity." Particularly, he hoped to make use of the heaven-sent opportunity to secure the nation's financial base. On the eve of the Thirty-First Diet (December 26, 1913–March 23, 1914), the minority forces that had helped to topple the third Katsura cabinet and precipitate the Taishō political crisis had made fiscal reform an integral component of their quest for "constitutional government."[132] While suppressed by the Yamamoto cabinet and the Seiyūkai majority in the Diet, their proposal to abolish business taxes found widespread support among business interests nationwide and had become the focus of discussion again during the Thirty-Third extraordinary Diet (June 22–28, 1914) under the new Ōkuma regime. Inoue's memorandum to Prime Minister Ōkuma and Field Marshal Yamagata, then, urged a cessation of the year's "noisy debate" on tax relief. Even before augmenting Japanese interests in Asia, the war, the marquis hoped, would "completely eliminate party debate" in Tokyo.[133] He and Yamagata were later to refer to such debate as a domestic "calamity" that they looked to the war to eliminate.[134]

Yamagata Aritomo

Yamagata's initial reaction to the outbreak of war in Europe was far less sanguine than that of his fellow *genrō* from the former Chōshū domain. The field marshal had immediately recognized the danger of Katō's command of the Foreign Ministry at such a time of international crisis. From the foreign minister's initial decision for war against Germany, he groused and grumbled at every initiative emanating from Kasumigaseki. Historians have frequently taken Yamagata's criticism of Katō's policies to signify a genuine concern for their substance. But in the first month of the war, Yamagata could only ponder the implication of Katō's actions for his own political power. Simply stated, Yamagata could not countenance Katō's comportment as the "number one diplomat in Japan."[135] He reacted to news of Katō's unilateral orchestration of a cabinet decision for war in "virtual amazement."[136] And his numerous protests against Katō's initiatives in the first week after the decision were so contradictory in substance that they assume the character of opposition for opposition's sake. In the August 8 *genrō*-cabinet conference, for example, the field marshal denounced a hasty war against Japan's former national model, Imperial Germany. Three days later, he urged Katō to send Japanese troops to Europe in response to French and Russian requests.[137] On August 13, Yamagata demanded that Prime Minister Ōkuma shelve all plans for mobilization.[138] The following day, he described the inclusion of a reference in the ultimatum to Germany to an eventual return of Jiaozhou to China as a "disgraceful" capitulation.[139]

Yamagata clearly shared Katō's fervor for strengthening Japan's position in China. But he could not welcome Katō's orchestration of cabinet decisions without *genrō* consent, stand by as the foreign minister conducted briefings in a cryptic clutter of English-language documents, or forgive his disregard for the advice of the once most powerful men in the nation. The contradictory character of the field marshal's advice only confirmed Katō's long-held doubts about oligarchic competence. "What do the old men know of the delicate skill of diplomacy?" he had wondered after his long battle for an Anglo-Japanese alliance.[140] In August 1914, Yamagata lamented that Katō considered him and his fellow elder statesmen "senile."[141]

Gotō Shinpei

The battle between Katō and Yamagata defined the main political drama in Tokyo in the first month of war. But Katō's initiatives were to have a far-reaching political effect among a wide spectrum of Japanese elites. Like the elder statesmen, bureaucrat-cum-politician Gotō Shinpei's political fortunes had plummeted during the Taishō political crisis. The fall of the Katsura cabinet in 1913 and sudden death of Prince Katsura had deprived him of an important political mentor. The baron's defeat to Katō Takaaki in the subsequent battle for the Dōshikai presidency robbed him of a potential political base. The setback appeared decisive when Katō refused, despite Gotō's intensive lobbying efforts, to reserve a place for him in the Ōkuma cabinet in April 1914.[142] Gotō was subsequently to approach the Dōshikai's principal political rival, the Seiyūkai, and become one of the Ōkuma cabinet's most vocal critics.[143]

In the summer of 1914, however, Gotō focused his attention, like many of his fellow statesmen, on the critical arena of China policy. Gotō had risen to political prominence as the civilian administrator of Taiwan and president of the South Manchuria Railway. At a time of political distress, he naturally chose to play his hand again in imperial affairs. In addition to appealing for greater Sino-Japanese economic unity, his proposal for an Asian development bank, in other words, had a political function. It aimed to place him back into the decision-making process. Indeed, Gotō circulated his plan to elder statesmen Yamagata, Matsukata, and Inoue and received the approval of Ōkuma. Inoue subsequently twice nominated the baron to serve as the high-level Japanese envoy to China considered by the *genrō* essential for negotiating a comprehensive settlement with Beijing.[144] But Katō was impressed neither by Gotō's economic expertise nor by his enthusiasm for a voice in the nation's imperial affairs. The foreign minister's monopoly of China policy from August 1914 effectively excluded the baron from a decision-making role until his assumption of the Home Ministry portfolio in the fall 1916.

Tanaka Giichi

Gotō Shinpei represented the bureaucratic elite who hoped imperial expansion abroad would be accompanied by a return to military-bureaucratic political dominance at home. But Gotō's power was limited. More central to the decision-making process were members of the armed forces, particularly, the Imperial Army leadership. By the Russo-Japanese War, the army had become a powerful independent force in Japanese domestic politics. Military ordinances promulgated after the war had continued the Meiji legacy of increasing military autonomy from civilian rule.[145] And the army increasingly competed with Foreign Ministry prerogatives by sending private diplomatic agents to Beijing and Manchuria. By the end of the Russo-Japanese War, the Imperial Army ranked second only to the elder statesmen in political influence in the Japanese polity.

But peace and the Taishō political crisis had the same effect upon the power of the army as it had had on *genrō* prerogatives. Japan's generals had been able, soon after the Russo-Japanese War, to increase their peacetime force levels from thirteen to nineteen divisions. But the anti-tax mood in the peacetime Diet stalled completion of the additional six divisions outlined in the 1907 Basic Plan of National Defense. The Saionji cabinet's refusal to authorize funds for two new divisions in the 1912 fiscal year marked the first in a series of crushing blows to army prerogative, which had seemed unassailable immediately after the war with Russia. Admiral Yamamoto Gonnohyōe aggravated the problem when, as we have seen, his cabinet promoted naval expansion while slowing the flow of funds to the army. Under Yamamoto's prime ministry, the active-duty rule for uniformed cabinet members that had enabled War Minister Uehara Yūsaka to bring down the Saionji administration was also abolished. And Yamamoto intruded into army sacred ground in Manchuria when he authorized the appointment of Seiyūkai party members to the leadership of the South Manchuria Railway. Indeed, by 1913, the Imperial Japanese Army stood on the defensive against increasing naval and cabinet encroachments upon its prerogatives.

It was thus that members of the army leadership also viewed the outbreak of war in Europe as more than an opportunity to promote Japanese continental interests. They saw it, as well, as a chance to shore up army authority at home.[146] By August 1914, Chōshū Major General Tanaka Giichi had already been actively engaged in the struggle to restore the political power of the Imperial Army. In fact, if Tanaka's ideas for Japanese national power anticipated the unbridled ambitions of the young officers of the 1930s, his political activity set the standard for the political adventurism of his successors. In this sense, he may be identified as the most tangible link between Japanese imperialism in the 1910s and that in the 1930s.[147] For while Tanaka mentor Yamagata forecast the 1930s with his ambitious plans for Japanese power in China, the elder statesman's politics were fundamentally conservative. He responded to the decline in army authority by expanding the scale of army operations—by enlarging the defense perimeter and raising the target number of troops.

By contrast, Tanaka responded to the new realities of peace by redefining the nature and function of the army. In Tanaka's hands, Japan's ground forces were transformed from the principal tool of Japanese imperialism into a spiritual guide for the entire nation. As commander of the Third Infantry Division from 1907 to 1909, Tanaka revised the rational European-style management of the army along the lines of a family. Following the pattern of Confucian relationships, the company commander played the part of the strict father, his aides the affectionate mother, and the noncommissioned officers the older brothers, in a "family of soldiers who suffer and rejoice together and live or die as one."[148] At the same time, in November 1910, Tanaka created the Imperial Military Reservists Association that dramatically expanded the mobilization potential of the Imperial Army and, through the establishment of local branches, brought a martial spirit and the values of loyalty and filial piety to the village level.[149] If the Reservists Association sustained the martial spirit of men retired from active duty, a national youth corps cultivated that spirit before induction into the services. By September 1915, Tanaka persuaded the Ōkuma administration to create a youth corps of three million members to "solidify the foundation of the State and maintain stability" in an era characterized by "moral depravity."[150] Ironically, then, while the young officers who would lead Japan to war in the 1930s reviled Tanaka in the 1920s as the last remnant of the Chōshū army clique (*gun-*

batsu), they owed their characteristic exaltation of the spirit to his pioneering efforts in military reform and organization of a military reserve and national youth corps.

Just as he spawned the new spiritual emphasis of the post-Russo-Japanese War army, Tanaka pioneered a political role for the service that typified the activities of the junior officers of the 1930s. As chief of the Military Affairs Bureau, Tanaka nurtured the office to its true potential— as the political arm of the Ministry of War, entrusted with the mission of asserting the political authority of the war minister.[151] In his most celebrated use of the office, Tanaka in 1912 encouraged War Minister Uehara Yūsaku to resign over the cabinet refusal to sanction a two-division expansion for the army, thereby sparking the Taishō political crisis. As vice chief of the Army General Staff, as we shall see, Tanaka reached his political apogee as the principal architect of Japan's China policy.

By the beginning of the Taishō period, then, Tanaka commanded the army offensive against the rising tide of democracy. His personal political situation on the eve of the Great War, furthermore, mirrored the general decline of the Imperial Army. Just as the Taishō political crisis had forced Japan's ground forces into a devastating political retreat, it sent Tanaka into temporary exile in Europe. His efforts to reemerge from this political asylum symbolized the larger campaign by the army to restore its sagging political authority.

While in Europe, Tanaka laid the groundwork for the Military Reservists Association by studying comparable European institutions. But more representative of the larger goals of the Imperial Army were his activities in China before his departure for Europe. While convalescing in China from a bout of dysentery, Tanaka chose to make his mark on an issue that had long since become the core of army planning, continental expansion. After two and a half months of discussions in Manchuria with local Japanese military personnel, Tanaka published and distributed a 24,000-character memorandum in Tokyo titled "Impressions While in Manchuria," which outlined the cardinal importance of South Manchuria and Eastern Inner Mongolia to the fate of the empire.[152] Both areas had long been the focus of Japanese expansion on the continent. As such, they were the principal justification both for the presence of the Imperial Army on the continent and for its political authority at home. They were, in other words, essential to the army's very reason for being. By fortifying Japan's position in these territories, then, Tanaka aimed not simply to strengthen Japan's position on the continent. He hoped to restore the army, and himself, to a central place in the Japanese polity.

General Tanaka's "Impressions While in Manchuria" bemoaned the tendency of domestic politics to divert attention from the army's mission in China. "At this moment, the world is focused upon the East," he declared. "The China problem, like the Turkish problem, is where the blood of the powers flows." Although Japan, as a rising force, stood shoulder-to-shoulder with the great powers in the competition in China, she had many interests that did not coincide with theirs. Nor did she match their strength. "In this position, the Empire requires great schemes and meticulous measures to plan its development." But regrettably, a majority of Japanese were "preoccupied with domestic affairs and do not think about the long-range plan of the State."[153]

Of immediate concern to Tanaka was Prime Minister Yamamoto's recent replacement of the president and vice president of the South Manchuria Railway with members of the Seiyūkai party.[154] Just as the perpetrators of the Manchurian Incident would call in the 1930s for an extra-party official to permanently occupy the presidency of the railway, Tanaka in 1913 objected to plunging the "central mechanism of Manchuria-Mongolian colonization and racial development" into the "maelstrom of party strife." "I cannot help but feel strong regret for the State and government," he cried.[155] And he urged the unification of Japanese administrative mechanisms in Korea and South Manchuria under the authority of someone who would "stand outside the political strife in Japan." The new governor-general would receive instructions from the prime minister on civil matters but would be responsible directly to the emperor.[156]

Tanaka hoped also to tackle the interservice rivalry that had eroded military authority in the face of growing party strength. The "likes of party politicians," he warned, were consolidating their power and attempting to interfere in imperial defense. "We, the army and navy, who carry the heavy responsibility of protecting national policy, should never again commit the folly of constructing walls [between us]. We must strive to retrieve the situation through mutual aid and reliance."[157]

Tanaka's principal prescription for rejuvenating the Imperial Army was to attain the peacetime force levels proposed for the army in 1907 and a massive expansion of the railway network in Manchuria. He recommended sending four new divisions to Korea and adding one to the existing division in South Manchuria, for a total of six divisions on the continent. A target of 1,600 kilometers of rail would increase the existing network in South Manchuria by 150 percent.[158]

As with the 1907 Basic Plan of National Defense, Tanaka cited the persistence of a Russian threat to justify the enormous expansion of the army's continental presence. But although much of the Russian army had remained intact in North Manchuria after the Russo-Japanese War, by 1913 Tanaka and the Imperial Army elite worried little about a threat from the north. Signals from St. Petersburg soon after the 1905 Portsmouth Conference confirmed that Russia desired to come to a negotiated agreement with Japan on respective spheres of influence in North Asia. As we have seen, Tanaka and mentor Yamagata responded eagerly to these "amorous glances" and promoted three conventions with St. Petersburg governing Japan's interests in Manchuria and Mongolia.

It is a singular irony of Japanese military history that, until the Pacific War, the Japanese army continued to regard Russia, later the Soviet Union, as their number one potential enemy.[159] This was not, as some historians have suggested, the consequence of an overwhelming fear of Russia. On the contrary, even when the Soviet Union boasted its greatest strength in the Russian Far East in the late 1930s, Japanese troops in Manchuria would boldly attempt to advance north.[160] Rather, the Russian enemy was a political necessity for the army. It was the principal foundation for the army's conceit of serving as the first line of imperial defense. The navy's success in 1923 at replacing Russia with the United States as Japan's number-one potential adversary shifted the principal focus of national defense from the army's continental stronghold in Manchuria to naval possessions in the Pacific and would be bitterly contested by Japan's generals throughout the 1920s and 1930s.[161]

The Great War increasingly revealed the absurdity of the notion of a Russian "threat." By 1917, after all, Imperial Russia ceased to exist as a political entity. Tanaka clearly grasped the difficulty of the tsar's position in August 1914.[162] And yet, as we have seen, he submitted to War Minister Oka Ichinosuke a plan for expanded Japanese army influence in Manchuria and China that far outstripped the agenda of his "Impressions While in Manchuria," whose strategic justification rested principally upon the idea of a Russian challenge.

Tanaka's initiative in August 1914, in other words, must be seen as the product not simply of strategic calculations. It emerges in the context of his long-term struggle to restore Imperial Army authority. War in Europe offered an unprecedented opportunity to shore up army power by greatly expanding its area of operations on the continent. The major general hoped, as well, that a stronger army would catapult himself to the center of decision making. Tanaka deplored the domestic political implications of Foreign Minister Katō's initiatives as much as he did their effect upon Japan's international posture. What grieved him most about the unprecedented opportunity presented by the war, in fact, was his exclusion from the policymaking process. "I cannot bear to be shut out of the situation," he informed General Terauchi at the end of August, "at this time when the world trembles and forecasts the fate of the empire."[163]

Terauchi Masatake

Tanaka surmounted his impotence soon enough. When he became vice chief of the Army General Staff in October 1915, he seized decisive command of Japan's China policy. And he proved in that capacity to be by far the most aggressive proponent of Japanese, and particularly army, prerogatives on the continent. But in August 1914 he was not alone in his dramatically expanded vision of Japanese and army rights. As we have seen, Terauchi Masatake, the governor-general of Korea, had a colossal vision of the Japanese emperor's rule over all of Asia. And he, too, had a specific ambition for Japanese politics in the context of war in Europe. In a letter to Gotō Shinpei at the beginning of August, Terauchi lamented recent developments in both Japanese politics and foreign policy. Like many of his fellow decision makers, he worried about the erosion of Japanese rights in Manchuria, Mongolia, and China. But he expressed equal concern for the "criticism of domestic politics." Just like Japan's foreign policy failures, such criticism, he lamented, had weakened Japanese national authority. And like elder statesman Inoue Kaoru, he felt particular anguish over the intensifying debate in the Diet over taxes. Such debate, after all, struck at the heart of army power by stalling completion of army force levels outlined in the 1907 Basic Plan of National Defense. It was time, then, to "cease the minor matters of domestic strife, argue about things such as lessening taxes some other day, and redirect internal discord outward."[164] The general sought a domestic political consensus that would guarantee army prerogatives at home as it reaffirmed them on the continent.

The Imperial Navy

Japan's admirals were as excited as her generals at the opportunity offered by the war to pursue Japanese interests on the continent. In 1914, Imperial Navy prerogatives, after all, depended as much upon continental empire as those of the army. The same 1907 Basic Plan of National Defense that had defined the protection of Japan's interests in Manchuria and Korea as the first order of defense and established a twenty-five-division peacetime target for the army had justified a fleet of eight battleships and eight battle cruisers (the so-called 8-8 fleet) for the navy. Indeed, in the leap from a defense of the Japanese archipelago to the protection of continental interests after the Russo-Japanese War, the army not only improved its own fortunes but formally recognized for the first time the indispensability of naval strength to national security.[165] Japan's generals and admirals cooperated closely for the first time in devising the 1907 Basic Plan and, thereafter, requests for naval funding referred to the need to protect Japan's continental interests.[166]

It is no surprise, then, that the Naval General Staff adopted a plan of operations for the Japan Sea two days after Germany declared war on Russia on August 1, 1914. The draft included a "plan first to attack, in concert with the army, the enemy's base at Qingdao" for the purpose of "permanently extinguishing Germany's power in Asia and eliminating its ambition."[167] Arguing for a postponement of operations in the kaiser's Pacific territories, the Naval General Staff seemed trained squarely upon a continental agenda.

Naval interests, however, were not identical with those of the army. Japan's admirals found soon after 1907 that compromises reached with the army in the Basic Plan of National Defense did not guarantee the construction of an 8–8 fleet. Budget cuts in the Twenty-Fourth Diet (December 28, 1907–March 26, 1908) demonstrated the impossibility of even the immediate goal of a 5–7 fleet by 1913. To make matters worse, the appearance of the dreadnought in Britain in 1906, followed by the super dreadnought in 1912, threatened to render the entire Japanese fleet obsolete.

Under the circumstances, naval authorities began thinking outside the framework of the 1907 compromise. The Naval General Staff presented Prime Minister Katsura with a "Proposal for Naval Expansion" in May 1910, which added four battleships to the original 8–8 plan, for a prospective 8–4–8 fleet. The 1907 Basic Plan of National Defense had subordinated Japan's sailors to her soldiers by designating the army's principal continental rival, Russia, the number one potential adversary. But the navy's proposal of 1910 based its requests upon the necessity to "accomplish the duty of the first line of defense."[168]

Failure to obtain budgetary approval for this plan, or even for a 4–4 fleet target under the second Saionji cabinet, compelled the head instructor of the Naval Academy, Rear Admiral Satō Tetsutarō, to push even further. In January 1912 he proposed two 8–4 fleets, to be supported by pruning the army to its immediate post-Sino-Japanese War strength of nineteen wartime divisions.[169] Japan's admirals, in other words, responded to the diminution of their domestic and international authority resulting from budgetary constraints by redefining their position vis-à-vis the army.

Satō's plan never reached the cabinet level. But the army had tangible cause for concern when the Diet, through the instigation of Prime Minister Admiral Yamamoto Gonnohyōe, abolished the active-duty rule, recently used to the army's advantage, and proposed a 60 million yen increase in the naval budget in December 1913.[170] This corresponded to a 4–4 fleet schedule and fell well within the framework of the 1907 Basic Plan. But Yamamoto did not at the same time allocate funds for the army's immediate goal of two additional divisions. The neglect, as we have seen, cost him his cabinet. And Yamagata's subsequent success in forcing Admiral Yamamoto and his deputy, Navy Minister Saitō Makoto, off the active duty list stripped the navy of its driving force.[171]

But despite the budgetary and personnel setbacks, naval authorities continued to stake their own territory in opposition to army supremacy. Admiral Katō Tomosaburō sabotaged Yamagata-backed Viscount Kiyoura Keigo's attempt to form a cabinet by refusing to serve as navy minister without a guarantee for supplemental naval funds. Persistence by the new navy minister, Yashiro Rokurō, and Vice Minister Suzuki Kantarō's negotiations with the Seiyūkai procured the unanimous passage of a supplemental navy bill in June 1914.[172] Responding to queries in the Peers budget committee, Yashiro revealed that the navy's solution to budgetary restrictions lay in revising the army's continental definition of national defense. To meet the financial restraints, he argued, "we must bear with a minimum of national strength. . . . What I mean by a minimum of national strength is not possessing the will to invade other countries or create potential enemies. It is simply the strength to carry out the duty of protecting the country."[173]

The reaction of Japan's admirals to the outbreak of war in Europe also reflected a conscious distancing from army objectives. The above-mentioned plan of operations by the Naval General Staff calling for a joint army-navy offensive at Qingdao did not envision a protracted occupation on the continent. Rather, it warned against "violating the neutrality of China."[174] Furthermore, this "Operational Outline" represented only one contingency, and a less preferred one for the high command.

Naval authorities favored the government proclamation of neutrality on August 4, recognizing "the advantage of keeping an eye on the situation." They argued that Japan was not restricted by the Anglo-Japanese alliance but could determine her attitude based upon her own interests. Their wait-and-see approach clearly rested upon a maritime definition of the empire's interests. "To maintain peace in the Far East and develop maritime commerce is in Japan's interest and is thus a means to fulfill Japan's national policy," they declared. "Therefore, it is best to first advocate neutrality and propose the cessation of belligerent actions in the Far East."[175]

Navy Minister Yashiro reflected these sentiments when he proposed, during the joint cabinet-genrō conference of August 8, that Japan refrain from belligerency. The main portion of the German fleet appeared headed for home via South America, he noted. With a change in the situation thus imminent, a desire to await developments had gained strength within the navy.[176] On August 13, Yashiro urged the cabinet to postpone a declaration of war and, instead, to send an ultimatum to Germany to restore Qingdao to China and withdraw the German fleet from the China Sea.[177] Beyond the expulsion of the German fleet, in other words, naval leaders perceived few advantages to military action in the Far East.

In fact, the disadvantages of hostilities in Asia became increasingly clear to Japan's admirals with the landing of imperial troops in northern Shandong on September 2. Even before the embarkation, Japan's generals demonstrated their enthusiasm for the opportunity afforded by the European war by planning an invasion of Fujian province. Foreign Minister Katō headed off the attempt in mid-August.[178] But he was less successful in limiting the army's area of operations in Shandong province. While Foreign Ministry Secretary Obata Yukichi had informed Beijing on August 31 that Japanese troops would maneuver east of Weixian, by October 6, the Eighteenth Division had occupied the entire Shandong Railway to Jinan.[179]

While the Imperial Army was rapidly taking advantage of the opportunity to expand its interests in China, the navy began revising its strategy toward Germany's South Pacific islands. Until early September the Naval General Staff had confined operations at sea to the blockade of Qingdao, the transport of Japanese troops to Shandong, and the surveillance of German ships, postponing a decision upon operations in the South Pacific. But on September 12, the navy drafted an operational plan to crush the enemy fleet in German Micronesia and destroy the ground facilities there.[180] The plan, "On the Matter of Activities by the Fleet Sent South," initially rejected a prolonged presence in the South Pacific, calling instead for a withdrawal soon after the completion of operations. But with the army rapidly advancing toward a new stronghold in Shandong, Navy Minister Yashiro and the chief of the Naval General Staff, Shimamura Hayao, agreed on September 21 to delete the demand for a quick retreat.[181] One day before facing off with the army in an appeal before the recently established Military Affairs Council for a wartime budget, Yashiro demanded cabinet approval for a "perpetual occupation" of the territories.[182] The cabinet ultimately authorized only a limited occupation of the Marshall, Mariana, and Caroline Islands, with their eventual disposal to be decided at a later date. But by December, Foreign Minister Katō informed his British allies that Japan desired to maintain the islands in perpetuity. Spurred by the army's drive for a new area of operations on the continent, the navy embarked upon an assertive campaign in the South Pacific.[183]

THE GENRŌ VERSUS PRIME MINISTER ŌKUMA, SEPTEMBER 1914

While the outbreak of hostilities in Asia provided an opportunity for an army takeover of Shandong and a naval occupation of German Micronesia, it did not benefit the genrō in their political battle with Foreign Minister Katō. Katō's ultimatum to Germany had proven to be wildly popular. Despite the parliamentary pressure from 1907 for a reduction of taxes, the Thirty-Fourth Diet (September 4–9, 1914) unanimously approved a war budget.[184] This included the long-awaited approval of monies for ten new destroyers for the navy. Questions from the opposition during the parliamentary session confirmed not only that the ultimatum was popular, but that sentiment leaned toward a more aggressive posture. The Seiyūkai's Ōoka Ikuzō questioned not the demands made of Germany but the restrictions placed upon them. "What is the meaning of limiting our demands of Germany simply to Jiaozhou, without covering the South Pacific and elsewhere? What is this, restricting the area of operations of our independent country upon declaring war? What do you intend by returning Jiaozhou to China? Has not Britain already occupied German territory in the South Pacific?"[185] The routinely antigovernment Tokyo Asahi shinbun testified that the entire world would "rejoice" over Japan's ultimatum to Germany and over the "extinguishing of German ambitions."[186]

In a bid to salvage genrō authority, Marquis Inoue circulated a second memorandum to Ōkuma, Yamagata, and Matsukata on August 20 and met with the prime minister twice in September to urge alliances with France and Russia and a solution to the "Katō problem." Count Ōkuma, however, continued to sidestep both issues.[187] Field Marshal Yamagata himself remained disinclined to follow an Inoue initiative on a Russo-

French-British-Japanese alliance but, like Inoue, resented Katō for ignoring his own August proposal on China. Katō's monopolization of the
mechanisms of foreign policy became especially critical for Yamagata
when, in an audience with the emperor in early September, the monarch
referred to information received from Katō to which Yamagata had not
been privy. The elder statesman was "aghast" to realize that, at this rate,
his own words amounted to a mere report rather than advice to the emperor.[188]

Ōkuma guessed from conversations with Inoue and Inoue's secretary
Mochizuki that he could not continue to deflect the approaches of the elder statesmen.[189] He asked the marquis on September 21, therefore, to arrange a meeting of the emperor's advisers.[190] The subsequent gathering of
Ōkuma, Yamagata, Inoue, Matsukata, and Ōyama Iwao at Inoue's residence on September 24 became an opportunity for the genrō to make a direct presentation of their fundamental conception of the national essence.

Primarily a reaction to a powerful foreign minister and an emboldened
navy, the official account of the meeting in five articles, nonetheless,
placed the problem outside the narrow confines of power politics. The
elder statesmen defined the concern not as a simple decline in their personal authority but as a grave matter for the fortunes of the state. The
solution lay in a complete overhaul of Japanese domestic and foreign affairs along the lines of the Meiji Renovation. "Since the death of the former Emperor and the reign of his present Majesty, Japan's authority
among the powers has shown tendencies of decline," the genrō began.
"Even the London Times of our ally now prints opinions that cling to fears
for Japan's future. Not only can the prime minister and all of the elder
statesmen not set aside their fears in serving the previous Emperor, but
we do not at all do justice to the present Emperor, who has yet to grow
accustomed to his political duties. We have yet to reach the object with
which we established the Ōkuma cabinet, the hope of a second Renovation." The time was ripe for action. "This rare occasion is a great chance
for Japan to turn the calamities of domestic and foreign policies into
fortunes." The genrō commanded the prime minister to immediately effect national unity by following their presecription for domestic and foreign affairs.[191]

Domestically, the *genrō* called for nothing less than excluding Katō from the political process. Four of the five articles of the conference record referred explicitly to the foreign minister and attempted to relegate him to the role of mere receptacle of policies devised by the prime minister and *genrō*. Article 2 stipulated that Katō "obey the consensual opinions on diplomacy negotiated with the prime minister and the *genrō*." Article 3 held that the prime minister would "make the fundamental decisions on foreign policy and compel the foreign minister to comply." Article 4 required Katō to consult with the *genrō* before all important negotiations with foreign powers. Finally, article 5 charged Ōkuma to recognize "Baron Katō's excessively bureaucratic nature" and his own responsibility for the lack of mutual understanding between Katō and the *genrō*.[192]

If the *genrō* directed their political energies principally toward relegating Katō to the margins of the policymaking process, Yamagata hoped, as well, to redress the budgetary priority given to the navy since 1911. A separate memorandum sent by the *genrō* to Ōkuma outlining "important diplomatic matters" called for an Army General Staff–Foreign Ministry committee to end the "lack of mutual understanding" between the two offices.[193] Such a committee would, Yamagata anticipated, help build Foreign Ministry support for the army's demand for two new divisions.[194] At the same time, he protested the cost of new ships and referred in a separate memorandum to the navy's "exorbitant demands" that had complicated the budget process.[195]

If the *genrō* worried primarily about the political challenge of continuing budgetary priority to the navy and Katō's monopolization of the foreign policy decision-making process, they hoped that Katō's expulsion would also mark a substantive change in the nation's diplomacy. A separate draft of pending questions issued on the occasion of the *genrō*-Ōkuma conference reiterated the drastic solution to Japan's quest for influence in China that Yamagata and his allies had aggressively pressed for since the outbreak of war—an alliance with Russia.[196] The elder statesmen stopped shy of dismissing the Anglo-Japanese alliance outright. Strengthened ties with Russia, it was proposed, would lead to a four-part alliance in the future with Russia, Britain, and France. But the *genrō* could not hide their displeasure with their current ally. The above-mentioned memorandum on "important diplomatic matters" included "Britain's oppression of our interests in southern China" among items of concern.[197] And the same memorandum stressed the principal threat to Japanese continental interests that Yamagata had already argued could not be handled by the Anglo-Japanese alliance alone. "Take care," it read, "not to easily believe that America will not intervene between Japan and China."[198] Ultimately, Yamagata and his fellow elder statesmen sought regional hegemony through a stronger relationship with China. The draft of pending questions summarizing the genrō-Ōkuma conference appealed, as the elder statesmen had continued to appeal, for a special envoy to be sent to Beijing to obtain the trust of Chinese president Yuan Shikai.[199]

SYNOPSIS

Japan greeted the outbreak of war in Europe in August 1914 with the same fanfare that animated Paris, London, and Berlin. It was, according to one of the empire's most authoritative statesmen, "divine aid." Following the precedents of the Sino- and Russo-Japanese Wars, contemporaries viewed the war as the perfect occasion to redefine the nation. It was the opportunity to resolve, once and for all, the tumultuous debate over the national essence that had plagued Japan since the war with Russia and the death of the Meiji emperor.

In foreign policy terms, Japanese statesmen aimed to reinvigorate Japan's international status by strengthening her interests in China. The main architect of Japan's declaration of war against Germany, Foreign Minister Katō Takaaki, hoped to force the kaiser to transfer German interests in Shandong province to Japan and to use this to extract concessions from China in areas of greatest interest to Tokyo, Manchuria and Mongolia. Other would-be policymakers showered the administration in the first few weeks of the war with numerous proposals for a comprehensive new agreement with China.

Katō's decisive action in response to the war, culminating in the presentation of a list of "pending problems" for negotiation with Beijing in January 1915, has marked him as a particularly aggressive proponent of Japanese continental interests. But his actions fell well within the established trajectory of Japanese diplomacy and great power relations in

China from the latter part of the nineteenth century. Katō remained steadfast in his faith in the Anglo-Japanese alliance. And, in accord with the British model of free trade imperialism, he stressed diplomatic negotiation and economic interests over autonomous military action and territorial gain.

By contrast, Kato's greatest political rivals, members of Japan's military-bureaucratic elite, envisioned bold new foreign policy departures as the great powers withdrew their attention from Asia to Europe. For these men, the most salient issue in Japanese foreign affairs was not the Anglo-Japanese alliance, but the prospect of a future "race war." Indeed, their insistence on "intimate" Sino-Japanese cooperation, by which they meant complete Japanese hegemony in Asia, raised the prospect of future conflict with the fastest growing power in the region, the United States. They placed less weight upon relations with Britain, then, than upon ties with powers better positioned to check the advance of American power. Above all, they stressed stronger ties with China and a common front to check the spread of American influence in Asia. In an ominous hint of the future, Tanaka Giichi in September 1914 went so far as to suggest that Japan "take on" the United States while American power remained undeveloped.

The diplomatic positions of Katō and members of Japan's military-bureaucratic elite can only be confused if one does not attend to the other essential element in their vision for the Japanese nation: domestic politics. Japan's entrance in the war was as significant for domestic politics as it was for foreign policy. If the war sparked universal enthusiasm for continental expansion, Japanese policymakers scrambled, as well, to promote their particular conception of domestic politics. The fundamental debate over who was to rule the nation had, after all, intensified as Japan's rising political parties chipped away at the political hegemony of the architects of the Meiji state. In 1912, the debate raged in full view as a campaign to replace the unrepresentative rule of a minority "clique" with "constitutional government." After August 1914, the battle took the form of a contest over the planning and execution of the most important foreign policy item facing the nation. He who could best promote Japanese continental interests would control the power.

As the first to take advantage of the diplomatic opportunity of the war, Katō Takaaki became its immediate political victor. Katō has secured a place in the history of modern Japan primarily as a foreign policy actor, not a politician. But the baron's greatest impact on that history lies less in his promotion of Japanese interests in Asia than in the battle against his principal political rivals in Japan. If Katō's diplomacy belonged squarely within the tradition of an earlier age (the age of imperialism), his politics were truly innovative. As foreign minister for the Ōkuma cabinet, he seized the prerogative of diplomatic decision making from the *genrō* and placed it squarely in the hands of the cabinet and Foreign Ministry. In so doing, he placed himself at the vanguard of the principal movement for political reform in Japan, the battle against oligarchic rule.

The objections to Katō's initiatives in the first month of the war by his chief rival for power, Field Marshal Yamagata, then, owe more to the political shock of being upstaged by the foreign minister than to a fundamental conflict of policies. Indeed, the greatest drama in Tokyo through September 1914 was less Japan's declaration of war per se than the political battle that unfolded between Katō and Yamagata. By completely controlling the timing and terms of Japan's participation in the Great War, Katō made the strongest bid to date for "constitutional government" over oligarchic rule. His success so struck Yamagata that the field marshal spent the next year attempting to remove the foreign minister from office.

The war carried political implications for other important Japanese elites, as well. Like Yamagata, fellow *genrō* Inoue Kaoru and bureaucrat Gotō Shinpei had looked to the conflict to restore a sense of national unity and the principle of oligarchic rule, which became ever more precarious in the wake of the Taishō political crisis. But, as with Yamagata, these men found themselves powerless in the face of Katō's relentless political offensive.

Japan's armed services, too, had hailed the war as an opportunity to restore the luster lost to military service after the Russo-Japanese War. But unlike the failures of their bureaucratic compatriots, military operations offered real opportunities for gains for the Imperial Army and Navy. Japan's generals quickly added Shandong province to their area of operations on the continent while her admirals established a new base in

the South Pacific. But these victories reflected the persistence of one of
the more troubling aspects of political tension in Taishō Japan, the unregulated competition between the two services. There was no clearer illustration of the increasing divergence of army and navy aims than the
picture of the navy projecting its power east across the Pacific as the
army fanned out west across the Shandong Railway. Like Tanaka's appeal to engage the United States in battle, it was a glimpse of things to
come.

War in Europe transformed the political canvas in Tokyo almost
overnight. The elder statesmen had created the Ōkuma cabinet in April
1914 to contain the political power of the Seiyūkai, the Satsuma faction,
and the navy. But the international crisis produced an even greater political foe from among the many new contenders for power: Foreign Minister Katō Takaaki. Katō's threat to the elder statesmen and the principle
of oligarchic rule was so potent that the quest to depose the foreign minister assumed an importance equal to the principal war aim of strengthening Japan's position in China. Unlike the quest for influence in Beijing,
however, the bid to revive oligarchic rule would become one of the first
casualties of the war.

3   Imperialism in the Service of Democracy: Katō Takaaki and the Twenty-One Demands

A sea of fire in front of the Imperial Palace. The city saw a burst of activity as, greeting the felicitous news of the fall of Qingdao, residents suddenly arose in excitement, flags in hand, lanterns displayed, and, unable to wait for the morrow, clamored for the immediate commencement of a parade.

—*Jiji shinpō*, November 9, 1914

Japan's confrontation with Germany was the only battle of the Great War that not only confirmed but bettered initial projections. British, French, German, and Russian soldiers had raced to the front lines certain that they would return victorious within several months. But the combatants soon realized that they would be crouching in trenches as the Christmas fires kindled back home. As the futile Allied and German race to the North Sea froze the boundaries of the Western front, Japan declared victory over the German fortress at Qingdao, China. For all intents and purposes, November 7, 1914, marked the end of Japan's battle against Germany. Exactly eight weeks had passed since the initial clash of troops north of the German leasehold. A "sea of fire" engulfed Hibiya Park before the Imperial Palace as bands and lanterns and banzais celebrated the third great military triumph for Imperial Japan.[1] Following her earlier engagements with China and Russia, the war proved that Japan was back on track to becoming the "leader of Asia."

Accompanying the victory procession to the Imperial Palace in early

November were expectations of great Japanese initiatives in China. The great powers, after all, were deadlocked in Europe. And Japan had just acquired a new leasehold, with a fortified harbor and railroad to the interior, in a Chinese province contiguous with the Japanese empire. By the standards of late-nineteenth-century great power competition in China, this was a triumph. While their European allies positioned themselves for a long and bloody struggle for survival, then, Japanese policymakers conjured great plans to capitalize upon the "one in a million chance" afforded by the "European war."

The consolidation and expansion of Japanese interests in China had, of course, constituted the original object of Japan's entrance in the Great War. A great number of would-be policymakers had, as we have seen, flooded the Ōkuma cabinet with proposals for a comprehensive agreement with China in the first month of hostilities. And Field Marshal Yamagata had reminded Foreign Minister Katō that Japan held no grudge against Germany. As soon as victory over Germany was secured, then, the main business of Japanese war aims was at hand. In January 1915, that business would take the form of a set of demands presented to Chinese president Yuan Shikai by Japan's minister in Beijing.

THE TWENTY-ONE DEMANDS IN INTERNATIONAL CONTEXT

Fig. 10   The army presents Katō with Qingdao

The Twenty-One Demands leap out of the historiography of modern Japan as the paramount symbol of Japanese aggression in the early twentieth century, conceived by the most belligerent elements in the Japanese polity and ultimately tied to the Japanese invasion of China in the 1930s.[2] Indeed, the demands were the most comprehensive Japanese essay for power in China to date. And their presentation, along with Japan's efforts to maintain their gains in the Paris Peace Conference of 1919, would play a pivotal role in the rise of Chinese nationalism in the twentieth century.[3] They are said, furthermore, to have had a decisive effect in turning the sympathy of American president Woodrow Wilson away from Japan.[4]

But despite their obvious international impact, the demands were neither a dramatic departure from established diplomatic practice in China nor the product of "extremist" elements in Japan. Rather, they belong squarely in the tradition of great power competition in China and are the handiwork of Japan's consummate practitioner of nineteenth-century imperialism in the British mode, Katō Takaaki.[5]

Great power competition in China was transformed with Japan's military defeat of China in 1895. Under the "treaty port imperialism" that had materialized after the Opium War, the great powers had enjoyed such rights in common as extraterritoriality and low tariffs on their goods. These privileges had rested upon confidence in Beijing's ability to guarantee them. But China's unexpected military defeat had destroyed that confidence. And the great powers abandoned their search for common privileges in favor of special rights in particular territories in China over which they could exert greater independent control. These areas were known as "spheres of influence," and they included such special rights as railway and mining concessions, leased territory, naval bases, and pledges from China not to grant comparable privileges in the same area to any other power.[6] Still new to the game of East Asian power politics, the United States was excluded from this scramble for spheres and attempted, at the turn of the century, to obtain assurances from the great powers that such spheres did not preclude equal opportunity for trade and investment for all.[7] But while the great powers had paid lip service to American appeals for an "open door," they maintained special rights in particular areas and expected all others to respect them. Thus, at the turn of the century, the French considered themselves dominant in Yunnan, Guangxi, and Guangdong; Germany in Shandong; Russia in Xinjiang, Mongolia, and Manchuria; and the British in the Yangzi valley and Hong Kong.

Aspiring to be a player in East Asian affairs, Japan naturally joined this scramble by seeking concessions in areas contiguous to her possessions. Thus in 1898, Tokyo obtained a promise from China not to cede Fujian province to another power. The territory lay directly across the straits from Japan's newly acquired Taiwan. Then in 1905, after the Russo-Japanese War, Tokyo assumed Russia's concessions in South Manchuria, bordering her protectorate in Korea.

The designation of "sphere of influence" was not necessarily cut and dried, especially since all great powers continued to pay lip service to the idea of equal opportunity embodied in the concept of the "open door." Nor did political instability help to clarify matters. Thus, Britain refused to concede predominant Russian influence in Xinjiang because of claims by the Indian government there. In 1900, the United States attempted to obtain a naval base and territorial concession at Samsah Bay in Japan's stake in Fujian. And Anglo-American financial interests tried to penetrate the supposedly Russian and Japanese spheres of influence in Manchuria between 1905 and 1911. Likewise, French and Japanese interests began to venture into presumed British territory in the Yangzi in 1911.

The new post-1895 imperialism in China, in other words, was a highly fluid affair, with the great powers constantly jockeying to maintain and expand their respective positions. Having come to the scramble for concessions in China late in the game, Japan was at a relative disadvantage. While France, Germany, Britain, and Russia had all staked out spheres of influence by the turn of the century, Japan did not obtain a leasehold until 1905. In 1914, therefore, Japanese policymakers viewed their position in China as still very much in the process of formation. War in Europe afforded the opportunity to secure rights still in flux. As the title of Katō's blueprint, "Solution of Pending Problems," suggests, moreover, his negotiations with China pinpointed areas to which Japan had, for the most part, already laid claim.[8]

There were five such areas: Shandong, South Manchuria, Eastern Inner Mongolia, the Yangzi Valley, and Fujian.[9] Most immediate was the question of the disposition of Shandong. The ejection of Germany from the province was, as we have seen, the reason Japan had initially declared war. And while, as stated in the ultimatum to Berlin, Foreign Minister Katō was prepared to return the province to China, he would do so only after a guarantee that Japanese presence in the area could remain strong. Group 1 of the Twenty-One Demands, therefore, called for Chinese assent to the transfer of all German rights to Japan, Japanese rights of residency, commerce, and rail construction in Shandong, and a promise not to cede territory in the province to any other power.

The most important area of Japanese interest in China was the Guandong (Kwantung) leasehold in South Manchuria. This had been Japan's first foothold on the continent and the main item of concern in Katō's discussions with British foreign secretary Grey in January 1913. Although Japan had assumed the Russian leases on the ports and railways in South Manchuria following the Russo-Japanese War, she had never negotiated lease agreements with China. The present leases were due to expire in ten to twenty-five years.[10] More significantly, since 1905, the United States had attempted several times to contest Japan's privileged position in the region.[11] Group 2 of the demands, then, hoped to establish South Manchuria as unambiguously a Japanese sphere of interest. It did so in the familiar manner of asking for preferential rights on railways, mines, and loans, and the right to send advisers to the area.[12]

A third, more recent area of Japanese interest was Eastern Inner Mongolia, which bordered Manchuria and ran along the northern side of the Great Wall. In the 1930s, this region would be better known by the names of the three provinces comprising it, Rehe (Jehol), Chahar, and Suiyuan. A lieutenant general by the name of Tōjō Hideki would gain his first substantial military experience there when, in the aftermath of the Manchurian Incident, he would lead two Guandong Army brigades on a blitzkrieg run across the Mongolian desert to establish control for Japan.[13] Japan had first laid claim to this territory in the Third Russo-Japanese Convention of 1912. But China had not recognized this arrangement. On the contrary, although the area had originally been a part of Mongolia, it had gradually been incorporated into China through successive extensions of the northern boundary of Zhili province.[14] And beginning in 1913, rumors circulated that Beijing planned a series of railways built and financed by the British that would connect the Chinese capital to the entire area. The Russians had obtained Chinese recognition of their monopoly control in Outer Mongolia in 1913 and 1914. Group 2 of the demands, then, aimed to gain the same type of recognition for Japan's position in Eastern Inner Mongolia.[15]

Group 3 of the demands dealt with an area considered by the British as their sphere of influence, the Yangzi valley. But Japanese concerns had purchased coal and iron ore from the Daye iron mines near Hanyang in the middle Yangzi since 1899. They were the largest and most important coal and iron properties in China, and the most important source of such supplies for Japan. Mitsui Company in Shanghai had originally proposed a loan to the owner of the mines, the Han-Ye-Ping Company, in response to a request from Sun Yatsen in December 1911 for Japanese weapons aid. By January 1912, the second Saionji government had arranged for a loan from the Yokohama Specie Bank in return for a tentative promise for joint management of the company.[16] But by 1914, Chinese president Yuan Shikai had begun preparing for the nationalization of iron ores.[17] Group 3 of the demands, then, hoped to salvage the 1912 agreement to assure Japanese control over the mines.

Group 4 covered the Chinese province just across the straits from the Japanese territory of Taiwan. Tokyo, as we have seen, had pursued monopoly rights in Fujian soon after acquiring Taiwan in the Sino-Japanese War. But although Beijing had promised in 1898 not to cede the province to another power, the United States had attempted to obtain a naval base there in 1900.[18] Again on the eve of the First World War, rumors circulated that the Bethlehem Steel Corporation had secured a contract from the Chinese government to construct a naval dock at Ma-Moi near Fuzhou. The rumors turned out to be false.[19] But Group 4 of the demands aimed, by securing a general promise from Beijing not to cede any territory on the China coast to another power, to reclaim Fujian for Japan.[20]

The Sino-Japanese negotiations of 1915 are frequently attributed to sinister motives in Tokyo, the work primarily of nationalist groups such as the Amur River Society (Kokuryūkai), which intended ultimately to turn China into a Japanese protectorate. At its "most influential stage in its history," the Kokuryūkai could not, apparently, be ignored.[21] Foreign Minister Katō, one study has argued, "deferred to a combination of militarist pressure and nationalist opinion" and hoped to "improve his bargaining hand domestically by assenting to extreme conditions."[22]

Group 5 of the demands has been particularly singled out by contemporaries and historians as "extreme." Some specialists are convinced that Katō would never have willingly agreed to such conditions but for strong "outside influences."[23] Indeed, it was primarily in response to this portion of Katō's demands that U.S. secretary of state William Jennings Bryan issued a twenty-page note to Japan's ambassador in Washington on March 13, 1915. The note reaffirmed the principles of the open door and warned against "political, military, and economic domination over China."[24] Field Marshal Yamagata would ultimately tell both Hara Takashi and Takahashi Yoshio that while Japan's rights in Manchuria and Mongolia were worth fighting for, to mobilize troops for the sake of Group 5 would be to "besmirch Japan's international reputation."[25]

But like the rest of the demands, the items in this group outlined privileges already enjoyed by other powers in common or in their spheres of influence. Foreign Minister Katō objected strongly to Chinese complaints that items in Group 5 threatened Chinese national existence. Each one of them, he declared in February, reflected the type of privileges already granted to other powers. That Japan's requests were particularly harmful was "difficult to understand."[26] Indeed, articles 1, 2, and 7 of Group 5, calling for engagement of influential Japanese advisers to the Chinese central government and granting Japanese subjects the right to establish hospitals, schools, and churches and to travel freely, reside, and own land in China simply placed in writing what had already become general practice among the great powers.[27] U.S. secretary of state Bryan found the provisions governing travel, residence, and landownership entirely unobjectionable.[28] Article 5 reiterated Japanese claims to railroad construction in the Yangzi Valley, originally made in January 1913, and article 6 reemphasized claims in Fujian province. While the British had, as we have seen, long claimed exclusive rights in the Yangzi, Japan had already financed two railroads in the area.[29] And the Japanese had, for some time, pursued further concessions that would incorporate these lines into a larger network of rails connecting the middle Yangzi with the south China coast. In the spring of 1914, however, Beijing had concluded several agreements with London that granted British firms exclusive rights to lines that would connect these Japanese railroads.[30]

Articles 3 and 4 of Group 5, which called for joint Sino-Japanese police protection in certain areas and joint management of an arsenal in China were undoubtedly the most problematic of all the demands. But they hardly aimed, as the U.S. note of March 13 suggested, for Japanese political and military domination of China. Rather, Tokyo hoped to apply article 3 specifically to South Manchuria to maintain legal control over Japanese subjects, who would, according to Group 2 of the demands, reside outside the main concession areas of Dairen and Port Arthur, where extraterritoriality remained in effect.[31] Finally, the stipulation in article 4 for either Japanese arms supplies to China or a Chinese arsenal jointly managed by Japan and China aimed for greater Sino-Japanese defense cooperation to replace the extensive defense privileges already enjoyed by Germany in Beijing.[32]

The notion, then, that the sinister hand of the Kokuryūkai was the motive force behind Katō's demands and that the foreign minister was operating only under severe duress ignores the international political and historical context of the Sino-Japanese talks. Given the pattern of great power competition for influence in China since 1895, these items were not the "extreme" object of some intractable radical fringe in Tokyo. Rather, they were goals shared by the most responsible Japanese policy-makers and opinion-leaders based upon a rational calculation of Japanese interests. Even noted China specialist and foremost champion of democracy in Japan, Yoshino Sakuzō, considered the desiderata the "bare minimum" necessary.[33] The demands, furthermore, were widely regarded in foreign capitals as "the natural outcome of recent events."[34] Contemporary American and British objections to the negotiations reflected less anxiety that the items exceeded acceptable behavior than concern over the boost to Japan's position in China that they would inevitably bring.[35]

Foreign Minister Katō pursued a comprehensive agreement with China not as a temporary expedient to placate domestic political enemies. He hoped to fulfill the highest responsibility of his office: to promote Japanese interests according to the accepted canon of international power politics. The demands as finally drafted by Japanese minister to China Hioki Eki and the chief of the Political Affairs Bureau of the Foreign Ministry, Koike Chōzō, incorporated a number of items from a variety of sources. And they clearly exceeded Katō's original aim of trading Germany's concession in Shandong for greater concessions to Japan in Manchuria and Eastern Inner Mongolia. But given the history of Japanese interests in China, and in the context of Japan's recent military victory over Germany, they in no way mark a sudden capitulation by Katō. The foreign minister believed firmly in the legitimacy of each item on the list, arguing strongly, as we have seen, even for the desiderata in Group 5. He would, as well, continue to defend the entire package until his death in 1925. Katō saw himself, in other words, as playing the game of imperial politics by rules that were widely accepted in the capitals of Europe and even in Washington.

If in his talks with China Katō was simply playing by the accepted rules of power politics in China, the same cannot be said of many of his principal domestic rivals. Weighed against the schemes of these men, Katō's vision of Japanese interests in China was modest. Katō sought Chinese assurances of special Japanese rights in Shandong, South Manchuria, Eastern Inner Mongolia, the Yangzi Valley, and Fujian. This was an impressive wish list, but well within the bounds of the scramble for spheres of influence since the Sino-Japanese War. Katō, like his principal model, Great Britain, sought special privileges that were chiefly economic in character.[36] He neither envisioned Japanese political control in Beijing nor sought an excuse for Japanese military action on the continent.

By contrast, Japan's most powerful elder statesmen and the army elite held little regard for Chinese sovereignty. Rather, they presumed the Chinese incapable of self-government and considered Japanese tutelage the ideal form of Sino-Japanese relations.[37] Thus, as we have seen, Inoue Kaoru spoke of placing Yuan Shikai in Japan's pocket. Yamagata Aritomo urged Chinese consultation with Japan on all political and economic matters involving third countries. Terauchi Masatake pictured an Asia under the rule of the Japanese emperor. Tanaka Giichi recommended overwhelming Japanese military presence in northern China's major cities and preparation for a war against the United States.[38] And Vice Chief of the Army General Staff Akashi Motojirō urged annexation of South Manchuria and Eastern Inner Mongolia.[39] While Katō's aims belonged squarely in the tradition of nineteenth-century imperialism, these men anticipated the spectacular ambition of the perpetrators of the Manchurian Incident. If they objected to the substance of Katō's aims in China, it was to their limited, not their ambitious, scope. Indeed, in August 1914, Yamagata had grumbled about the foreign minister's "short-sighted" diplomacy that pressed simply for a solution to already pending problems on the continent.[40]

Fig. 11   "The reason why Foreign Minister (Katō) is disliked"

THE POLITICS OF THE TWENTY-ONE DEMANDS

If Katō's diplomacy was anchored solidly in the past, his politics aimed boldly for the future. If the negotiations with China represented a new departure, they did so in the political, not the diplomatic, sense. For, just as with the declaration of war on Germany, in his talks with Beijing, Katō monopolized the foreign policy decision-making process. The principal importance of the talks, in other words, lies not in what they foretell of future Japanese aggression. It rests in what they reveal of Katō's continued success at promoting cabinet and Foreign Ministry supremacy in the making of Japanese foreign policy. As with the declaration of war against Germany, with the Twenty-One Demands, Katō was able to exclude the elder statesmen and their military and bureaucratic allies completely from the formulation and implementation of Japanese foreign policy.

The fall of Qingdao carried important political, as well as diplomatic, implications for Japan's decision-making elite. In political terms, it exposed the contrasting fortunes of Katō and his chief domestic rival for power, Field Marshal Yamagata. Yamagata reacted to the German surrender in plaintive verse:

Autumn passes,
The mountain winds shift.
Both leaves and the enemy
Fall to earth.[41]

To a man who had served as personal military adviser to the Meiji emperor and who had directly overseen military operations against Russia in
1904 as chief of the Army General Staff, the fall of Qingdao was particularly bittersweet. The field marshal later informed Hara Takashi that the
campaign had been entirely an army operation. He had only received
word after the event.[42] As the first instance of a military victory for Imperial Japan achieved outside Yamagata's direct management, Qingdao's fall
highlighted the continuing erosion of the elder statesman's political
authority.

By contrast, Katō greeted the Japanese victory with confidence. The
foreign minister had, as we have seen, worried about the effects of a
military engagement on the army's domestic political power. For that
reason, he had initially aimed for concessions from Germany short of
war. This had proved impossible, as had his subsequent attempt to limit
the Imperial Army's area of operations. Katō had hoped, subsequently,
for a swift German capitulation, to minimize the opportunity for army
action. The early surrender of Qingdao enabled the foreign minister to
recapture the policy initiative without serious interruption. While Yamagata reeled from the political defeat represented by the declaration of war
and the German capitulation, Katō stood poised to claim further victory.
When the white flag went up at the German fortress, the foreign minister was ready with a political strategy that would guarantee his command
of foreign policy decision making well into the new year.

The strategy revolved around the substance and timing of the negotiations with China. Katō entrusted the main burden of drafting Japan's
negotiating stance to the Japanese minister to China, Hioki Eki, and the
chief of the Political Affairs Bureau of the Foreign Ministry, Koike
Chōzō. But while these men incorporated suggestions that had circulated
from a wide variety of sources, Katō retained the last word on the substance of the final draft. He refused, furthermore, to entertain any direct
advice from the outside. He deflected as "completely off base" proposals
for an agreement on Japanese rights in South Manchuria submitted by

two successive Guandong governors-general.[43] And, as with the declaration of war upon Germany, he kept the *genrō* entirely at bay. Katō ignored Yamagata's "Opinion on China Policy" of August, and Prime Minister Ōkuma declined to sign the draft for discussions with Yuan Shikai circulated by the *genrō* after their September 1914 meeting with him.[44] As with the cabinet decision for war, the *genrō* would learn of a cabinet decision for negotiations with China only after the fact. They would be apprised of the details of those talks, furthermore, only after instructions had been sent to Minister Hioki in Beijing.[45]

Katō's control of the substance of negotiations with China depended largely upon their timing. A vital part of Katō's political strategy with the demands, then, involved a strict regulation of the hour of their presentation. Suggestions for a comprehensive agreement with China had already flooded the Ōkuma regime, as we have seen, in the first few weeks of the war. But Katō's first resolution regarding a prospective accord with Beijing was to begin negotiations only after victory in Shandong. He would wait, as well, until the army's mobile divisions had left the scene of military operations. The lingering of operational troops, after all, risked army interference in delicate negotiations with China. Katō took no initiative on an agreement with Beijing, then, in the first weeks of war. He responded to the queries of his minister to Beijing, Hioki Eki, with instructions to maintain an open channel for discussions "until a good opportunity arrives."[46]

As we have seen, public opinion in Tokyo deemed the fall of Qingdao a fitting opportunity to proceed with Japan's principal war aim. Having speculated since August on a wondrous new relationship with Beijing, and now flush from the excitement of a successful military engagement with Germany, Japanese policymakers and opinion leaders expected a bold initiative to consolidate the empire's new gains. Katō had, indeed, already tried the patience of his fellow policymakers by deferring movement on an agreement with China until the fall of Qingdao.[47] He moved swiftly in the aftermath of the German capitulation, therefore, to meet the tremendous expectations of his countrymen. In so doing, however, he ensured that policymaking remain entirely in his hands.

On November 10 and 11, just days after the German capitulation, Katō obtained a cabinet consensus on military government within the declared war zone. By the end of December, the Eighteenth Division was replaced by occupation forces. And Katō secured a voice in the occupation by negotiating a position for a Foreign Ministry representative within occupational command.[48] While thus clearing the ground of a potential military obstacle to Foreign Ministry command of China policy, Katō moved to preempt renewed demands for an approach to China. On November 11, without *genrō* approval, he orchestrated a cabinet decision to send a Japanese representative to China for talks with Beijing.[49] The following day, the foreign minister ordered Minister Hioki home from Beijing for negotiating instructions.

Hioki did not receive official instructions until December 3.[50] And Katō did not give the green light for the commencement of talks until mid-January. Historians have paid little attention to this delay.[51] But the timing constitutes an important element in the story of Katō's unwavering political offensive against his domestic political enemies. The foreign minister intended, as we have seen, to substitute occupational for operational forces in Shandong before the commencement of talks. But he had another potential political adversary in mind in choosing to delay: the Imperial Diet.

The Thirty-Fifth Diet (December 7–25, 1914) was, following customary practice, scheduled to convene in December 1914. Katō arranged, therefore, for an early commencement, hoped for a quick adjournment, and aimed to begin talks once Japan's MPs had left the capital. Prior to and during the session itself, Katō kept the focus of deliberations on the defense budget, away from negotiations with China. At a Seiyūkai party conference on December 3, Hara Takashi described the German surrender at Qingdao as an opportunity to begin a thorough discussion of the "China problem."[52] As long as the European war continued, Katō retorted, Japan "should not neglect national unity."[53] In his opening remarks to the Lower House on December 8, the foreign minister said nothing of his instructions to Hioki. Regarding China, he intimated only that "the Imperial Government continues to hope for the stability of the Republic of China and the security of her peace."[54] When Seiyūkai leader Ogawa Heikichi criticized the promise to return Jiaozhou to China and demanded a more aggressive pursuit of rights in Shandong, Katō deferred the matter "to future discussions."[55]

Katō, of course, had no intention of holding such discussions. In fact, he and Prime Minister Ōkuma had devised a clever strategy that would not only force a quick adjournment of parliament but deal crippling blows to all three of the cabinet's principal rivals for power, Field Marshal Yamagata, the Seiyūkai, and the army.

Preparing the Political Ground for the Twenty-One Demands

Yamagata began a political offensive of his own in the fall of 1914. As we have seen, among his charges for the Ōkuma cabinet had been the implementation of the long-awaited two-division expansion for the army. Since June, Ōkuma appeared on the way to fulfilling *genrō* expectations. In that month, the cabinet had established a Military Affairs Council, which had sanctioned the immediate expansion goals of both services, an 8–4 fleet for the navy and two divisions for the army.[56] The cabinet approved both proposals in mid-October. In the meantime, Yamagata's deputy, Tanaka Giichi, appealed to Seiyūkai party president Hara Takashi to support army expansion in the upcoming Diet session.[57] The field marshal, then, waited expectantly for the government to steer his cherished bill through parliament.

But Yamagata had another pressing concern in the fall of 1914. While his long crusade for two divisions appeared close to bearing fruit, there remained one serious problem: Foreign Minister Katō. Having been unable in August 1914 to exert any influence on the policymaking process, Yamagata vowed to remove from power the one responsible. As soon as parliament sanctioned his two divisions, he was poised to reshuffle the cabinet.[58]

Yamagata was, however, no match for Katō in political savvy. While the foreign minister understood the new political realities after the Taishō political crisis and knew how to use them to his benefit, Yamagata seemed trapped in the assumptions of an oligarchic polity. Still confident of his own power as the premier kingmaker, the field marshal never doubted that he could use the cabinet to implement his own agenda and then abandon it when his work was done. It took his younger deputy, Tanaka Giichi, to suggest that perhaps the government had read through his intentions and had made other plans.

Tanaka was every bit Katō's equal in political acumen. Just three years the foreign minister's junior, Tanaka, like Katō, appreciated the new political realities of the Taishō era and, as we have seen, helped to establish the ground rules. In a late November meeting with Yamagata, Tanaka suggested that the cabinet's support for two army divisions was not what it seemed. Prime Minister Ōkuma had not abandoned his pro-navy stance. Rather, cabinet approval in October for the army proposal was part of a larger plan to kill two birds with one stone. As the opposition party, the Seiyūkai would be compelled to fight the government endorsement of two divisions in the Diet. Seiyūkai opposition would justify a dissolution of the Diet, which the cabinet hoped to follow with a general election that would destroy Hara Takashi's parliamentary majority.[59] At the same time, Hara's opposition in the Diet would kill the army bill, which Foreign Minister Katō continued to view as unpalatable.[60]

Recognizing now the full import of a dissolution of the Diet, Yamagata rallied at the end of November to check the cabinet strategy. He did so by borrowing a chapter from his own recent political past: the two-division expansion battle of 1912. Once again, Yamagata attempted to force a showdown between the minister of war and the cabinet to bring a change of government. In 1912, the field marshal had helped to destroy the Saionji cabinet by supporting War Minister Uehara Yūsaku's refusal to abandon army expansion. In November 1914, he would have War Minister Oka Ichinosuke resist a parliamentary dissolution and force a cabinet resignation instead.[61] The field marshal thus urged Oka to oppose any attempt by the government to dissolve the Diet.[62] Deputy Tanaka Giichi followed with several appeals of his own, including a seven-point memorandum presented to the war minister in early December.[63]

But the cabinet showed no signs of wavering from the path toward parliamentary dissolution. In fact, both Katō and Ōkuma seemed set on a confrontation with the Seiyūkai. On December 4, Katō warned of "strong action in retaliation" if the opposition "acts in a manner contrary to our wishes."[64] Prime Minister Ōkuma continued to refuse negotiations with Hara Takashi, declaring that he hated compromise.[65] Meanwhile, to avoid a Seiyūkai preventive strike before the government could dissolve the Diet, Agriculture and Commerce Minister Ōura Kanetake began bribing Seiyūkai members in the Diet in early December to support the government on a possible no-confidence motion.[66] Tanaka warned Yamagata that Ōura's actions would have adverse consequences for army expansion.[67]

Clearly unable to dampen the cabinet's enthusiasm to dissolve parliament, Yamagata determined to work on the other side of the equation: the Seiyūkai. Again, it was Tanaka who persuaded him to do so. Tanaka arranged for Seiyūkai president Hara Takashi to visit Yamagata secretly at his Odawara residence on December 19. What followed was a three-hour discussion on how best to evade the cabinet's frontal assault. Hara suggested a withdrawal of the army expansion bill, a change of government, or replacement of the bill with another item. Predictably, Yamagata could not abandon his plans for expansion. But Hara could not promise full Seiyūkai support for the army bill. The two men decided, therefore, to postpone the legislation for one year, with the proviso that the original proposal be realized in full the following year.[68]

It was soon apparent, however, that a Yamagata-Hara understanding had little effect in the face of the relentless political offensive by Ōkuma and Katō. The day that Hara obtained Seiyūkai approval for his agreement with Yamagata, Ōkuma vowed to keep the Seiyūkai at arm's length. He could not agree to a compromise that would violate the cabinet's publicized policies, he informed financier Shibusawa Eiichi. A meeting with Hara would be "nothing but useless" and open to misinterpretation by the public.[69] Nor could Hara envoy Mizuno Rentarō gain access to Vice Minister of War Ōshima Ken'ichi to brief him on the Yamagata-Hara compromise.[70]

Unable to follow through on his deal with Yamagata, Hara decried the "insincerity" of the government and spurred his party on to a "spirited advance" in the December 25 plenary session of the Diet.[71] That evening, after more than eight hours of rancorous debate, the Seiyūkai and Kokumintō (Constitutional Peoples' Party) united to defeat the government's army bill by a 213 to 148 vote. Prime Minister Ōkuma immediately dissolved the Diet.[72] Army expansion had again become, as Yamagata and Tanaka had feared, engulfed in the whirlwind of party politics.

The Negotiations Begin

By the end of December 1914, then, Katō had cleared the slate of potentially disruptive challenges from all three of his chief domestic political rivals: the *genrō*, the Seiyūkai, and the army. He could proceed with the widely anticipated negotiations with China, then, assured that he could maintain control of the nation's most critical foreign policy interest. Indeed, Katō refused to accede to *genrō* suggestions for a special envoy of distinguished stature, one close to themselves, to conduct negotiations with China. By entrusting the responsibility for talks to Japan's minister to Beijing, Hioki Eki, Katō once again asserted Foreign Ministry supremacy in the conduct of the nation's foreign affairs. He also ensured that he would personally control the critical talks, through direct correspondence with Hioki.

The drama of Katō's actual negotiations with Beijing has been recounted elsewhere.[73] Japanese minister Hioki presented Chinese president Yuan Shikai with a list of "pending problems" in five groups on January 15, 1915, with a demand for negotiations. Using every means at his disposal, Yuan resisted committing himself on paper to the expansion and consolidation of Japanese privileges.[74] When Beijing finally refused Japan's revised demands on May 1, Tokyo issued an ultimatum, although with the most problematic Group 5 excised. Having obtained a major concession from Tokyo and unwilling to risk an unwinnable war, China's chief negotiator, Minister of Foreign Affairs Lu Zhengxiang, informed Hioki on May 9 that China would accept the ultimatum. Treaties and related agreements were signed on May 25.

The record of Katō's negotiations is marked by criticism from all quarters within Japan, censure that has been presented as further evidence of either Katō's relatively aggressive posture or of his debt to particularly belligerent elements in Tokyo. Yamagata claimed that war had been averted only because the *genrō* had stepped in to moderate Katō's demands.[75] Marquis Inoue called Katō a "stupid fool" who "knows nothing of diplomacy."[76] And Seiyūkai leader Ogawa Heikichi led the condemnation in the Thirty-Sixth Diet (May 20–June 9, 1915) of the new level of anti-Japanese sentiment in China that the foreign minister seemed to have produced.[77]

But the initial reaction of the military-bureaucratic establishment to Hioki's presentation of demands was highly favorable. Major General Tanaka spoke of obstacles to "the solution of the [January 18] proposal" as if the proposal were his own.[78] Vice Chief of the Army General Staff Akashi Motojirō expressed his own hopes for a "solution" to Katō's plan.[79] And while the governor-general of Korea, Terauchi Masatake, worried that some "difficult problems" had been included in the demands, he wished that the government had submitted "a proposal like this one" to the Chinese earlier.[80]

Elder statesmen Inoue and Yamagata, likewise, identified with the substance of Katō's terms. After describing the provisions in a letter to patron Inoue Kaoru, Mochizuki Kotarō rejoiced that "your opinions and appeals from last April [with respect to foreign policy] are increasingly coming to fruition."[81] Field Marshal Yamagata had responded to Katō's first private briefing of his initiative that he was "fundamentally opposed" to Katō's position.[82] He expressed, nonetheless, "general agreement" with the foreign minister's aims and requested that he be consulted on the final draft of Japanese terms.[83] Soon after the beginning of negotiations, moreover, the field marshal expressed his "great satisfaction" to fellow Chōshū general Miura Gorō that "the cabinet has decided along the lines of my ideas."[84] To Lieutenant General Akashi Motojirō, he noted his particular enthusiasm for the items covering Manchuria and Mongolia.[85]

The heated domestic discussion over negotiations with China in the first half of 1915 becomes a clash of foreign policy ideas only if one views the talks as a foreign policy event in isolation. In fact, beneath the surface of negotiations brewed a dramatic political battle that concerned Japanese policymakers as much as the actual direction of the nation's China policy and that had a direct effect upon their view of the discussions.

Hara Takashi and his Seiyūkai, as we have seen, fell victim to Katō's relentless political offensive when the Ōkuma cabinet dissolved the Diet in late December. In the foreign minister's initial orchestration of the cabinet decision for war, Hara had recognized and feared the potential opportunity that war afforded Katō. The declaration of war, he had observed in August 1914, aimed to "buttress the cabinet by directing public sentiment outward."[86] And when Katō agreed in early March to apply military pressure on China, Hara identified domestic politics as paramount among the foreign minister's motives. "It is," he declared, "an absolute abuse of power and patriotism."[87]

Both Hara and Katō maneuvered on the eve of the election to use the talks with China for their political purposes. As Hara noted, Katō had given the green light for negotiations in mid-January, hoping that their successful completion would catapult him to victory in the general elections in March.[88] But while he had been able to outmaneuver all of his chief domestic rivals at home, the foreign minister had much less success against his principal political rival abroad, Yuan Shikai. Perhaps recognizing the difficulty of the task, Katō urged Hioki in early February to hasten discussions along, "even if it means working day and night."[89] By the eve of the election, he had become desperate. On March 24, with no conclusion to the talks in sight, the foreign minister advised Hioki of the "extreme" necessity of an immediate completion of the discussions.[90]

Hara, for his part, had already seized the political opportunity afforded by the delay of a solution in China. "China policy is the core of the Empire's diplomacy," he declared at a March 22 Seiyūkai party rally. "One mistake, and the repercussions are almost unimaginable."[91] On the eve of the election, he described the Ōkuma cabinet as acting "blindly with no consideration but for promoting its own popularity," and declared Katō's diplomacy "not external but internal diplomacy."[92]

His worries notwithstanding, Katō's failure to reach an agreement with China by mid-March ultimately did not affect his prospects at the polls. Having maintained a parliamentary majority for fifteen years, the Seiyūkai had lost its luster as the party of change. The electorate retained, on the other hand, its faith in the original promise of the Ōkuma cabinet to bring fruition to "constitutional government" in Japan. Indeed, Ōkuma had campaigned that the "power of public opinion will control the fate of the Empire."[93] Together with the massive electoral intervention by Home Minister Ōura Kanetake, this added up to a decisive defeat for the Seiyūkai. By the latter 1920s, the party of Itō Hirobumi would become adept at using the "China card" to its own political advantage. Its criticism of Prime Minister Wakatsuki's failures in China would topple the Kenseikai cabinet in 1927 and ultimately help destroy party government in Japan. But in 1915, it lost its majority party status in the Diet for the first time over an issue that would continue to pose difficulties for its conservative legislators through the mid-1920s: domestic political reform.

While Katō delivered to the Seiyūkai its greatest political defeat, he continued to confound his political enemies among the elder statesmen and the army. The foreign minister's skillful forging of the groundwork for negotiations with China in the fall of 1914 had, like his orchestration of a decision for war, stunned Field Marshal Yamagata and his supporters in the army. Particularly disturbing had been the pivotal role played by War Minister Oka Ichinosuke in ensuring Katō's political victory. Oka was the first minister of war from the Chōshū domain since General Terauchi Masatake had yielded the portfolio to become governor-general of Korea in 1911. His father had been close to Chōshū patriarch Yamagata, and Oka owed his rise in the ranks to the elder statesman, including his present appointment as minister of war. As vice minister of war in the second Saionji cabinet, Oka had worked assiduously for the two-division expansion promoted by Yamagata and the army establishment. As minister of war, then, he was expected to further the agenda of the Yamagata faction.

To the faction's great surprise, however, Oka proved willing to side with the cabinet against Yamagata and his supporters on the most fundamental issues of national policy. On China policy, he assented to the November 11, 1914, cabinet decision to send an envoy to Beijing. He approved, furthermore, Katō's draft for negotiations with Beijing. Politically, Oka chose to support Ōkuma and Katō's crusade against the Seiyūkai rather than to defend Yamagata's compromise with Hara Takashi. It was Oka who, on December 22, had prevented Hara envoy Mizuno Rentarō from briefing the vice minister of war on the Yamagata-Hara compromise.

The inability to count upon the support of a war minister who hailed from the former Chōshū domain revealed further serious erosion in Yamagata's political authority. The field marshal cursed Oka's "breach of etiquette" and sent Tanaka Giichi to signal his displeasure.[94] To ally with the foreign minister on the "Manchuria-Mongolia problem," Tanaka warned, spelled disaster for the future position of the army. Compromise on such a fundamental matter would only lead to concessions on the army's most vital concern, national defense. If Oka merely followed the lead of the cabinet, he would "lose sight of the country, the army, and your future."[95]

But Oka not only sanctioned Katō's plan, he actively promoted the cabinet's political agenda. After preventing Mizuno from briefing the vice minister of war, Oka met with members of the Dōshikai to devise a new strategy for army expansion.[96] Hara Takashi noted that Oka appeared to be "controlled by Ōkuma and company."[97] Oka was acting, Tanaka observed, like a "Dōshikai minister." He seemed "wholeheartedly out to conquer the Seiyūkai," and some suspected that he had "broken from his superiors" to consort with Ōkuma and Katō.[98] Yamagata himself reviled Oka for having "forgotten the position of the army and become a Dōshikai cabinet minister" and urged Tanaka to force his resignation.[99]

But the idea that Oka had become a lackey of the cabinet was wholly exaggerated. He had simply discovered in his new position as minister of war a novel means by which to satisfy army needs. Before Oka's tenure, the Imperial Army considered Japanese minsters of war to be responsible, not to the cabinet, but to army command. Indeed, this is what pitted War Minister Uehara Yūsaku against the Saionji cabinet over the expansion of two divisions in 1912 and subsequently spurred Prime Minister Yamamoto to abolish the active-duty rule. But Oka learned from his experience with the two-division campaign that confrontation was counterproductive. He was, in any event, temperamentally better suited for a quieter and more circumspect promotion of army interests. While the flamboyant Tanaka Giichi had in 1912 trumpeted the cause of army expansion in the public spotlight, Oka had plodded methodically behind the scenes.[100] As war minister, then, he continued the campaign for two divisions and pressed the army agenda for a comprehensive agreement with China.[101] But he recognized that the most constructive and enduring means to satisfy army needs was to cooperate with the cabinet. He determined to follow the government timetable on this agenda.

In so doing, Oka may be described as a pioneer in the opposite sense of Tanaka Giichi. Tanaka developed a political role for the army that would inspire young officers to engage in a direct assault upon party government in the 1930s. Oka, on the other hand, was one of the first to demonstrate, on the model of the British cabinet system, the civilian function of the minister of war: as an army representative responsible to the cabinet. As we shall see, even Tanaka would assume this civilian role as war minister in 1918. The increasing appearance within the army of such diametrically opposed visions of army-cabinet relations would seriously complicate army politics in the 1920s.

If War Minister Oka's complicity with the cabinet alarmed Field Marshal Yamagata and members of the army leadership, so too did Katō's method in pursuing Japanese interests in China. These men, as we have seen, had rejoiced at the consequence for Japanese power that a successful solution to Katō's "pending problems" promised. But Katō's insistence upon a diplomatic solution to the China problem precluded any policymaking role for the Imperial Army. Diplomacy without military action, in other words, threatened to exclude the army from its own continental agenda.[102]

Even as they hailed Katō's daring in presenting a comprehensive list of demands, then, Japan's generals wished for more than a peaceful bid to enhance Japanese interests. In late January, Terauchi lamented Katō's failure to begin negotiations before the withdrawal of operational troops from Shandong.[103] Major General Tanaka urged readiness to take up arms, particularly in Manchuria, but bemoaned the unlikelihood of a show of force "with the authority of the military vis-à-vis the Foreign Ministry the way it is at this moment." The situation required great resolve to "strengthen the unity of the military."[104] Lieutenant General Akashi Motojirō pressed for a solution to the China problem "by way of the splendor of our power."[105] Vice Minister of War Ōshima Ken'ichi warned the Foreign Ministry that "there is no appropriate diplomacy besides [the use of] force."[106] And Field Marshal Yamagata strongly advised Katō at the end of December that in the event of Chinese resistance, the cabinet should be prepared, "even by resolutely resorting to military power," to obtain agreement on Japanese demands regarding Manchuria and Mongolia.[107]

The principal conflict between Katō and members of the military-bureaucratic elite over the foreign minister's negotiations with China, then, focused upon not substance but means. Far from fretting over the extreme nature of Katō's demands, these men hoped for a decisive use of force. Their anxiety over War Minister Oka's complicity with the cabinet grew exponentially with Oka's refusal to promote military operations against China. The war minister's hesitation on the use of arms made him, in Yamagata's eyes, "an obstacle to the progress of national business."[108] And Tanaka Giichi could not agree more. The empire should "resolve not to shy away from the use of force," he advised General Terauchi at the beginning of February. Otherwise, a solution was hopeless. But with Oka "at the beck and call of Katō," such a display of power would be difficult. "There is little hope," he cried, "for the application of the principle that peace can be preserved through arms."[109]

The Army General Staff, therefore, maneuvered immediately after the beginning of negotiations with Beijing to ensure that arms would remain a viable means to the empire's ends. Vice Chief of Staff Akashi Motojirō informed Terauchi on February 3 of a plan for military action in two stages. First, the army would send fresh troops to Manchuria and Qingdao during the regular rotation period without disengaging the old divisions. Subsequently, part of the Guandong Army would occupy vital points in northern China and two or three regiments from the detachment in Korea would be deployed in Manchuria to ready for a multidivisional assault on Beijing.[110] With Terauchi's blessing, Chief of the Army General Staff Hasegawa Yoshimichi sent a "Plan of Operations Against China" to the commander of Japanese forces in Korea on February 22.[111]

Foreign Minister Katō resisted army involvement in China diplomacy throughout February, even as Minister Hioki began suggesting the use of military threats. Katō cautioned Hioki on February 18 that both sides had yet to begin a thorough discussion of the proposal.[112] But by March, the talks had gone nowhere. The March 1 Ōsaka Asahi shinbun voiced regret over the lack of agreement on all but one article and urged an increase in the stakes. "We cannot deal with this China by common means," it declared. "At times, it is necessary to demonstrate stern authority to such a spoiled child."[113]

With the army prepared for action and an election around the corner, Katō cabled Hioki on March 5 that means to pressure China were now under review. The following day, the cabinet approved overlapping troops in Manchuria and Shandong during the regular rotation period.[114]

But Katō refused to implement the second stage of operations proposed by the Army General Staff. When War Minister Oka, in deference to staff demands, secretly petitioned the throne to send troops to China, the foreign minister had the petition immediately withdrawn.[115] Through the end of negotiations, Katō would insist that Japan "make every effort to gain acceptance of our position through diplomatic means."[116]

Yamagata's Second Offensive, June 1915

Field Marshal Yamagata's objections to Katō's negotiations with China have served as critical evidence in the recent reevaluation of the elder statesman as a voice of caution in Japanese foreign affairs. But if there was a substantive difference between Yamagata and Katō on China policy, it was Katō, not the elder statesman, who exercised the conservative voice. The field marshal's "Opinion on China" of August 1914, it will be recalled, went well beyond Katō's eventual negotiation of primarily commercial rights on the mainland by urging Chinese consultation with Japan on all political and economic matters involving foreign countries. Even before the commencement of talks, Yamagata, as we have seen, had urged immediate preparation for a display of force. And he would clarify his hopes for an alliance with Russia to replace Japan's reliance upon Britain in a February 1915 memorandum titled "For a Russian Alliance."

But the chief contest between Yamagata and Katō over the negotiations with China was, as it was with the army leadership, a battle for power, not substance. The elder statesmen's August and February policy papers, plus a second one on China policy in March, were all drafted and submitted to key members of the cabinet in the short interval between the outbreak of war and the conclusion of talks with China. Such productivity reflected Yamagata's particular interest in the opportunity afforded by the war. But the memoranda were also part of a desperate bid by the field marshal to remain in touch with the policymaking process. Thwarted by Katō at every turn, the field marshal hoped to defeat the foreign minister with a barrage of policy pronouncements. He was understandably disturbed, then, when each of his initiatives was ignored. Katō, he had observed in September 1914, considered the *genrō* senile. And when Ōkuma made no attempt to address his February memorandum for a Russian alliance, Yamagata decried the prime minister's "irresponsibility." There was, he told fellow *genrō* Matsukata, "no sign of a resolution" to the China problem. And he reminded the Satsuma elder that he had warned of the danger of Ōkuma at the outset of the cabinet. "Now my fears are completely confirmed."[117] Katō did not bother to reply to the field marshal's policy paper on China of March 1915.[118]

The political confrontation over China between Yamagata and Katō would reach a climax in May 1915. The foreign minister had refused to consult with the elder statesmen through the entire duration of the negotiations with Beijing.[119] And he had rebuffed Minister Hioki's suggestion on April 23 for an ultimatum to China because of the opportunity that it would grant the *genrō* to interfere in the talks.[120] But by the beginning of May, continued Chinese obstinance and overwhelming public pressure in Japan had forced the foreign minister's hand. On May 2, he, Foreign Ministry Secretary Matsui Keishirō, and Political Affairs Bureau Chief Koike Chōzō gathered at Katō's private residence to draft an ultimatum to China.[121] Cabinet approval came readily on the morning of May 4. But an ultimatum also required the sanction of the *genrō*. Katō braced for a fight as Yamagata and fellow *genrō* Matsukata and Ōyama joined the cabinet on the afternoon of the fourth to discuss the foreign minister's progress in Beijing.

Yamagata did not disappoint. Upon arriving at the prime minister's residence, he assumed the seat of Home Minister Ōura Kanetake, absent on business, directly across from the foreign minister. From this vantage point, he responded to Katō's cool explanation of the situation with an invective fueled by eight months of neglect. Katō knew, he began, of his fundamental disagreement with the foreign minister. And yet, why had he and the finance minister failed to heed any of the elder statesman's numerous verbal and written policy recommendations? Katō, the field marshal pressed, should make a personal trip to Beijing "to clear matters up." Navy Minister Yashiro interjected that Katō would be more useful at home at such a time of crisis. But Yamagata warned Yashiro to "stop making excuses!"[122] Katō and Ōkuma gave their own reasons for retaining the foreign minister in Tokyo. But Yamagata continued to press the baron until, flush with anger, Katō announced that he would take full responsibility and resign.[123] In the final stage of talks with China and with Japanese opinion clamoring for a show of strength, the *genrō* could not afford the sudden departure of their foreign minister. Faced with Katō's bluff, they could only make an honorable exit. "I have stated my opinion for your reference," declared Yamagata. "You should discuss it and make a decision."[124]

Yamagata's insistence here that Katō make a personal trip to Beijing before delivering an ultimatum is frequently offered as evidence of the field marshal's caution, particularly, his objection to the foreign minister's insistence upon Chinese acceptance of Group 5 of the demands. Indeed, the draft ultimatum submitted by Katō to the cabinet and *genrō* demanded Beijing's approval of all negotiating items. Yamagata would later inform Hara Takashi that, while Manchuria and Mongolia were a different matter, he had objected to taking arms against China over Group 5.[125] And, after the offensive clause was eliminated from the ultimatum and the demands accepted by Yuan Shikai, the elder statesman would boast that *genrō* objections had prevented Japan from going to war over Group 5.[126]

When Katō decided in early March for a display of force, Yamagata had, indeed, counseled against fighting over Group 5. But what would become the focus of great power censure was by no means the field marshal's chief preoccupation in March, or even at the critical *genrō*-cabinet meeting of May 4.[127] The general tone of his advice from December 1914 fell not on the side of caution but of resolve. In his December 30 meeting with Katō, for example, the field marshal expressed surprise at the foreign minister's lack of preparation for a display of force. If Beijing refused Japan's most cherished desiderata over Manchuria and Inner Mongolia, he urged at the time, the cabinet should decide on immediate military action.[128] Likewise, while excluding Group 5, when Katō solicited the elder statesman's approval of a revised version of Japanese terms on April 21, Yamagata advised preparation for a "final [act of] resolution" (*saigo no kesshin*) in case of Chinese obstinance.[129]

In the May *genrō*-cabinet conference, Yamagata focused his attack on the need to send Katō to China to "express the sincerity of the empire." This would help "maintain the trust of the powers and gain the sympathy of the people."[130] But the field marshal was neither advocating a softening of Japan's position nor discounting an eventual use of force. Rather, he hoped for Chinese acceptance of all of Japan's demands through a personal appeal to the justice of the empire's cause. If Yuan continued to object, Japan could take up arms knowing that it had at least clarified its position.[131]

The field marshal, in other words, worried in early May not about the severity of Japanese aims but of the signal of weakness sent by a Japanese compromise. The same can be said of Marquis Inoue. In a memorandum solicited by Yamagata and enthusiastically presented by the field marshal at the meeting,[132] Inoue underscored not the importance of compromise but the need to demonstrate Japanese resolve. Simply yielding on Group 5 without such a demonstration, Inoue argued, would embolden China to force a second compromise on the empire. Before agreeing to any concessions, then, Japan should clarify to China and the great powers that she is "bear[ing] the unbearable" for the sake of "peace in the Far East." Should China persist in her recalcitrance, it should be amply clear that Japan would resort, although "regrettably," to "autonomous action."[133]

Inoue and Yamagata did fret about Katō's aggressive posture in one sense, that is, in the political sense. If the pros and cons of Group 5 did not concern them, the foreign minister's relentless promotion of his own agenda at the expense of genrō authority certainly did. As with the last genrō-cabinet conference the previous August, Yamagata viewed the May 4 meeting as an opportunity to chasten Katō for his impudence, most recently, his refusal to answer his own April memorandum. Katō had called the present meeting to obtain genrō approval for a policy conceived entirely by himself and his Foreign Ministry aides after having intentionally ignored the advice of the elder statesmen. As a matter of principle, the genrō could not now simply bestow their blessing on it.

The cabinet would ultimately drop references to Group 5 in the final ultimatum, but not in response to genrō demands. Rather, they deferred to strong reservations recently expressed by Japan's ally, Britain.[134] Far from gratifying the elder statesmen, the compromise amplified their fundamental concern, that is, their anxiety regarding the expansion of Katō's power. China's favorable response to Japanese terms on May 8, after all, capped a critical chapter in Katō's diplomacy. The conclusion of a Sino-Japanese agreement on Japanese continental rights marked the long-awaited completion of the gamble embarked upon by the foreign minister in August 1914. He had met widespread expectations regarding the strengthening of Japanese rights in China and had done so entirely on his own terms. He had kept the talks in the hands of the Foreign Ministry, deflected army and *genrō* calls for a display of force, and transformed his accomplishments into majority party status in the Diet.[135] Yamagata responded to the conclusion of discussions, then, not with applause but with censure. "China diplomacy," he grumbled, "is not something that should be negotiated by the likes of Minister Hioki."[136] Ten days after China accepted the revised ultimatum, the field marshal apprised Hara that "we will have to destroy the Dōshikai."[137]

Yamagata would not pursue such an ambitious enterprise. But his outburst revealed a decisive shift of political focus between the advent of the Ōkuma cabinet and May 1915. The *genrō*, it will be recalled, had entrusted Ōkuma in April 1914 with the principal charge of destroying the Seiyūkai majority in parliament. The field marshal now recognized, however, a greater political enemy. The realization would ultimately prompt a surprising conversion by the elder statesman in 1918 into a chief sponsor of a Seiyūkai cabinet.

In the meantime, while he could not destroy the Dōshikai, Yamagata would again bring full pressure to bear on its president, Katō. He did so in a repeat of his September 1914 response to the foreign minister's original coup with the declaration of war. In mid-June, just as in the previous September, the field marshal summoned his fellow *genrō*, including a physically ailing Inoue, for a series of private conferences with Prime Minister Ōkuma. Yamagata's planning for these conferences featured him in true form as the political schemer that his contemporaries frequently described. He impressed upon Matsukata the need for a cabinet change and informed Inoue of Katō's refusal to submit diplomatic papers to the marquis because of his fear of an Inoue leak.[138] Matsukata declared that he would no longer support the cabinet while Katō remained in office.[139] And Inoue reacted to Yamagata's news with anger "like a raging fire," protesting that this was tantamount to being treated like a "tsarist spy."[140] He later pressed Ōkuma to replace Katō with Japan's ambassador to Russia, Motono Ichirō, and Minister Hioki with former minister in Beijing and personal friend of Yuan Shikai, Ijūin Hikokichi. If the prime minister refused, the marquis threatened to cut all political ties, call his son

Katsunosuke home from London where he was serving as Japan's ambassador, and retire from political life.[141]

Having amply roused the ire of his venerable colleagues, Yamagata now led Matsukata, Inoue, and Ōyama in presenting Ōkuma on June 25 with three basic demands. Foreign Minister Katō should be removed from office; the cabinet should always consult the genrō before acting on such important matters of diplomacy as the nation's China policy; and Japan should immediately respond favorably to Russian requests for an alliance.[142] Here in their most distilled form were Yamagata's most fundamental wishes for Japanese domestic politics and foreign policy. Katō would have to go, the genrō argued, because he was responsible for a dramatic rise in anti-Japanese sentiment in China. But the real reasons to eject Katō had little to do with public sentiment on the mainland. Rather, they were clearly embodied in the second and third demands presented to Ōkuma. The foreign minister was an obstacle because he held a conception of Japanese politics and foreign policy fundamentally different from that of the genrō. While the elder statesmen considered themselves the final arbiters of the nation's foreign policy, Katō had excluded them and insisted upon the cabinet as the principal locus of decision making. Thus the second command urged vigilance against "arbitrary action" by the cabinet. And where Katō had faithfully believed in the Anglo-Japanese alliance as the core of Japanese diplomacy, the genrō's third demand urged a diplomatic reorientation toward Imperial Russia.

Following the last private discussion with Prime Minister Ōkuma nine months earlier, then, the genrō again produced here a vision of Japanese domestic and foreign affairs striking in its contrast with Katō's. But the elder statesmen did not advance their interests here any further than they had in their previous meeting with the prime minister. Ōkuma responded by threatening to scuttle the cabinet. And to the frustration of Inoue and the complete dismay of Matsukata, the field marshal "changed his opinion midway" and now advised caution.[143] To oust Katō was one matter. To form a new cabinet posed another array of problems. Yamagata worried that, incited by other men from the former Satsuma domain, Matsukata had designs on the prime ministry.[144] And he suspected that a cabinet dissolution would be "used by the parties" and "result in a repeat of the failure of 1912."[145] Hara Takashi later noted that Yamagata, "in his usual selfish way," desired to keep Ōkuma in power to place him under his "complete control."[146]

But with Ōkuma standing by his foreign minister, the genrō conferences ended in failure in the first week of July. Upper House member Masuda Takashi observed that "even the genrō no longer have the power to move the government."[147] But Yamagata would not accept defeat. No sooner had the genrō conferences failed, than he began a new offensive on a Russo-Japanese alliance. Having been completely excluded from a role in Japan's critical negotiations with China, Yamagata retained only his original proposal on Russia with which he could make any impact upon the nation's foreign affairs. And he hoped, in part, that such pressure for a redirection of Japan's foreign policy would place Katō in an untenable position and finally eliminate the greatest political threat that the genrō had ever faced.[148]

But Yamagata had no greater success pressuring the cabinet on a matter of policy than he had had in confronting the prime minister directly about his insurgent deputy. The prime minister and foreign minister assured the elder statesman in two private meetings that they would study the matter of a Russo-Japanese alliance. But later inquiries revealed no movement on the issue.[149]

Ironically, in only a few weeks, Katō gave the genrō what they had struggled for for a full year but could ultimately not obtain on their own. Having failed to oust Home Minister Ōura Kanetake with a no-confidence motion in parliament in June, the Seiyūkai had begun working with its political allies in the courts to apply pressure on the home minister. Thanks to the enthusiasm of Chief Prosecutor Hiranuma Kiichirō, the home minister was found guilty of vote-buying in the March 1915 general election and forced to resign.[150] Foreign Minister Katō took the opportunity in 1915 to exit the cabinet. Since the government had entrusted Ōura with the task of "managing" Diet members for the election, he argued, the entire cabinet should assume responsibility for the election fraud.[151] In spite of Ōkuma's appeals, he, Finance Minister Wakatsuki, and Navy Minister Yashiro followed Ōura's exit in a cabinet reshuffling on August 10.

After a year of bitter partisan warfare, Katō's willingness to deliver to his political enemies exactly what they had desired seems curious. His departure was more than an appeal for responsible parliamentary government or an expression of loyalty to an old friend. Rather, it was based,

as all of his public actions were based, upon a distinct political calculation. With the Sino-Japanese treaties, the foreign minister had dramatically realized the highest goal of his office: consolidation of Japanese interests in China. Politically, there remained one final step: the creation of
his own cabinet. To do so, he would have to establish some distance between himself and the Ōkuma cabinet.[152] Given the recent spectacular
Dōshikai electoral victory and the successful conclusion of talks with
China, the timing seemed perfect.

But Katō's success at working parliamentary government to his benefit had given him a false sense of the strength of the system. As head of
the majority party in the Diet, he had assumed that the *genrō* would be
forced to nominate him to succeed Ōkuma. But the preeminent kingmaker, Yamagata, would do nothing of the kind. In the wake of Ōkuma's
fall in October 1916, the elder statesman called for a national unity cabinet to deal with the crisis presented by the war. The result would be the
long-awaited political debut of General Terauchi Masatake. What was
Katō's only tactical error in his year of battle with the *genrō* would prove
to be the greatest political miscalculation of his career. He would subsequently wait nine years before assuming the prime ministry. In the in-
terim, he would look on as his main political party rival, Hara, and a
string of statesmen without party affiliation formed their own governments and delayed the progress of representative government in Japan for
almost a decade.

SYNOPSIS

After widespread celebration of the Japanese victory against Germany
on November 7, 1914, the Ōkuma regime turned to the main task of
Japanese continental aims. Those aims, known as the Twenty-One Demands, and their chief proponent, Katō Takaaki, have assumed notoriety
as harbingers of a new level of Japanese aggression on the continent. But
these "demands" fell well within the pattern of great power competition
in China since the Sino-Japanese War. As a continuation, moreover, of
Japan's established route to great power status, they were widely popular
in Tokyo.

Katō's negotiating terms were, in fact, modest compared to many of
the proposals for a comprehensive agreement with China that circulated

in Tokyo in the fall of 1914. These plans envisioned political hegemony and Japanese military action in China, not primarily the economic supremacy promoted by the foreign minister. It was these proposals, chiefly the product of members of Japan's military-bureaucratic elite, that broke with the accepted norms of great power behavior in China and anticipated Japan's unbridled expansion of the 1930s.

If the Twenty-One Demands were unexceptional in terms of their foreign policy implications, they were revolutionary from the perspective of domestic politics. Just as he had with the declaration of war, Katō conducted negotiations with China in a manner intended to solidify cabinet and Foreign Ministry supremacy in the making of foreign policy. He delayed talks until able to dissolve the Diet and replace the mobile Eighteenth Division in Shandong with occupation troops. He personally directed discussions in Beijing through his Foreign Ministry representative. And he refused to authorize a show of force as the army had desired. It was, moreover, the first instance of a major foreign policy initiative undertaken exclusively by a foreign minister without prior consultation with the preeminent wielders of state power, the *genrō*.

The principal importance of Katō's talks with China in 1915, in other words, lies not in what they foretell of future Japanese aggression. It rests in what they reveal of Katō's continued success at excluding the original wielders of state power in Imperial Japan from the formulation and implementation of Japanese foreign policy. The May conclusion of the Sino-Japanese treaties represented an unmistakable political, as well as diplomatic, victory for the foreign minister. Field Marshal Yamagata, despite concern about Katō's unilateral actions since the outbreak of World War I and his persistent efforts to eject the foreign minister from the cabinet, could neither oust Katō nor force a fundamental change in policy. The Dōshikai victory in the March 1915 elections only reinforced Katō's command.

Paradoxically, however, Katō's electoral victory may have done more to bring about his downfall than any of Yamagata's initiatives since August 1914. Certain that the Diet majority now guaranteed his ascendance to the prime ministry after Ōkuma, Katō broke from the cabinet in August. To his surprise, his resignation did not become the first step on a direct road to Japan's first party cabinet. It was, rather, the last act of a dramatic demonstration of "constitutional government" before the return of military-bureaucratic rule. Deprived of its driving force, the Ōkuma regime soon fell prey to the extra-cabinet wielders of state power. Yamagata described Katō's resignation as "advantageous for the State in terms of its China diplomacy."[153] He would soon embark upon a diplomatic offensive aimed at restoring genrō prerogative in, and redressing the excessive pro-British orientation of, the empire's foreign policy.

4 Anticipating a New Order in Asia: Yamagata Aritomo, Tanaka Giichi, and an Autonomous Foreign Policy

We will not reach our objective if we simply follow the flow of events in China. Rather, we must think of shaping the situation ourselves.

— Vice Chief of the Army General Staff Tanaka Giichi, May 1916

In pondering the future of the empire, we should not await the arrival of an opportunity. We must create the opportunity.

— War Minister General Ugaki Kazushige, January 1931

The spring of 1915 brought renewed Allied attempts to break the stagnation of the Western front. New offensives against the Germans beginning in May at Artois and Champaign in northern France aimed for final victory "whatever the cost." The cost would surpass the carnage of the Somme and Verdun. But victory would be nowhere in sight.

While British and French soldiers suffered a growing sense of desperation, Japanese generals observed developments in Europe with fascination. Their own battle against the kaiser had been a gentlemanly affair. Japanese officers had sent messages into the Qingdao garrison wishing their German friends and tutors luck and safety during the siege. And when German POWs arrived in Japan to spend the duration of the hostilities in Japanese camps, the emperor sent an army representative to receive them and enthusiastic crowds greeted the arrivals with "banzais" and fluttering German and Japanese flags.[1] Of all the Western powers, after all, Imperial Germany had served as the principal model for the Meiji Renovation. German victories in Europe and her frustration of Allied offensives, in one sense, served to affirm Japan's chosen path of empire, arms, and oligarchic rule.

As Field Marshal Yamagata maneuvered in June 1915 to drive Foreign Minister Katō Takaaki from office, then, Major General Tanaka Giichi found in the growing evidence of German strength in Europe cause for celebration. At home, Katō's political offensive had, following the Taishō political crisis, suggested the inexorable advance of parliamentary politics. But German military victories proved the enduring strength of authoritarian rule. "Since the last extraordinary Diet session," Tanaka informed General Terauchi Masatake in June, "there seems to be a great awareness by respectable gentlemen that the evil of domination by the likes of politicians is unbearable. On the other hand, on the war situation in Europe, they recognize the superior power and influence of Germany." The time had come, Tanaka declared, "to correct the maladministration inspired by petty political concerns, to improve the national character, and realize national morality." To promote this antiparty agenda inspired by German power, the major general envisioned a new cabinet headed by the respected army elder General Terauchi himself.[2]

Tanaka mentor Yamagata was to echo Tanaka's enthusiasm for the kaiser when he informed Hara Takashi in January 1916 that Japan "should be learning not from Britain but, at least for the next few years, from Germany."[3] But Japanese generals and field marshals were not alone in their expressions of fondness for Japan's ostensible enemy. In the August 1915 issue of the monthly *Chūō kōron*, Tokyo Imperial University professor and opinion leader Yoshino Sakuzō noted that "to admire Germany and forget Britain and America is the most worrisome tendency in our country's press today." Among the nation's "German admirers," Yoshino saw an "unmistakable sickness." That was "the tendency, through extreme adoration of German 'power,' to exaggerate that power and praise other abhorrent characteristics which those with this 'power' tend to possess." It was necessary, Yoshino conceded, for Japan in the new age of the twentieth century to promote great national strength like Germany. "But I think we must also learn the strong points of Anglo-Saxon civilization and build a noble and complete, gentlemanly national character."[4]

As Tanaka and the "German admirers" hailed German national power as evidence of the strength of authoritarian rule, then, Yoshino looked to Britain to validate a very different conception of the state. Like Katō Takaaki, Yoshino considered the principal strong point of Anglo-Saxon civilization to be "constitutional government." Five months later, he would publish in the same journal what would become the central manifesto of the "Taishō democracy" movement, "Preaching the Essentials of Constitutional Government and Discussing the Road to Its Fulfillment."[5] In this lengthy essay, Yoshino traced the history of parliamentary politics in Britain to argue for government for the people, *minponshugi*, in Japan. Nothing could have been further from the wishes of Tanaka Giichi and his mentors.

THE LINGERING INFLUENCE
OF KATŌ TAKAAKI

The second half of the Ōkuma cabinet is relatively quiet in the historiography of Japanese politics and diplomacy. Political discussions center around the prime minister's battle in his final days to ensure Katō Takaaki's place as his successor. And like Japan's entrance into World War I, the two major foreign policy initiatives of this period, the movement to depose Chinese president Yuan Shikai and the Russo-Japanese Convention, are overshadowed by the drama of Katō Takaaki's negotiations with China. But the relative silence is hardly justified. For the period saw an intensification of the political battle between the civilian cabinet and members of the military-bureaucratic Yamagata faction that had raged since the outbreak of war in Europe. Political historians have generally overlooked this battle because, as during Katō's stint as foreign minister, it was waged primarily in the realm of foreign policy. A pivotal member of the Yamagata faction, General Terauchi Masatake, seized the prime ministry in October 1916. But long before the appearance of Terauchi's "transcendental" cabinet, the energetic vice chief of the Army General Staff, Tanaka Giichi, had reestablished control for the Yamagata faction of the most critical policy issue of Japanese interests in China. In fact, given the unexpected disintegration of Yamagata-faction unity with the ascension of the Terauchi cabinet, Tanaka's campaign to depose President Yuan, together with a new convention signed with Russia in 1916, would mark the peak of the faction's power during the Great War.

These two initiatives also provide another glimpse at the ambitious international aims of the most powerful leaders of the Yamagata faction. For if presenting the Twenty-One Demands belongs, as a diplomatic venture, in the context of nineteenth-century imperialism, the movement to depose Yuan and the Russo-Japanese Convention of 1916 represent bold new departures. The policy against Yuan aimed to establish a decisive Japanese physical presence in China. The Russo-Japanese agreement sought to replace Britain with Russia as the central focus of Japanese foreign relations. From Russia, Yamagata and his associates hoped to obtain recognition of vastly expanded Japanese continental interests and support against the most likely challenger to those interests: the United States.

The contrast between the policies of Yamagata and Katō is visible in the first few months after Katō's resignation. The ex-foreign minister was able initially to maintain a strong hand in policymaking by controlling the disposition of personnel within the Foreign Ministry. The *genrō* had aggressively lobbied for Japan's ambassador to Russia, Motono Ichirō, to succeed Katō. As a career Foreign Ministry official, Motono had spent twenty years in various European capitals, twelve of those in St. Petersburg. He was, as well, on good terms with Yamagata. He appeared the perfect candidate, in other words, to promote the field marshal's plan to replace Britain with Russia as the cornerstone of Japanese diplomacy. It was no accident that he was chosen to head the Foreign Ministry under General Terauchi in October 1916.

But in the fall of 1915, Katō fought vigorously to keep Motono from the Foreign Ministry portfolio. He was, Katō maintained, "too committed to the Russian government."[6] Instead, Katō anointed a career bureaucrat and longtime friend, the ambassador to France, Ishii Kikujirō, as his successor. For vice minister, he arranged for Minister Shidehara Kijūrō's relocation from the Hague. As Prime Minister Katō's foreign minister, Shidehara would, of course, become *the* symbol of a circumspect China policy in the 1920s. But Field Marshal Yamagata already worried in 1915 about the effect that the close relationship between these two men would have on the nation's foreign policy.[7]

The effect of Katō's lingering influence at Kasumigaseki was, of course, to keep Japanese foreign policy squarely centered on the Anglo-Japanese alliance. In the wake of Katō's resignation, Field Marshal Yamagata had immediately moved to fulfill his hopes for stronger Russo-Japanese ties. After securing the understanding of Vice Minister of War Ōshima over the head of War Minister Oka, he enthusiastically informed Prime Minister Ōkuma in mid-August of the army's willingness to increase arms aid to St. Petersburg. Soon after the fall of Qingdao, Japan had sent to Russia field artillery used in the campaign and batteries seized from the Germans. Now, Yamagata noted, Japan's generals were determined to expand Japan's arsenals and "work night and day" on weapons manufactures. An "immediate commencement" of operations, he reminded the prime minister, would require the encouragement of the government.[8] Meanwhile, Yamagata took advantage of the temporary leadership vacuum at the Foreign Ministry to press Vice Minister of Foreign Affairs Matsui Keishirō directly on an alliance with Russia.

The pressure for stronger Tokyo–St. Petersburg ties came, as well, from abroad. Russian foreign minister Sergei Sazonov had recommended a Russo-Japanese alliance to British foreign secretary Grey after he had learned of German overtures to Tokyo regarding a separate peace.[9] He had also received information from the Russian ambassador to Japan of substantial pro-German sentiment in Tokyo.[10] Grey had subsequently broached the subject with then foreign minister Katō.

Katō had, however, steadfastly resisted a stronger relationship with St. Petersburg. He had argued that a new alliance could obligate Japan to send troops to Europe. But the foreign minister worried primarily about the effect that such an arrangement could have on the alliance with Britain. It would, he maintained, inevitably weaken Anglo-Japanese ties, like "dilut[ing] whiskey with water."[11]

While Yamagata began a new offensive for a Russo-Japanese alliance, then, the cabinet, with Katō's encouragement, moved to strengthen Japanese ties with London. On the route home to Tokyo to assume the Foreign Ministry portfolio, Ambassador Ishii first called upon British foreign secretary Grey. Eight days after Yamagata's appeal for an increase in arms aid to Russia, the cabinet approved instructions to Ishii in London designed to deflect the pressure for a stronger relationship with the tsar. Japan, Ishii was to make clear, "is already aiding [Russia] to the best of its ability." There was "no prospect" of any assistance over and above this.[12] And the envoy was advised to "refrain from making a commitment" regarding Russia's possible inclusion in the Anglo-Japanese alliance.[13] Nor did the Foreign Ministry respond favorably to Yamagata's direct overtures for a bilateral alliance. Vice Minister of Foreign Affairs Matsui informed the field marshal that, because the matter required caution, a decision could not be made until Ambassador Ishii returned to Tokyo.[14] Yamagata could only express his fear that an opportunity would be missed.[15]

The Ōkuma cabinet snubbed Yamagata again by deciding on September 23 to adhere to the London Declaration. Britain, France, and Russia had proclaimed their solidarity against Germany in September 1914 with a pledge not to pursue a separate peace with the kaiser. Since July 1915, British foreign secretary Grey had proposed that Japan, too, join the pledge. As an answer to Grey's recommendations, then, the Japanese decision reaffirmed Japan's commitment to the Anglo-Japanese alliance. As a renunciation of the right to make a separate peace with Germany, it alarmed Japan's "German admirers." Most important, the cabinet chose to sign a declaration to avoid a deeper commitment to Russia. It was the least binding of three options discussed by Ishii and Grey aimed at satisfying Russia's desire for a closer relationship with Japan. By signing the declaration, the cabinet denied Russia membership in the Anglo-Japanese alliance and rejected an independent alliance with St. Petersburg.[16] Well aware of *genrō* displeasure, the government concluded matters through an exchange of notes in London without first submitting them, as was standard procedure for international treaties, to the Yamagata-chaired Privy Council.[17]

Fig. 12
China the
mad horse

THE TROUBLESOME POLITICS OF JAPAN'S CHINA POLICY

Five days before Japan signed the London Declaration, the reshuffled Ōkuma cabinet made its first important decision regarding China. It resolved to warn the president of the Chinese Republic, Yuan Shikai, against assuming the status of emperor. Yuan's capitulation to Japanese pressure with the Sino-Japanese treaties in May had shaken his reputation at home. It had also sparked widespread hostility toward Japan that would play a critical role in the rise of Chinese nationalism. To tap that rising sentiment and prevent a further erosion of his own political authority, Yuan had moved three months after the Sino-Japanese treaties to resurrect the aura of imperial Chinese rule. The Society for Planning Peace was formed in late August to lay the ground for the triumphal return of absolute authority to the Forbidden City.

The Ōkuma regime had no intrinsic reason to reject Yuan's bid for monarchy. The second Saionji cabinet had, after all, promoted constitutional monarchy in Beijing after the Chinese Revolution for the validation that it would bring to Japan's own experiment with monarchic rule. The end of republicanism in China now might help to erase Japan's diplomatic defeat to American republicanism in Beijing in 1911. Indeed, Ōkuma initially broached no objection to Yuan's initiative. China's reversion to monarchy, the premier advised the *Jiji shinpō* in September 1915, was a natural step after four years of unsuccessful republicanism.[18]

The October cabinet decision to warn Yuan explained that a sudden transformation to monarchy would spark rebellion in China and threaten the stability of Yuan's regime. Japan hoped by restraining the Chinese president to "prevent disturbances" and "solidify the foundation of peace in the Far East."[19] But their proclamations notwithstanding, Japanese policymakers in the 1910s, as in the late 1920s and 1930s, were not merely the victims of circumstances in China. Like their counterparts among the great powers, they aimed as much to shape international events as to be shaped by them. This was as true of Prime Minister Ōkuma as it had been of Katō Takaaki. It would also be true for Tanaka Giichi, who would shortly come to command the policy directed at President Yuan.

Contrary to the official text of Japan's warning to Yuan, reports from Japan's ministers and even military representatives in China in the fall and winter of 1915 downplayed the significance of opposition movements on the continent.[20] In December, the Army General Staff's representative in Beijing, Banzai Rihachirō, noted the probable failure of an anti-Yuan movement if opposition forces did not accelerate their activities. A majority in China, after all, leaned toward support of the Chinese president.[21] The text of the Japanese warning to Beijing itself recognized the apparent absence of "major opposition" to a monarchical system in China. But it insisted that this accurately described only the outer situation. "On the inside," it offered in almost desperate hope, "opposition is unexpectedly widespread. We cannot deny that an unstable situation is gradually spreading to all areas."[22]

What truly alarmed Ōkuma at this time, as it would Prime Minister Tanaka Giichi in 1927 as Chiang Kaishek proceeded to unify China under the Nationalist banner, was not the weakness of the Beijing regime. It was, rather, its strength. Katō and the cabinet had taken credit in May for the conclusion of a long-sought comprehensive agreement with China. That agreement had highlighted Japan as the preeminent player in East Asian power politics. By October 1915, however, Japanese power to influence events in China was facing renewed challenges. Soon after the conclusion of talks, Beijing had begun taking advantage of loopholes in the May treaties to demand a reduction of Japanese privileges. Claiming that under article 5 of the South Manchuria, Eastern Inner Mongolia Treaty Japanese civilians in Manchuria were now legally covered under

Chinese police law, the Chinese government advised the removal of Japanese police stations in Chouyang in Liaoyuan county.[23] Negotiators in Mukden (present-day Shenyang) argued that Japanese police posts outside the railroad and concession areas would have to be eliminated before the treaties went into effect in September. Foreign Minister Katō responded curtly in late July that there was "absolutely no change" regarding Japanese police and court protection of its own citizens in Manchuria.[24]

Of more immediate concern to the cabinet in October was Chinese disregard for Japanese legal jurisdiction over Korean residents in Jiandao, near the Sino-Korean border. The cabinet had ruled on August 13 that the new treaties superseded the Jiandao Treaty of 1909, which had assigned dominion to China. But by the beginning of October, the Japanese press reported Chinese claims to their former rights.[25] By midmonth, Japanese authority had been rendered meaningless by pressure applied by the Chinese government on Koreans seeking legal action.[26]

Tokyo Asahi reporter Negishi Tadashi, a China specialist with extensive contacts in the Foreign Ministry,[27] emphasized the seriousness of the situation in a conversation with Hara Takashi in late October. The incompleteness of the recent treaties with China, Negishi observed, was jeopardizing Japanese rights in Manchuria and Mongolia. China was shutting Japan out by actually enforcing the treaties, bringing greater disadvantage to Japan than before the talks with Beijing. The Foreign Ministry, he noted, was "in anguish."[28]

The October cabinet decision to warn Yuan Shikai against donning imperial robes, then, aimed to minimize the political fallout of evidence that, contrary to the impression imparted by the Sino-Japanese treaties, Beijing, not Tokyo, was setting the agenda in China. With its own popularity on the wane since the March 1915 general election and parliament scheduled to convene in December, the Ōkuma government hoped to avoid a further loss of face and to ensure the future manageability of Yuan. As Negishi explained to Hara, the decision to call for a postponement of monarchy in China had emerged from domestic political circumstances. First, the cabinet wanted to avoid the criticism that Ōkuma was a "stooge" of the Chinese president. Second, it aimed to resolve its internal political problems "by directing the attention of the Japanese public outward." Finally, members of the cabinet hoped to force Yuan to make appeals to Japan, to which the empire would respond with advantageous conditions attached. Ultimately they hoped to "place Yuan in Japan's debt."[29]

TANAKA GIICHI AND THE PLOT FOR CIVIL WAR IN CHINA

The October cabinet decision marks only the beginning of a posture of direct confrontation with Yuan Shikai that would lead to a second resolution in November and culminate in a final decision in March 1916 to aid opposition movements against the Chinese president. Together these are known as the "anti-Yuan policy" (han-En seisaku) and are described in the scholarship, as they were later described by Ōkuma's successors, as evidence of the Ōkuma cabinet's interventionism in China's internal affairs. But these three initiatives can only be thought of as three aspects of the same policy if analyzed outside the larger political context of the turbulent domestic political battle over the national essence. The March decision was not simply a more potent version of the sanctions against Yuan outlined in October and November. Its aims were as different from the two previous decisions as the aims of Katō were from those of members of the Yamagata faction at the outbreak of war in Europe. The March decision was, in fact, the product of Yamagata-faction lieutenant Tanaka Giichi. It represents, in other words, a gradual shift in the locus of China policy decision making from Katō to Tanaka by the beginning of 1916. It offers, in turn, a tangible illustration of the drastic alternatives to Katō's initiatives in China pursued by his principal rivals for power.[30]

Tanaka, as we have seen, had deplored his inability in August 1914 to capitalize on the opportunity represented by the war in Europe to make an impact on the nation's China policy. But as Katō outmaneuvered the army in foreign affairs, Tanaka remained actively engaged in expanding the role of Japan's soldiers back home. By September 1915 he had persuaded the Ōkuma administration to create a national youth corps of three million members. And by October, he had advanced to the rank of lieutenant general and assumed the powerful post of vice chief of the Army General Staff. From this new vantage point, and through his intimacy with army patriarch Yamagata, Tanaka would steadily work his way to the center of China policy decision making.[31]

From October 1915 to March 1916, then, a momentous political battle pitting Tanaka against the cabinet raged around the formulation and implementation of policy concerning Yuan Shikai's proposed enthronement. Tanaka initially attempted to enter the policymaking process through War Minister Oka. A few days before the cabinet decision on a warning to Yuan, Tanaka delivered to Oka a memorandum outlining his own ideas for a response to the Chinese president. At first glance, this policy appears more moderate than that proposed by the cabinet. Rather than a warning to Yuan, it proposed eventual recognition of imperial rule in Beijing and a policy of "cracking down on revolutionaries and their associates within our jurisdiction."[32] But in the context of Tanaka's suggestion at the outbreak of war in Europe to depose Yuan, this hardly qualifies as evidence of his moderation. As we shall see, this was far from the appeal for nonintervention in China that it was later made out to be.

The point, here, however, is that Tanaka's first foray into China policy decision making as the vice chief of the Army General Staff ended in dismal failure. Thinking that he had secured the agreement of War Minister Oka for his plan,[33] Tanaka was astonished to hear that the cabinet on October 14 had decided on warning Yuan Shikai instead. The Yamagata faction's Ichiki Kitokurō, serving as home minister, objected in the cabinet debate to the demand for a postponement of monarchy. But he could not sell the idea of a reconciliation with Yuan Shikai.[34] Tanaka cried foul and cited the concurrent opposition of the navy. Yamagata grumbled that Ōkuma was again ignoring his own policy suggestions on China.[35] But the press sympathized with the government. "As the kindness of a good neighbor and from the perspective of self-defense," the October 29 Tokyo Asahi declared, "ultimately [our government] cannot simply stand by [as Yuan establishes monarchy]."[36]

As had Katō with the Sino-Japanese negotiations, the cabinet had outmaneuvered Yamagata and the army with a bold initiative in China. But just like Katō earlier in the year, the cabinet found in October that they faced one variable entirely out of their control: Yuan Shikai. Far from submitting to the pressure and granting concessions to the Japanese government, the Chinese president proclaimed on November 2 that a change of government was purely a domestic matter and represented the "irresistible movement of the [Chinese] people."[37]

The Ōkuma cabinet would publicly respond to Yuan Shikai's proclamation as a problem of policy. But the most serious implications were political. The Chinese president's disregard of Japan's official posture posed a serious problem of credibility for the cabinet and offered fresh grounds for attack by the government's political enemies. Indeed, Justice Minister Ozaki Yukio warned that the "army clique" would use the opportunity to destroy the cabinet.[38] Foreign Minister Ishii, in a meeting with China's minister to Tokyo on November 6, accused Yuan of embarrassing the Japanese government by donning imperial robes while the Japanese Diet convened. Minister Hioki, on leave in Tokyo, advised Minister Lu to delay the coronation for four or five months until the Japanese Diet recessed.[39] And rumors circulated at the beginning of November that Yamagata's bureaucratic allies planned to oust Ōkuma after the upcoming enthronement of the Taishō emperor.[40] Fearful of the appearance of being snubbed by the Chinese president, Foreign Minister Ishii warned Minister Lu that if Yuan proceeded with his plans, Japan would have to adopt "suitable measures," which could not be communicated to China.[41] Ozaki suggested a strong posture in concert with the Allies and persistent warnings to Yuan.[42] Two weeks later, the cabinet adopted Ozaki's plan to negotiate with the great powers the withholding of recognition in the event that Yuan established a monarchy before peace in Europe.[43]

If Yuan Shikai's obstinance threatened the cabinet's hopes to outmaneuver its chief domestic political rivals, so too did the energy of the new vice chief of the Army General Staff. After the cabinet's rebuff on October 14, Tanaka had abandoned the attempt to influence policy through the regular channels of parliamentary government. Instead of relying upon the war minister as the principal representative of army policy in the cabinet, Tanaka assumed personal responsibility for promoting army demands. He intended to do so through Katō's successor as foreign minister, Ishii Kikujirō.

Despite heading one of the most powerful ministries in the cabinet, this was Ishii's first stint at the helm. Ishii lacked the broad diplomatic and political experience of Katō and did not have the strong sense of policy goals or the political savvy of his predecessor. He was, further-more, three years younger than Tanaka's fifty-two. The vice chief of the Army General Staff chose to guide policy, then, through daily meetings with the malleable new head of the Foreign Ministry.[44]

The success of the strategy was immediate. For despite the November 18 cabinet decision to withhold recognition of monarchy in China until the end of war, Tanaka secured Ishii's consent to inform Yuan Shikai through Tanaka's representative in Beijing, Colonel Banzai Rihachirō, that Japan "never aimed to interfere in China's state affairs or desired an unlimited postponement [of monarchy]." Banzai was instructed to sug-gest to Yuan a coronation for the following March or April.[45] Tanaka also extracted Ishii's consent for a special envoy from Beijing to honor the Taishō emperor's own enthronement. Japanese reception of the mission would constitute the first step toward recognizing Yuan's new polity.[46]

Despite his seemingly charitable attitude toward China, Tanaka's promise of Japanese neutrality in China's domestic affairs carried an im-portant proviso. In his initial decision to support Yuan Shikai's bid for monarchical rule, he had reserved the right of "self-defense" in case of civil disturbance in China.[47] In his December instructions to Banzai, he guaranteed Japanese noninterference on the continent "as long as there is no disturbance."[48] What Tanaka did not inform Yuan, or Banzai for that matter, was that he had taken steps to ensure that a disturbance was im-minent.

For while Tanaka was relaying goodwill messages to the Chinese president through Banzai, he was instructing the commander of Japanese forces at Port Arthur, Lieutenant General Aoki Nobuzumi, to incite op-position to Yuan in southern China.[49] Subsequently, Aoki arranged for revolutionary leaders Liang Qichao and Zai Ao to travel to southern China from Shanghai via Japan. Six days after Zai's arrival in Yunnan on December 19, the provincial government declared independence.[50] The following week, a Major Yamagata Hatsuo of the Army General Staff, who was Zai's former teacher, arrived in Yunnan.[51]

The contradiction of offering symbolic support to Yuan Shikai while inciting opposition to his rule had its own logic. Like the cabinet, Tanaka sought Yuan's dependence on Japan and the great powers' recognition of Japanese authority. Indeed, he could not hide his excitement over the apparent effect of the November 18 cabinet decision to arrange with the great powers a second warning to Yuan. "It seems," he informed Banzai, "that Britain and the other powers have recently come to understand the international significance of our country. We are in the amiable situation that they finally follow our lead in foreign policy." Tanaka instructed his envoy to "continue your efforts to bore into Yuan and get him to understand the international significance of our empire."[52]

In place of the policy of outright confrontation chosen by the cabinet, then, Tanaka proposed to drive the Chinese president into Japanese arms by covert means. He offered to recognize the monarchy and even to provide Yuan with financial aid.[53] A rebellion in southern China would then give Yuan the final push to seek assistance in Tokyo.[54] Confirming the wisdom of the strategy, Banzai predicted on January 14 that whether the rebellion in Yunnan spread or not, "it is certain that the Yuan government will begin to feel financial difficulties" because of the disturbance. He advised Tanaka to consider in advance what rights, such as mines, that Japan should demand as collateral in the likely event that the Chinese made a request for a loan.[55]

But Yuan Shikai was no more responsive to Tanaka's prods than he had been to the cabinet's threats. While promising Foreign Minister Ishii through Minister Lu in Tokyo "to consult only with Japan,"[56] he continued discussions with the great powers. Soon after Tanaka's message that Japan would accept the establishment of monarchy in March or April, Yuan announced that his enthronement would proceed on February 9, 1916.[57] Tanaka wired Banzai on December 28 that "the actions of the Chinese government lack sincerity."[58]

By early January 1916, Yuan had contained the rebellion within Yunnan province and declared confidence in his ability to crush the rebels, provided that they received no foreign aid.[59] The veiled reference to Japanese complicity was transparent. So too was Yuan's determination to manage his internal political troubles without Japanese help. Tanaka complained bitterly to Banzai on January 17 of Beijing's attempt to "guarantee domestic tranquility and assume the responsibility on its own." Continuing to press for monarchy in defiance of the situation in the south "ignores the face of Japan and the other cooperative powers and is highly disturbing." "If Yuan is sincere about Sino-Japanese friendship," the vice chief of the Army General Staff warned, "I earnestly hope that he considers maintaining peace in the Far East in concert with Japan."[60]

Yuan's failure to take the bait of southern rebellion to seek Japanese aid compelled Tanaka to revoke one of his incentives. Foreign Minister Ishii instructed Minister Hioki to postpone the dispatch of a special envoy from China because of "the suspicion that China's attitude is trampling on Japan's honor." Tanaka then ordered Banzai to explain "frankly" to Yuan that "for China to consider only its own advantage and to purposely ignore the position of Japan and the other powers will complicate international relations and place Japan in an unavoidable position."[61]

The threat, plus a subsequent cabinet decision on January 19 to withhold recognition of Yuan's imminent enthronement, brought the Japanese government full circle, back to its position of the previous November. The important difference, however, was that Tanaka was now in charge. The decision was based on a four-point memorandum from Tanaka to the foreign minister on January 15 that had stipulated that "the Imperial Government will not recognize the monarchy at present." It had also called for "measures of self-defense to meet the natural consequences of nonrecognition."[62] Three days after Banzai delivered Tanaka's warnings on the eighteenth, President Yuan announced an indefinite postponement of his coronation.[63]

Yuan understood the scale of the machinations against him. Soon after the Chinese president's announcement, Tanaka sent another warning through Colonel Banzai denying a series of accusations by the president. "There is absolutely nothing like a scheme in the works at this time," Banzai was to inform Yuan. "He who contemptuously suspects others brings doubt upon himself." Yuan had apparently uncovered General Staff envoy Aoki Nobuzumi's plot, for Banzai was to warn Beijing that the "suspicion" of Lieutenant General Aoki was completely without foundation.[64]

Especially disturbing to the Army General Staff were fresh rumors that Yuan was working with the British on an accommodation with the south. The January 30 *Tokyo Asahi shinbun* reported that Yuan had approached the British minister in Beijing, Sir John Jordan, with a mediation plan. Despite Chinese and British denials, the *Asahi* continued in early February to fan the speculation.[65]

The General Staff responded by warning Lieutenant General Aoki in Shanghai that rumors of negotiations brokered by London were "stirring up public opinion in our country. As a result, they have caused a rift, not only in Sino-Japanese relations, but between Japan and Britain." It was the responsibility of the Chinese government, the memorandum declared, to deny the rumors publicly. If it did not, "it will bring a disadvantageous situation to the government of China."[66]

Simultaneous with reports of British complicity in a mediation plan came warnings from General Staff representatives in the field that victory for Yuan in the civil war was imminent. Adviser to the Hubei Regular Army, Colonel Teranishi Hidetake, wired General Staff Second Division Chief Fukuda Masatarō on February 1 that if the Japanese government did not decide by mid-month to support the revolutionary party, "it is very likely that Yuan will pacify Yunnan and establish imperial government." If Yuan did so, Britain and Russia would probably recognize the new regime and Japan would be forced to follow suit without a single gain. "We may thus be despised and ridiculed by Yuan and scorned by the Chinese people."[67]

Tanaka's attempt to drive the Chinese president into Japan's arms simply by dispatching Army General Staff advisers to China's revolutionaries was, in other words, bound to fail. According to Teranishi, the situation required a clear military and financial commitment to the south by the Japanese government. In early February, he sent repeated petitions to Tanaka and Chief of the Army General Staff Uehara Yūsaku to "topple Yuan and establish our influence in China by any means." To thus take advantage of the "exceptionally opportune European war (*senzai ichigū no Ōsen*)" was, he urged, critical for the nation's future and for the future of Japanese military and economic development.[68]

Soon after Teranishi's petitions, Tanaka hinted that he was moving beyond simple repudiation of Yuan's bid for monarchy. The Chinese president was losing public support by the day, he informed General Terauchi. "Even those thought to be his confidants have turned against him.

The situation does not bode well." It was becoming increasingly clear that Yuan could be forced to abandon the presidency. In such an event, "Japan cannot commit suicide with him." Japan had no alternative but to "devise a new path."[69]

Having failed to incite a rebellion against Yuan in Yunnan, in other words, Tanaka now exaggerated the probability of insurrection to prevent an increasingly likely escalation of the Chinese president's power. The sense of urgency expressed by Teranishi in his petitions was reflected in Tanaka's immediate call for a "new path." The day that he impressed upon Terauchi the need for change, Tanaka advised Foreign Minister Ishii that Japan could waver no longer in devising a new strategy.[70] The following week, he solicited the cooperation of War Minister Oka. "It would be advantageous to think of means to oust Yuan and establish our political influence," he suggested.[71] On February 28, soon after another warning from Teranishi that there was little chance of victory for the Yunnan army, and that Guangzhou and Guangxi would not join the rebellion without a supply of Japanese arms,[72] Tanaka forwarded to Oka a plan to aid the rebels. It was necessary, he informed the minister of war, because "there is increasingly little hope at present in trusting and using Yuan."[73]

But a consensus on formal support for the south was less forthcoming than Tanaka had hoped. War Minister Oka neither responded to Tanaka's draft nor approached the foreign and navy ministers about the matter as Tanaka had requested. Navy Minister Katō Tomosaburō did not quarrel with Tanaka's proposal, but he remained sidelined with a cold.[74] The Foreign Ministry continued to hesitate on a cabinet decision.[75] General Terauchi, who had consistently advocated working with Yuan, refused to cooperate, even after the eventual cabinet decision to drive the Chinese president from office. He warned Uehara in May that Tanaka was directing China policy "conspiratorially."[76] Hara Takashi, to whom Tanaka appealed in early March, scoffed at Tanaka's argument that Japanese public opinion now called for a rejection of Yuan. "In reality," he noted in his diary, "there is no such Japanese public opinion." To him it was clear that the Army General Staff was unnecessarily inciting Japan's China adventurers, the so-called rōnin, to assemble and push for Yuan's ouster.[77]

By the beginning of March, Tanaka had run out of patience. So too, apparently, had his mentor Yamagata. Most studies of the movement to depose Yuan Shikai point to Yamagata's reservations about this most clandestine of Japanese foreign policy operations during the Great War as further evidence of the contrast between the *genrō* and army upper echelon "caution" and General Staff belligerence on China policy.[78] Tanaka was, indeed, the chief perpetrator of the covert enterprise. Yamagata, moreover, did express reservations. But the field marshal made no attempt to contain the actions of his principal deputy. Rather, he offered tacit approval, which Tanaka attempted to use to his benefit. If the Japanese government did not act, Tanaka warned War Minister Oka, Japan would simply repeat the failure at the time of the first Chinese Revolution. "Old Prince Yamagata also worries that if we do not determine government policy as quickly as possible, we will miss the opportunity."[79]

By the beginning of March, Tanaka and Yamagata had to wait no longer. Overcome by a battle with cancer, War Minister Oka had, by that time, lost his will to fight. Relieved of the last major domestic hurdle to Yamagata faction supremacy, Tanaka orchestrated a cabinet decision on March 7 to remove the greatest overseas obstacle to Japanese hegemony in China, Yuan Shikai. "The Empire," the decision read, "should at this time establish superior influence in China and build a foundation for Sino-Japanese friendship by making the Chinese people conscious of the Empire's influence." Since Yuan was an "obstacle" to that object, "it would be convenient for Yuan to withdraw from Chinese jurisdiction. . . . There is no doubt that no matter who replaces Yuan, he will be far and away better for the Empire than Yuan." To drive the Chinese president from office, the cabinet agreed to formally recognize the southern army and tacitly support aid from the Japanese private sector to anti-Yuan movements throughout the continent.[80]

Tanaka secured the cooperation of Foreign Minister Ishii in this decision by promising Foreign Ministry supremacy in promoting the anti-Yuan agenda. The cabinet decision stipulated that the ministry "carry primary responsibility" for policy implementation.[81] To coordinate army and navy activities under ostensible Foreign Ministry supervision, a special task force composed of bureau chiefs from the two service ministries and division chiefs from the two general staffs soon began weekly and sometimes twice-weekly discussions in the office of Political Affairs Bureau Chief Koike Chōzō.[82] But Kasumigaseki's reaction to these concessions was subdued. The Foreign Ministry, Tanaka learned, "hopes that matters will not become any worse."[83]

Indeed, it was increasingly clear that the Foreign Ministry, under Ishii's leadership, had lost the policy initiative to Tanaka. Ishii answered protests regarding the new policy from Foreign Ministry representatives in the field by arguing that tacit government support for anti-Yuan movements would "unify those actions."[84] But while the ministry organized financial aid to the revolutionaries,[85] it was Tanaka, the vice chief of the Army General Staff, who had become the unifier and ultimate arbiter of the anti-Yuan agenda.

It was, indeed, an ambitious agenda. For, contrary to what the foreign minister may have believed, this was not a plan simply to remove Yuan Shikai from power. The aim, rather, was to expand Japanese influence on the continent. As Tanaka put it to Banzai Rihachirō in early March, Japan should "seize the chance to touch the heart of political power" in Beijing.[86] This, of course, was another way of saying that Japan should create a new regime in China. But, as we saw during the Sino-Japanese negotiations of 1915, the army elite desired, more specifically, to increase Japanese military presence on the continent. Having decided in February 1916, then, to depose Yuan, Tanaka hoped to do so in a manner that would create the opportunity for a major deployment of Japanese troops in China.

Tanaka cautioned Banzai, therefore, against disposing of Yuan too hastily. "It is best," he explained, "to make Yuan hesitate [to withdraw from power] until he has reached his absolute end."[87] As he instructed the chief of staff of Japanese forces at Qingdao, Major General Morioka Morishige, in mid-May, Japan should press Yuan's abdication only "when the north and south look to a military solution."[88] The main object, in other words, was a civil war in China.

Civil war offered two excuses for Japanese army intervention: as catalyst and check. First, Japanese officers would continue, in greater numbers, to fan opposition movements against Yuan to ensure greater civil strife. Tanaka worried that Yuan might "avoid an armed resolution" for fear of great power intervention. In such a case, Japan would have to "create the appropriate situation" by mobilizing revolutionary forces in Shandong and Manchuria.[89] Once Japan had incited civil war, it would be time for Japanese troops to make a triumphant public entrance to the rescue. As Tanaka informed Lieutenant General Aoki, Japan should appear to be "intervening by necessity, not of her liking, after the opportunity for armed conflict between the north and south finally arrives and various foreign countries, feeling the danger, urge Japan to intervene."[90]

Beginning in mid-March, with a cabinet guarantee for arms and funding, and under the direct orders of Tanaka, army representatives embarked for Manchuria, Shandong, and Yunnan to fan the flames of rebellion in anticipation of Japanese armed intervention. One of the four officers sent to Port Arthur, Major Koiso Kuniaki, a man who himself would help plan one of the great conspiracies of the 1930s, recognized the scheme as a "plot" and judged the likelihood of success to be "slim."[91]

Indeed, Tanaka's plan for Manchurian independence led by Zhang Zuolin collapsed when Yuan Shikai brought the Chinese general under his authority in mid-April by designating him Mukden garrison commander.[92] With "no prospect for success"[93] in securing Zhang's cooperation with the south, Tanaka subsequently concentrated on coordinating and placing the anti-Yuan forces in south and central China, especially in Shandong, on a war footing. As he explained to Colonel Itogawa Tatsuzō in early June, command of the Jinan-Pukou Railway, the main line of transport south of Beijing, would allow Shandong's rebel forces to stop an advance of Yuan's army in its tracks.[94] Tanaka assured Major General Morioka in Qingdao that, if necessary, reinforcements could easily be sent from Port Arthur.[95] Indeed, preparing Shandong to fight with the south against northern encroachment promised to strengthen Japanese control in the province. By May 23 a Chinese rebel force armed and transported via the Japanese-run Shandong Railway dislodged the Beijing-backed Chinese army from Weixian.[96]

Like Ōkuma and Katō, however, Tanaka discovered a formidable obstacle to his best laid plans in China: Chinese president Yuan Shikai himself. Although it would be the last time that Yuan would prove a thorn in Japan's side, his sudden death on June 6 stopped Tanaka's scheme cold. Just three days earlier, Tanaka had instructed Colonel Itogawa to urge upon southern revolutionary Cen Chunxuan "a resolution through armed might."[97] Unable now to count on a major civil war as a pretext for Japanese intervention, the vice chief rallied to ensure Japanese influence with the new administration of Li Yuanhong in Beijing. On June 7, the Army–Navy–Foreign Ministry task force within the Foreign Ministry approved Tanaka's plan to "take measures to make him [Li] dependent on us." This included possible loans to Li and Japanese responsibility for "the maintenance of public order" in China on request.[98]

Tanaka could not easily abandon the hope for a substantial army role in promoting "mutual dependence" between Japan and China. A "Draft Opinion on China," presented to the Army–Navy–Foreign Ministry task force in June, stipulated that Japan advise the great powers to "rest assured" that Japan would guarantee public order in Beijing and protect the lives and property of foreigners on the continent. For this purpose, the empire would immediately increase its troop strength at Tianjin by one infantry regiment and, if necessary, by one division.[99] On June 10, two days after Lieutenant General Fukuda Masatarō was ordered to Europe to atone for the failure of Tanaka's original plan,[100] the first movement of troops from Port Arthur to Tianjin and Tianjin to Beijing began. On the same day, Minister Hioki in Beijing informed Foreign Minister Ishii that Major General Saitō Suejirō and Colonel Banzai were "filling Li Yuanhong with all kinds of secret demands and opinions."[101]

Despite the failure of Tanaka's original scheme, the Foreign Ministry, therefore, faced the full consequences of allowing the initiative on China policy to slip into army hands. When Prime Minister Ōkuma stressed the "danger of foreign policy disunity" at a cabinet meeting on June 13, new war minister Ōshima Ken'ichi countered with a threat to "evacuate everything."[102] Understandably, Foreign Ministry Political Affairs Bureau Chief Koike was "not in high spirits" in the Army–Navy–Foreign Ministry task force meeting of June 12.[103] Foreign Minister Ishii's objections finally held Japanese troop movements near Beijing to a minimum. But in response to criticism from the field regarding the "conspicuous actions" of the army, Ishii could only reaffirm Tanaka's policy initiative.

"The Imperial Government," he instructed the Foreign Ministry's representatives, "is determined to aid this [new administration in Beijing] in full, directly and indirectly."[104]

Fig. 13
"The keystone of Asia"—
The Russo-Japanese Convention

YAMAGATA ARITOMO AND THE QUEST TO CONTAIN THE UNITED STATES

At about the time that Ishii had begun to cede the China policy initiative to Tanaka in January 1916, a royal delegation arrived in Tokyo on the invitation of the foreign minister's most powerful political rivals. Grand Duke Georgii Mikhailovich disembarked in Tokyo on January 12, 1916, amid great fanfare. It was the first visit by a member of the Russian royal family since the near-assassination of Tsarevich Nicholas at Ōtsu in 1891. General Terauchi, designated master of ceremonies for the occasion, accompanied the grand duke as he was met at Tokyo station by a distinguished welcoming party of three imperial princes, Prime Minister Ōkuma, War Minister Oka, Navy Minister Katō, and Foreign Minister Ishii, all in full ceremonial attire.[105] During his ten-day official visit, the grand duke enjoyed a full array of fêtes and audiences with Japan's most distinguished political, military, and economic leaders, and imperial titleholders. He laid, as well, the foundations for a fundamental reorientation of Japanese foreign policy. By July 3, Japan had strengthened ties with the tsar in a manner that Yamagata and his supporters had vigorously championed since the outbreak of war in Europe.

If the anti-Yuan policy typified Tanaka Giichi's vision of an autonomous Japanese diplomacy, the Russo-Japanese Convention of July 1916 symbolized Yamagata's own quest for an independent path on the continent. Some historians have identified the agreement as symbolic of Yamagata's policy of great power cooperation.[106] But it reflected, rather, the field marshal's growing appetite for Japanese continental power and his long-term desire to break away from the alliance with Britain. Like Tanaka's scheme to topple Yuan Shikai, it stands in stark contrast with Katō's vision of limited Japanese interests in China based upon great power cooperation.

Following the first three agreements with St. Petersburg after the Russo-Japanese War, the fourth accord had as its most immediate aim an expansion of Japan's sphere of influence in northeast Asia. Tokyo's first and second pacts with the tsar had obtained Russian confirmation of and a promise to aid Japan in defense of the Guandong concession and South Manchuria Railway, which Japan had secured in the Russo-Japanese War. The third agreement expanded Japan's sphere of interest to Eastern Inner Mongolia.[107] In December 1915, Japan's ambassador to St. Petersburg, Motono Ichirō, spoke of extending Japanese jurisdiction in South Manchuria northward, as "compensation" for Japanese participation in the Great War.[108] Following indications of probable Russian concessions, Motono proposed to stretch Japanese authority beyond the current boundary of Changchun to the Sungari River. Expectations in Tokyo, however, ran even higher. Upon his arrival in Japan in January, Russian Foreign Ministry Far Eastern Bureau Chief Grigorii Kozakov announced St. Petersburg's willingness to transfer rights to the Manchurian railway south of the Sungari. But Japan's former minister to Mexico, Adachi Mineichirō, appointed by General Terauchi to accompany the Russian delegation as official translator, inquired about the railway north of the Sungari to Harbin.[109]

Foreign Minister Ishii responded to Kozakov's personal presentation of the Russian agenda on January 14 with a declaration of the immense value of the entire plain up to the chief Russian outpost of Harbin:

The soil in Manchuria becomes increasingly rich as one moves northward. If we are able to use the Changchun-Harbin Railway and make the wide expanse of fertile field from Changchun to Harbin our sphere of influence in reality, the natural resources of the Jilin plain will come entirely under our control. As a result, we will bring remarkable growth to the South Manchuria Railway area of operations. The strategic and commercial advantages to us will likely be enormous.[110]

In April, the governor-general of Korea, Terauchi Masatake, branded useless any agreement with Russia that did not permit Japanese trains to run to Harbin.[111]

Yamagata described Foreign Minister Ishii's celebration of the Jilin plain as an "eminently fair argument."[112] But he made clear, as well, that he hoped to obtain in a fourth agreement with the tsar much more than an extension of Japanese interests in South Manchuria. As we have seen, by the outbreak of war in August 1914, the field marshal had developed quite an ambitious vision of Sino-Japanese relations. His appeal at that time for Beijing to consult Tokyo on all political and economic problems involving foreign countries shows that his thinking had evolved well beyond the concern for spheres of interest that had guided the great powers in their quest for influence in China since the Sino-Japanese War. Yamagata and many prominent members of his faction now perceived Japan not as one power among many in the scramble for influence in China but as the preeminent force in Asia. Thus, the field marshal instructed Ishii in 1916 to negotiate an agreement with Russia that did not just defend Japanese interests in Manchuria and Mongolia. He proposed an accord that guaranteed "the preservation of China."[113] At the same time, Vice Chief of the Army General Staff Tanaka Giichi proposed revising the 1907 Basic Plan of National Defense to define Chinese security, for the first time, as Japan's principal strategic goal.[114]

But Yamagata's dreams of Japanese power exceeded even the borders of China. In addition to calling for the "preservation of China," he urged Foreign Minister Ishii in January 1916 to suggest to Russia that the Japanese take responsibility for maintaining security in the entire Russian Far East. "The empire will guarantee peace east of the Ural mountains," he proposed, "and we will immediately support Russia if an uprising, etc., occurs in Siberia."[115]

Yamagata's dreams of becoming the guardian of Siberian security would, as we shall see, have to await the Allied intervention in Siberia in August 1918. But the Fourth Russo-Japanese Convention would meet the field marshal's expectations by defining the area of concern as China. If it thus exceeded the framework of great power relations in China since the Sino-Japanese War in the projected scope of Japanese power, it did so, as well, in terms of Japanese alliance politics. Yamagata made clear in February 1915 that what he desired in a fourth accord with Russia was an alliance. Historians have interpreted his concurrent expressions of support for relations with Britain as evidence that he had no intention of pursuing closer ties with St. Petersburg at the expense of the Anglo-Japanese pact. But while the field marshal took care in formal pronouncements to stress the continuing utility of Anglo-Japanese relations, he could not mask his growing disenchantment with the alliance after the fulfillment of its original objective.

Unlike fellow *genrō* Inoue and Itō Hirobumi, Yamagata had originally supported an accord with London to check Russian power in northeast Asia. Soon after the Russo-Japanese War, however, he had looked to project Japanese power south of the Great Wall, where it could easily conflict with Britain's established sphere of influence in the Yangzi valley.[116] Indeed, Japanese attempts at financial penetration of the region beginning in 1912 had met resistance in London, spurring *genrō* criticism at the September 1914 *genrō*-Ōkuma conference of Britain's "oppression" of Japanese interests in central China.[117]

The China policies pursued by London and Tokyo became increasingly antagonistic after the Chinese Revolution. There was widespread disappointment in Japan over Britain's unilateral mediation of a settlement of the revolution in 1911.[118] After the outbreak of war in Europe, London had attempted to limit Japanese operations in Asia, had raised objections to Group 5 of Katō's demands of China, and most recently, had appeared to support Yuan Shikai in the face of Japanese efforts to postpone Yuan's bid for monarchy.[119] Yamagata and his supporters increasingly imagined a British public hostile to Japan. Japan's representative to the Court of St. James, the son of *genrō* Inoue Kaoru, had confirmed that British foreign secretary Grey was privately anti-Japanese. "The sentiment of the British government and people," the field marshal had concluded in July 1915, "is not at all what it used to be."[120]

Yamagata, then, saw increasingly less benefit in the Anglo-Japanese alliance for Japanese interests in China. Not only did it seem an obstacle to further Japanese expansion, it was clearly of little use in dealing with the fastest growing presence in the region: the United States. Thanks to the appeal of "manifest destiny" and the opportunity of the Spanish-American War, the United States had catapulted from relative obscurity in the late nineteenth century to a position of major importance in East Asian affairs. Its influence in East Asian politics was demonstrated first by Theodore Roosevelt's mediation of the Russo-Japanese War. But a series of postwar agreements between Tokyo and Washington covering respective interests in the Asia-Pacific region attest to Japanese recognition of America's increasing importance.[121] That presence became particularly problematic with the advent of the Taft administration and the beginning of a direct challenge to Japan's self-proclaimed sphere of influence in South Manchuria. Japan's three agreements with St. Petersburg after the Russo-Japanese War were expressly intended to counter American initiatives in China.[122]

Yamagata had increasingly looked to St. Petersburg for aid in Japan's relations with the United States in part from the recognition that the Anglo-Japanese alliance could not serve the same purpose. London had provided valuable financial support and prevented a third-party challenge to Japanese ambitions in Asia in the war against Russia. But there was no sign that Britain's promise to aid Japan in the event of an outside challenge would be honored if that challenge were to come from the United States. Indeed, in response to American concerns over such a possibility, Whitehall had, in negotiations for a third Anglo-Japanese alliance in 1911, obtained an arbitration clause designed to preclude the possibility of waging war with the United States. Washington later failed to ratify the arbitration treaty with London that would have given the new clause full legal effect. But British persistence during negotiations with Japan confirmed the suspicion that London would not come to Tokyo's aid against America.[123]

Yamagata had greeted this revelation with concern. It was not, he had informed the cabinet in a July 1911 memo, unexpected. But in light of the probability of a clash between the United States and Japan in the future, it was disturbing:

Although the likelihood of an outbreak of war between the United States and Japan is, at this point, almost unimaginable, the world will witness a sudden change in a few years. We do not know when and what type of transformation will occur, especially given that recent U.S. policy in the Pacific often carries points of friction with the empire's interests and [in light of] the unavoidability of a mutual clash sooner or later if the present trends continue.[124]

The outbreak of war in Europe in August 1914 was indeed the "sudden change" that Yamagata had anticipated in 1911. And the European call to arms triggered the greatest worries over probable consequences for American power. In his "Opinion on China Policy" presented to the prime minister soon after Japan's ultimatum to Germany, the elder statesman had singled out relations with the United States as a "key consideration" in the formulation and implementation of Japan's China policy. He feared that the war in Europe, by diverting the attention of the great powers from East Asia, would enable the United States to increase its influence in China and secure a "monopoly on the prize."[125] Terauchi cautioned that if Japan looked passively on, the United States would, without fail, "intervene in China and begin to seize rights."[126] And Yamagata protégé Tanaka Giichi warned in September 1914 that regardless of the outcome of the war, Russia, Germany, Britain, and France would reach a state of exhaustion while the United States alone would "increase its strength and extend its power to China."[127]

The probable decline of every major European power and the concomitant increase in U.S. strength called for a major revision of Japan's strategic priorities. Tanaka hinted at the substance of that revision in a memorandum sent to elder statesman Prince Ōyama Iwao sometime in 1915. The 1907 Basic Plan of National Defense had named Russia, the United States, Germany, and France as the empire's four most likely enemies, in that order, and the accompanying "Tactical Outline" had determined the deployment of troops accordingly. Tanaka's 1915 memorandum described diplomacy after the Russo-Japanese War as "increasingly complicated" and offered a new "Tactical Outline" to respond to mounting anti-Japanese activity in China and to clarify operations against the United States. The outline specified joint land and sea operations in China and on Luzon Island to destroy the U.S. Navy's base of operations in the Philippines.[128] Vice Chief of the Army General Staff Tanaka's "Policy for National Defense" the following year confirmed the shift from the 1907 definition of strategic priorities by replacing the clear reference to the threat of Russia, the United States, Germany, and France with an unnamed enemy. The empire should be prepared, he noted, to come to Beijing's aid "if China is subject to invasion by *another power*."[129]

It is within this context of changing strategic priorities vis-à-vis the United States and the inability to turn to the British as a counterweight to growing American influence in China that Yamagata drafted "For a Russo-Japanese Alliance" in February 1915. "The European War has brought change to the strength of the powers," the Field Marshal declared. To rely exclusively upon the Anglo-Japanese alliance to effect lasting peace in East Asia was not "sound policy."[130] The field marshal and his supporters would ultimately fail to obtain an explicit Russian guarantee of aid in the event of an American challenge to Japanese interests. But, in addition to widening the scope of concern to cover all of China, the secret clause of the Fourth Russo-Japanese Convention offered indirect support against just such a threat. And it would exceed all previous arrangements in suggesting the military character of mutual aid. Each signatory promised to send troops in the event that China fell under "the political hold of a third country possessing an aggressive tendency" toward either power.[131] In January 1916, soon after Grand Duke Georgii's departure from Tokyo, Yamagata explained to Hara Takashi that Japan could no longer "depend upon the British way or on Britain."[132]

If Yamagata and his supporters sought an alliance with the tsar to aid in a future conflict with the United States, his Russian counterparts held starkly contrasting motives. The ambiguity of the "third country" clause has given rise to a good deal of debate over the ultimate target of the 1916 convention. In the wake of the Russian Revolution, the Bolsheviks publicized the secret compact and identified Britain and the United States as the principal focus. The two foreign ministers who negotiated the pact, Sergei Sazonov and Ishii Kikujirō, on the other hand, later described the enemy as Germany.[133] While Japanese scholars have, for the most part, accepted the validity of Bolshevik claims, the pact still stands in the English-language literature as being directed against Germany.[134]

The confusion may, undoubtedly, be attributed to the fact that Tokyo and St. Petersburg each had their eye on a different challenge. If Yamagata and his supporters spied the United States on the horizon, Russian foreign minister Sazonov sought stronger ties to anchor Japan squarely in the Allied camp in the fight against Germany. The most telling aspect of negotiations for the 1916 convention lies not in the two parties' arrival at an agreement for stronger relations. It rests in the protracted dispute over specifying a common enemy. Sazonov's stubborn insistence on a direct reference to Germany in an agreement attests to the depth of Allied anxiety over Japan's loyalty in the fight against the kaiser. Japan's ultimate refusal to include such a reference testifies to Yamagata's principal concern with the United States and highlights Tokyo's increasing departure from the Anglo-Japanese alliance.

St. Petersburg's most immediate incentive for an agreement with Japan was to expand the quantity of arms and ammunition that left Japanese factories for Russian troops. Japanese aid had played a crucial part in the Russian war effort. And Foreign Ministry Far Eastern Bureau Chief Grigorii Kozakov's first request when he arrived in Kagoshima with the entourage of Grand Duke Georgii in January 1916 was for a doubling of Japan's weapons support.[135] But Russia had a more general concern that had prompted her to seek a stronger commitment from Japan for the Allied war effort. Japan's war against Germany had, for all intents and purposes, ended with the fall of Qingdao in November 1914. And in the wake of the German capitulation, there were signs of a German-Japanese rapprochement. St. Petersburg was aware, from eavesdropping on Japanese ambassador Motono's communications with Tokyo and from Foreign Minister Katō's direct disclosures, that Germany had approached Tokyo from January 1915 about a separate peace.[136] In his July 1915 report of the increasingly positive sentiment in the Japanese capital for a Russo-Japanese alliance, Russian ambassador Nicholas Malevski-Malevich warned Foreign Minister Sazonov, moreover, of the strength of pro-German sentiment in Tokyo.[137] Sazonov responded to this and to information received from Ambassador Motono with a recommendation to British foreign secretary Grey for a Russo-Japanese alliance to prevent Japan from approaching Germany.[138] On July 27,

Motono confirmed that Russian overtures stemmed from a need for arms and a "desire to prevent a German-Japanese rapprochement after the war."[139]

Kozakov's initial approaches to Japanese Foreign Ministry personnel during Grand Duke Georgii's visit, then, stressed the seriousness of the German threat to Japanese and Russian interests in China. Kozakov reminded Adachi Mineichirō of Kaiser Wilhelm II's meeting with Tsar Nicholas II at a Baltic port in June 1912. Wilhelm had, on that occasion, recalled for Russian foreign minister Sazonov that he had been the first to foresee the Yellow Peril and had urged Russia to "unite with China to repel Japan."[140] Later, Berlin had approached China with a plan to "check and repel both Japan and Russia."[141] Relaying a message from Foreign Minister Sazonov to Ishii, Kozakov urged that Japan, Britain, Russia, and France devise a policy to resist Germany's attempt to "taint its hands with China and make it a second Turkey." A Russo-Japanese alliance, he suggested, was the most effective means toward this end.[142]

But Yamagata refused to allow this anti-German sentiment to determine the character of a strengthened Russo-Japanese relationship. He did not even address the matter of Germany in responding to Foreign Minister Ishii's description of the January 14 meeting with Kozakov. Rather, he instructed Ishii, as we have seen, to suggest in an agreement provisions for a military alliance in Siberia and an article covering the preservation of China.[143] Ishii later presented Yamagata a draft reply to Sazonov's proposals for an alliance aimed at allaying St. Petersburg's concerns about Germany. It was clear from the Russian foreign minister's plan, he noted, that Russia felt substantial anxiety over the prospect of China's succumbing to German influence and becoming a "second Turkey." Ishii suggested adding a clause to a prospective agreement explicitly outlining frank communication and appropriate action by Japan and Russia "as a means of preventing China from falling into the palm of Germany in the future."[144] But Yamagata preferred a less restrictive reference to a common enemy. A prospective agreement, he responded, should simply stipulate that Japan and Russia cooperate to "preserve the peace of Asia. In the event that another country violates this [peace], both countries will strive to attain this common objective through continual mutual help."[145]

Foreign Minister Ishii's instructions to Ambassador Motono to begin negotiations followed Yamagata's preference for ambiguity on this point.[146] Russian foreign minister Sazonov described the proposal in general as a "reasonable" one, but questioned the ambiguity of this clause by urging the necessity for Japan and Russia "to sufficiently cooperate to expel German influence from the Far East during the war and in the future."[147] On February 21, Motono advised Tokyo to name Germany explicitly because it would provoke suspicion not to do so.[148] But Foreign Minister Ishii answered the alternative draft agreement sent by the ambassador that specified Germany with the curt admonition that "your draft agreement runs completely contrary to our proposal."[149]

Unable to secure a clear indication of Japanese loyalty in the fight against Germany, Sazonov offered Motono on March 21 a counterproposal that downgraded the prospective alliance to a simple "convention." And he made clear that, while the Japanese may have had a different potential enemy in mind, the tsar would not be dragged into a war that did not have the approval of Russia's or Japan's other ally. The attempt of a third power to put China under her political control, Sazonov explained, did not constitute a *casus foederis* under either the Franco-Russian Treaty or the Anglo-Japanese alliance. It was safest, therefore, for Japan and Russia to exchange military assistance only with the approval of France and Britain. For the same reason, Sazonov hoped to make the terms of the Russo-Japanese agreement coincide with those of the Anglo-Japanese alliance and to reflect any amendment or abrogation of that accord.[150] He undoubtedly had in mind the inclusion of an arbitration clause in the most recent version of the Anglo-Japanese pact that prevented British assistance to Japan in the event of a war against the United States.

But Tokyo resisted any "complicated explanatory provisions" in the "third country" clause and refused to include a stipulation for mutual consultation before either party signed an "international agreement" covering its special interests in China.[151] Foreign Minister Ishii noted that Sazonov appeared concerned that Japan "may conclude a treaty with a third country that will result in direct or indirect injury to Russian rights and interests." He instructed Motono to assure St. Petersburg that in proposing an agreement, Japan "places complete emphasis upon the Russian foreign minister's opinion" regarding "the probability of China sub-

mitting to the political authority of Germany."[152] But when pressed by
the Russian foreign minister to offer the assurance in writing, Ishii declined.

Throughout the negotiations, Tokyo deflected St. Petersburg's attempts to extract a written Japanese commitment to the fight against
Germany.[153] Instead, Japan obtained, if only indirectly, what it could no
longer count on its British allies to deliver: a guarantee to come to Japan's
aid in the event of an American challenge to its growing influence in
China.[154] In terms of Japanese policy, then, the 1916 Russo-Japanese Convention is significant for expanding the scope of Japanese continental interests and rejecting the Anglocentrism that had marked Japanese diplomacy since 1902. More particularly, it marks the growing continental aims
and declining enthusiasm for the Anglo-Japanese alliance of a specific
group of policymakers in Japan: Field Marshal Yamagata and his supporters in the army and bureaucracy. Like the movement to depose Yuan Shikai, in other words, the Russo-Japanese Convention stands as further evidence of the ambitious goals of Katō Takaaki's principal political rivals.
And like the campaign against Yuan, Japan's negotiations with Russia
were accompanied by a subplot of domestic politics that would have a significant impact upon the subsequent history of modern Japan.

THE POLITICS OF THE 1916
RUSSO-JAPANESE CONVENTION

That subplot, it will be recalled, is the story of the Yamagata faction's
struggle to reclaim the foreign policy initiative after having been decisively shut out by Foreign Minister Katō in negotiations with China in
1915. As we have seen, it took Tanaka Giichi several months to commandeer the nation's China policy in the wake of Katō's resignation. Likewise, Yamagata's eventual success in negotiating a fourth convention with
Russia was by no means guaranteed.

Foreign Minister Ishii, after all, had received the royal entourage from
Russia in January with decidedly less enthusiasm than had Yamagata and
his associates. Two days after the delegation's arrival, Ishii listened cor-
dially to Yamagata's ideas for a Russo-Japanese agreement. But he and

Prime Minister Ōkuma arranged a January 20 meeting with the three *genrō* in palace chambers to clarify their own agenda. The foreign minister presented Yamagata, Ōyama, and Matsukata an outline of possible points of discussion with Russia but remained equivocal on the idea of a new agreement with the tsar.[155]

Yamagata was not amused. The field marshal had, as we have seen, renewed his offensive for stronger Russo-Japanese ties in the wake of Katō Takaaki's resignation in August 1915. But the new foreign minister not only resisted a new agreement with St. Petersburg. His outline of points of discussion did not even mention what Yamagata considered a critical first step in that direction, an expansion of Japanese weapons aid. The field marshal pressed Ōkuma and Ishii to prod War Minister Oka on the matter.[156] Later, during a break in a state luncheon for the Russian grand duke, he urged Ishii to talk with Vice Minister of War Ōshima and Vice Chief of the Army General Staff Tanaka.[157] Ōkuma and Ishii responded by inviting Yamagata to an afternoon session with Oka, where the minister of war repeated Ishii's 1915 communication to British foreign secretary Grey. Since Japan was exerting itself to the limit on arms aid to Russia, she could not respond any further to St. Petersburg's requests. To Yamagata's suggestion to talk with the vice minister of war, Oka replied that the result would be the same. Declaring that he had nothing left to say, the field marshal retired in defeat.[158]

Emboldened by this successful rebuff of Yamagata in the afternoon, Foreign Minister Ishii met Kozakov at 5:30 P.M. on January 20 to formally reject the need for a new agreement with Russia. The prospect of a resurgence of German influence in China did not constitute sufficient grounds for an accord, Ishii argued. And he was unable, he insisted, to "arouse the curiosity" of Japan's army leadership on more weapons for the tsar.[159]

The effect on Yamagata was immediate. The field marshal found Ishii's actions "almost unbelievable" and scrambled to repair the damage. Two days later, he urged General Terauchi to "appeal" to Kozakov "for the sake of the future."[160] Terauchi assured Grand Duke Georgii that day that Japan would send 20 million rounds of ammunition to St. Petersburg in the next three weeks.[161] Accompanying the delegation on its return through Korea at the end of January, Terauchi offered Kozakov a host of promises, to the extent that he himself feared that he had "said too much."[162] Tanaka assured the governor-general that his words would facilitate the matter by spurring a vigorous debate.[163]

The main boost to the campaign for a Russo-Japanese alliance, however, came with the sidelining of War Minister Oka due to serious illness. Unable in the critical days following Terauchi's assurances to Kozakov to marshal the support of their key ally in the battle against the Yamagata faction, Ōkuma and Ishii presided over the February 14 cabinet decision that called for continued arms aid to Russia and the establishment of an "alliance relationship."[164] Tanaka immediately called upon the Russian ambassador, Malevski-Malevich, to explain the War Ministry's delay and promise maximum effort on aid.[165] To Terauchi, he joyfully reported, "Absolutely everything is as the army advocated."[166]

Subsequent negotiations in St. Petersburg did not, as we have seen, entirely satisfy army demands. The Russians downgraded the proposed alliance to a "convention" and refused to cede the Changchun-Harbin Railway north of the Sungari River. But Japan did gain an indirect guarantee of Russian aid in the event of an American challenge to her interests in China. And the final conclusion of an agreement on July 3 signified the triumphant return of Yamagata and his military-bureaucratic associates to the foreign policy decision-making process. The field marshal undoubtedly had this political, as well as the policy, victory in mind when he penned a poetic sigh of relief soon after the agreement:

> I take in hand
> The text, though late.
> But when I look
> My brow eases
> For the first time.[167]

The decisive political victory for Yamagata and his army protégés represented by the Russo-Japanese Convention marked the beginning of the end for the Ōkuma cabinet. The prime minister struggled for some time to stay in power. And when this appeared impossible, he attempted to nominate Katō Takaaki to succeed him. But the agreement with the tsar revealed that the political momentum in Imperial Japan had dramatically shifted. The friends of parliamentary government had yielded the policy initiative to those whom Yoshino Sakuzō had labeled "German admirers," men who had long ago lost faith in the utility of Japan's association with Britain and had, rather, exalted the national power of Imperial Germany and the domestic political power of Kaiser Wilhelm. Buoyed by his diplomatic coup with the Russo-Japanese Convention, Yamagata decided that the time was ripe for a long-awaited domestic political stroke. He would replace the old symbol of "constitutional government," Ōkuma, with his own protégé General Terauchi Masatake. Since the fall of the second Saionji cabinet, Yamagata and his followers had planned for a nonpartisan Terauchi cabinet to deal a decisive blow to the escalating calls for responsible government. They were to find their bid for "national unity" under Terauchi, however, doomed from the start. If Katō had erred in believing that the age of responsible cabinets had arrived, Yamagata and his associates blundered in their conviction that the political momentum could be contained.

SYNOPSIS

After a year of bloodshed, a desperate fight for survival continued to preoccupy Allied generals in Europe. In Tokyo, by contrast, the principal battle remained that between two contrasting visions of the national essence. Yoshino Sakuzō described the battle in terms of a struggle between "German admirers" and those who valued the strong points of "Anglo-Saxon civilization." The "German admirers," such as Major General Tanaka Giichi, celebrated German power and sought to revitalize in Japan the zeal for empire, arms, and authoritarian rule that Meiji Japan's founders had originally introduced from Imperial Germany. Admirers of "Anglo-Saxon civilization," such as Katō Takaaki, on the other hand, remained faithful to the Anglo-Japanese alliance and championed parliamentary politics at home.

For a time after Katō's departure from the Ōkuma cabinet, the former foreign minister was able to preserve the pro-British orientation of his policies against the continuing pressure for change from the "German admirers" of the Yamagata faction. The September 1915 decision to adhere to the London Declaration rejected Field Marshal Yamagata's idea for an alliance with Imperial Russia. And the October warning to Chinese president Yuan Shikai not to crown himself emperor aimed to halt the Ōkuma cabinet's eroding domestic authority in the face of continuing challenges from Beijing.

In light of the political ascendance of the most politically savvy member of the Yamagata faction, however, the reconstructed Ōkuma cabinet would soon surrender to the command of some of Japan's most powerful "German admirers." After assuming the office of vice chief of the Army General Staff in October 1915, Tanaka Giichi would commandeer the nation's China policy from Katō's less experienced successor, Baron Ishii Kikujirō. By March 1916, he had transformed that policy from a mere warning to Yuan to an elaborate plan to depose the Chinese president and establish a pretext for Japanese military intervention in China.

At the same time, War Minister Oka Ichinosuke's incapacity because of serious illness enabled Tanaka, and mentors Yamagata and Terauchi, to move forward on a long-awaited plan to reorient Japanese foreign policy from the alliance with Britain to closer ties with Russia. Since the Russo-Japanese War, Japan had strengthened her position in Manchuria and Eastern Inner Mongolia through a series of agreements with the tsar. Japanese relations with Britain, by contrast, had steadily soured over conflicts of interest in China. It had become increasingly clear, moreover, that the British alliance would be useless in the event of a conflict with the most rapidly rising power in East Asian politics, the United States.

While the Russians hoped through strengthened ties with Japan to guarantee Tokyo's allegiance in the Allied fight against Germany, the principal Japanese architects of the 1916 Russo-Japanese Convention, then, envisioned a very different enemy. After the fall of Qingdao, the "German admirers" of the Yamagata faction feigned little interest in the campaign against the kaiser. They hoped, rather, to fortify Japan's continental position against the more obvious potential threats of the United States and Great Britain. At home, they sought to strengthen their own authority in the face of the rising celebration of "Anglo-Saxon civilization."

With the Russo-Japanese Convention, the Yamagata faction came close to satisfying its foreign policy goals. It had reoriented Japanese diplomacy from the increasingly less reliable Britain to the tsar. In October 1916, members of the faction would also celebrate the attainment of a long-awaited domestic political goal: the formation of a "national unity" cabinet headed by one of their own, General Terauchi Masatake. The war in Europe, it seemed, had finally restored the security to Japan's international position and to the domestic political posture of her military-bureaucratic elite that had been anticipated in August 1914. It would not take long, however, for both the new relationship with the tsar and the illusion of "national unity" to vanish against the backdrop of a rapidly changing international and domestic political order.

5 Last Chance of an Opportune War: Preempting Woodrow Wilson in Asia

Away, then, with the alien and repulsive slogan, "democratic!" Never will the mechanical-democratic state of the West be naturalized with us.

—Thomas Mann, *Reflections of a Nonpolitical Man*, 1918

The American president's propagation of democracy throughout the world in the wake of military victory has given a strong push [to parliamentary government and universal suffrage]. . . . For better or for worse, we are truly up against a time of crisis.

—Mori Ōgai, 1918

The principal belligerents entered the third year of war in the fall of 1916 reinvigorated for battle. The heroes of Germany's eastern campaign, General Paul von Hindenburg and Major General Erich Ludendorff, became in August the chief of the German General Staff and quartermaster general, respectively, and refused to accommodate Russia by renouncing German gains in Poland. In France, General Robert Nivelle, architect of recent spectacular advances at Verdun, assumed the role of supreme commander on the Western front in November and announced that "victory is certain."[1] In London, the Liberal Party's David Lloyd George, who had called in parliament for a "knock-out blow" against the Germans, in December formed a "national unity" cabinet and promised to prosecute the war with vigor.

While the French and British thus focused on crushing the German menace, their Japanese allies had turned their attention to a very different challenge. That challenge was graphically described in the title of a special three-part series in the monthly *Chūō kōron* beginning October 1916: "A Study of America, Which Is Extending Its Expansionary Wings over the Pacific and East Asian Continent." Japan's most prominent intellectuals, businessmen, and soldiers gathered in the fall of 1916 for a forum not on how to defeat Germany in the present but on how to confront the United States in the future. Like Japan, Kyōto University professor Suehiro Shigeo explained, the United States had not only avoided the destruction of the war but had actually benefited economically.[2] If the conflict had dramatically raised Japanese national power and international authority, it promised to do the same for the United States.

What did a boost to American international authority mean for Japan's future? Waseda University professor Ōyama Ikuo clung to the desperate hope that the United States would "remain forever the peacemaker of the world."[3] But Suehiro was less sanguine. "Will not Japanese-American relations," he wondered, "become in the future, in a certain sense, similar to British-German relations before the war?"[4] Representatives of Japan's two services described the rapid wartime growth of America's army and navy and demanded an equivalent augmentation of Japan's armed forces.[5] And the champion of Japanese democracy, Yoshino Sakuzō, noted the high probability of American expansion in China and the likelihood that this would lead to conflict with other powers with a stake on the continent.[6]

The tension between Japanese and American wartime goals would, indeed, become increasingly marked under the cabinet of General Terauchi Masatake. The cabinet would emerge in September 1916, after all, as the Yamagata faction's antidote to the movement for "constitutional government." And under Terauchi, the faction's bid for an autonomous Japanese diplomacy would reach its fullest fruition. The United States, on the other hand, would enter the war in April 1917 in a bid to make the world "safe for democracy." It would, as well, offer international cooperation over the balance of power as the primary object of international affairs.

The present chapter focuses on the principal foreign policy initiatives of the Terauchi cabinet: the Nishihara loans, the Sino-Japanese Military Agreement, and the Siberian Intervention. Each of these ventures has been treated separately in meticulously researched papers and monographs. But like Japan's other diplomatic initiatives between 1914 and 1919, they must be viewed within the larger context of the Great War and the turbulent political struggle over the national essence in Imperial Japan. In particular, they belong together as products of a transcendental cabinet, of the military-bureaucratic forces that had been cavalierly brushed aside by Foreign Minister Katō Takaaki in his relentless bid for his own solution to the nation's foremost diplomatic concern, relations with China. These were the same forces that had criticized Katō for disturbing Sino-Japanese harmony in his aggressive negotiations with China in 1915. But, as we shall see, given the opportunity to shape policy without any interference from the political opposition, these men devised schemes that far outpaced Katō's orthodox pursuit of Japanese continental interests. These were the men who had, from before the outbreak of war in Europe, envisioned an eventual conflict with the United States. And it was their vision of Japanese domestic and foreign affairs, not Katō's, that would come to contrast most sharply with President Woodrow Wilson's new conception of politics and diplomacy.

Fig. 14
"After the windbag,
the saber"

GENERAL TERAUCHI MASATAKE'S QUEST FOR NATIONAL UNITY

The Terauchi regime, like the Lloyd George cabinet in Britain or the Clemenceau government in France, was a product of the Great War. It was, like its European counterparts, a bid for national unity at a time of crisis. But whereas London and Paris were engaged in a struggle for national survival, Tokyo was absorbed in a battle for national identity. After all, Japan's fight against the kaiser had, for all intents and purposes, ended with the fall of Qingdao in November 1914. The war over the legacy of the Meiji era, by contrast, continued unabated. Field Marshal Yamagata and his supporters had, since 1912, waged a desperate battle to salvage the legacy of empire, arms, and oligarchic rule. By decisively capturing the foreign policy prerogative in August 1914, Foreign Minister Katō Takaaki had made a powerful bid for responsible government and civilian control. With Katō gone after August 1915, the Yamagata faction had reestablished the military and bureaucratic thrust of Japanese diplomacy.

When in his final days as prime minister Count Ōkuma proposed to yield the reins of government to Katō, Field Marshal Yamagata balked. Japan may have eradicated the enemy from the Far East. But she was still at war. It was time, Yamagata declared, to promote the empire's external posture by developing Japanese "internal strength." He desired not a prime minister "inclined toward a particular party" but a "neutral" candidate to "unify and guide the people without bias."[7] That candidate was the Yamagata faction's second in command, General Terauchi Masatake.[8]

The foreign policy initiatives of the Terauchi cabinet must, in other words, be analyzed in the context of this essential bid to buttress military-bureaucratic rule in Japan. The attempt was, from the beginning, marred by complications. For the Japanese public reacted angrily to the blatant reversal of the momentum for political reform. Indeed, they had had every reason to believe that the Dōshikai-supported Ōkuma government would yield to a strengthened Dōshikai cabinet. Katō Takaaki's party, after all, retained preponderant strength in the Diet and was slated to capture an absolute majority through a merger with the Chūseikai (Association for Impartiality) and Kōyū Club (Friends' Club) parties.[9]

When Terauchi vowed that cabinet appointments would be divorced from party affiliation,[10] Ōkuma advised the new prime minister not to conduct matters in a "German fashion."[11] The press, which had hailed the Ōkuma cabinet in 1914 as a triumph of "constitutional government," now lambasted the appointment of a general without party affiliation as a "blatant reversal" of the same.[12] "This disturbs the principle of constitutional government and ignores the majority will of the people," grumbled the *Tokyo Mainichi shinbun*. To the *Yorozu Chōhō*, a Terauchi cabinet marked "the triumph of militarism in Japan."[13] Yoshino Sakuzō delivered a twenty-page "stern criticism" in the November *Chūō kōron*, characterizing the change of government as "the emergence, with the protection of the *genrō* and from a mistaken, stubbornly conservative constitutional theory against the trend of the times, of one group of bureaucrats thirsty for power."[14]

If contemporaries described the Terauchi cabinet as a step backward politically, diplomatic historians have spoken of the regime as a new departure diplomatically. In his first formal statement on China policy, delivered in January 1917, Terauchi, after all, repudiated his predecessor's interference in Chinese domestic affairs. And he reoriented Japan's posture vis-à-vis China from Tanaka Giichi's emphasis on armed intervention to a preference for financial diplomacy. The classic study of Japanese army policy during this period stresses the philosophical differences between the Terauchi and Ōkuma cabinet China policies and describes the aim of aid to Chinese premier Duan Qirui as Chinese unity, not support for one faction in the ongoing Chinese civil war.[15]

But while the Terauchi cabinet did mark a reversal of the movement for political reform, it did not represent the interests of the Yamagata faction as originally anticipated. Nor did the new cabinet mark a sudden shift to noninterference in Chinese domestic politics. Rather, Terauchi proved to have a political agenda of his own. And his professed rejection of interference in China affairs signaled less a change of substance than one of form. In substantive terms, in fact, Terauchi's policies would rival the most ambitious plans of those of his fellow members of the Yamagata faction.

Politically, the new cabinet would disappoint its main sponsors in the Yamagata faction. Despite the long-held hope of faction heads that Terauchi would restore their political authority, the new prime minister refused from the outset to play Yamagata's stooge. Advised by the factional patriarch in May 1915 to ready himself for the prime ministry, the general had countered that he saw "no need for preparation."[16] During discussions with Ōkuma in July 1916 over the transfer of power, he had informed Yamagata that he was no longer a child and could not, therefore, listen to everything that the elder statesman said.[17] Indeed, on matters of both personnel and policy, Terauchi pursued his own agenda.

Terauchi's most important initial personnel decision was to turn for support not to Yamagata protégé Hirata Tōsuke, but to his old friend from the second Katsura cabinet, Gotō Shinpei. Hirata had, on behalf of the elder statesman, worked energetically in the weeks leading to Terauchi's appointment for an accommodation between the new cabinet and the Dōshikai.[18] Gotō, on the other hand, had lobbied just as resolutely against a Dōshikai link. It was thanks to Dōshikai president Katō, after all, that the baron had spent the last three and a half years in political exile.[19]

The formation of the new cabinet in early October marked Gotō's victory in the duel to win over Terauchi. Not only did the Dōshikai fail to receive any seats in the cabinet, the Seiyūkai's Nakashōji Ren and Gotō obtained portfolios despite Katō Takaaki's warning that to include the two Dōshikai renegades would constitute "picking a fight" with his party.[20] This, in turn, destroyed any chance for Hirata, who had staked his reputation on a Terauchi-Dōshikai compromise, to join the cabinet. "The military way will not do," the field marshal chided Terauchi. The new prime minister should have consulted the elder statesman prior to the cabinet appointments.[21] Indeed, Terauchi's fait accompli was disturbingly reminiscent of the methods of Yamagata's greatest political rival, Katō.

AN EXPANSIVE DEFINITION
OF JAPANESE RIGHTS IN ASIA:
THE NISHIHARA LOANS

Yamagata breathed a sigh of relief that Gotō had assumed the helm at the Home rather than the Foreign Ministry. At Kasumigaseki, the field marshal had apprised Hara Takashi, there was "no telling what he will do."[22] But Gotō did not intend for a domestic political assignment to contain his principal interest in Japan's continental affairs. Upon accepting the Home Ministry portfolio, he informed his vice minister, Okuda

Yoshito, that he would leave the daily operation of the ministry entirely in Okuda's hands. He himself would devote his time to the more ambitious enterprise of China affairs. Having earlier been nominated by elder statesman Inoue Kaoru to serve as Japan's special envoy to China, Gotō envisioned, in particular, a triumphant voyage to China to personally work out a "smooth resolution" to Sino-Japanese relations.[23]

Gotō Shinpei's Quest for Autonomy in China

Gotō would not visit China as planned, but he emerged even before the formation of the new cabinet as the principal architect of a break with the previous government based on a reorientation of the empire's China policy. The change, as already indicated, was less one of substance than of form. Indeed, Katō Takaaki observed that, despite the rhetoric, "there is no difference with [the policy of] all other cabinets."[24] The new regime's first official statement on China in January 1917, in fact, closely resembled Katō's agenda in his negotiations with China, covering four of the five geographic areas in which Katō had sought concessions. It urged the promotion of Japan's "special interests" in South Manchuria and Eastern Inner Mongolia; the preservation of the empire's "special relationship" with Fujian province; and the transfer of all prewar German interests in Shandong to Japan.

Like his predecessors, in other words, Terauchi sought to strengthen Japan's foothold on the continent in areas in which Japan had had a growing interest since the Russo-Japanese War. There was, nonetheless, one distinctive feature of the new cabinet's approach to China: its emphasis on financial loans. Japan's policymakers had long dreamed of competing in the game of financial diplomacy in China. That game had become popular in the aftermath of the Sino-Japanese War as the great powers discovered that they could buy exclusive rights to Chinese territory by funding the construction of railroads throughout the continent. Having only recently joined the ranks of modern nation-states, Japan had had neither the military nor the financial strength to profit from the scramble for spheres of influence in China after 1895. Relative financial weakness had even led to serious discussions in Tokyo in 1905 of forgoing a sphere of influence in newly acquired South Manchuria in favor of joint management with the United States.[25] As late as September 1914, Tanaka Giichi had fretted over Japan's financial weakness relative to the great powers and argued that Japan had no alternative but to resort to that tool of diplomacy that she wielded with increasing effect: arms.[26]

But the economic boom brought by the Great War finally gave Japan the capacity to compete in the world of international finance. The withdrawal of the great powers to Europe had opened new markets for Japanese arms, shipping, and textiles; and by mid-1916 Japan had produced its first balance of payments surplus since 1909 and the largest in its history.[27] Gotō had long held an interest in the financial aspects of empire. He had, as we have seen, submitted a proposal for improved Sino-Japanese relations on the eve of the war that envisioned intimate economic cooperation around an Asian development bank. By November 1916, he urged Prime Minister Terauchi to devise an "original policy" that would reflect the new financial situation.

Historians are, of course, correct in highlighting the resulting series of loans to the Duan Qirui regime in Beijing as a new departure in Japanese diplomacy. No previous Japanese cabinet had had the capacity to engage in financial diplomacy on such a scale. But to identify the departure as a turn toward a more modest posture in China is to misunderstand the aims of the chief architects of the Nishihara loans. The Terauchi cabinet's attempt to buy influence in Beijing pales in comparison to Tanaka Giichi's bid for armed intervention. But like Tanaka's China policy, the loans had an object much larger than Katō's aim with the negotiations with Beijing. Katō, as we have seen, attempted to negotiate concessions in the manner that had become accepted by the great powers since the Sino-Japanese War. Both Gotō Shinpei and Nishihara Kamezō, however, like Prime Minister Terauchi and other members of the military-bureaucratic elite, conceived of Sino-Japanese relations in entirely novel terms. Indeed, while four out of five points in the January 1917 statement on China policy closely paralleled Katō's outline of negotiations with Beijing, point 5 called for great power recognition of Japan's "superior position" in all of China.[28]

While he focused on financial aid, Gotō's ideas for Japanese influence in China, like those of other members of the military-bureaucratic elite, were based upon a racial conception of international affairs and were unlimited in their ambition. His plan for an "original" China policy presented to Terauchi in November 1916 outlined a Sino-Japanese economic alliance aimed at strengthening Sino-Japanese political, economic, and cultural ties to the exclusion of the Western powers. Japan, the home minister urged Prime Minister Terauchi, should "stand outside the restrictions of the four-power consortium" that had provided loans to China since 1912 and begin unilateral funding. As a start, he suggested founding a new bank that would channel 100 million yen to Beijing. Collateral for the loan could come from the Chinese government monopoly on opium.[29] Ultimately, Gotō aimed to alleviate the problem of Japanese "subservience" to Western diplomatic initiatives on the continent and to "open new vistas in terms of the ultimate ideal relationship between the yellow and white races."[30]

Nishihara Kamezō's Quest for the Kingly Way in China

As home minister–designate, Gotō was instrumental in launching the new financial orientation of the Terauchi regime. But it was ultimately Terauchi's hand-picked negotiator, Nishihara Kamezō, who would become the main architect of that policy. Nishihara was an enterprising businessman and longtime proponent of aggressive Japanese expansion. He was a close associate of nationalist politician Kōmuchi Tomotsune from the Kensei Hontō party, who had, in the 1890s, campaigned against the Itō cabinet's weakness on treaty revision and, in 1902, founded the Counter Russia Association (Tai-Rō dōshikai) to press for war against the tsar. Nishihara was a charter member of the association and one of the first to take advantage of the political and economic hegemony that Japan enjoyed in Korea as a result of the Russo-Japanese War. It was during his extended stay in Seoul from 1905 to early 1916 as adviser to the Seoul Chamber of Commerce that he became acquainted with Japan's first governor-general to the peninsula, General Terauchi, and the chairman of the Bank of Korea, Shōda Kazue.[31]

Like Gotō and other members of the military-bureaucratic elite, Nishihara's aspirations for Japanese power recognized few bounds. While he expressed dismay at the "naïveté" of the ambitious designs of Army General Staff representatives in China, he proposed schemes of his own that anticipated the unbridled Japanese expansionism of the 1930s. With letters of introduction from Terauchi, Nishihara had traveled to Beijing in June 1916 to discuss the continental situation with Japanese military and diplomatic personnel and members of the new Chinese government. There he found military attaché Major General Saitō Suejirō eager to incite rebellion along the banks of the Yangzi as an excuse to send four Japanese divisions to "unify" the country. Nishihara condemned the idea of militarily unifying and "assimilating" a country of 400 million people as the "height of difficulty." With only two divisions, he countered, it would take at least forty to fifty years to assimilate Korea completely.[32] But Nishihara's own prescription for stronger Sino-Japanese ties envisioned nothing less than complete Japanese economic hegemony on the continent. In his "Outline of Economic Mechanisms in Response to the Situation in China," presented to Terauchi on July 3, he proposed not only a 10 million yen loan to Beijing, but also the introduction of Japanese currency into China. Only a mixture of yuan and yen and the pursuit of the Kingly Way (ōdōshugi), Nishihara argued, would enable Japan to overcome its financial inferiority relative to the great powers in China. The currency mix would initially be implemented in areas under direct Japanese police control and would be facilitated by a rejuvenated Transportation Bank and Japanese financial advisers in Beijing.[33] The idea of a currency mix and the appeal of ōdōshugi in China were ahead of their time in 1916. The Japanese government would eventually make yen and yuan notes convertible on a one-to-one basis in Manchuria in 1931. And the Neo-Confucian idea of the Kingly Way, signifying a harmonious state free from the divisive individualism and materialism of the capitalist West, would be used to describe social relations in the new creation of Manchukuo after 1932.

Like other members of the military-bureaucratic elite, Nishihara's unlimited vision of expansion on the continent was integrally linked with the expectation of conflict with the other rapidly rising force in the Asia-Pacific: the United States. In a "wish" list presented to Terauchi on October 2, Nishihara proposed an expanded Japanese presence both in China and across the Pacific. In China, Nishihara anticipated the creation and cultivation of a base "to last a hundred generations." Overseas, he hoped to send one-fifth of the archipelago's annual population growth, 100,000 Japanese, each year to Mexico and South America for use, in part, "in our policy vis-à-vis the United States."[34] An October 11 memorandum suggested unifying the administrative, financial, and transportation networks of South Manchuria and Korea and proposed the "economic territorialization" (*keizai-teki ryōdoka*) of Manchuria and Mongolia.[35] By mid-November, Nishihara hinted at the same goal promoted by the army representatives whom he had earlier ridiculed. If China could not support itself, he advised Terauchi, "we cannot avoid annexation."[36]

The Nishihara loans utterly failed to achieve the basic goals of their chief architects. Rather than strengthen Japanese influence in Beijing, they fortified Chinese president Duan Qirui against his domestic political enemies, and by implication, against Japan itself. Rather than kowtow to his Japanese sponsors, Duan devoured Tokyo's largesse for his own political purposes without offering any tangible benefit in return. Instead of falling into the obvious snare embodied by the Japanese proposals, he and his advisers kept a wary distance. During negotiations in December 1916 for a loan to the Chinese Transportation Bank, for example, Transportation Minister Cao Rulin accused the Japanese representatives outright of planning to annex Manchuria if the "Sino-Japanese friendship" and "eternal peace in the Far East" so highly touted by Nishihara failed to materialize.[37]

Japanese statesmen would struggle in vain for the next twenty years to obtain repayment of their loans. It is perhaps due to the singular failure of Japan's first attempt at financial diplomacy on such a large scale that it is customarily overshadowed, like most other Japanese diplomatic initiatives during the First World War, by Katō's more successful negotiations with China. But it is worth remembering that the loans originally aimed, like the movement to depose Yuan and the Russo-Japanese Convention of 1916, to establish a dramatic new level of Japanese influence in China. They offer another glimpse of the spectacular ambitions entertained by some of Katō's principal rivals for power.

THE POLITICS OF THE NISHIHARA LOANS

The Nishihara loans are a familiar chapter in the basic narrative of Japanese diplomacy in the twentieth century. But like Japan's other diplomatic initiatives during the First World War, they have a political significance that is often overlooked. If, in the history of Japanese diplomacy, the Terauchi cabinet's loans attest to the spectacular imperial ambitions held by some members of the Japanese elite, in political terms, the loans vividly illustrate the complexity of Taishō era politics. For while the loans may be classified together with the initiatives of Yamagata and Tanaka as exceeding the boundaries of great power politics followed by Katō Takaaki in his negotiations with China, they also demonstrate that the anti-Katō forces were by no means monolithic in their attempt to forge a new path in China. On the contrary, if on the diplomatic level the loans aimed to vastly increase Japanese influence in China, politically, they mark Terauchi's attempt to outmaneuver a longtime supporter and fellow member of the Yamagata faction, Tanaka Giichi. For even before their ascension to power, Terauchi and his immediate backers recognized Tanaka's enormous influence in Japanese foreign policy and the need to neutralize his presence. The Nishihara loans, then, are as much a story of the political struggle between the core members of the new Terauchi cabinet and the chief architect of China policy in the latter half of the Ōkuma cabinet (Tanaka Giichi) as they are an illustration of unbridled ambition in Tokyo.

In helping to found the new cabinet, home minister–designate Gotō Shinpei paid particular attention to repudiating the previous regime's China policy. In early August, he commissioned Nishihara to present evidence of the Ōkuma cabinet's clandestine support of Chinese revolutionaries to a forum of seventy to eighty peers. Because the March 7, 1916, cabinet decision had not been made public, Nishihara's findings caused a considerable stir.[38] The home minister–designate followed with a plea to Terauchi on October 3 for an immediate purge of the principal China-policy actors of the reshuffled Ōkuma cabinet. They included Ōkuma, Foreign Minister Ishii, Vice Minister Shidehara, Foreign Ministry Political Affairs Bureau Chief Koike Chōzō, Governor-General of Guandong Nakamura Satoru, and Vice Chief of the Army General Staff Tanaka "and his associates."[39]

Tanaka Giichi's conspicuousness as the chief architect of Ōkuma's China policy after Katō Takaaki's resignation won him particular censure from Gotō and other Terauchi advisers. Two days before his formal appointment as communications minister, House of Peers member

Baron Den Kenjirō warned the prime minister of the "failure of Tanaka Giichi's schemes" and suggested demoting him to division chief.[40] Chōshū general and Privy Council member Viscount Miura Gorō urged Terauchi to oust "the epitome of the China problem, the likes of Tanaka Giichi," to demonstrate a complete break from the former cabinet's approach to China.[41]

Emboldened by the advice, Terauchi summoned Tanaka in early October to chasten him for his reckless schemes on the continent. Was he, asked the new prime minister, prepared to deal with the consequences of his support for the Chinese revolutionaries, that is, to go to war with China?[42] But Terauchi could not easily dismiss a fellow member of the Yamagata faction who retained the favor of Yamagata. He informed Miura in early November that "there is another means."[43]

That means was to work around Tanaka and the Army General Staff by redirecting the thrust of the empire's China policy. Tanaka had controlled the approaches to China through a network of military ties with various anti-Yuan factions on the continent. Terauchi's civilian advisers now proposed an exclusive relationship with the new Duan Qirui regime in Beijing through an approach that they could hope to command, financial diplomacy. The new financial thrust of the Terauchi cabinet's China policy, in other words, was not simply the result of the availability of a new weapon in Japan's struggle for influence on the continent. It was also devised in order to outmaneuver the most powerful players in China affairs at the time, Tanaka Giichi and the Army General Staff.

The battle to seize command of the nation's China policy was a tumultuous one, requiring all the ingenuity of the two chief adversaries. Nishihara Kamezō moved soon after Terauchi's appointment to initiate the new cabinet's first important diplomatic contact with the new regime in Beijing, the dispatch of a special Chinese envoy to Tokyo. To do the honors, Nishihara chose Cao Rulin, Prime Minister Duan Qirui's transportation minister, whom he had met in June and with whom he expected to work closely on revitalizing the Transportation Bank. Nishihara sounded out Foreign Ministry Political Affairs Bureau Chief Obata Yūkichi, Chief Cabinet Secretary (and Terauchi son-in-law) Kodama Hideo, and Vice Finance Minister (and longtime acquaintance from Nishihara's days in Korea) Shōda Kazue and broached the idea with

China's minister to Tokyo, Zhang Zongxiang, even before discussing the matter with Terauchi. Zhang announced the upcoming dispatch of Cao Rulin on November 1.[44]

But to Nishihara's dismay, the mission never materialized. The network of continental adventurers assembled by Vice Chief of the Army General Staff Tanaka to stir up unrest under Chinese president Yuan Shikai remained active, in spite of the Ōkuma government's decision after Yuan's death to withdraw support to these men. Lieutenant General Aoki Nobuzumi, Major General Saitō Suejirō, and Kawashima Naniwa had all played key roles in Tanaka's scheme and continued their support for the Guomindang opposition to Duan Qirui's cabinet.[45] Nishihara suspected that Aoki and civilian accomplices Kamei Rokurō and Sawara Tokuzō were behind the Guomindang refusal to sanction Cao's visit in early December. He urged Terauchi to recall these men and all Japanese officers in China "participating in revolution."[46]

Having failed in this first attempt to develop a close rapport between the Terauchi and Duan cabinets, Nishihara organized a second trip to Beijing, this time as the personal envoy of the Japanese prime minister. In discussions with Premier Duan and his associates, Nishihara discovered fresh evidence of Japanese army complicity in movements aimed against Duan. In a series of letters to Terauchi, he described the efforts of Kawashima to assemble, with funds intended for the clean-up of failed revolutionary movements, a corps of army reserves in South Manchuria's major cities with ties to the Manchurian independence party, the Zongshedang, and to Mongolia. In Shandong, the Japanese army was facilitating the movement of rebel forces by refusing passage to the Chinese Regular Army on railroads under Japanese Army control. Kamei Rokurō, who had promoted unrest in concert with Lieutenant General Aoki and the Guomindang, continued to operate the daily *Shuntian shibao* with Japanese Foreign Ministry money as if it were the mouthpiece of the Guomindang. Finally, Lieutenant General Aoki himself was rumored to have been involved in an uprising against Duan sponsored by the Guomindang in Zhejiang Province.[47]

Nishihara urged the prime minister to replace all Japanese army field commanders and military attachés in China.[48] But in the immediate term, he attempted to wrest control of China policy by negotiating with Duan's regime a loan to a depository for Chinese government specie and the official bank of the Chinese National Railway, the Transportation Bank. While Nishihara thus maneuvered in Beijing to build the foundation for a "new" China policy, Prime Minister Terauchi attempted to regroup forces back home. In early November he had confirmed to Viscount Miura Gorō the new economic orientation of the empire's posture toward China. Japan, he proposed, could dispense up to 100 million yen in loans to Beijing.[49] On January 9 of the new year, Terauchi received cabinet approval for the government's first formal statement on China policy.

The statement, as we have seen, closely resembled Katō's negotiating points with Beijing two years prior. But its principal purpose was to mark a clear departure from the Ōkuma cabinet. This it actually did, but from a particular member of that cabinet. The stipulation in the third clause that the empire "not interfere by any means in the internal political disturbances [of China]" was meant as a rejection of the March 7, 1916, cabinet decision to recognize and support revolutionary movements against Yuan Shikai. It was intended, in other words, as a repudiation of the activities of the principal architect of that policy, Tanaka Giichi. With this January statement, Terauchi formally declared that it was he and his personal advisers who would now direct Japan's most important foreign policy agenda, not Tanaka Giichi or his henchmen of the Army General Staff in the field.[50]

Viscount Miura had urged Terauchi in November to circumvent the power of Tanaka by securing the support of the three major party heads for his China policy initiatives.[51] Having now obtained cabinet approval, the prime minister assembled Katō, Hara, and Kokumintō party president Inukai Tsuyoshi on January 15 to discuss the five-point plan. It was the first of a series of meetings that would lead to the establishment of the Advisory Council on Foreign Affairs (Gaikō chōsakai) in June 1917.[52] The Gaikō chōsakai is often described as an attempt by the "transcendental" Terauchi cabinet to cultivate broad support for its foreign policies in lieu of an independent power base in the Imperial Diet. But it was formed, in other words, with another more specific aim in mind; namely, to strengthen Terauchi's command of the approaches to China in light of Tanaka Giichi's continuing influence there.

If control of the approaches to China remained a critical component of the battle for political supremacy in Tokyo, the impossibility of ultimately swaying events on the continent continued to confound the best laid plans of Japan's policymakers. We have already witnessed the difficulties experienced by Katō, Ōkuma, and Tanaka in guiding events in China. Complications would multiply as Japan deepened her involvement on the continent in the latter 1920s and 1930s. Likewise, the emerging battle between Nishihara and Tanaka to steer events across the Japan Sea continued to produce unintended consequences.

Nishihara's effort to obtain Chinese participation in the war, for example, would destabilize politics in Beijing and present Tanaka a fresh opportunity to recapture command of Japan's China policy. Nishihara had considered a Chinese break with Germany under Japanese auspices essential to solidifying Terauchi's relationship with the Duan cabinet and to establishing Japanese leadership in China. He devoted his third trip to Beijing in February 1917, therefore, to negotiating China's participation in the war. Beijing subsequently severed ties with Germany on March 14.

The action brought applause in Tokyo as evidence of the growing international authority of the empire. But the political results in Beijing were disastrous. Far from stabilizing Chinese affairs and Sino-Japanese relations, Chinese participation in the war exacerbated tensions between Chinese prime minister Duan Qirui and president Li Yuanhong. Before Beijing severed ties with Germany, Duan had resigned the premiership in response to Li's opposition to the move. He subsequently resumed the post at Li's request, only to face renewed resistance over the actual declaration of war from Li, Sun Yatsen, and members of the Guomindang in parliament. When Li refused to dissolve the parliament after failing to secure a vote for war, seven military governors organized a general staff in Tianjin and threatened to sever relations with Beijing unless parliament was dissolved. The new turmoil marked the greatest setback to date for Terauchi's China policy. It threatened the new cabinet's investment in Duan. And it granted the cabinet's preeminent political rival, and the one against whom the new orientation in China policy had been directed, a new opportunity to make his mark in China affairs.

Over the strenuous objections of Nishihara, Tanaka had, in January, secured the appointment of Army General Staff officers Lieutenant General Aoki Nobuzumi and Lieutenant Colonel Taga Muneyuki as military advisers to Chinese president Li Yuanhong and vice president Feng Guozhang, respectively.[53] Both Li and Feng were sympathetic to China's revolutionaries and had occupied important positions in the vice chief's plans for China before the Terauchi cabinet. Tanaka had cultivated Feng to control Nanjing during the movement to oust Yuan Shikai.[54] After Yuan's death, he had targeted Li as the centerpiece of Japan's approaches to China.[55] Nishihara had nullified this latter initiative when he had designated Prime Minister Duan Qirui the recipient of Japanese largesse. Now Tanaka was poised to reclaim command by revitalizing his ties with Duan's domestic rivals for power.

Prime Minister Duan's mounting political problems in March compelled Tanaka to attempt some hands-on diplomacy by way of an extended tour of China in May and June. As he informed Terauchi toward the end of his tour, he had offered advice to a variety of people in an "unofficial" capacity to lay the ground for Japan's future China policy.[56] "Unofficial" or no, the danger of Tanaka pursuing an independent path on the continent compelled the prime minister to attempt to reroute the vice chief of staff to St. Petersburg soon after his arrival in Qingdao.[57] But protests from Army Chief of Staff Uehara spared the vice chief from banishment to Russia and enabled him to work on an alternative to Duan's rule in Beijing.

Tanaka's first important call in China was upon Anhui military governor Zhang Xun. Like Duan, Zhang belonged to the Beiyang clique formerly led by Yuan Shikai, but he had made his own bid for power after Yuan's death by sponsoring a series of interprovincial conferences at Xuzhou (Jiangsu province). These were ostensibly aimed at promoting Beiyang unity in the face of southern opposition. In actuality, the conferences became planning sessions for a Manchu restoration under Zhang's leadership, a prospect that threatened Tanaka's plan to make President Li the new locus of power. Tanaka assured the governor that, as a Japanese and a soldier, he "deeply welcomed" the prospect of a restoration of the throne. But such an agenda threatened to "provoke a great upheaval and plunge the country into an ever more dangerous state." Tanaka would not countenance, in other words, a Zhang Xun monopoly on power in Beijing. To take full advantage of the "heaven-sent great happiness" that the war offered by diverting the great powers from their "oppression" of Asia, close Sino-Japanese cooperation to "strengthen the Far East" was required. And this necessitated "national unity" in China. Tanaka counseled Zhang to become, together with the civilian leader of the Beiyang clique Xu Shichang, the "central figures for national union" under the leadership of President Li. If opposed by a "rebellion-loving gang," he advised, "it is just to resolve the issue at *this* time by a use of force." Tanaka promised his "sincere goodwill" if Zhang accepted his advice.[58] One week later, Zhang hosted the fourth Xuzhou Conference, setting the stage for his march on Beijing and restoration of Manchu emperor Puyi in June.[59]

Meanwhile, Tanaka proceeded to Nanjing on May 16, where he chided Vice President Feng Guozhang for failing to support President Li more actively. Feng had initially sided with Li in opposing Premier Duan's push for a break with Germany, but he had worked for Duan's return to office after the prime minister resigned in March. His support was needed to help Li shed the restrictions placed on his authority after the return of Duan.[60]

After receiving Feng's assurance that he would "cherish" the idea for national unity, Tanaka continued to Shanghai, where he solicited the support of Sun Yatsen for Li's rule. Sun refused to participate in discussions in Beijing with a government unwilling to compromise. But soon after the Guomindang leader's meeting with Tanaka, Li dismissed Prime Minister Duan for the second time. Eager to obtain Sun's reaction to the new developments, Tanaka paid him a second visit, this time securing his agreement to travel to Beijing to work with Li. This was the break Tanaka had been waiting for. In a burst of excitement, he ordered Lieutenant Colonel Taga on May 28 to inform Feng Guozhang that Sun, fellow republican Tang Shaoyi, and southern sympathizer Cen Chunxuan had all expressed willingness to cooperate with Li after Duan's departure.[61]

But while Prime Minister Duan's ouster paved the way for southern support for Li's regime, it did so at the expense of cooperation from northern warlords. Less than a week after Duan's dismissal, the governor of Anhui, Ni Sichong, and the military governor of Shaanxi, Chen Shu-fan, severed relations with the Beijing government. Tanaka rushed to Beijing on June 5 to urge Li Yuanhong to remain firm in his position as president. Vice President Feng Guozhang had promised to work with Li for national unity, he argued. And there were indications that Zhang Xun had left Xuzhou for Beijing to mediate a settlement together with Xu Shichang. On June 7, Tanaka ordered Lieutenant Colonel Taga to obtain Vice President Feng's support "to prevent all of China from falling into a state of confusion."[62]

But Feng would not commit himself to a losing cause. It was not the time to work openly for mediation, he informed Tanaka.[63] Four days later, it became clear that Tanaka's other hope for strengthening Li's position vis-à-vis the northern generals, Zhang Xun, intended to proceed with his monarchical plans in Beijing. Tanaka cabled a frantic message to Feng on June 12 and twice again the following day. It was "absolutely necessary" that he come to Beijing to "advise" the president and prevent Zhang's move. "As vice president, is it appropriate for you to be excluded and have nothing to do with deciding future measures?"[64] Zhang Xun marched into the nation's capital on June 14, just as Feng cabled Tanaka that the situation in Yunnan and Guangdong was as yet too unstable to warrant a trip north.[65] Two days later, the vice chief warned Duan Zhigui, a member of the Beiyang clique and protégé of Xu Shichang, that if Zhang's interference was not resolved by the time Tanaka returned to Tokyo, the lieutenant general would have to take "appropriate measures."[66]

Meanwhile, Nishihara had slipped into China unannounced on June 8 to revive the mainstay of his own China policy, the Duan regime. Two days after his arrival, he cabled Finance Minister Shōda Kazue that Tanaka was attempting to control the situation by supporting President Li. In so doing, he was "suppressing" Premier Duan and Xu Shichang, with whom Li was at odds, and promised to "further complicate the situation." Nishihara urged Shōda to have Prime Minister Terauchi halt Tanaka's scheme and persuade him to work on Xu's behalf.[67]

In fact, the problem of Tanaka's activities in China was soon resolved independently of Nishihara's initiatives. By his scheduled date of return

to Tokyo, Tanaka had made little headway in steering events. Still un-
aware of Nishihara's presence in Beijing, he fumed over the "schemers"
that were instigating Zhang Xun and moving President Li in an "impossible drama" to restore Duan Qirui to power. "It is transparent that this
drama is a plot especially to use your cabinet, as well as [to use] Japan,"
he informed Terauchi the day before his departure. It was time for Japan
to begin steering events in China rather than being led by developments
out of their control.[68]

After Tanaka's departure and three and a half weeks of discussions
with Duan Qirui, Xu Shichang, and Cao Rulin regarding legal and financial means to facilitate their return to power, Nishihara witnessed a
fortuitous turn of events.[69] On July 2 Duan and his troops began moving
toward Beijing to remove Zhang Xun. On the same day, after designating Duan the prime minister, Tanaka's hope for China, President Li
Yuanhong, approached the vice chief's agent and military attaché in Beijing, Major General Saitō Suejirō, to request political asylum.[70] Nishihara welcomed the imminent realization of his objectives as a "break of
dawn."[71] Ten days later, Duan's troops captured Beijing. On July 20, the
Japanese cabinet reaffirmed its position against support for the "southern
faction" and formally approved Nishihara's policy of aid to the restored
Duan regime.[72]

Tanaka viewed the failure of his personal mission to China with
exasperation. "The instantaneous downfall of Zhang Xun was truly a
laughable affair," he wrote Lieutenant General Akashi. "But we can
no longer stand by and watch. It is time to take some kind of decisive
action."[73] The vice chief of staff began with a policy statement designed
to demonstrate that his recent defeat to the practitioners of economic
diplomacy did not reflect his own lack of sensitivity to financial matters.
In fact, his statement, "A Personal Opinion on the Management
of China," seemed intent upon proving Nishihara's piecemeal offers of
aid mere child's play. In a text exceeding 21,000 characters, Tanaka
argued for the "harmonic union of the Chinese and Japanese people"
by means of "joint management" of China's economic and intellectual infrastructure.[74] Included was the establishment of a Japan-China Association to oversee all Chinese educational institutions and the media; the

development of a unified system of hospital care in China under Japanese management; the unification under joint Sino-Japanese supervision of China's silk and textile industries and, in the form of a giant steamship company, of all Chinese railways and steamship lines; and the establishment of a colossal Sino-Japanese steel company to regulate all Chinese production of steel and oil. All this would protect the "eternal peace of the Far East" from the "various pressures" to come with the end of war in Europe.

Even in political defeat, in other words, Tanaka's ambitions for Sino-Japanese relations recognized few bounds. While Katō Takaaki's negotiations with China had outlined exclusive privileges for Japan in specific areas of China (Shandong, South Manchuria, Eastern Inner Mongolia, the Yangzi valley, Fujian), Tanaka now proposed Japanese management of the entire country. Nor did he stop there. The giant steamship company would serve as the "foundation for [our] activity in the East and South Pacific region," in the same manner that the South Manchuria Railway stood as "the marrow of our continental management."[75]

Nishihara was not eclipsed by Tanaka's ideas any more than he was by Tanaka's politics. As Tanaka drafted a plan for Japanese management of the Chinese economy and for expansion in the South Pacific, Nishihara nurtured his own visions of aggressive expansion southward. In negotiations with Chinese transportation minister Cao Rulin in July, he offered to alleviate Beijing's fears of Japanese designs on Manchuria. Japan would, he informed Cao, look to the Dutch East Indies instead. As Nishihara later informed Transportation Minister Den Kenjirō, the Dutch minister to China had "fortunately" slandered China at the time of Zhang Xun's restoration attempt. Nishihara urged Cao to expel the minister and send troops to the Dutch East Indies to protect her citizens. China would then obtain the permission of the great powers to "recover" the colony and, after concluding a military pact with Japan, secretly contract to transfer the territory to Tokyo. Japan would bankroll the operation and subsequently relinquish "what should be relinquished" of her hold on Manchuria. Cao indicated probable agreement if the Manchurian problem could be resolved, and Nishihara broached the matter with Terauchi in early September.[76]

Fig. 15
"Wilson
whoipping
Kaiser"

AMERICA ENTERS
THE WAR

Neither Tanaka's nor Nishihara's plans for expanding the Japanese empire to Southeast Asia and the Pacific would materialize. But like the movement to depose Yuan Shikai and the Russo-Japanese Convention of 1916, they were indicative of the boundless ambitions entertained by some of Tokyo's most powerful policymakers at a time when Japan's major international competitors were preoccupied with war in Europe. In the summer of 1917, they could also have reflected a sense that the great freedom of action enjoyed by Japan since the outbreak of war was about to end. For one of Japan's competitors, a power whose potential to spoil Japanese dreams had been recognized and feared since before the outbreak of war, was poised for a dramatically expanded voice in world affairs. After having tried to secure peace since 1914, the United States in April 1917 formally declared war on Germany.

Studies of U.S.-Japanese relations in the early twentieth century invariably highlight friction over issues of immigration and race as central in the rise of tensions between the two countries.[77] The 1905 San Francisco School Board segregation of Japanese students, the 1907 Gentlemen's Agreement to restrict Japanese labor immigration, Woodrow Wilson's rejection of Japan's proposed racial nondiscrimination clause in the Covenant of the League of Nations at the Versailles Conference in 1919, and the 1924 Immigration Act, which effectively banned all Japanese immigration to America, are all familiar signposts in the history of U.S.-Japanese relations. Rarely do scholars focus on

America's entrance into the First World War and her subsequent military victory as ground-breaking events in the rise of U.S.-Japanese tensions.[78]

But U.S. belligerence and victory in the Great War was, arguably, more pivotal than all of the rancor surrounding Japanese immigration and race combined in terms of the ultimate effect on Japan. For America's new voice in international affairs, like the arrival of Commodore Perry sixty-four years earlier, did not simply forecast a shift in the balance of power in Asia. It had a direct effect on the debate already raging in Japan over national identity.

To be sure, American belligerence had the most visible immediate effect on the balance of power in Asia. It raised serious questions about the viability of Japanese interests in the face of a dramatic rise in American influence. Already in the fall of 1916, Japan's most respected educators and opinion leaders had, as we have seen, fretted over the possible effect on Japanese interests of a drastic rise in American power. Washington's appeal to all belligerents in January 1917 for a statement of war aims demonstrated exactly what that effect could be. The Allied response to Washington's initiative contained some disturbing omissions. At a party conference in early February, Kokumintō party president Inukai Tsuyoshi acknowledged Allied appeals for a German withdrawal from Belgium, the Balkans, and the Dardanelles. But there was no mention of the kaiser's Asian and Pacific territories. "If the peace conference were held today," Inukai bemoaned, "we would have to return Qingdao, Jiaozhou Bay, and the South Pacific." To Inukai, the omission seemed, in part, racial. The great powers' opposition to Turkish possession of any European territory seemed to indicate that although "Caucasians" could possess territory in Asia and Europe, Asians could not.[79] Writing in the March 1917 *Chūō kōron*, even Yoshino Sakuzō observed that the great powers might take Japan's contribution to the European war lightly and disregard Japan's rights at the peace conference. "We must," he argued, "request the skill of those concerned to get our allies to sufficiently respect our demands."[80]

If the American entrance into the war raised serious questions about the fate of Japanese gains already secured, it complicated Japanese diplomacy in the present. Nishihara Kamezō, as we have seen, negotiated

Chinese participation in the war in February 1917. The Ōkuma cabinet had discouraged Chinese belligerence out of concern that it would strengthen President Yuan Shikai's political power and Beijing's autonomy from Japan. After Yuan's death, however, Nishihara had viewed a Chinese break with Germany through Japanese auspices as essential to solidifying Terauchi's relationship with the Duan cabinet and establishing Japanese leadership in China. As he originally informed the Japanese minister to Beijing, Hayashi Gonsuke, on his second voyage to the continent, Chinese belligerence would guarantee great power cooperation with Nishihara's plan for economic reform in China and, by implication, Japanese authority over China.[81]

But the United States threatened to undermine Nishihara's entire scheme when it severed diplomatic relations with Germany on February 3. At that time, President Wilson invited all neutral parties, including China, to take similar action. Anxious not to be forced to follow America's lead, Nishihara immediately embarked for Beijing.[82] By March 14, he had ensured that it was Japan, not the United States, under whose auspices China entered the war. To minimize the consequent strengthening of China's voice at an eventual peace conference, the Foreign Ministry subsequently obtained British, French, Russian, and Italian recognition of Japanese rights to the former German possessions in Shandong.

These efforts, as we shall see, ensured that Japan obtained great power recognition of all of her wartime gains at the Paris Peace Conference. American participation in the war did not, in other words, affect the balance of power in Asia as gravely as Japanese statesmen and opinion leaders had anticipated. The impact of Versailles upon the ever pressing question of Japanese national identity, however, was considerable. For in declaring war, Woodrow Wilson completely transformed the definition of the modern state.

In the age of empire, a nation's international standing had been determined by its success in war and the possession of colonies. But Wilson now identified military prowess and territorial expansion as specific causes of the Great War. He singled out undemocratic polities, such as that in Germany, moreover, as strongly inclined toward militarism and imperialism. The United States joined the war against the kaiser, then, not merely to end the immediate conflict. Wilson sought to eliminate war for all time. To do so, he proposed to eradicate the fundamental threat to world peace. He aimed to destroy "German militarism" to make the world "safe for democracy."

Nothing could have been further from the aims of the Japanese government. Modern Japan's founders had fashioned their country expressly after the militarism, imperialism, and authoritarian rule of Imperial Germany. The Russo-Japanese Convention of 1916 was a classic imperialist treaty along the lines of what Wilson now described as the "old diplomacy": secret negotiations for the purpose of territorial gain. And Yamagata had orchestrated the transcendental cabinet of General Terauchi expressly to stem the tide of democracy in Japan. Prime Minister Terauchi, then, greeted Wilson's declaration of war aims with alarm. The point, he thought, was "to punish the high-handedness of the German and Austrian armies," not to fight for such abstract political ideals as democracy and internationalism.[83] The United States and Japan, after all, had fundamentally different national polities. While the United States was a democracy, Japan was a monarchy. The Japanese monarchy, in fact, was "unparalleled" in the antiquity of its unbroken imperial line, the loyalty and patriotism of its subjects, and its identity as a union of throne and state. The danger of America's insistence upon a new world order was real. "The tidal wave of world thought may," the prime minister warned, "destroy all order and damage the essence of our National Polity." Germany's "aggressive militarism" had sparked a "surge of democratic thought" throughout the world, and the American announcement had excited this and set it aflame. "If at some point German militarism is destroyed by this, we must prevent the misfortune of this engulfing the empire."[84]

Wilson's pronouncements in 1917, in other words, were the equivalent of Perry's "black ships" in 1853: they breathed new life into the fundamental rethinking of the national polity that had wrenched Japanese politics since the death of Emperor Meiji. Just as Perry's arrival had unveiled the power of the modern nation-state, America's participation in the Great War demonstrated the weight of a modern democratic regime and the vision of a peaceful world order. After having expressly rejected republicanism for a constitutional monarchy and developed an unflinching faith in military might, Japan's established elite now discovered that their national model of choice, Imperial Germany, no longer stood at the vanguard of modern civilization.

Rather, just as Perry had incited and strengthened the enemies of the Tokugawa regime in the 1850s, the appeal of democracy and internationalism in 1917 stirred the opponents of Terauchi's national unity cabinet. Veteran champion of political liberalization in Japan Yoshino Sakuzō welcomed Wilson's pronouncements as confirmation of the inexorable march away from militarism and imperialism to a new liberal world order. Abandoning his earlier misgivings about the American trajectory, Yoshino declared in May that Wilson's ideas would "have an important bearing on the advance of civilization after the war."[85]

REVOLUTION IN RUSSIA

The impact in Japan of America's entrance into the war is overshadowed in the historical literature by another major international event just three weeks prior to Wilson's announcement: the Russian Revolution. While specialists of Japan have generally overlooked the Great War itself as a critical turning point in the twentieth century, they have not underestimated the connection between the Russian Revolution and events after 1945. The political challenge of the Soviet Union, after all, shaped the history of the Cold War.[86]

The impact of the Russian Revolution upon Japan was, indeed, genuine. The demise of Imperial China and emergence of republican government in Beijing, as we have seen, had already raised troubling questions about Japan's own monarchy. In 1917, as well, Japanese elites stood dismayed as another well-established imperial regime collapsed. "No one imagined," General Terauchi exclaimed, "that the [Russian] Imperial Household, which possessed an enormous army and international renown, would meet in an instant such a fate." Added to the fall of the Qing and the growing crisis of the Hohenzollerns of Prussia, the Romanovs' demise marked a disturbing pattern. The prime minister scrambled to assure his countrymen that Japan's imperial household would not meet a similar fate. It was, after all, "coeval with heaven and earth." And Japan's national polity would not be damaged by Allied calls for the extermination of German militarism. "But it is natural that antipathy for the nobility and men of wealth will follow. Our noblemen and wealthy must begin to take precautions."[87]

Field Marshal Yamagata echoed this concern for the integrity of Japan's unique polity. Since the Chinese and Russian Revolutions, he declared in June 1917, the "old idea of socialist fallacy, propagated mistakenly since the beginning of Meiji," had spread widely among the "low, ignorant classes." And many Japanese did not understand that words of moral decline, self-indulgence, and utility would "bring doubt upon the monarchical system, malign militarism, and cause the destruction of the State."[88]

Like Woodrow Wilson's declaration of war, in other words, the Russian Revolution sparked the greatest worries in Japan over the viability of the Meiji polity. But contrary to the impression imparted by the available literature, these fears did not outweigh the calamity that was Woodrow Wilson. It was the United States, after all, that played the decisive role in bringing the war to a conclusion. And it would be Wilson's ideas of democracy and internationalism, not Lenin's appeal for socialism and anti-imperialism, that would govern the peace talks in Paris. In the context of long-term Japanese worries over the rise of American power, the transformation of the United States by 1919 into the preeminent voice in international affairs was truly alarming.

THE OPPORTUNITY
OF INTERVENTION
IN SIBERIA

The Russian Revolution typically enjoys greater exposure than Woodrow Wilson in the historiography of modern Japan because of another pivotal event with which it is associated: the Siberian Intervention. Since the mid-1950s, the intervention has been the subject of several monographs. And along with Katō Takaaki's negotiations with China in 1915, it receives regular coverage as one of Japan's major diplomatic initiatives during the First World War. But, like the Russian Revolution, the Siberian Intervention owes its historiographical significance primarily to the post-1945 context of the Cold War. The expedition's original examiners sought in the initiative lessons on how to deal with the Soviet Union in the present.[89] The Russian Revolution and the Siberian Intervention have, in other words, become integral components of the absorbing tale of the arrival of socialism in Asia.

In light of the end of the Cold War, it is likely that historians will begin to reevaluate the significance originally attributed to the Russian Revolution in the history of modern Japan. The collapse of the Soviet Union is, as well, an opportunity to reconsider the importance of the Siberian Intervention. Until now, the deployment of Japanese troops to the Russian Far East has been described primarily in the context of the Russian Revolution and as a foreign policy event.[90] Few studies have highlighted it as an integral component of Japanese domestic and foreign affairs during the First World War. But the Siberian Intervention is incomprehensible outside the context of World War I. In foreign policy terms, it represents the culmination of Japan's principal war aim: the strengthening of her position on the continent. Politically, it marks the completion of the Yamagata faction's quest to reestablish command of the foreign policy decision-making process.

In the context of the Russian Revolution, the Siberian Intervention is often described as a counteroffensive against the spread of Bolshevik influence east. This was, indeed, the common refrain of European statesmen as the reality of Bolshevik power became clear. Diplomatic historians note that Japanese policymakers also expressed concern about the possible spread of German influence east in the wake of the separate peace between Russia and Germany concluded at Brest-Litovsk. But this, the greatest influx of Japanese troops on the continent during the Great War, must be seen primarily not as a defensive reaction to a formidable international threat. It was, rather, an offensive maneuver eagerly engaged in as the exploitation of an unprecedented opportunity.

The collapse of Imperial Russia did give Japan's established elite a powerful jolt. The Russo-Japanese Convention, to which Yamagata and his supporters had looked as a guarantee against the rising power of the United States, was, like tsarist Russia's other foreign treaties, immediately denounced by the Bolsheviks as a relic of the imperialist past. And the disintegration of another formidable imperial dynasty, as we have seen, raised troubling questions about the future viability of the Japanese monarchy and state. But Field Marshal Yamagata and his supporters would soon recover from their surprise. For there was opportunity for Japan in the misfortune of the Romanovs.

The most tangible benefit that Japanese decision makers had sought in the Russo-Japanese Convention of 1916 had been, as we have seen, an expansion of Japanese control in Manchuria. In particular, they had sought Japanese operation of the Changchun-Harbin Railway. The Kerensky regime agreed to sell the Japanese this line as far as the Sungari River, but the Bolsheviks assumed power before the deal was closed. Yamagata and his supporters may have initially considered this with some regret. But their misfortune did not preoccupy them for long. For the rights that they had finally arranged to purchase paled by comparison with the rights they were now in a position to seize, rights that the Japanese Army had sought earlier by more clandestine means. On the occasion of both the Chinese Revolution and Katō Takaaki's negotiations with China in 1915, Japan's generals, supported by army elder Yamagata Aritomo, had planned a major expedition of troops to China proper. In both cases, these plans had been frustrated by the civilian cabinet. In 1916, Vice Chief of the Army General Staff Tanaka Giichi had again aimed for a major troop deployment in China, only to be foiled this time by the death of Yuan Shikai. In negotiations with Russia in the same year, the army leadership, for once, attempted to enlarge their area of operations through negotiation. But the potential payoff for good behavior was slim. In any event, the collapse of Imperial Russia nullified Japan's proposed negotiated claim to more territory on the continent.

On the other hand, political chaos and a military vacuum in the Russian Far East again offered the possibility to seek a greater continental presence outside the restrictive framework of international treaties. It is not surprising, then, that there was widespread excitement in Tokyo at the opportunity presented by the Russian Revolution.

Terauchi's chief foreign policy agent, Nishihara Kamezō, was the first to envision the enormous potential of a political vacuum in the Russian Far East. Inspired by the ideas of journalist Ōtani Masao and the Committee for the Development of the National Destiny created soon after the Bolshevik coup in October, Nishihara immediately began setting the stage for a major expedition of Japanese troops to North Manchuria and Siberia. With Terauchi's blessing, he apprised one of Duan's generals, Jin

Yunpeng, at the end of November that Japan would likely take action in response to the new situation in Russia. Tokyo, he advised, expected Beijing to cooperate.[91] A week later, he began discussions with Foreign Minister Motono on an expedition of Japanese troops to Siberia.[92]

Nishihara was particularly intrigued by the proposal of a young member of the new Committee for the Development of the National Destiny, Nakano Jirō, for an independent Siberia under Japanese tutelage. He soon began mustering funds to send a group of Russian émigrés and Japanese adventurers, including Nakano, to the continent to assess the prospects.[93] At the same time, he pressed Terauchi and Motono on the urgency of a military agreement with China and a Japanese occupation of Siberia.[94] His motives had little to do with the threat of an eastward movement of Bolshevik or German power. Rather, like his idea for a Japanese takeover of the Dutch East Indies, Nishihara spied an opportunity for a substantial expansion of Japanese influence. Like Yamagata and members of the army leadership, he envisioned Japan as the principal arbiter of events in Asia, unencumbered by Western interference. He called for a "fundamental union" of Japan and China, to ensure "Eastern self-sufficiency" and "prevent, for all time, the intrusion of European power in the Japan Sea."[95]

As Nishihara proceeded with his strategy for "Eastern self-sufficiency," the Army General Staff formulated its own plans to capitalize upon the new political situation on the continent. Soon after the Bolshevik coup, the staff drafted a "Plan to Send Troops to the Russian Far East to Protect Foreign Residents," proposing an expedition of one Japanese brigade to North Manchuria and one to the Russian Maritimes. While the ostensible purpose of the deployments was to protect Japanese nationals in these areas, the memorandum charged the troops to "guard the railways and telegraph facilities" to prepare "for military operations which may be undertaken later."[96] The liberation of North Manchuria and Siberia from central Russian authority offered the perfect opportunity to extend the drive for empire north.

The Sino-Japanese Military Agreement

Tanaka took the opportunity in the immediate term to negotiate a military agreement with China. Like the Siberian Intervention itself, the

Sino-Japanese Military Agreement of 1918 is often analyzed in terms of strategic exigencies. In particular, it is described as a response to the nullification of the Russo-Japanese Convention by the new Bolshevik regime.[97] But like the intervention, the pact represented less a protection than a projection of Japanese interests. Its context was not primarily the sudden political vacuum in the Russian Far East but the long-expressed desire of members of Japan's military-bureaucratic elite to substantially boost Japanese influence and physical presence in China.

A general consensus in Tokyo, it will be recalled, had looked to the outbreak of war in August 1914 as the opportunity to enhance Japan's position on the continent. Among the most energetic promoters of Japan's continental position were Field Marshal Yamagata and his associates in the Imperial Army, who had, in their proposals for a comprehensive agreement with Beijing, argued for all manner of Japanese political and military privileges in China. Katō's 1915 negotiations with Beijing had stressed economic rights and fallen well short of these plans for Japanese political and military hegemony. At any rate, the foreign minister had not tolerated any *genrō* or army interference in his program. The sudden collapse of Imperial Russia and opening of a political vacuum in the Russian Far East, however, now offered a second chance for Katō's principal political rivals to take bold action in China. With the ascension of Yamagata protégé, Terauchi, to the prime ministry, the opportunity was irresistible.

In January 1918, therefore, Yamagata again called for a dramatic new relationship with Beijing. While he had emphasized foreign affairs and economics in his 1914 "Opinion on China Policy," the vast military opportunities presented by the collapse of Russian power in the Far East inspired the *genrō* in 1918 to stress the military aspects of Japan's relations with China.[98] Particularly, in anticipation of a large expedition of Japanese troops to Siberia, Yamagata hoped for full military cooperation from China in Manchuria. He appealed for an "offensive-defensive entente" that would grant Japanese troops unlimited freedom of movement in the province. Reminiscent of his hope in 1914 for Katō to assume the posture of the foreign minister of both China and Japan, he spoke now of combined Sino-Japanese military operations, "as if one country, with different bodies but of the same mind."[99] And he was just as willing as he had been in 1915 to use force if necessary to obtain Chinese compliance with Japanese demands.[100]

If Yamagata and his supporters desired generally to increase Japan's say in Chinese domestic affairs, they hoped specifically to expand the Japanese Army's area of operations on the continent. In particular, Vice Chief of the Army General Staff Tanaka, who directed the negotiations with China, hoped to push Japanese influence even farther north in Manchuria than had been possible through negotiations with Russia. Tokyo, as we have seen, had only been able to arrange with St. Petersburg Japanese control of the Changchun-Harbin Railway up to the Sungari River. With Russian power in the region now shattered, the vast expanse of both Siberia and North Manchuria stood ripe for the taking. Tanaka hoped to conclude a military agreement with China, in particular, that would offer de facto Chinese recognition of Japanese command of the core of Russia's former presence in the region, the Chinese Eastern Railway.

Rather than fret over the uselessness of the agreement to purchase the Chungchun-Harbin line to the Sungari River, then, Tanaka spied an opportunity. The political instability in St. Petersburg had removed one more obstacle to Japanese expansion in Manchuria. On December 22, Tanaka instructed the War Ministry's Military Affairs Bureau chief, Major General Nara Takeji, to inform Minister Ōshima that Japan "must take over" after the Russian withdrawal from the Chinese Eastern Railway.[101]

The Wang Shizhen regime harbored no illusions regarding Japanese aims. Soon after expelling the Bolsheviks from Harbin on December 25, 4,500 troops from the Jilin Regular Army fanned out along the Chinese Eastern Railway zone. The Chinese commander at Manzhouli, Major General Liu Fuman, later noted that, had China not done so, Japan would have occupied the area.[102] Chinese suspicion of Japanese motives prevented any progress on a military agreement before March. In mid-February the Wang cabinet agreed that the Japanese army was promoting the agreement in an attempt to seize North Manchuria. It decided to negotiate military cooperation outside Chinese borders, namely Siberia. But within her borders, particularly North Manchuria, Chinese troops would operate alone.[103]

Wang eventually agreed to discussions on Tanaka's terms after the latter pledged to withdraw Japanese troops upon the completion of combined operations. But the original draft for negotiations presented in late March again confirmed Beijing's suspicions. It proposed Japanese Army deployments in North Manchuria, Eastern Inner Mongolia, and the Russian Far East to eastern Siberia, with Chinese troops in this area to operate "under the direction of the Japanese Imperial Army authorities." Japan would be responsible for "transporting and distributing men, horses, and supplies" to Chinese units in this area, a stipulation interpreted by Beijing as sanctioning Japanese control of the Chinese Eastern Railway. Finally, provisions for Japanese military advisers and cooperation between the respective military authorities on matters of grand strategy "as world conditions, particularly the situation in East Asia, develop" would guarantee Japanese command of all aspects of Chinese military planning.[104]

Unable to move Premier Duan Qirui with such a glaring violation of Chinese sovereignty, Tanaka authorized a compromise. The main text of the final agreement, as signed on May 16, 1918, called for Chinese aid to Japanese troops and Japanese "respect" for the "sovereignty of China" in "military areas" left undefined. All Japanese troops in Chinese territory were to be withdrawn as soon as military operations ceased, and Japanese military experts would be provided "only if China requested the assistance." Article 8 specifically referred to the use of the Chinese Eastern Railway, requiring that "the provisions in the original treaty regarding the management and protection of said railway shall be respected."[105]

But Tanaka had by no means abandoned Japan's claim to the important railway. A War Ministry memorandum of April 21 that urged greater support for White Russian generals Horvath and Semyonov (who were fighting from Manchuria for an independent Siberia) dramatized its centrality. Aid to these generals, the memorandum argued, should include sending men and capital and "actually taking over the operation of the railroad." It should "save for us the military power of the Chinese Eastern Railway." The memorandum concluded with an exhortation to proceed "on the basis of further developing the present excellent conditions in the Far East, and above all along the Chinese Eastern Railway."[106] Tanaka, who continued to pursue negotiations with China in close consultation with the War Ministry, was by April convinced of this strategy to aid Semyonov and Horvath to halt Chinese inroads in the Chinese Eastern Railway zone. In an April 23 letter to Terauchi, he urged an illicit 500,000 to 600,000 yen in additional military aid to Semyonov, lest "the plan for along the Chinese Eastern Railway come to naught."[107] At the same time, he lobbied aggressively for a reorganization of the railway's board of directors at Harbin. By the end of April, a thorough restructuring had placed General Horvath, with whom the Japanese had established a close working relationship, and his Russian protégés in senior positions on the board.[108] And in anticipation of Horvath's eventual exodus to Siberia to establish an independent regime, Tanaka negotiated an adjunct to the military agreement calling for a Sino-Japanese committee to coordinate with the board the transport of Japanese, Chinese, and Czechoslovak troops along the railway.[109] Three weeks after the May 16 signing of the military agreement, Tanaka informed War Ministry Military Affairs Bureau Chief Nara Takeji that Prime Minister Terauchi had approved the dispatch of one hundred heavily armed Japanese troops to Harbin.[110]

The Quest to Become the "Great Master" of Asia

By this time, the military agreement with China had become but part of a progressively expanding vision of action for Japanese troops in the Russian Far East. Tanaka had concurred with Nishihara's plan to send Russian émigré Andreev and Japanese adventurer Nakano Jirō to Siberia in December to assess the viability of an independence movement.[111] Simultaneously, the General Staff dispatched several junior officers to reconnoiter on both sides of the Siberian border.[112] In January, Tanaka arranged the transfer of two senior officers, Lieutenant Colonel Sakabe Toshio of the Army General Staff and Russian specialist Major General Nakajima Masatake, to Vladivostok to seek out "moderate elements" to support against the "eastward advance of German and Austrian power."[113] By founding a Joint Committee on Military Affairs on January 28, Tanaka firmly established the momentum for an expedition to the Russian Far East. Under his chairmanship, the committee immediately began coordinating General Staff and War Ministry preparations.[114]

Diplomatic historians have often described the Japanese expedition to Siberia as a response to the threat of the eastward movement of German power in the wake of Brest-Litovsk.[115] Indeed, contemporaries, particularly Field Marshal Yamagata and members of the Imperial Army, spoke of it in those terms. But while Germany served as a handy pretext after the disintegration of the army's former number one potential enemy, Russia, the prevailing sentiment in 1918 was one of enthusiasm for an opportunity, not fear of an external challenge. Like the Sino-Japanese Military Agreement, the Siberian Intervention belongs less in the context of a sudden change in the balance of power in East Asia in 1918 than against the backdrop of the energetic efforts of members of the Yamagata faction since the outbreak of the war in 1914 to substantially boost Japan's continental position. In light of the repeatedly frustrated efforts by these men to enhance Japan's military posture on the continent, the opening of an enormous political and military vacuum in the Russian Far East appeared as an unprecedented boon. Particularly, with the war in Europe clearly winding down, an expedition to Siberia offered a final chance for a long-sought dramatic display of Japanese power on the continent.

Vice Chief of the Army General Staff Tanaka Giichi could hardly contain his joy in 1918. Soon after the initial dispatch of troops in August, he hailed the "extremely convenient situation for attaining our goals." Having actively pursued Japanese supremacy in Asia, the chance for a major Japanese military operation that the great powers not only did not resist but actively supported seemed to fulfill his greatest aspirations. Japan, Tanaka rejoiced, was poised to achieve "great effect with little effort." To encounter such a situation was "divine aid," and to refrain from seizing the opportunity "would leave a thousand regrets." It would be particularly regrettable because the war in Europe was coming to an end. An expedition of Japanese soldiers to the wide expanse of the Russian Far East, a "display of national authority" as Tanaka called it, promised to be the "crowning act of the empire" at the conclusion of the European war.[116] Indeed, Lieutenant General Ōi Shigemoto, commander of the Twelfth Division, which was sent to Siberia in August 1918, would later describe the Allied proposal for an expedition as the "perfect pretext" at war's end to deploy Japanese troops on the continent.[117]

As part of their reappraisal of Field Marshal Yamagata as a voice of caution in Japanese diplomatic affairs, historians have highlighted his initial resistance to an expedition of Japanese troops to Siberia. Indeed, the field marshal reserved final approval for such an expedition until June 1918. But his hesitation offers another glimpse not of the elder statesman's circumspection but of his ambition. As early as February 1918, Yamagata had impressed upon Prime Minister Terauchi the "importance" of an expedition of Japanese troops to the Russian Far East.[118] Six weeks later, he explained:

Britain and America have already become great masters. Their houses are spacious, their assets abundant. So they can provide amply for several families with ease. But we are a small house recently provided. Our rooms are small, our assets meager. Moreover, our resources are as yet inadequate to support our many children. . . . An opportunity lost will not come again.[119]

An expedition of troops to North Manchuria and Siberia was, in other words, an opportunity to expand the parameters of the Japanese "small house" to become truly a "great master." As Tanaka had indicated, the importance of doing so was all the more apparent with the prospect of peace in Europe. Yamagata was perfectly prepared to follow British and French wishes on provisions for peace in Europe. "But with respect to the Far East, the Empire is the master and they are the guests."[120] In anticipation of the peace conference, Japanese leadership of an expedition to Siberia would demonstrate to the great powers exactly who was master of Asia.

Yamagata hesitated to give final approval for an expedition to Siberia not out of deference to the Allies but out of an unwavering suspicion concerning their intentions in Asia. As we have seen with his attitude at the outbreak of war, the obverse of his grand ambitions for Japan to become the "master" of Asia was a fear that the great powers would attempt to foil his efforts. Far from guaranteeing great power recognition of Japanese leadership in Asia, it appeared during initial discussions for an expedition that the Allies hoped to use the venture to contain Japanese power. Thus, Yamagata cautioned Prime Minister Terauchi that "it is important not to be incited by Westerners."[121] Britain and France, he explained to Gotō Shinpei in March, were working on a "desperate plan" to solicit U.S. participation in order to control Japanese ambitions. In their frequent talks with the United States and their requests for Japanese troops, London and Paris either called for an American technical corps

to accompany the Japanese military or insisted upon combined operations with White Russian forces. "It seems," Yamagata observed, "that
they do not want to entrust [the expedition] to the empire." While recognizing the difficulty of acting without Allied support, Yamagata insisted that Japan meet any security threat in the Russian Far East "on her
own power."[122] He desired an autonomous expedition, unencumbered by
restrictions placed upon Japan by the world community.

Yamagata and his supporters in the Imperial Army were not the only
ones to jump at the opportunity for a dramatic display of Japanese power
in Siberia. Nishihara Kamezō, as we have seen, became an energetic early
promoter of an independent Siberia. Foreign Minister Motono urged
prompt action in Siberia and North Manchuria to establish a "predominant position in the Orient."[123] In February, without cabinet approval, he
sought Allied sanction for an independent Japanese expedition. "To delay," he warned the French ambassador, "is dangerous. Eventually Japan
will become impatient."[124] Home Minister Gotō called in December 1917
for one million Japanese troops to occupy Russia east of Lake Baikal at a
cost of 5 billion yen a year.[125] After succeeding Motono as foreign minister in April 1918, he lobbied aggressively for an independent Japanese expedition. To cover the cost of such an operation, he pushed in August for
an extraordinary Diet session to pass a 300 million yen supplemental
budget.[126] The prime minister maintained a lower profile on an expedition than his energetic deputies. But he continued to express interest after first agreeing in December 1916 to a Nishihara plan to occupy Manchuria, the Maritime Provinces, and Siberia in the event that Russia
withdraw from the war.[127]

THE POLITICAL
PUSH FOR A
SIBERIAN EXPEDITION

The prevailing sentiment in the Terauchi cabinet from early 1918 on,
then, was enthusiasm for an unprecedented opportunity. If the Japanese
architects of an expedition to Siberia feared any danger, it was an internal
political, not an external strategic, concern. Recent analyses of army policy during this period have located such a political interest in the desire to

build the domestic foundations for general mobilization. Taking to heart the lessons of the first total war, Japan's generals, like their European counterparts, sought more effective means of tapping the energies of the entire nation for war. To do so, they hoped to increase the authority of the army both at home and abroad.[128]

Plans for general mobilization did, indeed, take shape concurrently with the embarkation of Japanese troops to Vladivostok. But to consider general mobilization the be all and end all of Japanese army policy from 1918 is to miss an important basic political dynamic behind calls for both general mobilization and an expedition of troops to Siberia. There were important political reasons to appeal for general mobilization, just as there were for an expedition to Siberia. At a time when the war in Europe was winding down and the military budget seemed far from secure, both enterprises offered fresh justification for a major increase in army funding.[129]

Restoring the Army as the First Line of National Defense

The army, as we have seen, had lost to the navy in the heated budget battles that accompanied the fiscal austerity following the Russo-Japanese War. Tanaka and his associates had looked to the outbreak of war in Europe, in part, to escape this losing cycle. But the new opportunity for military action only exacerbated the tension between Japan's generals and admirals. After August 1914, each service had expanded the parameters of its respective operations and attempted to carve out a larger share of the national defense pie.[130] The army succeeded in creating a new sphere of influence in Shandong, but it seethed at the continuing budget priority given to the navy by Prime Minister Ōkuma.

Unable to obtain a greater portion of the defense budget, Tanaka vowed in 1915 to restructure the allocation process altogether. In a memorandum to Field Marshal Ōyama, then major general Tanaka lamented a situation in which the nation's coffers were "unable to satisfy the demands of both [services]." This had led to conflict and antagonism and a "mutual desire to expand one's own power without compromise." Each service had solicited the support of politicians and public opinion against the other with disastrous results. For it had "made the tempo of military preparedness and substance of national defense a matter of personal discussion for politicians." It had, furthermore, falsely led the general public to assume that national defense, like other state affairs, was open to public discussion. Tanaka urged a revision of the 1907 Basic Plan of National Defense and designated force levels to "disperse past feelings between the army and navy, frankly devise a unified, long-range plan for the State, and clarify the foundation of the military." This, he hoped, would help "maintain the sacred nature of national defense."[131]

Tanaka made no further progress during the Ōkuma administration on a major redefinition of strategic priorities. But he did receive Prime Minister Terauchi's approval soon after the formation of the new cabinet to draft a revision of the 1907 Basic Plan. Six months later, Tanaka informed Terauchi that the army leadership had reached an agreement on a "Draft for Army Preparedness."[132] The terminology was suggestive, for the new defense plan was an effort to commit both the navy and the government to an unprecedented program of expansion for the army. The proposed force levels were enormous. Creating a new class of division composed of six rather than the four regiments typical of the old standard, the plan called for a peacetime force equivalent of thirty-three old divisions and a wartime mobilization strength equal to 61.5 old divisions. This represented a 30 percent increase over the previous mark of twenty-five divisions and 20 percent growth in the former fifty-division target. Compared to the present twenty-one divisions, the thirty-three-division mark represented a 60 percent expansion.[133]

The problem for the army was that, with her traditional continental enemy Russia no longer a military factor after the fall of the tsar, there was little justification for the initial target of twenty-five divisions set in 1907, let alone for the new goal of thirty-three divisions. In their requests for funds in the 1918 budget, both services argued for expansion based upon the military lessons of the Great War.[134] But the navy, with a tangible threat in the three-year, 156-ship naval expansion program launched by the United States in 1916, easily proved the more persuasive of the two military branches. In budget deliberations in the Fortieth Diet (December 27, 1917–March 26, 1918), the government approved Navy Minister Katō's request for 280 million yen without amendment. The appropriation aimed at an expansion from an 8–4 to an 8–6 fleet and represented the maximum possible utilization of Japan's ship-building capacity.[135]

The army, on the other hand, chafed at the government's idea for an eighteen-year plan of 180 million yen based on the existing twenty-one-division structure. While this represented the best funding since the 1907 Basic Plan of National Defense, it was half of what the Army General Staff had asked for.[136] Yamagata called Prime Minister Terauchi's budget "meaningless" and pushed unsuccessfully for consideration of supplemental funds.[137] War Ministry First Bureau Chief Ugaki Kazushige sneered at the navy's success, calling the attempt to compete with the United States and the combined strength of the U.S. and Britain that Japan would most likely face in a conflict a "fool's dream."[138]

But Japan's admirals were no fools. Yamagata perceived in their expanding sights across the Pacific a fundamental threat to the continental basis of, and army superiority in, imperial defense. The number of new weapons to be employed as a result of the lessons of the European War was extremely great, he observed in June 1918. But if Japan were to apply these weapons to naval defense, army facilities would be rendered largely out of date. "It would not fit with [the goals of] securing the line of transport with the continent and protecting the important [continental] resources, which are the foundation of imperial defense."[139] For Yamagata, indeed, Japanese security had necessarily to rest on a continental definition of national defense. As he had insisted upon the foundation of the Imperial Army, the Japanese Navy was to transport and protect the army at the principal line of defense on the continent.

It was precisely at this time, when the army's prospects for growth and its raison d'être as the empire's first line of defense had substantially eroded, that opportunity knocked in the Russian Far East. It is no coincidence that Tanaka completed his "Draft for Army Preparedness" soon after the collapse of Imperial Russia. And Field Marshal Yamagata responded to the fall with more than grave warnings about the consequences for the Japanese monarchy. In the same memorandum to Prince Tokugawa Iesato decrying the political fallout of the collapse in Japan, Yamagata offered a positive appraisal of the opportunity afforded. "In today's world," he declared, "we fight for our existence by achieving national strength through arms." And in the postwar world, it would be the countries with "flourishing national power and vigorous popular will" that would prosper. Those with "weakening national power and decaying popular will" would decline. "Is it not at this time the heavenly bestowed duty of our empire to display the brilliance of our National Polity and have the people of the world grasp its righteousness?"[140]

In June of 1917, Yamagata was as yet unclear on the shape that a display of the "brilliance" of the Japanese national polity would take. But he clearly hoped for strong confirmation of the importance of armed strength. In this context, French Field Marshal Ferdinand Foch's original suggestion in December for an expedition of troops to Siberia must have seemed like a godsend. At the time of Foch's suggestion, the proposed revision of the 1907 Basic Plan of National Defense had lain dormant for nine months. The idea of a joint expedition of troops, however, provided Yamagata and the Army General Staff with tangible cause to re-anchor the empire's defense firmly on the continent and to justify an enormous expansion of army power. By the summer of 1918, navy representatives on Vice Chief of the Army General Staff Tanaka's Joint Committee on Military Affairs had agreed to a joint military operation whose centerpiece was the mobilization of ten army divisions to the Russian Far East.[141]

Nor was this the extent of the opportunity in 1918. In the 1930s, the choice of either a northern or southern advance by the Imperial Army on the continent would become a major point of strategic debate, with a decision on the southern option in 1940 ultimately leading to war against the United States. So enormous was the opportunity presented in 1918, however, that Japanese military planners saw no need to choose between north or south. Rather, as the Joint Committee on Military Affairs mapped out a strategy for operations in Siberia, Yamagata also found justification for a massive increase in Japanese force levels in his long-term hopes for an "inseparable spirit" between Japan and China. In an official explanation of the new strategic posture outlined in the revised Basic Plan of National Defense, Yamagata called for Japan to assume the responsibility to "protect and lead China by ourselves." While he described a threat to China in the probable return of American, German, and British power to the East, his principal hope was to use Japan's "enormous" troop strength to compel the Chinese to "incline toward us."[142]

The shifting strategic map, in other words, revealed brand-new vistas for Japanese power in Asia in 1918. In his initial reorganization of the Imperial Army in the 1880s, Yamagata had effected a dramatic expansion of the strategic mission to cover what he termed Japan's "line of advantage" in Korea in addition to her "line of sovereignty" demarcated by the Japanese archipelago. Now he proposed to extend that line of advantage to cover all of China. "The defense of our empire," he declared, "does not end simply with the protection of Imperial territory. It must progress further, to the defense of all of China." To secure the transportation routes to the continent, the elder statesman even suggested that Japan "cut off the Taiwan Straits or capture Singapore."[143]

Restoring "Militarism" in Public Consciousness

If assuming the burden of Chinese defense and dispatching troops to Siberia were essential components of the plan to restore primary responsibility of national defense to the army, there was also widespread hope that a troop deployment would revitalize public sentiment for the state. That sentiment, it seemed to members of the military-bureaucratic elite, had been irreparably damaged by the twin evils of economic prosperity and American appeals for democracy.

The rapid expansion of trade and industrial production sparked by the war had transformed Japanese society. From 1913 to 1918 Japan's urban population grew by 16.5 percent,[144] and a new level of prosperity translated into an increasing pursuit of leisure. In 1917 an unprecedented number of viewers flocked to Tokyo's sixty-nine movie theaters, Tokyo schoolgirls commonly wore makeup and silk kimonos, and a new level of eroticism permeated the arts, from the bare-legged dancers in the recently inaugurated Asakusa opera, to the painted and sculptured nudes on display at the Pacific Western Painting Exhibition in May.[145] Industrial growth brought a rapid expansion in the workforce and an unprecedented number of labor disturbances. In 1916 a mere 8,413 workers had participated in 108 strikes; in 1917, the number of strikers rose to 57,309 and the number of strikes to 398.[146]

The ill effects of rapid economic growth had become increasingly apparent after the Russo-Japanese War. In the January 1, 1915, issue of *Ni-*

hon oyobi Nihonjin, China adventurer Ioki Ryōzō described the ten years since Portsmouth as a history of the "corruption of the empire" by individualism and the worship of money.[147] When Gotō Shinpei emerged as one of the chief architects of the Terauchi cabinet's China policy in the fall of 1916, he had hoped in part that a new emphasis upon financial diplomacy would help absorb the new energy in Japan's private financial circles. Private participation in a Far Eastern Economic Union, he proposed, would awaken certain entrepreneurs from their "illusion" of privatization, lower taxes, and an eradication of floating loans.[148] Prime Minister Terauchi himself decried the "wind of luxury and frivolity" that had spread as a result of the wartime prosperity and urged an assembly of police bureau chiefs in October 1917 to promote a mood of "frugal industry and simplicity" and a spirit of loyalty and patriotism. The frequent occurrence of strikes, he warned, was "most troubling."[149]

The economic effects of the war by themselves posed a serious problem to the Terauchi regime. But U.S. participation in the war brought the crisis to a breaking point. Inside Diet walls, Woodrow Wilson's calls for democracy placed the transcendental cabinet in an increasingly difficult position. As Kenseikai orator Ozaki Yukio noted in January 1918, the Allies hoped to "destroy militarist politics like that of Germany and decide matters based upon the popular will." But the Japanese regime seemed trained upon an entirely contradictory aim:

Our Prime Minister Terauchi talks as if his ideas and feelings are in almost complete agreement [with those of the Allies]. . . . But the Terauchi cabinet is a transcendental, militarist cabinet that was originally formed without an emphasis upon the popular will. In other words, it is of a bent similar to the government that the Allies are trying to destroy. . . . While we declared war on the same enemy, if we look at the essence of the Terauchi cabinet, the object differs. Although the Western allies are trying to destroy militarism, the Terauchi cabinet is trying, at home and abroad, to strengthen and protect it.[150]

"The recent trend of the media flows clearly toward the reckless," Terauchi warned a gathering of local leaders in May 1917. "They purposely play with radical ideas, publish obscene articles, and tempt the minds of the people. We cannot guarantee that [they] will not ultimately mistake the principles of our National Polity, stain the respect for the Throne, and destroy our manner of simplicity and honesty."[151] To the assembly of police bureau chiefs in October, he added the "tendency to occasionally glorify the direction of the world, democratic thought," to the list of sins requiring the special encouragement of loyalty and patriotism.[152]

The appeal for national loyalty became an increasingly common refrain among Japanese policymakers after the dramatic events of 1917, particularly among members of the Terauchi regime, whose own political power was most threatened by the dissipation of the national focus. To these men, especially, a show of force in Siberia offered the perfect opportunity to repair the crumbling basis of their political power. Finance Minister Shōda Kazue advised Terauchi in late January to "use relations with Russia to direct domestic trouble outward."[153] Yamagata protégé and communications minister, Den Kenjirō, energetically lobbied for intervention by pointing to the examples of the Sino- and Russo-Japanese Wars. As in these conflicts, "once we send an expedition of troops," he confidently informed the Seiyūkai's Yokota Sennosuke, "national opinion will uniformly return to militarism."[154]

Home Minister Gotō specifically bemoaned the ideological threat of the United States. "If we probe the real intentions of the U.S. further," he warned Terauchi in March 1918, "it embraces what I call moralistic aggression. It is, in other words, none other than a great hypocritical monster clothed in justice and humanity." Apparently forgetting his earlier affection for Germany, the baron continued, "we cannot deny that the ideology of the German people and American democracy are, in the end, the same thing in different form."[155] The situation called for "an especially great effort at this time to adhere to the spirit of our State, unchanging for ten million years (senmannen), and to accomplish the original grand objective." Gotō urged the establishment of an autonomous Ministry of War Mobilization to "prepare the people for a world war," the formation of a Newspaper and Information Inspection Bureau, and the partial implementation of martial law in Japan's largest cities and throughout Hokkaidō to "display the reality of Imperial armaments." Abroad, Japan should offer aid to the destitute in Siberia to expose them to the grace of the empire and to shock America, "who proclaims a hypocritical humanity." Should some power attempt to obstruct the plan, Japan would "prepare an imposing force of arms," and, if necessary, "immediately take decisive measures to capture and occupy [Siberia]."[156]

Seiyūkai president Hara Takashi often emerges in analyses of the Siberian Intervention as the strongest force of moderation on a mobilization of troops.[157] Indeed, he made full use of the Advisory Council on Foreign Affairs to stress the dangers of an independent expedition. And unlike Gotō and others associated with the Terauchi cabinet, he did not envision an expedition as part of the campaign to battle American political and ideological power. Rather, he considered a joint operation a critical means of restoring the goodwill between Tokyo and Washington that had been strained by wartime developments.[158] But Hara did not disagree with one of the fundamental objects of a mobilization of Japanese troops. He shared with many of Japan's soldiers and bureaucrats a concern for the rising tide of democracy and an enthusiasm for measures that could moderate it. "The surge of democracy in the future will indeed be frightening," he had warned Miura Gorō in October 1917.[159] In December, he argued for more funds for imperial defense and stressed the need "to direct the spirit of the people to the idea that a military state does not come easily."[160]

The final arbiter of any action in the Russian Far East, Field Marshal Yamagata, was, perhaps, the most sensitive to the domestic political effect of economic growth and Wilson's calls for democracy and internationalism. He worried about the army's loss of "public sympathy" caused by the rise in the wartime economy.[161] And he objected fiercely to Wilson's vision of a new world order. According to the U.S. declaration of war and other subsequent Allied pronouncements, he observed in March 1918, the Great War aimed to "eradicate militarism for the sake of human freedom." There was also talk of destroying German imperialism and spreading republicanism throughout the world. Some even called for a peace without annexations or reparations. But, he queried, "I wonder if militarism and imperialism are really so hateful? And I wonder if republicanism is so wonderful and the principle of no annexations and no reparations so equitable and just?"[162] His answer was an emphatic no, and he had a plan to ensure that the Japanese people would agree. An expedition of troops to Siberia, he informed Hara in the same month, would help to "raise the idea of militarism among the people."[163] In case there remained any confusion on the point, the field marshal declared in June that, "the Great European War has done away with the delusion of the promoters of peace and demonstrated that the complete independence of all states must be preserved through enormous war preparations."[164]

The renewed emphasis on arms represented by both the Sino-Japanese Military Agreement and the Siberian Intervention had the immediate political effect of returning the core of the Yamagata faction back to the center of decision making under the Terauchi cabinet. Indeed, through their use of financial diplomacy, Terauchi and his personal envoy, Nishihara Kamezō, had, by the spring of 1917, succeeded in wrenching the initiative on China affairs from the hands of Vice Chief of the General Staff Tanaka Giichi and staff representatives in the field. But negotiations for a military pact with China and preparations for military operations in Siberia were the natural policy prerogative of the Imperial Army. Despite his early promotion of both initiatives, Nishihara stood helpless as Tanaka easily commandeered the leadership of both projects. Nor could Terauchi or the Advisory Council on Foreign Affairs (which was originally created, it will be recalled, to curtail Tanaka's influence in foreign affairs) prevent the realization of the chief foreign and domestic policies of the Imperial Army. Despite a government promise to the Advisory Council on Foreign Affairs in July to limit Japanese forces in Siberia to two divisions, the army moved quickly after the mobilization order on August 2 to execute its own agenda. On August 13, the cabinet announced the transfer of an arm of the Guandong Army to the Russo-Chinese border.[165] By mid-October, more than three and a half divisions occupied the Amur River basin, and the army secured the Siberian railway network by a pincer movement between Vladivostok and Khabarovsk in the east and Manzhouli and Chita in the west.[166] In early December, Japanese soldiers in the Russian Far East exceeded 50,000 men.[167]

Meanwhile, a memorial from the throne on September 13 conferred official sanction upon the army revision of the 1907 Basic Plan of National Defense, calling for forty-one wartime divisions (equivalent to 61.5 old divisions). The generals' request for the 1919 budget, presented on September 20 well after the submission deadline and after the resignation of Terauchi had been assured, outlined a fifteen-year schedule for the new divisions. The 300 million yen bid for 1919 represented 2.7 times the amount that Terauchi had held the army to in 1918.[168]

But if Yamagata and his chief deputy seemed to have succeeded in restoring their political power and creating a new foundation for Japanese militarism and imperialism, they immediately discovered that the foundation rested in sand. One day after the official announcement of Japanese participation in an expedition, discontent over the exorbitant price of rice, which had simmered in Toyama prefecture since the middle of July, leapt into the national headlines. The most dramatic product of Japanese wartime economic growth, the discontent erupted, over the next few weeks, in an orgy of burning and looting that brought two million Japanese subjects to the streets. By mid-September, the Terauchi government had restored order, but only with the help of over 100,000 troops.[169] The damage had been done. Instead of the rousing national endorsement of empire, arms, and oligarchic rule anticipated with the Siberian expedition, the rice riots showed that the national unity forged, if only briefly, by the Sino- and Russo-Japanese Wars was a thing of the past. "It is of unbearable regret," Yamagata lamented, "that an incident like this was provoked at such a time as the expedition. To completely renew this public sympathy will not be an easy task."[170] Lieutenant General Machida Keiu regretted that "the expedition of troops dispatched by this cabinet has received a cold stare from the public. Compared to the hearty send-offs and welcomes and cries of 'banzai' resonating at the train stations and ports each time the expeditionary forces passed in the last two great wars, there is really a world of a difference."[171] Yamagata spoke for most of his protégés in the Imperial Army when he muttered that "with this situation, we cannot discard our regrets and anxieties for the future of the Empire."[172]

SYNOPSIS

As British and French forces entered the third year of the Great War reinvigorated for battle against the kaiser, their Japanese allies worried about an entirely different challenge. Like Japan, the United States seemed to benefit from the crisis in Europe. As the great European powers destroyed the human, cultural, and material resources of a continent, the American economy boomed. Even such cautious Japanese observers as Yoshino Sakuzō spied in the parallel wartime advantages to the United States and Japan seeds of future bilateral conflict.

Katō Takaaki and the Twenty-One Demands stand out in the historiography of U.S.-Japanese relations as a principal source of tension between Tokyo and Washington during the Great War. But the main foreign policy initiatives of the new "transcendental" Terauchi regime from October 1916—the Nishihara loans, the Sino-Japanese Military Agreement, and the Siberian Intervention—offer a glimpse of far greater Japanese diplomatic ambitions. Indeed, while promoted by the very men who had criticized Foreign Minister Katō Takaaki for his aggressive stance vis-à-vis China in 1915, these policies reveal an entirely new level of commitment to the long-term goal of strengthening Japan's continental influence. These men envisioned political and economic hegemony on the continent on a scale never seen before and to degrees that anticipated the voracious continental appetites of their successors in the 1930s. Thus, in promoting the financial aid to China that would become known as the Nishihara loans, Home Minister Gotō Shinpei hoped for an intimate bilateral relationship that would secure an unassailable position for Japan in a future "racial war." Terauchi adviser Nishihara Kamezō envisioned Japanese financial domination of China governed by a mystical appeal to the supposed Asian value of the Kingly Way.

The military-bureaucratic supporters of the Terauchi cabinet were, by no means, a monolithic bloc. On the contrary, the principal political battle under Terauchi was waged not between these men and the rising power of the political parties but within the most powerful nonrepresentative political force, the Yamagata faction. This faction had long anticipated a regime headed by its second in command, Terauchi. But upon assuming power, Terauchi demonstrated that he had his own political and foreign policy agendas. In fact, the financial diplomacy promoted by the general and his advisers was more than simply a reflection of the new financial power gained through wartime economic growth. It marked an explicit attempt to work around the network of Army General Staff personnel on the continent that Vice Chief of the Army General Staff Tanaka Giichi had employed to monopolize the making of China policy in the reshuffled Ōkuma cabinet. Conversely, the return to a military solution in China represented by the Sino-Japanese Military Agreement and the Siberian Intervention symbolized the return of Yamagata and his henchman Tanaka Giichi to the command of Japan's most critical foreign policy aim, continental expansion.

The Sino-Japanese Military Agreement and the Siberian Intervention are typically analyzed in the context of changes in Japan's international strategic environment. But both initiatives were less a response to sudden international events than a culmination of long-term Japanese continental goals. Members of the Yamagata faction promoted a military agreement with Beijing and an expedition of Japanese troops to the Russian Far East not primarily to defend against the spread of Bolshevik or German power east. Rather, they hoped to seize an extraordinary opportunity to promote a dramatic expansion of Japanese power on the continent.

If the architects of the Siberian Intervention envisioned a threat, it was chiefly one of domestic, not foreign, origin. The most energetic promoters of an expedition, the Imperial Army leadership, in particular, relished the boost that a major military operation would give their slipping political position at home. For while the outbreak of war had raised the stock of Japan's generals with a new area of operations in Shandong province and two new divisions, military funding continued to prioritize the navy. With the destruction of the principal raison d'être for the army's presence on the continent, Imperial Russia, army expansion faced a new crisis. In this context, the idea of a Bolshevik or German threat offered a fresh opportunity to re-anchor the nation's defense squarely upon the continent and upon the shoulders of a vastly expanded ground force.

In the context of Japan's wartime economic prosperity and America's entrance into the war, an expedition to Siberia assumed even greater political significance. The Seiyūkai's Hara Takashi was unusual in regarding the intervention as an opportunity to strengthen ties with Washington. For the most part, members of the military-bureaucratic elite viewed a military engagement in the Russian Far East as an ideal opportunity to confront the increasingly menacing presence of the United States. Woodrow Wilson had declared war in April 1917, after all, condemning all that the modern Japanese state had stood for since its creation. In the place of militarism and imperialism, the American president had heralded a new world of democracy and internationalism. Prime Minister Terauchi and his supporters saw a major deployment of Japanese troops on the continent as an ideal way to restore the centrality of military virtues and national service that had eroded with wartime economic growth and Wilson's pronouncements.

Unfortunately for these men, this, Japan's last great opportunity for military action during the First World War, aroused not widespread public enthusiasm but criticism. Just as Japanese troops poised to embark for the continent, a wave of riots responding to the wartime inflationary spiral of rice seized Japan and the attention of its subjects. Yamagata and his protégés in the Imperial Army viewed the timing of the disturbances with profound regret. For two million voices of protest demonstrated that imperial expansion no longer served the automatic unifying function that it had in the Sino- and Russo-Japanese Wars.

6 Versailles in the Context of National Renovation: Wilson Arrives in Japan

The surge of democracy in the future will indeed be frightening.
—Hara Takashi, October 22, 1917

The new trend of the world is, in domestic policy, the perfection of democracy. In foreign policy, it is the establishment of international egalitarianism.
—Yoshino Sakuzō, January 1919

Jubilant crowds swarmed the streets of New York, London, and Paris on November 11, 1918, to celebrate a momentous occasion: the conclusion of an armistice with Germany. After more than nine million lives lost and over $180 billion in direct costs, peace could not have come a moment too soon. But while French newspapers captured "all faces drunk with joy" and British parsons sang "lustily" with Union Jacks in their silk hats,[1] Japanese crowds seemed tempered in their cheer. Novelist Nagai Kafū noted the strong presence of labor activists in the celebrations, colorfully dressed and marching in file in Hibiya Park. But he could not detect the buoyancy that had characterized festivals marking the transfer of the national capital from Kyōto to Tokyo in 1897, or the annexation of Korea in 1910. "The scene of the throngs around Hibiya and Marunouchi," he observed, "is, unlike earlier times, a display of a kind of painful emotion."[2]

Indeed, while the armistice meant for Japan's allies an end to slaughter and destruction on a scale never known before, for Japan it marked the passing of an opportunity. For the first time since the beginning of the scramble for spheres of influence in China in the late 1890s, Japan had enjoyed a free hand to pursue her continental interests unimpeded. Japanese businesses, as well, had enjoyed unprecedented prosperity, supplying the Allies with badly needed materiel and breaking into markets abandoned, at least temporarily, by the European powers. The end of the war would no doubt bring a steady return of some of that power to Asia. What, Japanese policymakers and opinion leaders asked, would be the effect upon Japan's wartime gains? More important, how would the dramatic rise of American power at the end of the war affect Japanese prospects for the future?

Fig. 16
The peace belongs
to Wilson

VERSAILLES AND THE CHALLENGE OF A NEW WORLD ORDER

While the Great War plays a minor part in the narrative of twentieth-century Japanese history, historians have generally created a space for the celebrated conclusion of the conflict. The Versailles Peace Conference, like its two predecessors, the Shimonoseki Conference capping the Sino-Japanese War and the Portsmouth Conference crowning the war with Russia, serves, on the one hand, as a reminder of the distinct rise of Japan's international status. The Japanese victory in 1895 made her in the eyes of the West the "pioneer of progress in the Orient." Her defeat of Russia in 1905 paved the way for the elevation of her foreign missions to embassies. Now, at the conclusion of the Great War, Japanese delegates would sit as equals in the councils of the Big Five victors of the war.

Like Shimonoseki and Portsmouth, however, the story of Versailles includes a more somber tale that, in fact, often supersedes the chronicle of diplomatic success. It is the story of Japanese victimization upon the international stage that is marshaled to explain Japan's ultimate defiance of the world order in the 1930s. At Shimonoseki, Japan acquired Taiwan and the Pescadores Islands. But she was forced to relinquish Liaodong Peninsula (Manchuria) by the Triple Intervention. At Portsmouth, she established a foothold in Manchuria and achieved preponderant influence in Korea. But she only acquired half of Sakhalin Island and no indemnity. And at Versailles, she stood tall as one of the five great powers of the world. But the principle of equality was rejected with the defeat of Japan's proposed racial nondiscrimination clause in the covenant of the League of Nations.

References to the racial nondiscrimination clause, often mistakenly referred to as the "racial equality" clause, continue to dominate discussions of Japan at Versailles.[3] Even the Shōwa emperor, reminiscing in 1946, described the pivotal importance of the clause's defeat for subsequent events. "The cause (of the Greater East Asia War) lies concealed far off in the substance of the peace treaty following World War I," he noted. "The great powers did not accept the racial equality clause proposed by Japan. Discriminatory sentiment between the white and yellow races remains. This and the rejection of immigration to California were enough to anger the Japanese people."[4] At the very least, historians have documented the widespread Japanese media coverage of the "race problem" (jinshū mondai) from the beginning of the Versailles Conference in January 1919 through the defeat of the clause in April.[5]

Most diplomatic historians, however, recognize the clause as secondary to the main preoccupation of Japan's delegates to the conference, Shandong province.[6] Japan entered the war hoping to increase her influence in China. At Versailles, her plenipotentiaries aimed to obtain great power recognition of Japan's principal wartime gain. While they maintained a now legendary silence on matters outside their immediate interest, on the disposition of Shandong and Germany's former possessions in the South Pacific, Japan's delegates spared no effort.

But the primary significance of the Versailles Conference for the history of twentieth-century Japan lies no more in Shandong than it does in the racial nondiscrimination clause. Despite Wilson's reluctance to accept any product of "imperialist diplomacy," Japan's delegates, after all, obtained at the conference recognition of all her wartime territorial gains. The quarrel over Shandong weighs much more heavily in the histories of the United States and China.[7] For the American president's compromise with Japan over the Chinese province played a critical role in both the U.S. Senate rejection of the peace treaty and the rise of Chinese nationalism.

Studies that do not highlight Japan's humiliation at Versailles seem content to relegate the peace conference, like the Great War itself, to an obscure corner of modern Japanese history. Despite widespread recognition of the 1920s as an era of considerable change in Imperial Japan, one is hard-pressed to find in surveys of modern Japanese history that which is standard in the histories of the great Western belligerents and China: chapters or sub-headings devoted to the Great War and its denouement.[8] But the peace conference had an impact upon Japan every bit as dramatic as the Shandong problem in the United States and China. That impact did not come from such relatively minor matters of race or territory. It sprang, rather, from the more fundamental question of national identity. Wilson's appeal for a new order packed a force equivalent to Perry's "black ships" in 1853. For his exaltation of democracy excited the ongoing domestic debate over oligarchic rule in Japan. And his celebration of internationalism spurred an entirely novel discussion about imperialism. Like the patriots of the Satsuma and Chōshū domains in the 1860s, Seiyūkai president Hara Takashi proposed to meet Wilson's challenge by transforming Japanese society. Like elder statesman Inoue Kaoru, who had in April 1914 begun a campaign to destroy the Seiyūkai, Hara himself called for a "complete reform" (*issai no kakushin*) on the model of the "civilization and enlightenment" movement following the Meiji Renovation.[9]

If the outbreak of war in 1914 had raised widespread expectations in Tokyo for a substantial increase in Japanese power in China, the end of hostilities excited equally broad hopes that the great powers would recognize all of Japan's wartime gains at a future peace conference. Washington's appeal for a clarification of war aims in January 1917, as we have seen, had spurred a lively discussion in the Japanese Diet and media about possible great power disregard of Japanese territorial gains at the negotiating table. When the new cabinet of Hara Takashi convened the

Advisory Council on Foreign Affairs in November 1918 to deliberate on Japan's position at the upcoming peace conference in Paris, then, there was little dispute over what Japan should bargain for. Yamagata associate and coauthor of the Meiji constitution Itō Miyoji called for the perpetual occupation of Qingdao and the seizure, "by all means," of the vast resources of Shandong province.[10] While Prime Minister Hara insisted upon the eventual restoration of Qingdao to China as promised by Foreign Minister Katō at the outbreak of war, he suggested substantial Chinese concessions in Shandong in return for monetary compensation.[11] And War Minister Tanaka Giichi warned of the grave loss that the surrender of railroad rights in the province would represent. "We will have lost the artery for the future expansion of our empire's authority," he advised.[12]

Navy Minister Katō Tomosaburō naturally became the most energetic spokesman for Japanese gains in the German South Pacific islands. As with Shandong, Japan had obtained British, French, and Italian recognition in 1917 of her rights to this territory. At the December 2 meeting of the Advisory Council, Katō reminded his colleagues of British assurances and stressed the indispensability of the islands to the empire. New studies since the Japanese occupation in 1914 had revealed great potential for the cultivation of coconut trees, sugar, and cotton. And among the indigenous population were people "of the same race" as the Japanese. Militarily, Katō reiterated his appeal for the islands to become the "eternal possession of our empire."[13]

The principal charge to Japan's delegates to the peace conference, then, was to obtain great power recognition of these two new additions to the empire. Negotiating instructions approved by the Advisory Council on December 22 called for the transfer to Japan of all German rights and possessions in Shandong and the South Pacific islands "without compensation."[14] Eventual restoration of Shandong to China, it had been decided earlier, would proceed as a matter "strictly between China and Japan."[15] Japan's plenipotentiaries would push most energetically at Paris to retain her right to dispose of Shandong as she wished. They would ultimately secure their wish by threatening to bolt the conference if denied a "satisfactory settlement" of their demands.[16]

If Shandong and German Micronesia had been the extent of Japan's concerns for the peace settlement, Versailles could, indeed, pass as a minor event in the history of modern Japan. But Wilson's pronouncements for peace were replete with meaning for much more than simply the immediate issue of war booty. They redefined the essential character of foreign policy and domestic politics in the twentieth century. They amplified the debate already raging in Japan about the nature of the national polity.

That debate, as we have seen, had rocked Japan since the Meiji Renovation and had centered on the elder statesmen's construction of empire, arms, and oligarchic rule. Large military appropriations were, from the first session of the Imperial Diet, vigorously contested in the national assembly. The widespread enthusiasm sparked by the Sino- and Russo-Japanese Wars had temporarily quieted that debate and facilitated large expansion programs for both services. But peace had inevitably spelled an end to the national enthusiasm for war and to monies available for armaments.

The First World War, like the campaigns against China and Russia, facilitated the growth of both the army and the navy. But Wilson's pronouncements packed a force far greater than any peacetime Diet. For while Imperial Diets had spiked the flow of military funds because of a temporary return to civilian priorities, Wilson provided theoretical justification for a permanent check on military expansion. Wilson, after all, hoped to do much more than end the Great War. He aimed to eliminate war for all time. To do so, he condemned two central components of nineteenth-century international relations, the balance of power and the large investment in arms on which the balance was maintained. In Wilson's eyes, military hardware was as much a cause as a solution to international conflict. Among his famed fourteen points, then, was a plea to reduce the level of armaments. British prime minister David Lloyd George went even further to call for an end to military conscription.

To a Japanese military establishment already struggling to reach the force levels outlined in the 1907 Basic Plan of National Defense, this came as an insufferable blow. Tanaka Giichi refused to accept the devalued estimation of the armed forces. In a memorandum presented to the

Advisory Council on Foreign Affairs in January 1919, he insisted that Japan had been able to "maintain a position among the powers" chiefly because of her military strength.[17] Nor did he believe in the direct connection between military strength and national aggression implied by Wilson and Lloyd George. The Japanese military and the conscription on which it was based were designed strictly for national defense. And in light of the doubtful ability of the international association of states proposed by Wilson to regulate international conflicts justly, they were a basic necessity. Wilson's world vision exacerbated the military's deteriorating position within Japanese society. But it also seemed to worsen the army's position vis-à-vis the navy. The attempt to abolish conscription while touting the freedom of the seas, Tanaka argued, marked an unfair unilateral regulation of ground power.[18]

If Wilson's pronouncements threatened one of the main pillars of Japanese foreign policy, they also resonated with the most pressing political concerns of the early Taishō state: the struggle against oligarchic rule. The advent of republican government in China in 1912 had raised questions about Japanese claims to stand at the vanguard of political modernization in Asia. And the toppling of an oligarchic cabinet by a coalition of political parties in Japan the following year sparked doubts about the viability of the Japanese monarchy itself. Now Woodrow Wilson suggested that political systems such as Japan's were the direct cause of the greatest war in history. For if the balance of power and the competition over armaments had, according to the American president, contributed generally to the outbreak of war, it was nonrepresentative governments that were particularly likely to resort to arms. Such "selfish and autocratic" countries, after all, easily engaged in "intrigue" and "conquest." Although Wilson had been referring specifically to Germany and Austria, by his standards, Japan belonged in the category of "selfish and autocratic." Indeed, she had borrowed many of her political institutions from Imperial Germany. From the perspective of Japan's military-bureaucratic elites, then, Wilson's appeal to make the world "safe for democracy" translated into a plea for the destruction of Imperial Japan. As Prime Minister Terauchi had put it, a "tidal wave" of democratic thought was threatening to "destroy all order and damage the essence of our National Polity."[19]

Perhaps the most momentous of Wilson's declarations for Japan lay at the heart of his new vision of foreign policy. The president's appeals for arms reductions and democracy resonated with long-term movements within Japan. But his petitions for a new diplomacy were entirely original and greatly complicated the political struggle that had long raged in Tokyo. Wilson's critique of balances of power condemned not only the arms race, but also the race for territorial acquisition that lay at its core. In pushing for a Japanese withdrawal from Shandong, he challenged not simply Japan's wartime gains. He called into question the very means by which Japan had gained international respectability in the nineteenth century: imperialism. And in place of imperialism and organized rivalries among states, Wilson called for an "organized common peace" for the benefit of all humanity. The new diplomacy, he hoped, would rest not on a balance of power but on a "community of power," on the peaceful cooperation of states organized in a League of Nations.

Yoshino Sakuzō in July 1918 hailed the complete transformation of "world culture" implied by the League and the new spirit of international "trust and cooperation." But he recognized it as "the equivalent of a giant alarm" ending the "idle slumber" of the Japanese people. In the past, after all, Japan had been, in words, "the most stubborn opponent of the world situation."[20] Indeed, as plenipotentiary-designate to Paris Makino Nobuaki reminded fellow members of the Advisory Council on Foreign Affairs in December, Japan had raised suspicions during the war with her sympathies for Germany and her conduct in China and Siberia.[21] If Wilson's pleas were followed, fellow council member Inukai Tsuyoshi made clear, "we may no longer demand even an inch of land for the acquisition of territory. . . . It is like saying that we cannot promote any path of development for the empire except economic relations."[22]

HARA TAKASHI AS SYMBOL
OF POLITICAL REFORM

Japanese policymakers and opinion leaders alike, then, recognized the American position at Versailles as a fundamental challenge to the prevailing conception of the state in Japan. But the Great War had already transformed international politics and society long before the start of the

peace conference. In Japan, that transformation most immediately affected the domestic economy, inviting an unprecedented level of prosperity, but also accompanying discontents. The nationwide disturbances
over the inflationary spiral of the cost of rice were the most dramatic side
effect of wartime prosperity. The "rice riots," in turn, produced the most
spectacular political development of the war: Japan's first true political
party cabinet.

Since the late 1960s, scholars have rightly hailed the emergence of
"commoner premier" Hara Takashi and a Seiyūkai party cabinet in September 1918 as decisive steps in the arrival of democracy in Imperial Japan.[23] Indeed, Hara not only retained a seat in the Lower House but also
stocked his cabinet with party members.[24] He would continue to extend
the reach of the Seiyūkai throughout local and national government: in
the many rural constituencies where the Seiyūkai boasted its greatest
strength, to the national bureaucracy, the Upper House, even to Japanese
colonial administration.

Although not typically analyzed in the specific context, the Hara
cabinet appears particularly progressive against the backdrop of the
Great War. Like the preceding Terauchi regime, it was very much a
product of the war and presents a conspicuous contrast to its predecessor. While Terauchi sprang from a period of "national crisis" at the
height of battle, the Hara government materialized in response to the escalating momentum for social and political change toward the end of
hostilities.[25] If the "transcendental" Terauchi regime anticipated the political shift to the right in European capitals in 1916, Hara anticipated the
general shift left toward the end of the war.[26]

Indeed, the rise of Hara highlights the decisive shift in the political
center of gravity in Tokyo during the war years. At the outbreak of hostilities, Japanese politics had revolved around the battle between the established power of the Yamagata faction and the rising political force of
the Seiyūkai. Elder statesmen Yamagata and Inoue had sponsored the
Ōkuma cabinet in April 1914 to destroy the majority party, which had, in
the previous year, led the first coalition of political parties to topple an
oligarchic cabinet. As the war came to a close, however, Yamagata was
compelled to recognize the preeminent power in the Diet and shift his
attention from halting to moderating the momentum toward party rule.

Four years after a coalition of parties had pronounced the end of oligarchic rule and following two years of "transcendental" government by General Terauchi, the Japanese media greeted the arrival of party government in September 1918 with great fanfare. Editors of the *Chūō kōron* hailed the first cabinet "to emerge from the exigencies of the situation," and a forum of intellectuals in the same October issue lauded the first victory for representative government.[27] "As the beginning of the eventual conduct of politics truly based on the people," reveled political scientist Fukuda Tokuzō, "it is something we must celebrate."[28] Numerous studies since the 1960s have highlighted the liberal accomplishments of the Hara regime.[29] But in the context of the turbulent struggle for power that played out in the foreign policy arena during the war, one particular achievement stands out: the neutralization of the principal proponent of the Yamagata faction's domestic and foreign policy agendas, Lieutenant General Tanaka Giichi.

As we have seen, Tanaka was, in the aftermath of Katō Takaaki's departure from the Foreign Ministry, the driving force behind Japan's movement beyond the familiar game of great power politics in China and attempted return to a militarized national polity. On the international stage, he had promoted civil war in China, a Russo-Japanese alliance, the Sino-Japanese Military Agreement, and an "autonomous" Siberian expedition. Domestically, he had created a national youth corps and authored an enormous plan for military expansion that promised to militarize Japanese national consciousness while it ensured army superiority over the navy. Tanaka's assumption of the War Ministry portfolio in the new Hara cabinet naturally raised eyebrows. While he had succeeded General Terauchi as the new hope for the Yamagata faction and was thus a natural choice for the War Ministry portfolio, the image of the very symbol of extra-cabinet military-bureaucratic scheming sitting in an all-party cabinet proved incongruous at best. The "military-bureaucratic clique" retained an "enormous, ubiquitous authority" in the political world, warned Tokyo University professor Yoshino Sakuzō in the October *Chūō kōron* forum. What did the inclusion of the "champion of active expansionism" in the Hara regime augur for the future of Japanese diplomacy?[30]

Tanaka had earned his place in the new administration by serving as its political midwife. Having chafed at Terauchi's granting of budget priority to the navy over the army, Tanaka had helped to nudge the general out.[31] At the same time, he had approached Hara about creating a new cabinet.[32] Yoshino was right in suspecting, however, that the coincidence of political interests that had brought Tanaka into the new government would not force a fundamental change of character. The new war minister's initial impulse was to continue guiding policy through unofficial channels. He first reshuffled critical posts within the army to maintain the decisive influence in continental affairs as minister of war that he had enjoyed as vice chief of the Army General Staff. To preserve his leverage at the office, he arranged for Lieutenant General Fukuda Masatarō, who had coordinated his scheme to depose Yuan Shikai in 1916, to succeed him as vice chief. To ensure his authority within the Ministry of War, Tanaka had the former war minister, Ōshima Kenichi, who had defended Prime Minister Terauchi's paltry defense budget, dispatched to China to assume command of Japanese forces at Qingdao. Finally, Hongō Fusatarō, whom Terauchi had recommended to succeed Ōshima in Tanaka's stead, was transferred from Qingdao to a nondescript post within the War Ministry, where he could do no harm.[33]

The war minister relied in large measure upon the direct ties that he maintained to the continent to secure the reins of the new cabinet's China policy. Through his agents in the field, Tanaka reengaged the policy of north-south cooperation that he had pursued in the spring of 1917 to counter Nishihara Kamezō's exclusive support for Duan Qirui.[34] Both Premier Duan and President Feng Guozhang had recently resigned in the face of escalating southern resistance to northern rule, and the new minister of war had spied another opportunity.

But Tanaka learned quickly that the extra-cabinet stratagems that he had employed to seize the policy initiative during the reorganized Ōkuma and Terauchi cabinets would not work with Hara Takashi. Like Katō before him, Hara considered the formulation and execution of foreign policy the exclusive province of the civilian cabinet, particularly, the foreign minister in consultation with the prime minister. He moved swiftly, then, to respond to reports from Minister Yoshizawa Kenkichi in Beijing that Tanaka's agents were invading the operational parameters of the Foreign Ministry in the field. The new minister to China, Obata Yūkichi, was dispatched to the Chinese capital with instructions to "sufficiently command the army envoys" in China.[35] Only two days earlier, the Foreign Ministry leadership and the finance and agricultural ministers had stressed the need for "unity" in the empire's foreign policy. They also claimed for Kasumigaseki an exclusive right to conduct the empire's China loan policy. Hara subsequently summoned Tanaka to speak to him directly about the matter.[36]

Tanaka thus confronted for the first time the true constraints of parliamentary government. But he also recognized its possibilities. Hara had demanded that the war minister remain responsible to the cabinet. But Tanaka also realized that as long as he deferred to the prime minister, he could play an important decision-making role as a pivotal member of the government. Although he had incited Minister of War Uehara Yūsaku to defy the Saionji regime over military expansion in 1912, once he assumed the post himself, he began to conceive of the office of minister of war in entirely different terms. Following the example set by his former adversary, Oka Ichinosuke, Tanaka began playing the part of a minister in the British cabinet system. He would be responsible fundamentally to the cabinet, not the army.

Indeed, this was the beginning of a new political career for Tanaka. Having risen to power by creating an overtly political role for the army outside the framework of parliamentary government, Tanaka now tied his fortunes to working within that framework. He would henceforth behave less as a political soldier than as a soldier-politician. He would, in fact, ultimately assume the leadership of the Seiyūkai and, in 1927, cap his career in the office of prime minister. Unfortunately, Tanaka's successors in the Imperial Army would take as their model not his adaptation to the times but his earlier activities as a political soldier. In time they came to view Tanaka the soldier-politician as an obstacle to army authority at home and imperial glory abroad. Tanaka's metamorphosis, after all, would affect his policies as much as his politics.

Tanaka's position on the Siberian Intervention offers a case in point. Yoshino Sakuzō had justifiably raised questions in September 1918 about the effect of Tanaka Giichi upon the new cabinet's policies. As founder and chairman of the Joint Committee on Military Affairs from January 1918, he had, after all, led the campaign to send ten Japanese divisions to the Russian Far East. Soon after the initial deployment of troops, he had written enthusiastically of the need to "exert ourselves aggressively and be prepared to reach our objective by all means."[37]

But with Tanaka's assumption of the War Ministry portfolio came a dramatic policy reversal. Only two months after his appeal for an energetic offensive, with just three and a half divisions in place in the Amur Basin, Tanaka advised the new prime minister that there was no need for additional Japanese troops in the region. Japan could rely on Russian Cossacks to keep the peace and should not make further deployments west of Lake Baikal as requested by the British, French, and American governments.[38] In mid-October the new war minister warned Hara that the 100 million yen allocated for the expedition in 1918 would not cover the necessary expenses. But rather than recommend an increase in spending, he suggested a withdrawal of troops.[39] By December, he determined that half the 50,000 Japanese soldiers now occupying the Russian Far East should return to Japan, with the remainder to be placed in a state of peacetime deployment.[40]

Tanaka's aboutface on an expedition to Siberia has been described principally as the consequence of policy considerations. With the end of the war in Europe, it is argued, the new war minister recognized the necessity of renewed cooperation with the great powers.[41] But, as we shall see, the armistice did not prevent Tanaka from making a fresh appeal in September 1919 for more intimate Sino-Japanese relations to replace the Anglo-Japanese alliance. There is no reason to believe, in other words, that the end of the war altered Tanaka's fundamental wish for an autonomous Japanese diplomacy. Rather, his aboutface on Siberia owes more to political than policy considerations. It reflected, in particular, his new position at the helm of the Ministry of War.

As vice chief of the Army General Staff, Tanaka had commandeered Japan's China policy by directing clandestine military operations on the continent. But Hara had demanded not only that the minister of war be responsible to the cabinet. He required, as well, that all military operations be conducted with official cabinet approval. As long as such operations remained official, they were the responsibility of operational command, the General Staff. As minister of war, in other words, Tanaka was now excluded from the official line of command of military operations. He could no longer expect to direct a major deployment of troops on the continent. Such a deployment would, rather, shift the balance of power within the army to the General Staff. Tanaka lobbied for a reduction of Japanese troops in Siberia and their conversion to a peacetime footing, then, in a bid to retain control of the expedition in his capacity as minister of war. The operation should be left in his own hands, he advised General Staff Chief Uehara, because it had materialized from political considerations, not with the object of waging war.[42]

Fig. 17
*"Hara is a fogy
behind the times"*

HARA TAKASHI AS CONSERVATIVE REACTION TO WOODROW WILSON

Hara's ability to control the irrepressible Tanaka and the more frequently recounted story of Seiyūkai infiltration at all levels of local and national administration suffice to secure him an exalted place in the history of Japanese representative government. But scholars looking for the roots of democracy in Imperial Japan have dwelt on Hara to the neglect of other pivotal elements of the story. Particularly ironic is the fact that 1919 is identified not, following the histories of Europe and America, as the year of Versailles but as one year in the life of the Hara regime. For the most dramatic steps toward representative government in Japan in that year came not through Hara's efforts but as a consequence of the Great War and its denouement, the Paris Peace Conference. In fact, by 1919, the Seiyūkai and its president had surrendered their role as the most powerful champions of representative government in Japan to a much more formidable proponent: Woodrow Wilson. The political spectrum had, indeed, shifted to the left with the ascendance of Hara Takashi. But in the light of Wilson's dramatic calls for democracy and internationalism, the Seiyūkai, like its former arch-rival, Yamagata Aritomo, looked very much the product of an earlier age. In fact, it would now ally itself with the mightiest force for political conservatism, Yamagata, in an effort to stem the new tide of democracy now pervading Japan. In so doing, it would anticipate its pivotal role from the late 1920s in the eventual destruction of representative government in Japan.

The conservative thrust of Seiyūkai rule was not lost upon contemporaries. Celebrations of Hara's prime ministry in September 1918 were overwhelmingly tempered by concerns over his party's already distinct record of compromise with the enemies of party rule. While profound social and political changes had produced the new cabinet, none of Fukuda Tokuzō's colleagues in the October 1918 *Chūō kōron* wagered that Hara would actually meet the expectations raised by the wartime transformation of state and society. "Our welcome of the Hara cabinet," cautioned the editors, "is not necessarily due to our trust in the judgment of the person of the prime minister. Nor is it due to our agreement with the policies of the Seiyūkai." Rather, it came from the "hope for the immediate establishment of party government." "Presently, the people [of Japan] urgently [seek] to have government policy adapt to world trends. . . . Is the Hara cabinet prepared to reward this broad-mindedness of the people and not defy their expectations?"[43]

The Conservative Foundation of Hara's Politics

As we have seen, Yoshino Sakuzō was wrong to think that Tanaka Giichi's adventurism would steer the new cabinet. But he was right to recognize that Tanaka's inclusion in the Hara regime signaled a close working relationship with the military-bureaucratic faction of Yamagata Aritomo. It was Yamagata who had suggested that the prime minister appoint Tanaka, and Hara had acceded expressly to co-opt the power of the elder statesman. "To involve Tanaka in this cabinet," he had informed the Seiyūkai's Fukui Saburō, "is to include Yamagata. There is nothing mightier than to head a cabinet that includes Yamagata."[44]

Hara's collusion with Yamagata and his supporters is frequently offered as evidence of the Seiyūkai president's pragmatism.[45] His fundamental interests, after all, directly clashed with those of the elder statesman. While Yamagata struggled to sustain bureaucratic control of policymaking, Hara viewed the political parties as the true heirs of the Meiji Renovation. And, to the field marshal's great distress, Hara would

continue promoting party power in such sacred territory as the bureaucracy, the Upper House, and even in Japan's colonies.[46]

But Hara's political alliance with Yamagata and his supporters went
well beyond mere recognition of the faction's power. It was founded on a
genuine community of interests magnified by changes accompanying the
war in Europe, particularly in public consciousness. The first concurrence over the frightening prospect of change came in November 1916 in
the context of talk within Allied capitals about the possibility of peace.
Hara warned the field marshal that to meet the exigencies of the coming
peace, a "complete reform" on the model of the Meiji Renovation was required, particularly in the realms of religion and education.[47] The prosperity of the war had, after all, spurred a precipitous decline in public
morality. In his first major speech on "postwar management" given a
month earlier, Hara had described the "public spirit" as being infected by
a new level of "frivolity," a problem, he insisted, requiring "great attention."[48] Yamagata assured the party president in November that "there is
nothing in your point of argument with which I do not agree."[49]

America's entrance into the war to make the world "safe for democracy" magnified, as we have seen, the apprehensions of Japan's ruling elite
regarding the enormous changes stimulated by the European war in Japan.[50] Hara Takashi proved no less alarmed than Prime Minister Terauchi and Yamagata when he warned then home minister Gotō Shinpei in
September 1917 that, "with the sudden diffusion of democracy [min-
shushugi], we must secretly worry for the Throne."[51] Five weeks later, he
and Yamagata exchanged their fears of the United States. The field marshal described the future of the empire as "extremely worrisome." "The
recent actions of America, in particular, may have an unfathomable effect
upon our country." Hara noted that the real intention of the U.S. declaration of war remained obscure. But regardless, with the arrival of peace,
"U.S. power vis-à-vis the world will be astonishing."[52] When later apprised by the Privy Council's Miura Gorō of Yamagata's horror of U.S.
"domination," Hara replied that "the surge of democracy in the future
will indeed be frightening. On this, the bureaucrats and I equally
worry."[53]

It was thus that both Yamagata and Hara's plans for Japan's immediate future increasingly became a blueprint for softening the impact of an

American-led peace. And like Yamagata, Hara proposed to meet the new challenge with an old strategy. Yamagata, as we have seen with the Siberian Intervention, hoped to deal with the problem of public consciousness through a renewed emphasis on empire and arms. Hara, for his part, adroitly refashioned the Seiyūkai's old agenda for gaining power into a blueprint for maintaining control under extraordinary conditions.

That agenda comprised five elements: the introduction of small electoral districts, the expansion of the transportation network, the encouragement of trade and industry, the expansion of higher education, and the strengthening of national defense. The Seiyūkai had for many years advocated small electoral districts to expand its base of power. But in the context of the growing clamor for democracy, such districts came to be regarded as the most efficacious route to halting the expansion of voting rights. An immediate implementation of such districts was imperative, Hara warned, to stem the tide toward the most fearful probable consequence of the democracy movement: universal manhood suffrage.[54] Investment in transportation and the encouragement of trade and industry had been the centerpiece of the Seiyūkai's transformation into a national network after the Russo-Japanese War. Hara now hoped to continue dispersing public largesse to retain the loyalty of his constituents. Hara's plan to expand the national network of colleges had originally aimed to diffuse the pressure from a growing number of secondary-school graduates for more opportunities for higher education. It would now serve, as well, to advance the values of the state. As Finance Minister Takahashi later explained, the cabinet hoped to "reassure" the people "by promoting industry and the development of international trade and to exalt the spirit of our National Polity [kokutai] through a diffusion of education."[55] Finally, after the devastating defeat in the 1915 general election, Hara had committed himself to strong support for national defense. Indeed, his sudden conversion was critical in securing the support of the Yamagata faction for his cabinet. In the context of the increasing diffusion of public sentiment, it would also serve to focus national attention on the concerns of the state.

From the outset of his cabinet, then, Hara had placed himself firmly on the conservative side of change. While Yoshino Sakuzō, on the one hand, called upon the new regime to "befriend the populace" and promote reforms that would "spark vitality throughout all aspects of society,"[56] Hara announced a policy of business as usual. The European War threatened to "transform" the nation's state of affairs, he warned his party in an October 5, 1918, address. In devising policies to meet the new challenges, he promised, he would always consider "the will of the people."[57] But while Yoshino hoped the Seiyūkai would now "atone for its past sins" with a completely new path, Hara informed a gathering of the Tokyo Chamber of Commerce on October 11 that he did not see any need whatsoever for the Seiyūkai to change policies now that it had captured the premiership.[58] The old agenda for establishing a political base would now serve the important task of maintaining power.

The Conservative Foundation of Hara's Diplomacy

Like his domestic political agenda, Hara's foreign policy borrowed from an old formula and aimed to minimize the impact of radical change. As we have seen, American belligerency had sparked the Seiyūkai president's concern regarding the "diffusion of democracy" in Japan. But the U.S. declaration of war carried important foreign policy implications as well. Seven weeks after the announcement, Hara speculated that "in the future, America will take the lead in the world."[59] It was a lead, Hara felt, that Japan could not contest.

America's foreign policy goals were not, however, identical with those of Japan, especially with respect to China. Secretary of State Bryan had made this clear in his March 1915 note to the Japanese government warning against the coercion of Beijing and the "assumption of political, military or economic domination over China by a foreign power."[60] Since Secretary of State John Hay's declaration of an "open door" in 1898, the United States had challenged Japan's quest for power in Asia by pressing for equal access for all in China. When Woodrow Wilson in February 1917 invited all neutral powers to join the United States in severing ties with Germany, he offered China strong moral justification to fight Japan's wartime aggression.

As we have seen, Nishihara Kamezō quickly maneuvered on that occasion to ensure that the Duan regime declare war for the promise of Japanese funds, not for the sake of American ideals. But Wilson's injunction against militarism continued to reverberate on the continent, especially among the southern forces fighting the Japanese-backed Duan Qirui. In a conversation with Hara Takashi in April 1918, southern revolutionary Tang Shaoyi praised Wilson as "the greatest genius since Lincoln." The Seiyūkai president responded soberly that Japan would have to keep an eye on America's future actions in China.[61]

Hara's strategy for coping with a powerful and meddlesome America was to commandeer the moral high ground on the most pressing problem since the death of Yuan Shikai, China's civil war. Clearly, the Terauchi cabinet's exclusive support for one faction in the domestic battle promised to prolong the strife and breed the discontent that would drive China's revolutionaries into American arms. Hara counseled Terauchi in September 1917 to send a mediator of "appropriate authority" to negotiate an agreement between the north and south. If successful, he explained, Japan would enjoy the enviable position of being viewed by both parties as "virtuous." Even in the event of failure, Tokyo would arouse no ill feeling among the Chinese or the great powers.[62] Like Woodrow Wilson, whose example loomed vividly before him, Hara proposed to garner influence not through money or force, but by an appeal to the justice of a universally acceptable cause, the unification of China.

Hara placed a premium, therefore, on the appearance of propriety. When Prime Minister Terauchi proposed to supply the Duan regime with weapons in 1917, the Seiyūkai president urged him to ensure that both the Japanese and Chinese people understood the Chinese government declaration not to use the arms against the south. Japan, he suggested, should also make a public announcement to the great powers to that effect.[63] When Home Minister Gotō Shinpei proposed to sponsor Chinese students in Japan to compete with a similar American program, Hara suggested that the Terauchi government establish a private organization to channel the funds, to avoid violating the sensibilities of the southern faction.[64] Finally, Hara urged coordinating with the United States at every step in discussions leading to an expedition of troops to Siberia, viewing the expedition as "the beginning of Japanese-American cooperation in the future."[65]

Hara had by no means abandoned the traditional thrust of the empire's China policy. When the Terauchi cabinet, responding to growing mutual suspicions regarding respective goals in China, sent former foreign minister Ishii Kikujirō to the United States in July 1917 to negotiate an accommodation, Hara hailed the Japanese draft as a first step "to obtain American recognition of our superior interests [in China]." It would also help, he argued, to obtain southern Chinese leaders' recognition of those interests, since they had increasingly looked to the United States for support.[66] The following spring, Hara advised Terauchi that a north-south compromise was "the best excuse to begin infusing our power [into China]."[67] The first priority, he had advised earlier, was to "block the southern faction's avenue of seeking aid from the United States."[68]

Hara could not overstate the importance of arranging a north-south compromise before the end of hostilities in Europe. To permit the civil dispute to continue, he warned Terauchi in April 1918, would invite great "hardships" with peace.[69] The assumption, shared by much of Japan's ruling elite, was that an end to the European war would bring a dramatic increase in U.S. influence worldwide. It was imperative that Japan work its appeal for Chinese unity before the American injunction against militarism could erode Japan's wartime continental gains.

HARA TAKASHI, YAMAGATA ARITOMO, AND DEFENSIVE PREPARATIONS FOR PEACE

Armed thus with a defensive foreign as well as domestic policy, Hara maneuvered soon after his inauguration to temper the disruptions promised by the end of war. On October 7, he assembled the heads of Japan's wire services and the foreign correspondents' club and threatened to censor, ban, or otherwise penalize any publications that failed to "properly guide" public opinion.[70] Three days later, he warned southern revolutionary Zhang Shizhao that unless he quickly established a unified government, the end of war in Europe would bring a "troublesome" situation. "Not only is this not at all in China's interests, for Japan's sake as well, it should not be allowed."[71]

But Hara faced a formidable challenge. He agreed with Field Marshal Yamagata in early November that public opinion was becoming increasingly radicalized. "Because the people have naturally become infected by the atmosphere outside of the country," he stressed, "where there are in-stigators, they will arise. We can do nothing but deal appropriately with them."[72] More ominously, the Allies signed an armistice with Germany on November 11. Four days later, the Ōsaka Asahi shinbun published the reaction of southern Chinese leader Tang Shaoyi. China had aided the Allied side with the provision of labor during the war. "At the peace conference," Tang declared, "we will thus have our own demands. To be delivered from German oppression goes without saying. We also need consideration of the seriousness of the Chinese people regarding the preservation of Chinese territory."[73]

No sooner had Tang implicitly laid claim to Chinese territory cap-tured by the Japanese during the war, than the Hara government began deliberating on how best to maintain possession. The Advisory Council on Foreign Affairs, as we have seen, would ultimately approve instruc-tions to Japan's delegates to obtain the transfer of all German rights and possessions in Shandong and the South Pacific islands to Japan "without compensation" to Germany. Wilson's proclamations notwithstanding, Hara himself viewed the issue in strictly nineteenth-century imperialist terms. Why, he asked in the Advisory Council meeting of December 2, should Japan alone try to conform to the new standard for international behavior set by Wilson? Even Britain did not necessarily adhere to "civi-lizationism" (bunmeishugi). The British would, undoubtedly, present some "sharp" demands at Versailles. Japan should coordinate its steps with London and push for concessions in Shandong in return for mone-tary compensation to Japan.[74]

But despite the cabinet's efforts to maintain the focus upon the tradi-tional object of peace talks, Wilson's "new standards" continued to in-trude. Baron Makino Nobuaki, the recently appointed Japanese pleni-potentiary to Paris, surprised all in attendance when he spoke on behalf of the new diplomacy in a December 2, 1918, meeting of the Advisory Council on Foreign Affairs. "The respect for peace and rejection of high-handedness are trends of the world today," he exclaimed. "Americanism" was being propounded unanimously in all corners of the earth, and "con-ditions have unquestionably changed from the days of the old diplo-macy." Japan could no longer talk of Sino-Japanese friendship, he argued, while the Foreign Ministry, continental adventurers, and soldiers pursued diplomacy on three different fronts. It was time to "work to expel oppressive and scheming means, tread the path of righteousness (seidō), and make helping a weak country [China] our principle."[75] The following week, Makino made clear what the precepts of the new diplomacy ultimately required: the withdrawal of Japanese troops from China.[76]

Makino could not have given those lost in the "idle slumber" described by Yoshino Sakuzō a ruder awakening. The first to respond to this clearest definition of the new diplomacy, Kokumintō party president Inukai Tsuyoshi, protested, as we have seen, to the elimination of all but economics from the fundamental tools of international competition. War Minister Tanaka vehemently denied that the military and Foreign Ministry had been working at cross-purposes in China and warned that as long as the "self-indulgent uprisings" of China's "warlords" continued, Japan could not easily withdraw her troops.[77]

Yoshino urged the Hara regime to take the lead in helping to create an international association of states.[78] But the cabinet decided to maintain what the Tokyo Imperial University professor described as Japan's traditional role of followership. In the November 19 meeting of the Advisory Council on Foreign Affairs, Itō Miyoji warned that the West intended to preserve the "status quo of the Anglo-Saxon race" and "restrict the future development" of outside powers with the establishment of a League of Nations.[79] Hara countered that Japan should avoid the great powers' suspicions and even offered to advocate a League of Nations himself, "if it is proposed with the object of maintaining eternal peace and follows the principle of fairness."[80] But the prime minister did not, apparently, believe that that was Wilson's object. The council would ultimately agree to instruct Japan's delegates to postpone agreement on a concrete proposal for a League "as long as possible."[81]

Hara's reservations concerning a League of Nations reflected his general attitude toward the peace conference. He demonstrated no little concern for preserving Japan's rights and interests in China and the former German territories in the South Pacific. But these issues, Hara had originally felt, were matters that should be discussed directly with Germany, not in Paris.[82] He eventually agreed to allow consideration of such issues for the sake of "cooperation" with the great powers. But he publicly hinted that he did not place much import in or expect much from the peace conference.[83] By highlighting Japan's place among the world's great powers, the conference offered a chance to lift Hara's political fortunes. But the risks of peace loomed larger than the benefits.[84] Japan's delegation would have to return home with all of the demanded rights and interests in Shandong and Germany's South Pacific islands to avoid a recurrence of the post–Portsmouth Treaty (Russo-Japanese War) disturbances in Tokyo. Likewise, the cabinet would have to moderate the domestic impact of Wilson's pronouncements on democracy and internationalism.

Hara's preparations for the peace conference were, therefore, defensive. He appointed the venerable statesmen Marquis Saionji Kinmochi and Privy Council member Baron Makino Nobuaki to represent Japan at Paris for the authority they could command in a time of crisis. As Makino later recalled, the selection of delegates was important because Japan might be compelled to withdraw from the conference. Even if pressure from the great powers did not bring such drastic action, forced compromise at Paris could bring dissatisfaction at home.[85] Hara declined the advice of Yamagata, Hirata Tōsuke, and members of the Advisory Council to lead the Japanese delegation himself. It was impossible, he argued, for him to leave Japan in light of the present domestic social and political situation.[86] While Saionji and Makino braced for a fight in Paris, the prime minister would concentrate on damage control at home.

In that vein, Hara attempted first to lower Japanese expectations regarding the peace. He did so by downplaying the importance of the conference for the fortunes of the empire.[87] More important, the prime minister tried to neutralize the appeal of the "new thought" now sweeping the country. Despite his warnings to the press in October, signs of that new thought pervaded the media. A November *Yorozu chōhō* editorial, for example, titled "The Twentieth Century Renaissance," described a "new atmosphere" marked by the spread of "democratic thought" in Japan after the "destruction of dark German militarism."[88] To deal with such explosive ideas, Hara offered his own interpretation of the significance of the war. During the conflict, he informed an assembly of reporters in mid-November, the Allies determined that Germany was the enemy of mankind and engaged in mutual aid for the sake of justice and humanity. "To be kind and to help each other," concluded the prime minister, "this is an unusual temper. This temper is the new spirit of all mankind." Purposely ignoring claims that the war had been a struggle for democracy over militarism, Hara advanced the politically more palatable notion that the lesson to be learned was international cooperation.[89]

Meanwhile, Field Marshal Yamagata and his followers gathered to mull over ways to deal with the domestic and international changes that threatened the foundation of their conception of the state. Upper House member Den Kenjirō visited Yamagata at the beginning of December to discuss changes in the international balance of power after peace, labor unrest, the high price of rice, suffrage expansion, and ways to "Japanize" the democratic trend of thought (*minponshugi no shichō*).[90] Nine days later, Yamagata hosted an assembly of fourteen of his closest supporters to bemoan the "radical thought" (*kageki shisō*) that had, he held, permeated domestic and international sentiment as a result of the war. This thought would "harm the National Polity [*kokutai*]" and "break the peace," and the field marshal called for solutions to "prevent the sprouting of a calamity."[91]

Following the historiographical overestimation of the Russian Revolution, scholars have generally interpreted Japanese references at this time to "radical" thought to mean Bolshevism. But Cold War sensitivities should not interfere with our understanding of policymaking in the 1910s. Japanese statesmen during the Great War faced a greater challenge than the unlikely prospect of revolution. While Cold War era historians considered socialism the greatest imaginable threat, to Japan's military-bureaucratic elites in the 1910s, that distinction went to the momentum toward representative government. Indeed, in November 1918, Mori Ōgai noted that Yamagata and his followers worried about the effects, not of the Russian Revolution, but of Woodrow Wilson's public statements.[92] The reference in the December 1918 meeting of Yamagata's supporters was to the effect of the war in general, not to the Bolshevik Revolution in particular. And as Yamagata's discussion with Den Kenjirō on December 1 indicates, the elder statesman worried particularly about the expansion of suffrage and "democratic" thought. He had, in fact, charged Den Kenjirō in October with creating a third party in the House of Peers to prevent the primacy of the Lower House in the event of an institutionalization of party cabinets.[93] Of all the problems of "radical" thought, Den himself clearly considered the movement for universal manhood suffrage the most troublesome.[94]

By December 1918, not only had the "radical" thought permeated the nation's press, it had penetrated the political dialogue in anticipation of the convening of the Forty-First Diet (December 27, 1918–March 26, 1919). Addressing a Kenseikai rally in early November, party president Katō Takaaki declared that Germany had directed its will to the concentration of military might since its founding in 1870. By contrast, modern France and Britain had generally leaned toward peace. It was in these countries, characterized by the rule of both the people and the monarchy, where "virtuous democracy" reigned. "Should we not say that those who deem it dangerous thought when one proclaims this democracy have, ironically, succumbed to dangerous thought themselves?"[95]

The Kenseikai's Hamaguchi Osachi echoed this sentiment in early January 1919. "The defeat of Germany," he declared, "has deeply implanted the idea that bureaucratism and militarism have declined and that politics must be modeled entirely upon democracy. The great tide of democracy is overwhelming the entire world at this moment."[96] The Kenseikai posture for the Forty-First Diet stressed, among other things, "respect for human rights." And in a critique of Hara's emphasis upon Japanese rights in China and the South Pacific, it called for more attention to international matters outside Japan's immediate interests, namely, to the "establishment of lasting world peace."[97] Specific proposals for the forty-first session included expanding the electorate by lowering the tax requirement for voters to two rather than the Seiyūkai's plan for three yen and by reducing the intellectual requirement to a secondary education. Likewise, Kenseikai members in the Lower House expressed concern over the financial burden of Hara's four-point plan to invest in higher education, industry, national defense, and transportation.[98]

None of these protestations had any effect upon Hara's own legislative agenda. With Upper House approval of monies for his educational expansion program and Lower House sanction of his electoral reform law on March 25, Hara accomplished his two major goals for the Forty-First Diet without incident. Added to the unprecedented passage of the 1919 fiscal budget without revision, they attested to the prime minister's success at his self-appointed task of stabilizing the home front. It was, he sighed, a "blessing for the State."[99]

Fig. 18   "The tide of the thought"

THE SOCIAL AND
POLITICAL EFFECTS
OF WILSON IN JAPAN

But the greatest challenge to Hara and the military-bureaucratic clique with which he had found common ground simmered outside the walls of parliament. While Katō Takaaki declined to fight for universal manhood suffrage in the Forty-First Diet, lawyer and Dietman Imai Yoshiyuki trumpeted the cause to an enthusiastic audience at the first meeting of the newly established Reimeikai (Dawn Society) in January 1919. The wartime victory of "democracy" (*minponshugi*) over "bureaucratism" (*kanryōshugi*) had demonstrated that "when there are matters of state, they must be based upon the people," Imai argued. Together with the rice riots, which had proven the magnitude of the "power of the people," the war had provided an unprecedented opportunity to push for universal manhood suffrage. "I hope that we do not miss the opportunity. The general public should call loudly for universal suffrage, and we must strive to the end to accomplish that objective."[100] Two months later, 50,000 students, merchants, and factory and clerical workers assembled in Hibiya park in central Tokyo to rally for expanded voting rights. The *Tōyō keizai shinpō* dubbed it "Japan's first great political demonstration."[101]

Particularly disturbing to the Hara government was the participation of organized labor in this event. The Police Bureau had ordered organizers to avoid March 1, which was a labor holiday, but to no avail. Factory workers turned out in record numbers for the political rally, and among them were members of Japan's most successful early labor organization, the Yūaikai (Friendly Society). From its founding in 1912, the Yūaikai had stressed "harmony and cooperation between labor and capital." But on January 16, 1919, the union's Ōsaka and Kōbe chapters sponsored a "rally to promote official recognition of labor unions," in a first move toward a more confrontational posture vis-à-vis management.[102] Again, the motive force was the war in Europe, and clauses in the Treaty of Versailles guaranteeing the right of trade unions to organize and authorizing the creation of an International Labor Organization raised the Yūaikai's fortunes to new heights. "The world is changing," proclaimed the August 30, 1919, national conference commemorating the seventh anniversary of the Yūaikai. "And it is moving progressively forward, leaving only Japan behind. We, Japan's producers, therefore, proclaim to the world the following. So that the entire globe will be governed by peace, freedom, and equality, we, Japan's laborers, will live by the spirit of the League of Nations and its labor agreement and will not refrain from a struggle of martyrs." With this pronouncement, the single union Yūaikai became a national federation of unions, renamed the Greater Japan General Federation of Labor and the Friendly Society (Dai Nihon Rōdō Sōdōmei-Yūaikai). A twenty-point plan called for universal manhood suffrage, abrogation of the Public Peace Police Law, and the "democratization" of the educational system. Further provisions aimed to improve the immediate condition of labor.[103]

While the peace conference thus aroused sentiment for political accountability in government and industry in Japan proper, it also fanned the flames of self-determination in Japanese territories and in China. The very day that the universal suffragists swarmed Hibiya park, thousands of students, intellectuals, and the religious faithful assembled in Korea's major cities to support a proclamation by a committee of Buddhist and Christian clerics for Korean independence. Hara grumbled at the "empty slogan of self-determination" that he identified as the driving force of the movement.[104] But there was nothing empty about the magnitude of the protests. By the beginning of April, disturbances spread to fifty locations in eleven provinces and mobilized up to 40,000 demonstrators.[105] The event would become known as the March First Movement and mark a pivotal step in the rise of Korean nationalism.

The Hara government quelled the March First Movement by the end of April with the help of six infantry battalions and four hundred mounted military police secretly dispatched from Tokyo.[106] But next door, China's determination to resist Japanese chauvinism only intensified. "The recent Korean independence movement is grand, sincere, and tragic," wrote Beijing University professor Chen Duxiu soon after the event. "It literally marks a new era in the history of world revolution. With this glory manifesting in the Korean race, the embarrassment of the decay of the Chinese race is all the more apparent."[107] Chinese students, entrepreneurs, and others had showered their delegation to Paris in January with telegrams of support for an energetic fight to restore Japanese-occupied Qingdao and Shandong to China. Now, after the Korean independence movement and just before the Council of Five began deliberations in Paris on Shandong, demands in China for justice reached a deafening pitch. On April 20, between thirty and forty thousand people gathered at the palace courtyard in Jinan (Shandong) to demand the return of Qingdao and vow to "struggle to the death for Shandong rights." When word reached Beijing in early May that the Council of Five in Paris had decided to transfer all of Germany's interests in Shandong to Japan, three thousand students assembled in front of the Gate of Heavenly Peace to "fight for national rights abroad, punish national traitors at home."[108] The result was a national wave of protests, strikes, and anti-Japanese boycotts that would become known as the May Fourth Movement and mark a vital step in the rise of Chinese nationalism.

In Japan, Yoshino Sakuzō greeted the protests abroad with a call for partial self-government in Korea and an end to the Japanese association with the pro-Japanese faction in Beijing. The student leaders of the May Fourth Movement, he argued, bore no grudge against the Japanese people but shared their goal of liberating the country from their own "military-bureaucratic clique." The construction of a popular base for Sino-Japanese friendship depended upon the success of the "liberation movement" in both China and Japan.[109]

THE CONSERVATIVE BATTLE
TO RETAIN THE OLD ORDER

The Hara government reacted to these voices for reform at home and abroad by clamping down on public expression and underscoring Japanese diplomatic autonomy. At the end of February 1919, Home Minister Tokonami Takejirō increased personnel at his ministry and dispatched representatives to local government offices to "cultivate the power of the people." As outlined in the minister's instructions to local officials, he aimed to address the "increasing gravity to the empire's standing" caused by the great powers' attempt to "reconstruct a completely new world culture" after the war. Tokonami urged all Japanese subjects to exhibit unanimous self-restraint, a spirit of sacrifice and public service, and to "increasingly strive to exalt the brilliance of our National Polity [kokutai]." And echoing the previous cabinet's concerns over overproduction and privatization, he implored those same subjects to regulate their production and seek harmony through mutual aid. "We must deeply warn against pleasure, the wanton waste of capital, rashness, and things that may cause us to lose our way or, at the very least, obstruct the progress of the State." Through unity of the people and the state, the Japanese should strive for a "complete renovation."[110]

At the beginning of April, War Minister Tanaka urged "resolute determination" in domestic policy.[111] And Hara decried the "noisy change in public sentiment." "Unstable change" was a distinct possibility in the aftermath of war, he warned, and "ordinary determination" to deal with the situation would not suffice.[112] Hara and Home Minister Tokonami, then, solicited the support of Japanese religious leaders to reform public sentiment. Tokonami urged an ecumenical group of Buddhist, Shinto, and Christian clerics in May to promote "a flourishing sense of State, preparation as the people of a great country, and the perfection of national defense," in addressing their followers.[113] Hara added his caution regarding the "spirit of the people" in a discussion with these leaders on May 24.[114]

Regarding labor, Japanese representatives to the Committee for International Labor Legislation at Paris negotiated an escape clause in the Labor Charter to minimize Japan's obligation to the rights of workers. At the same time, Tokonami proposed the creation of a "trust and friendship society" to foster "harmony" between labor and capital. The incorporated body was founded in December, following Hara's request that the new organization be powerful enough to avoid an "extension of the power of labor."[115] Meanwhile, the cabinet appointed a representative of management, over the vehement objections of Japan's unions, as the empire's delegate to the first meeting of the International Labor Conference in October.

Hara had moved swiftly to quell the March riots in Korea through a secret dispatch of troops from Japan. But to ensure long-term stability, the prime minister urged reform of the "Western" model of colonial rule, which was designed, he maintained, to govern peoples of a different race, religion, language, and history. "Because Japan and Korea are the same country," he informed American bishop Herbert Welch in May, "we want to govern [both] by the same policies."[116] Hara envisioned, among other things, the establishment of civilian rule and the reconstruction of Korea's police and educational systems along Japanese lines. "I am absolutely opposed," he apprised Yamagata in June, "to allowing the self-government suggested by the [Japanese] public."[117]

Regarding China, Japan's delegates to Paris refused to compromise on Japanese rights in Shandong, threatening, as instructed, not to sign the peace treaty without a "satisfactory settlement" of their demands.[118] Simultaneously, after taking the lead in pressing China to end her civil war, the Hara government pushed to exempt Manchuria from the scope of a new four-power consortium proposed by the United States to channel loans to Beijing.[119] Proving no friend of the voices of "liberation" in China, the cabinet decided in early September to resume aid to the Xu regime regardless of the participation of the consortium.[120]

The signing of the Versailles Treaty on June 28 marked formal international recognition of everything that the Japanese had fought for in Shandong and the German South Pacific islands during the First World War. As the most ardent proponents of Japanese rights in these areas, Japan's military-bureaucratic elite had much to celebrate. But the mood of Japan's most powerful bureaucrats and the Imperial Army in the summer of 1919 remained decidedly defensive. Materially, the Japanese empire had benefited. But ideologically, the very foundation of that empire as this elite had built and sustained it was crumbling.

House of Peers member Den Kenjirō predicted a "monopoly of Britain and the United States" arising from the establishment of a League of Nations. He also feared an "overturning of social institutions" with the spread of "Western democratic thought" in the postwar world. "Will we be able, by ourselves," he queried in June, "to prevent this and preserve our State and social institutions?"[121] Lieutenant General Utsunomiya Tarō noted that the empire had become "an object of the world's jealous gaze." Because Japan was "besieged" by Britain, the United States, China, Korea, and the Bolsheviks, she had to be well prepared for a crisis. But the enthusiasm of the general public was "exceedingly low." Even the highest authorities viewed the present situation "as if viewing a fire on the opposite shore."[122]

Tanaka Giichi could see the fire at close range. It was clear, he warned in mid-June, that Britain and the United States were poised to expand in China after the war. But from the perspective of geography and the principle of "same culture–same race" (dōbun-dōshu), and from considerations of politics, economy, and national defense, Japan had long enjoyed more intimate relations with China than had the distant West. And there was a difference in the effect of "radical thought" (kageki shisō) in the West and in Japan. While it was of little concern in the West, the dissemination of subversive political ideas promised to have severe repercussions in Tokyo. In one of his most explicit proclamations to date of Japanese autonomy in China, Tanaka declared that, "without merely stressing cooperation with Britain and America, it is natural that the empire gauge international relations in China through an independent policy based upon Sino-Japanese cooperation. The Empire has reached a point where it must act resolutely to carry out its own policies regardless of the reaction of the powers."[123]

Yamagata sounded the loudest alarm of all. In a conversation with Den Kenjirō at the same time as Tanaka's memorandum, the field marshal spoke excitedly about British designs in Western China and U.S. aims in Manchuria. Pressured on both sides by these two great powers, China, he warned, would succumb to the same tragic fate as Turkey. It would be overcome by political turmoil and forced into the same situation as Russia by the pronouncements of Russian radicals. That would be a tragic event for East Asia. The responsibility for saving China rested exclusively with the empire, and Japan should be prepared, Yamagata urged, for international isolation in pursuit of this goal. It was of "deep concern for the State," he added, that in his conversation with Foreign Minister Uchida, the minister seemed to have no plan to deal with the situation.[124]

With the arrival of peace, in other words, Yamagata and deputy Tanaka longed for the readiness of war. Yoshino Sakuzō, for one, read through the martial bluster of these men. "Recently," he observed in a July Chūō kōron editorial, "I hear that among academics, soldiers, and journalists there are those who frequently talk of urging Foreign Ministry officials to take militant measures in Japan's relations toward China." What this crowd proposed, Yoshino offered, was to deepen the "spirit of war" among the people in order to quell the rising sentiment for armament reductions. They aimed to increase the "anti-American fever" to pressure those whom they perceived to be pro-American—the Japanese democrats (minponshugisha). And they would skillfully exploit the idea of punishing anti-Japanese movements in China to build public sentiment for the Chinese government's forceful repression of these movements.[125]

The reaction of men such as Yamagata to the wave of domestic and international changes spurred by the Versailles Conference, Yoshino was saying, was to fight desperately, using a weapon well tested in 1894 and 1905, to preserve a particular conception of the state. These men sought war to preserve a nation devoted to armed might, suppression of political dissent at home, and the subjugation of China. Yoshino, however, believed in the ultimate victory of an entirely different national trajectory. "The trend of the world," he loudly proclaimed on the first day of the peace conference, "is, in domestic policy, the perfection of democracy. In foreign policy, it is the establishment of international egalitarianism."[126]

SYNOPSIS

While the Allies in November 1918 greeted the end of war with Germany with great fanfare, the mood in Tokyo remained decidedly reserved. The cessation of hostilities for the Japanese, after all, meant not a reprieve from bloodshed but the end of an opportunity. Japanese policymakers and opinion leaders alike worried about the future expansion of the empire now that their free hand in Asia had come to an end.

Japanese delegates embarked for Paris, then, prepared to do battle for their wartime gains in Shandong and German Micronesia. Secondarily, they endeavored to include in the Covenant of the new League of Nations a racial nondiscrimination clause. But the principal challenge of Versailles for Japanese policymakers lay not in the quest for territory or racial equality. It rested in the altogether new definition of domestic and foreign affairs pronounced by American president Woodrow Wilson upon the U.S. entrance into the war. By denouncing German militarism and imperialism, Wilson condemned modern Japan's preferred path to national development and reinvigorated the debate over national identity that had complicated the politics of modern Japan since its founding. In the place of arms, the American president counseled arms reductions. Instead of "autocratic" government, he proposed "democracy." And in the place of empire, he advised economic, rather than territorial, expansion and a peaceful international association of states instead of a balance of power.

In the history of modern Japan, the year 1919 is celebrated not as the year of Versailles but as the first year of Japan's first true party government. Indeed, Hara Takashi and his Seiyūkai deserve credit for extending the reach of the political parties throughout all principal political and administrative institutions of Imperial Japan. And Hara's relationship with Yamagata faction henchman War Minister Tanaka Giichi reveals the moderating influence of the Hara regime even upon the most aggressive proponents of Japanese national rights and clandestine military-bureaucratic scheming at home. But the principal gains of representative government in Japan came not because of the efforts of Hara but due to the economic and political effects of the Great War. Economic growth spurred privatization at the expense of state enterprises. And Woodrow Wilson's call for democracy and internationalism added vigor to the voices of longtime critics of oligarchic rule. Hara, by contrast, attained power through an alliance with the mightiest force for political conservatism in Imperial Japan, Field Marshal Yamagata. And like Yamagata, the new prime minister devoted his efforts in the latter half of 1918 to moderating the domestic and international effects of the Great War on Japan.

Hara's preparations for the peace conference, then, were defensive. Guidelines for Japan's delegates instructed them to press vigorously for great power recognition of Japan's wartime gains. But regarding the centerpiece of Wilson's "new diplomacy," the League of Nations, the cabinet ordered Japan's plenipotentiaries to postpone an agreement as long as possible. Hara chose Japan's delegates to Paris in anticipation not of diplomatic success but political crisis. The prime minister himself would remain at home to moderate the impact of an undesirable peace.

The great powers would ultimately confirm at Versailles all of Japan's wartime gains. But neither Hara nor the most powerful members of Japan's military-bureaucratic elite found great cause for celebration. For while Wilson relented at Paris to Japanese possession of German territories in Asia and the Pacific, his proclamations resonated in Tokyo and elsewhere in Asia with the appeals of the government's greatest political adversaries. Thus, on the eve of the Forty-First Diet, Kenseikai party leaders reminded their constituents that the real essence of the "new thought" was democracy at home and a greater attention to world peace over national rights abroad. In March 1919, 50,000 students, merchants, and factory and clerical workers rallied in Hibiya park for universal manhood suffrage. In August, the single union Yūaikai became a national federation of unions and called for a "struggle of martyrs" for international labor rights. In the Japanese empire, the March First Movement brought 40,000 demonstrators to Korean streets in a loud call for self-determination. In China, the May Fourth Movement roused the nation in a wave of protests, strikes, and anti-Japanese boycotts that marked a critical step in the advance of Chinese nationalism.

Hara reacted to these events by ordering the Home Ministry to launch an intensified campaign of thought control; by appointing a representative of management to head Japan's delegation to the International Labor Conference; by establishing a new program to "assimilate" Korea with Japan; and by advocating unilateral Japanese assistance to Beijing. The prime minister's military and bureaucratic allies, likewise, reacted with a renewed sense of urgency regarding the need to preserve an empire devoted to armed strength, authoritarian rule, and territorial expansion. For the immediate term, Yoshino Sakuzō's vision of democracy at home and international egalitarianism abroad carried the moment. But the Seiyūkai would accelerate its battle against reform as its chief political party rival, the Kenseikai, would increasingly embrace the new political and diplomatic trends in the 1920s. And Imperial Japan's soldiers and bureaucrats would persist in their opposition to the new Wilsonian world order.

Fig. 19   Goddess of Peace

7 Conclusion

The present great disturbance in Europe is the divine aid of the new Taishō era for the development of the destiny of Japan.

—Marquis Inoue Kaoru, August 1914

The Manchurian Incident was a Heaven-sent tocsin signaling at home and abroad the epoch-making dawn of East Asia.

—War Minister Tōjō Hideki, September 1941

For all the continuing general interest in Japan in the United States, we are far from creating a serviceable image of Japanese leadership in the twentieth century. Remarkably, little has changed since Ruth Benedict originally spoke of a duality in the Japanese character. Just as Benedict discovered in 1946 a polite but overbearing, rigid yet adaptive, loyal but treacherous, aggressive and unaggressive people, caught between the contradictory poles of a chrysanthemum and a sword,[1] a broad cross section of current literature offers a vision of Japan striking in its contrasts. On the one hand, general studies of Japanese diplomacy and specific accounts of such tragedies as Hiroshima portray a land and people vulnerable to a steady stream of injustices in the twentieth century. On the other hand, mainstream Japanese texts on modern Japanese history and best-selling literature in the United States on Japan, especially on Japan's participation in the Second World War, unveil a record of unbridled aggression and heinous crimes, equal in magnitude to those of the undisputed champion of evil in the twentieth century, Nazi Germany.[2]

Each of these visions, of course, has some basis in fact. In no other country, perhaps, is there a juxtaposition of historical events as dramatic in their contrast as the Nanjing massacre and Hiroshima. Yet the problem of oversimplification remains acute, to the extent that we have a substantial body of literature devoted to exposing the long history of problematic Western images of Japan.[3] Much of this literature attributes the prevalence of stock racial and cultural formulas to a latent Western racism.[4] But perhaps more relevant in the study of Japanese politics and diplomacy is the difficulty of pinpointing the great decisions and decision makers in Japanese history. If the mid-1990s economic crisis highlighted the serious lack of transparency in the Japanese economy, it apprised outside observers of a similar challenge in identifying the critical struggles for power in Japanese domestic politics.

The lack of political transparency has led many to downplay the role of conflict in Japanese society and to assume an unusual unanimity in Japanese foreign-policy decision making. As A. Whitney Griswold declared in 1938, "Probably no people in the world were more thoroughly united on foreign policy than the intensely nationalistic, emperor-worshiping Japanese."[5] One may excuse Griswold for finding consensus at a time when Japan's appetite for conquered territory in China seemed insatiable. But as assuredly as war spawned the vision of a Japanese foreign policy juggernaut in the 1930s, bilateral economic tensions in the early 1990s had a similar effect. Another prominent American diplomatic historian in 1997 condensed U.S.-Japanese relations over the past 136 years to a "clash of two capitalisms" and Japanese foreign policy to a familiar refrain. "The Japanese," he argued, "were determined to break free of Western constraints and exert maximum control over their foreign relations."[6]

Recognizing, of course, the utility of locating general patterns in Japanese foreign policy over time, these works, nonetheless, demonstrate the critical need for renewed scholarly attention to the policymaking process in modern Japan. As John Dower has observed, such attention has been woefully lacking in recent analyses by Japan scholars.[7] Not only do researchers confront a lack of transparency, they must contend with a peculiar complexity in Japanese politics. Given the crash program of modernization and a lack of foresight by her creators, modern Japan has been plagued from the outset by serious political instability. Contrary to the vision of a consensus society and unified foreign policy, in other words, much of what has driven Japanese foreign policy in the modern era has been serious domestic political conflict. Students interested in locating critical changes and continuities in modern Japanese history, then, must first do the painstaking work of clarifying the continually shifting source of political power in Japanese society.

RESTORING AGENCY TO JAPANESE LEADERSHIP

This study has analyzed the principal Japanese wages of power for the pivotal period of the First World War. In so doing, it has attempted to place Japan's foreign-policy decision makers within a broad context, to recognize that domestic determinants of diplomatic decision making may equal, even outweigh, external stimuli. To shift the principal impetus of foreign-policy decision making from the distant external to the more immediate internal world is to restore a sense of agency to Japanese leaders engaged in the nation's foreign affairs. No longer may we be satisfied with the image of hapless Japanese elites captive to the inexorable flow of international events. We must view them as men who spied opportunities and actively sought to manipulate events abroad just as they ordered their world at home.[8]

In restoring agency to Japan's foreign policy actors, this study resembles similar recent attempts by historians to locate active human agency in the construction of national culture. Like foreign policy, culture has long been viewed less as a variable than a given. If historians have considered diplomacy primarily the product of external circumstances, they have regarded culture as principally the legacy of deep historical and geographic roots. Since the 1980s, however, Eric Hobsbawm, Benedict Anderson, and others have exposed the "invented" and "imagined" character of cultural "traditions."[9] Such inventions are, in fact, now understood to be an integral component of the modernizing process. In particular, as Hobsbawm has noted, the radical social, political, and economic changes between the late nineteenth and early twentieth centuries compelled even well-established nation-states to seek new forms of political legitimization.[10]

This study has stressed the centrality of this quest for political legitimization in Japan during the same period. Imperial Japan, after all, had only just embarked upon the enterprise of national unification in 1868. Japanese leaders were consumed in the first half of Japan's modern century with the task of nation-building. All policies, whether foreign or domestic, emanated from this fundamental concern. While recent studies of nationalism highlight the domestic component of nation-building efforts—the creation of social, cultural, and political "traditions"—few consider foreign policy as similarly dependent on the fundamental enterprise of national self-definition.[11] Nor have the effects of war on the universal enterprise of national reinvention been explored in depth. But the foreign policy choices of modern Japan's founders, like their political choice for constitutional monarchy, were a critical means by which these men sought to define their fledgling nation. And the dramatic changes in foreign affairs that Japanese leaders envisioned in 1918 were the direct result of the wartime transformation of the desired conception of the national essence.

THE POLITICS OF NATIONAL REINVENTION

Like the original "restoration" of imperial rule in 1868, the death of the Meiji emperor and advent of the Taishō era in July 1912 marked a time of deep soul-searching for Imperial Japan. During the reign of the Meiji monarch, modern Japan's founders had painstakingly forged a modern nation-state out of a disparate coalition of over 270 feudal domains. Allowed by the great powers the freedom to fashion both their own foreign and domestic policies, these men consciously chose to create a nation-state on the model of the fastest rising power in Europe, Imperial Germany. Like Germany, they hoped, Imperial Japan would become a great continental power supported by a large army and governed by a powerful central authority in the Japanese emperor and themselves as his immediate advisers.

To the distress of her architects, however, Imperial Japan did not evolve entirely as planned. Yoshino Sakuzō would observe in 1916, in fact, that the Japanese nation had developed along lines "completely counter" to the pains and wishes of the elder statesmen.[12] Although victorious wars against China and Russia had forged and legitimized a continental empire, large armaments, and the political authority of Japan's oligarchs, peace checked the enthusiasm for arms and oligarchic rule and raised the fortunes of a powerful new political force, the political parties. The death of the Meiji emperor exposed the basic tension of the Meiji years in full relief. Would Imperial Japan continue on the path of empire, arms, and oligarchic rule? Or would "democratic reform," in the words of journalist Ishibashi Tanzan, increasingly define the character of the modern Japanese state? Forty-five years after the fall of the feudal regime, the question of Japan's future national trajectory remained the subject of fierce debate.

It was amid this tumultuous debate in Tokyo over the national essence that war broke out in Europe in August 1914. Japanese policymakers and opinion leaders fashioned their responses to the war, then, with the principal aim of positioning themselves within this most fundamental domestic contest over the national trajectory. For Japan, in other words, the Great War was not so much an objective circumstance demanding an immediate strategic response. It was, rather, a golden opportunity, an empty canvas on which Japan's policymakers freely created their most cherished dreams for a new Japan. It was, in the words of elder statesman Inoue Kaoru, "divine aid." The variety of Japanese dreams for the future ensured a scramble for position the likes of which had not been seen since the Taishō political crisis. And the scale of some of these dreams hinted at a much more active future of expansion abroad and authoritarian politics at home.

This study distills the variety of dreams of state to the two principal sources of political conflict in wartime Japan, Foreign Minister Katō Takaaki and members of the military-bureaucratic Yamagata faction. In recent years, Japanese and Western scholars alike have admirably supplanted the "binarism" that long characterized our understanding of Japanese society—tradition/modernity, liberalism/militarism, state/society—with a picture of great complexity in Japanese life. We have learned valuable lessons about the "modern" creation of symbolism surrounding the "traditional" emperor, about the wide range of continental policies within the Japanese army, and about the convergence of public and private interests on issues of social reform in interwar Japan.[13]

The current vogue among Japan specialists for locating complexity, however, obscures what may be considered the central theme of modern

Japanese life. Tales of conflict among actors customarily considered allies identify a critical component of Japanese politics: turbulent conflict. They are less effective, however, in explaining the general logic of those politics, that is, in locating the essential source of political conflict. Recent studies of the modern uses of tradition and the convergence of bureaucratic and popular aims in interwar Japan, on the other hand, clearly identify a principal focus for the energies of Japan's varied political actors: the construction of a modern identity. They are equally ineffective, however, in delineating the fundamental lines of political conflict in modern Japan.

This study has attempted both to highlight the complexity of Japanese politics and to locate the basic lines of political conflict. It *is* relevant, as others have shown, that both Field Marshal Yamagata and Korea Governor-General Terauchi objected to fellow Yamagata faction member Tanaka Giichi's scheme to depose Chinese president Yuan Shikai in 1916. Historians *should*, as they have, record the Yamagata faction's ultimate disappointment with their own candidate for prime minister, Terauchi. This study offers ample new evidence of complexity in Taishō era politics: for example, War Minister Oka Ichinosuke's alliance with Foreign Minister Katō against his erstwhile supporters in the Yamagata faction and Imperial Army (Chapter 3); Foreign Minister Ishii's initial hesitation on a Russo-Japanese alliance but ultimate concurrence with Yamagata on the proposed terms of the agreement (Chapter 4); Prime Minister Terauchi's use of the Nishihara loans against fellow Chōshū general Tanaka Giichi (Chapter 5); and the transformation, on the one hand, of Lieutenant General Tanaka Giichi from the principal "champion of active expansionism" to an upstanding member of a civilian cabinet, and, on the other, of Hara Takashi from the chief proponent of party politics to one of the most conservative opponents of rapid political change (Chapter 6).

To recognize an enormous political complexity, however, should not keep us from pinpointing the most fundamental source of conflict in Imperial Japan. Although tensions frequently flared among members of the same political factions and the lines of conflict and compromise were never stationary, historians can and should identify the most fundamental source of tension and choose, as contemporaries readily chose (note the endpapers in this volume), a clearly definable roster of heroes and villains.

*Fig. 20
Decline of the
military clique
in Germany*

THE GREAT WAR IN THE CONTEXT OF NATIONAL REINVENTION

This study agrees with the most recent variant of "modernization" theory on Japan in recognizing the quest for a modern identity as a principal concern of Imperial Japanese statesmen and subjects alike.[14] But to identify a common search for progress among a wide range of Japanese actors is to accomplish only half of the task. One should be able to locate in the myriad of "competing modernities," as they have been described, the most fundamental source of political tension in modern Japan. This study, then, extracts from a wide range of hopes for the future of Japanese politics and foreign policy the two visions of the national essence (and their chief proponents) that became the principal focus of political tension from 1914 to 1919. On the one hand were dreams of free trade imperialism and parliamentary politics on the British model pursued by Foreign Minister Katō Takaaki in the first year of the war. On the other hand were hopes for continued exaltation, following the Meiji Renovation, of Imperial Germany—the pursuit of continental empire supported by large ground forces, and oligarchic rule at home—cherished by Katō's principal political rivals in the military-bureaucratic Yamagata faction.

Katō Takaaki has never received the scholarly attention that his principal political party rival, president of the Seiyūkai Hara Takashi, has enjoyed. For his success in expanding the power of the Seiyūkai throughout the Japanese countryside, the national bureaucracy, the Upper House, even to Japanese colonial administration, Hara rightly deserves his reputation as a pioneer of party politics in Japan. But Katō's political accomplishments during the Great War, added to his more widely publicized contributions to party rule during his subsequent tenure as prime minister in the mid-1920s, should confirm his place as Hara's equal in the fight for representative government in Japan.

Those achievements have been overshadowed by the foreign minister's association with the notorious Twenty-One Demands. Of all the diplomatic initiatives pursued by Japan during the Great War, the "demands" leap out of the historiography as a precursor to the unbridled aggression that was to bring Japan to blows against China and the United States two decades later. But Katō's terms for negotiation with the Chinese in 1915 are a harbinger of the unfettered imperialism of the 1930s only if one neglects the larger context of foreign-policy decision making during the Great War. The Twenty-One Demands were, after all, the quintessential expression of Katō's conception of the national essence. And that conception was as conservative diplomatically as it was progressive politically. Katō identified as much with the age of imperialism as he did with British parliamentarism. In negotiating the demands, the foreign minister championed both imperialist expansion as widely accepted by the great powers in the late nineteenth century and cabinet and Foreign Ministry supremacy in the making of Japanese diplomacy. Appropriately identified as Imperial Japan's most devout Anglophile, Katō hoped to fashion Japan into the Britain of East Asia—the champion of free trade imperialism in China and parliamentary politics at home.

If the essence of Katō's foreign and domestic policies was his identification with British free trade imperialism and parliamentary politics, his principal rivals in the Yamagata faction worshipped a starkly distinct conception of the national essence. Like the original architects of the Meiji state, these men looked chiefly to Imperial Germany for inspiration. As a central figure in the nation-building enterprise, after all, Yamagata had actively promoted the adoption of German models for both Japan's system of local government and the Imperial Japanese Army in the 1880s. Given the freedom to pursue their ideal foreign and domestic policies after the departure of Katō in August 1915, these men, in fact, took their conception of empire, arms, and oligarchic rule to new heights.

Displeased with the limits imposed on Japanese expansion by the accepted rules of international engagement in China since the 1890s, they sought nothing less than complete regional hegemony. At home, they aimed for unprecedented military-bureaucratic management of the nation's most fundamental domestic and foreign policies.

If the Great War magnified the tumultuous domestic battle between two incompatible visions of the national essence, it concluded with the arrival of a third, entirely novel, conception of the state. If the first year of the war belonged to Katō's vision of a Britain of East Asia, and the second through fourth years to Yamagata's exaltation of continental expansion on the model of Imperial Germany, then the peace went to the dramatic new concept of national power emanating from the United States. Woodrow Wilson's notion of democracy at home and peaceful economic intercourse abroad confounded all earlier projections of the future of Japanese power. In so doing, it brought even greater tumult to a fractious Japanese national polity. All subsequent formulations of domestic and foreign policies in Imperial Japan had to engage this most revolutionary definition of the state.

THE MANCHURIAN INCIDENT IN THE CONTEXT OF NATIONAL REINVENTION

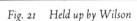

Fig. 21   Held up by Wilson

While highlighting Japanese diplomacy as a function of the larger campaign for national self-definition, then, a study of the turbulent battle for the national essence during the Great War offers telling clues of subsequent events. As the pivotal event in the history of the twentieth century, the Second World War, unlike the Great War, has attracted substantial scholarly attention among specialists of modern Japan. The general outline of Japanese aggression from the Manchurian Incident to 1945 is clear, and there is ample speculation as to its causes.

Recent diplomatic histories describe Japan's road to war in the 1930s chiefly as a response to dramatic external events. Echoing Ruth Benedict's classic formulation, an influential three-volume series on Japanese imperialism characterizes the evolution of Japanese empire-building from the nineteenth century to 1945 as "situational in origin."[15] Just as Benedict argued that Japan would remain peaceful in a peaceful world but resort to arms within a world organized into an armed camp,[16] this series, and others, strongly suggest that policymakers in Imperial Japan had, given the objective circumstances, little alternative but to resort to aggression in the 1930s. Those circumstances included the rise of Chinese nationalism, the international economic crisis, unfavorable U.S. trade and immigration policies, the threat of Soviet power, and the challenge of "total war." Among adverse internal developments, historians frequently stress rising Japanese unemployment and rural poverty and a generational change within the Japanese leadership.

Each of these factors undoubtedly played a role in the dramatic developments of the 1930s. But they should not be considered more than immediate catalysts to renewed aggression. For they transpired after the Great War, when, as we have seen, a particular segment of Japan's ruling elite had already pursued aims similar to the ones that would lead their successors into a war against China and the United States. Long before Chinese nationalism justified Japanese military expeditions to China, for example, Vice Chief of the Army General Staff Tanaka Giichi in 1916 envisioned a dispatch of imperial troops to spark civil war on the continent. Long before American trade policy, the international economic crisis, or the challenges of "total war" sanctioned the creation of an autonomous Asian economic bloc, Home Minister Gotō Shinpei pressed in 1916 for a Sino-Japanese economic alliance in opposition to American financial power. Long before the defeat of Japan's racial nondiscrimination clause at the Versailles Conference or passage of the 1924 U.S. Immigration Act, elder statesman Inoue Kaoru called in 1914 for Japanese solidarity with China in anticipation of a future "white alliance" against Japan. Long before the Soviet Union posed a threat to Japanese interests in South Manchuria, Field Marshal Yamagata Aritomo in 1916 pressed for Japanese expansion in North Manchuria and Japanese responsibility for "guarantee[ing] peace" in all of Siberia. And long before Washington slapped Japan with a de facto oil embargo in July 1941, Major General

Tanaka Giichi in 1914 urged a preemptive military strike against an increasingly powerful United States.

Before viewing the road to war in the 1930s as principally the product of challenges faced by Japan in the interwar period, then, one must probe the source of similar aims during the First World War, long before the presumed difficulties materialized. A wide gulf, of course, separates the seemingly analogous aims of the 1930s from those of the Great War. Many objects in the 1914 to 1919 years remained no more than aspirations and fell well short of the official policy that they were to become in the 1930s. But they should not be dismissed as the wild fantasies of a lunatic fringe that loosely resemble subsequent policies. On the contrary, these were the serious aspirations of some of Japan's most powerful and respected men during the Great War, many of whom appear in other contexts as representatives of a cautious older generation. And these aspirations reveal a pattern of domestic- and foreign-policy decision making that was to characterize Japan's bid for a New Order in Asia in the 1930s.

That pattern, as we have seen, derived from a particular conception of the state, one that originated in the nineteenth century as a quest for empire, arms, and oligarchic rule. In the twentieth century, both aspirations for great national and domestic political power expanded with each military victory abroad and political setback at home. By the outbreak of war in 1914, then, influential members of the military-bureaucratic elite desired complete Japanese hegemony in Asia and absolute control over the recalcitrant forces of the Imperial Diet, political parties, and the growing trend toward economic privatization at home. Just as the second Konoe cabinet sought in the summer of 1940 to construct a hierarchical Greater East Asia Co-prosperity Sphere centered around the Japanese throne, the governor-general of Korea, General Terauchi Masatake, appealed in August 1914 for an Asia "under the control of our emperor." And just as the same Konoe cabinet in October 1940 created the Imperial Rule Assistance Association to focus the energies of Japan's disparate political forces on the national goals of "assisting imperial rule" and constructing a national defense state, elder statesman Inoue Kaoru hoped that renewed national attention to war in 1914 would "completely eliminate party debate."

The quest for complete Japanese hegemony in Asia, we have seen, was grounded in a racial conception of international affairs distinguished by its tenacity. If Katō Takaaki sought to use all the diplomatic tools at his disposal to expand Japanese interests in China, he did so with the understanding that Japan was one among many powers maneuvering for position on the continent. Katō was an imperialist, not a pan-Asianist. His principal identification was not with China as a fellow Asian power but with the great Western imperialists, who viewed China as no more nor less than a vital stage upon which to flex their national muscle.

For Katō's greatest political rivals in the Yamagata faction, on the other hand, China assumed an almost religious significance. As the former center of East Asian civilization and fellow object of Western imperialism, China for these men served a critical function in their growing aspirations for a distinct modern identity. Troubled by the apparent limitations of associating with the imperialist West, they created a vision of cultural distinctiveness that, by definition, precluded genuine Japanese cooperation with the West and, at the same time, rendered "intimate" Sino-Japanese cooperation an absolute necessity, even a national security requirement. Recent studies of the pan-Asianist element of the Greater East Asia Co-prosperity Sphere describe such sentiment as mere "rhetoric" to "legitimize the establishment of domination."[17] But such characterizations not only overlook the long history of Japanese pan-Asianism before actual "domination" of China in the 1930s, they minimize the conviction held by its principal adherents. Indeed, the Hirota cabinet elevated pan-Asianism to official policy in August 1936 when the Fundamentals of National Policy called for "intimate cooperation" (kinmitsu naru teikei) between Japan, China, and Manchukuo to eliminate the "military rule" of the great powers in Asia. Similarly, an "inseparable spirit" (kyōdō itchi no seishin) between Japan and China to prepare for an inevitable future "race war" against the West was central to Field Marshal Yamagata's worldview during the Great War.

If the quest by Yamagata and his associates for complete Japanese hegemony in Asia derived in part from their conviction in Sino-Japanese "inseparability," it spurred creative solutions for alliances with Western powers. Recent studies of Japanese imperialism have suggested that "caution and conformity" characterized Japanese dealings with the West until rising unemployment and rural poverty in the 1930s introduced "a note of stridency" into Japanese politics and diplomacy.[18] But at least one segment of Japan's ruling elite had abandoned diplomatic caution, particularly vis-à-vis Britain and the United States, soon after the Russo-Japanese War. Confrontation between Japan and the Anglo-American powers had, in fact, become a basic tenet of the worldview of members of the Yamagata faction. For as long as these men sought complete regional hegemony, they knew that they would have to engage these, the two most powerful outside players in Asia.

Regardless of continual lip service to and, indeed, the persistent actual utility of the Anglo-Japanese alliance, then, Yamagata and his associates after the Russo-Japanese War pursued international agreements designed to aid Japan in the inevitable confrontation with London and Washington. To check British power in China, some members of the faction in the early 1910s contemplated an alliance with Germany. And to guard against increasing American inroads in Manchuria, Yamagata himself vigorously promoted a series of conventions with Imperial Russia. The irony is that the elder statesman's successors in the 1930s would not learn from the failures of these early attempts to confront, rather than cooperate with, the greatest outside powers in the region. By 1918, both nations to which the Japanese had turned to check Anglo-American power had disintegrated, the most conspicuous casualties of the Great War. And yet for the same goal of complete Japanese regional hegemony, Foreign Minister Matsuoka Yōsuke was in September 1940 to repeat the same mistake. He would abandon a relationship with obvious material benefits—with Japan's largest trading partner, the United States—to ally with a power with little capacity to influence events in Asia, Germany. This time, not only did the strategy of confrontation not bring Japan any gains, it worked positively to Japan's detriment. Rather than dissuade the United States from meddling in Asia, as Matsuoka had apparently intended, Japan's identification with Nazi Germany impressed on the Americans, for the first time, the seriousness of the Japanese challenge to the world order.

If the general pattern of domestic- and foreign-policy decision making in 1930s Japan was already visible among a particular segment of Japanese elites during the Great War, the motives of those earlier elites should shed light on the causes of subsequent events. This study has portrayed those motives as a product of the nation-building efforts that had consumed Japanese policymakers since the toppling of the feudal regime in 1868. Given the continuing fluidity of domestic politics in Taishō Japan, Japan's most prominent decision makers looked to the Great War as an opportunity to promote their particular conceptions of the state. For Japan, the war was more of a domestic political struggle over national identity than it was a strategic battle against a foreign enemy.

Others have suggested that later Japanese aims were, likewise, more invention than response to objective circumstances. Peter Duus has perceptively noted that Japan's ballooning expansionist goals in the 1930s were "based less on an evaluation of what Japan was capable of doing than on what particular elements in the army, navy and bureaucracy wished to do."[19] The observation, however, is confined to developments after 1936. Few currently active specialists of Japanese diplomatic affairs, Japanese or otherwise, accept the argument of Japanese Marxists, or American specialists writing several decades ago, that Japanese elites actively solicited war in 1931 as a creative opportunity.[20]

Although developments in the 1930s are beyond the focus of this study, there is ample evidence to suggest that in making their most fundamental foreign policy choices, Japanese leaders in the 1930s were as concerned with the fate of the national essence as their predecessors had been during the First World War. Contrary to widespread expectations in August 1914, after all, the Great War did not settle the question of national identity that the Meiji Renovation had initially posed. Rather, it seriously complicated it by widening the gulf between the two principal opposing forces in the debate. At the very least, both Japanese admirers of Great Britain and their chief rivals, men inspired by the example of Imperial Germany, agreed on one thing in 1914: the importance of Japanese imperialist expansion on the continent. But Woodrow Wilson raised fundamental questions about even this, the preeminent pillar of the Meiji state, by condemning territorial expansion and the balance of power as characteristic of the "old diplomacy" and proclaiming, in its stead, a new world of peaceful economic competition and international cooperation in the body of a League of Nations. If Japan's most bitter political enemies had, before 1914, been divided principally over the question of who had the right to rule in Japan—extra-cabinet military-bureaucratic elites or political party leaders in a civilian cabinet—after

1919, they stood across a much wider chasm dividing proponents of militarism and imperialism from champions of democracy and internationalism.

The 1920s would confirm the political supremacy of proponents of a new Wilsonian order in Japan. Japanese troops withdrew from Siberia and Shandong in 1922, civilian governments slashed the Imperial Army by four divisions by 1925 and pared the navy according to international standards agreed to at the Washington (1922) and London (1930) Naval Conferences, the Imperial Diet passed universal manhood suffrage in 1925, a succession of party cabinets seized political power from 1924 to 1932, and the Kenseikai and Minseitō cabinets pursued cooperative diplomacy with the powers in China. But the victory of democracy and internationalism did not destroy the champions of empire, arms, and authoritarian rule. On the contrary, members of the original ruling elite remained in positions of power and resisted every movement away from the earlier orthodoxy. Thus the Privy Council only reluctantly acquiesced to universal manhood suffrage to prevent the spread of "dangerous thought," the army debunked party politicians as "degenerate," members of the Privy Council and House of Peers decried the principle of nonintervention and cooperation in China as "weak and soft," and the Seiyūkai and the Navy General Staff damned the London Naval Treaty of 1930 as a "violation of supreme command." The tumultuous battle over the national essence that had marked the 1914 to 1919 years, in other words, continued, in fact, intensified throughout the 1920s. And like members of the Yamagata faction during the Great War, guardians of the old order looked for any opportunity to redirect the nation back to what they perceived to be the golden age of Japanese militarism and imperialism.

It is this larger context of the turbulent domestic political battle over the national essence within which the Manchurian Incident most belongs. External developments such as the rise of Chinese nationalism undoubtedly played a role in Japan's renewed expansionist drive on the continent. But that role was most likely the converse to what is typically assumed. As we have seen, Vice Chief of the Army General Staff Tanaka Giichi welcomed the prospect of political instability in China in 1916 as an opportunity to expand Japanese influence on the continent. Likewise, many in the Imperial Army in the latter 1920s viewed the rise of Chinese nationalism less as a threat than as a useful pretext for renewed activity in Manchuria.[21] Indeed, just as Tanaka in 1916 relished the opportunity of "shaping the situation ourselves" in China, War Minister Ugaki Kazushige noted on the eve of the Manchurian Incident that "in pondering the future of the empire, we should not await the arrival of an opportunity. We must create the opportunity."[22]

Ugaki was not specifically referring to Japan's China policy here. Rather, he was speaking of what was, in actuality, the most pressing issue of the day: the rise of party politics in Imperial Japan. Like members of the military-bureaucratic elite during the Great War and throughout the 1920s, Ugaki decried the worst manifestations of party rule—"corrupt elections, the frivolous appearance of the Diet"—and called for a Shōwa Renovation (Shōwa ishin) to restore a sense of "tension" and purpose to an increasingly fractious public discourse.[23] Analyses of interwar Japan have generally taken criticism of the "degeneracy" of political parties and the "decadence" of economic growth as true reflections of the unstable state of politics and economy in Taishō Japan. But, like similar criticisms leveled during the First World War, they reflect less instability of the polity than anxiety over change by some members of the established elite. John Dewey discovered the depth of that anxiety soon after the end of the Great War. On a tour of Japan in 1919, the American educator observed that the war had "dealt the militaristic and bureaucratic party in Japan the greatest blow it has ever had." To avoid a descent into political oblivion, he predicted, this group "must take steps to recover some of its lost prestige."[24]

Indeed, the problem for Ugaki and other members of the military-bureaucratic elite in the 1920s was not the weakness and degeneracy of party politics—it was their strength. The retrenchment of Japanese power from the continent and paring of the army and navy at home were, after all, the handiwork of Japan's rising political parties. In particular, it was the political party of the man who had done the most for political plurality during the First World War, Katō Takaaki, that led the charge for political reform in the 1920s. In its promotion of universal manhood suffrage, arms reductions, peaceful economic intercourse with China, and the rights of hitherto disenfranchised political forces such as urban labor and rural tenants, the Kenseikai (after 1927, the Minseitō) offered an entirely novel national identity for Imperial Japan. In so doing, like Katō in the first year of the Great War, it utterly eclipsed the guardians of a militarist, imperialist national polity, and even its principal political party rival, the Seiyūkai.[25]

Like many of his military-bureaucratic predecessors and contemporaries, Ugaki was consumed by this most formidable challenge to the traditional ruling prerogatives of the civilian and military bureaucracies. "The government," he insisted in August 1930, "is neither the possession of the Seyūkai nor the Minseitō but of the Japanese empire."[26] A group of field grade officers from the Army General Staff was even more explicit. Just days after a Privy Council deliberative committee approved the London Naval Treaty in September 1930, these men condemned the latest political party assault on military prerogatives and offered a dramatic solution. "The poisonous sword of the thoroughly degenerate party politicians is being pointed at the military," they declared. "It is obvious that the party politicians' sword, which was used against the navy, will soon be used to reduce the size of the army. Hence, we who constitute the mainstay of the army must . . . arouse ourselves and wash out the bowels of the completely decadent politicians."[27] Ugaki would subtly encourage these men, members of the Sakurakai (Cherry Blossom Society), to attempt a military coup in March 1931. But the failed coup was only one component of a larger campaign to "renovate" both Japanese politics and foreign policies. Six months later, the same men would aid the successful takeover of Manchuria by the Guandong Army.

In 1918, Yamagata Aritomo and his associates had looked to the Siberian Intervention as an opportunity to stem the decline of Imperial Army budgets and authority and restore "militarism" to public consciousness. Likewise, the perpetrators of the Manchurian Incident appealed to war in 1931 to check the reformist zeal of the greatest threat to Imperial Army prerogatives since the end of the Great War: the Minseitō. Twelve years after Dewey's visit to Japan, members of the Guandong Army and Army General Staff in Tokyo had fulfilled his prediction. They had acted decisively to recover the prestige lost with the death of their ideal national model, Imperial Germany.

In its proper context, then, the Manchurian Incident appears less an exercise in national defense than of national creation. Like the enemies of the Tokugawa *bakufu*, like the founders of the Meiji state, like the proponents of a military expedition to Siberia, the men who planted explosives on the South Manchuria Railway in 1931 sought principally not national security but national renovation. Aggression abroad became a vital component of reconstructing the nation at home. As Mitani Taichirō has recently pointed out, the Manchurian Incident and creation of an independent "Manchukuo" aimed to contest the dominant national model that had emerged in the aftermath of the Great War. Ishiwara Kanji and his fellow conspirators hoped to replace the internationalist state of the Minseitō with an "ultra-defense state," that would be poised for another great war. Unable due to the strength of the Minseitō vision of the state to carry out the operation from within, these men aimed for internal restructuring from without.[28]

Ishiwara and his associates were, in the immediate term, successful. The Manchurian Incident rekindled wild public enthusiasm for military conquest and effectively destroyed the greatest challenge to military-bureaucratic power since the defeat of German militarism in 1918: Japanese democracy. The selfish political aims of these men and their political and bureaucratic allies would, however, ultimately invite the annihilation of Imperial Japan.

RECONCEPTUALIZING JAPANESE LEADERSHIP IN THE TWENTIETH CENTURY

If the history of the Great War thus bears lessons for Japan's subsequent road to war in the 1930s, it also holds meaning for the more profound issue of Japanese leadership in the twentieth century. If Western scholars have often assumed a unanimity in Japanese foreign-policy decision making, they have also frequently described that process as principally a reaction to Western persecution and prejudice on the international stage. But Japanese imperialism from the latter half of the nineteenth century was driven less by fear of a terrible fate than recognition of unprecedented opportunities. Japanese decision makers suffered less from paranoia than euphoria. At the beginning of each new major foreign policy initiative, they spoke more of great opportunities than dire calamities.

Their attitudes were shaped less by the burden of the Triple Intervention or defeat of the racial nondiscrimination clause at Versailles, than by
the glorious memory of victories in the Sino- and Russo-Japanese Wars.

Contrary to the impression imparted by much of the current diplomatic history literature, in other words, the great tragedy of modern Japan lies not in a record of persistent diplomatic failures. Rather, it may
be found in the story of precocious success. Like most other domestic
and foreign observers, Lafcadio Hearn found a future "big with promise"
in Japan's spectacular victory over China in 1895. "Japan has neither fears
nor doubts," he declared soon after the war. But Hearn anticipated a
problem with such aplomb. "Perhaps the future danger," he continued,
"is just in this immense self-confidence."[29]

Indeed, while many responsible Japanese leaders took the victories of
the Sino- and Russo-Japanese Wars in stride, there was also an influential segment of the population that perceived such accomplishments as a
license to plan ever expanding schemes for Japanese power on the continent. Intoxicated with the national and personal political power spawned
by such unexpected military victories, these men could ultimately accept
nothing less than complete Japanese hegemony in Asia. Increasing fraternity with the West did little to dispel the fundamentally racial conceptions of the world order of these men. Rather, they ordered Japanese
domestic politics and foreign policy in anticipation of an eventual conclu-
sive battle between East and West.

The momentum for continental expansion clearly slowed in Japan in
the 1920s. But memories of great military victories remained. The Great
War may have, as we have seen, raised serious questions about the fate of
the established national trajectory. But there was one critical difference
between Japan's experience and that of the major European belligerents.
Japan fought the First World War, as she had fought her two previous
modern wars, on distant shores. The number of Japanese with firsthand
war experience remained small. In fact, fewer Japanese soldiers saw action in the siege of Qingdao than the number of casualties in the Battle
of Mukden during the Russo-Japanese War alone.

Sojourning in Europe from 1936 to 1938, Japanese historian Oka Yoshitake was struck by the "indescribable face of sorrow" of a gentleman
paying respects to the tomb of the unknown soldier at the Arc de Tri-

omphe in Paris. Almost twenty years had passed since the end of the "war to end all wars." "Does the Great War," Oka observed, "continue, nonetheless, to carve such deep wounds in men's hearts?" He could not help but sense "a world of difference between the feelings of Europeans and Japanese toward the Great War—no, toward war itself."[30]

There was one lesson, then, that the Japanese failed to learn from the First World War: the lesson of war's horrors. Even as Japan embraced peace in the 1920s, in other words, the taste for military might, the excitement for a glorious battle, initially sparked by Japanese victories against China in the 1890s, remained. It was, in fact, actively fostered. Oka found the difference in European and Japanese sensibilities toward war apparent in the contrast between displays at the Imperial War Museum in London and the Yasukuni Shrine in Tokyo. Yasukuni presented visions of "great heroism" and the "pleasure" of victory, with no reference to war's miseries. But the British museum labored to depict the Great War "realistically." Its grounds, furthermore, were blanketed simply with grass and flowers, not with the spoils of war found at Yasukuni.[31]

Indeed, the perpetrators of the Manchurian Incident and their successors in the China Incident, it is most likely, not only had little fear of Chinese nationalism. They had little fear of war itself. And the enthusiastic Japanese crowds that hailed every new account of conquest in China in the 1930s had little feeling for the pain exhibited by the man at the tomb of the unknown soldier in Paris.[32] The men who propelled Japan to war in the 1930s were consumed, in other words, not by fear but by hubris. It is the great tragedy of modern Japan that the ultimate antidote for such hubris would be the calamitous arrival of the horrors of modern war to Japanese shores.

Epilogue

The time has come to retrieve the Japanese sense of identity once more.
—Tawara Sōichirō, September 1998

The aggressive fourteen-year effort to transform the Japanese national polity, variously mislabeled the "Fifteen Years' War," the "China Incident," the "Pacific War," and the "Greater East Asia War," did, indeed, ultimately bring the horrors of modern war to Japanese shores. But it did not resolve the fundamental question of modern national identity that had plagued Japanese statesmen and opinion leaders since the founding of the Meiji state. Rather, like the Great War, the fourteen-year bloodbath for the national essence aggravated fundamental tensions. With the obliteration of Imperial Japan, Japanese elites embarked once again on the grand enterprise of national reinvention. In place of empire, arms, and oligarchic politics, they offered diplomatic dependence, economic might, and one-party rule. Rapid economic growth sanctified this new trajectory, just as military victories against China and Russia had validated the military-bureaucratic cast of Meiji Japan.

But consolidation of the basic institutions of the new state by 1955 did not resolve the fundamental debate over the national identity. On the contrary, the peculiar circumstances surrounding the creation of a new national polity (particularly, the international context of the Cold War), like the unusually concentrated rush for national unity in the nineteenth century, invited an artificial suppression of debate that ensured a fundamental tension in Japanese political life after the beginning of the "1955 system." Just as Imperial Japan's founders at the turn of the century resisted the political parties' vision of parliamentary rule, the architects of "postwar" Japan—the Liberal Democratic Party and its economic and bureaucratic allies—contained the progressive vision of popular government and unarmed neutrality after 1945.

Like Woodrow Wilson's appeals for democracy and internationalism in 1919, the promise of a peaceful, multipolar world order after the fall of the Berlin Wall lifted the cap from the suspended discussion on Japanese national identity in the postwar era. As in 1919, Japanese policymakers and opinion leaders in the 1990s had the opportunity to fully debate Japan's relations abroad as they rethought the structure of rule at home.[1] The principal pillar of Japan's postwar one-party rule, the Cold War alliance with the United States, was, by no means, off-limits in that discussion. On the contrary, with the Cold War over, a weakening of the U.S.-Japanese partnership, at least in the short term, seemed to offer the only means by which the question of Japanese national identity, which had plagued the modern polity since its founding in the nineteenth century, could finally be resolved.[2]

A study of Japan in the Great War cannot reveal the direction that the U.S.-Japanese alliance will take in the post–Cold War era. It does suggest, however, that one of the most important factors that will determine the shape of Asia in the twenty-first century will be an impassioned dialogue within Japan about the most fundamental question of national identity. The importance of a final resolution to the long-unsettled debate cannot be overstated. For the Great War and its aftermath demonstrate that peace in Asia depends first and foremost on a Japan at peace with herself.

Reference Matter

Notes

For full author names, titles, and publication data for works cited here in short form, see the Bibliography, pp. 325–44. The following abbreviations are used herein:

HKM   Hara Takashi monjo kenkyūkai, ed., *Hara Takashi kankei monjo*
HMM   "Hamaomote Matasuke monjo," in Kindai Nihon kenkyūkai, ed., *Kindai Nihon to higashi Ajia*
HN   Hara Keiichirō, ed., *Hara Takashi nikki*
ONS   Yamamoto Shirō, ed., *Dai-niji ōkuma naikaku kankei shiryō*
STH   Meiji Taishō Shōwa shinbun kenkyūkai, ed., *Shinbun shūsei Taishō hennenshi*
TNS   Yamamoto Shirō, ed., *Terauchi Masatake naikaku kankei shiryō*
UKM   Uehara Yūsaku kankei monjo kenkyūkai, ed., *Uehara Yūsaku kankei monjo*
YAI   Ōyama Azusa, comp., *Yamagata Aritomo ikensho*
YDH   Itō Takashi, ed., *Taishō shoki Yamagata Aritomo danwa hikki*

Preface

1. See Leitch et al., *Japan's Role in the Post–Cold War World*, p. 6.

2. One needs only look to the torrent of literature on Japanese aggression and war crimes that flooded the American market around the fiftieth anniversary of the Pacific War. See, for example, Iris Chang, *The Rape of Nanking*; Harris, *Factories of Death*; George Hicks, *The Comfort Women*; and Yuki Tanaka, *Hidden Horrors*.

3. A growing number of Japanese observers recognize the importance of the parallels between the First World War and the post–Cold War era for modern Japan. See Itō Yukio, "Dai-ichiji taisen to sengo Nihon no keisei"; and Kawada Minoru, *Hara Takashi to Yamagata Aritomo*. See also Dickinson, "Daiyon no 'kaikoku' wa jitsugen suru ka."

Introduction

1. Camille Mauclair, *L'Avenir de France* (Paris, 1918), p. 512; cited in Silver, *Esprit de Corps*, p. 27.

2. Gay, *Weimar Culture*, p. 9.

3. Dos Passos, *1919*, p. 34.

4. A recent example is the celebrated PBS series *The Great War and the Shaping of the 20th Century* (1996), which makes no mention of Japan in the context of the war in eight one-hour episodes (although the final episode on the legacy of war describes veteran Harry Truman's eventual decision to drop the atomic bomb on Hiroshima). Martin Gilbert's 615-page *The First World War: A Complete History* devotes sixteen sentences to Japan.

5. William Randolph Hearst's newspapers, for example, published a series in 1915 titled "Japan's Plans to Invade and Conquer the United States." Hearst would subsequently produce the film *Patria* in 1917, which showed Japanese and Mexican troops looting, murdering, and raping during an invasion of the United States (see LaFeber, *The Clash*, p. 120). In May 1916, the *North American Review* reported that Japan had answered American protests over the Twenty-One Demands by assembling a threatening naval force in Mexican waters (Neumann, *America Encounters Japan*, p. 145). The first wave of war hysteria followed Japan's surprising victory over Russia in 1905 and increasing bilateral tension over Japanese immigration to California. Among the sensationalist literature of the time was Homer Lea's *Valor of Ignorance* (Harper, 1909), which argued that tension over the mistreatment of Japanese immigrants in California could easily push Japan to war with the United States, and Ernest Hugh Fitzpatrick's *The Coming Conflict of Nations, or The Japanese-American War* (H. W. Bokker, 1909). For a fascinating analysis of these and other classic studies of bilateral relations in the context of rising tensions between two burgeoning empires, see Iriye, *Pacific Estrangement*.

6. Hagihara, "What Japan Means to the Twentieth Century," p. 20.

7. Terauchi monjo 441-10, "Ōshū taisen to kokumin no kakugo," Apr. 1917, in TNS, 1: 886–89.

8. See Hobsbawm and Ranger, *The Invention of Tradition*; and Anderson, *Imagined Communities*.

9. See Stephan Tanaka, *Japan's Orient*; Fujitani, *Splendid Monarchy*; and Vlastos, *Mirror of Modernity*.

Chapter 1

1. See Borton, *Japan's Modern Century*, p. 8.

2. See Huber, *The Revolutionary Origins of Modern Japan*, p. 17. Compare this with the earlier assumption that "without pressure from the West, which revealed its military and political weakness, the Tokugawa system might have continued another century or more" (Fairbank et al., *East Asia*, p. 188).

3. Seki, "The Manchurian Incident, 1931," p. 143.

4. As W. G. Beasley, the distinguished authority on Japanese foreign relations, has described it, Japan's "politically feudal" and "economically backward" nature

made her "easy prey for powerful intruders" (Beasley, *Japanese Imperialism*, p. 14). A recent study of nineteenth-century Japanese imperialism proposes the creation of a special category of "late" imperialism to describe the particular political, economic, and ideological disadvantages faced by Japanese empire-builders vis-à-vis their more powerful Western counterparts (see Duus, *The Abacus and the Sword*). Even Michael Barnhart, who regularly stresses the importance of domestic political struggles in modern Japan's foreign-policy decision making, ultimately prioritizes the "hostile and always chaotic international environment from Perry's arrival in 1853 at least until the commencement of the American Occupation in 1945" (Barnhart, *Japan and the World Since 1868*, p. 2). In Japanese, the most extreme expression of Japan's harrowing struggle on the international stage remains Hayashi Fusao's classic, *Daitōa sensō kōtei ron*.

5. For a brief account of this episode, and the Kanghwa incident of 1875 that preceded it, see Duus, *The Abacus and the Sword*, pp. 43–49.

6. Russia, France, and Germany joined hands in what became known as the Triple Intervention.

7. By the Taft-Katsura agreement of July 1905, Tokyo recognized American control of the Philippines, and Washington accepted Japanese suzerainty over Korea. By the Root-Takahira agreement of November 1908, the United States and Japan agreed to maintain the status quo in the Pacific and respect the independence and "integrity" of China. See Griswold, *The Far Eastern Policy of the United States*, chap. 3.

8. This is how Taft's irascible secretary of state, Philander C. Knox, privately described the agenda (ibid., p. 175).

9. The best account of America's history of exclusion against the Japanese remains Daniels, *The Politics of Prejudice*.

10. For an in-depth look at this facinating episode in the history of Western imperialism in the Pacific, see Paul M. Kennedy, *The Samoan Tangle*.

11. Walter LaFeber (*The Clash*, p. 65) offers "blatant racism" first among reasons for the transition from U.S.-Japanese friendship to enmity between 1900 and 1912.

12. See Fairbank et al., *East Asia*, pp. 179–82.

13. For China, see Fairbank, *The Chinese World Order*; for Japan, see Toby, *State and Diplomacy in Early Modern Japan*.

14. For a useful summary of this scholarship, see Toby, *State and Diplomacy in Early Modern Japan*, p. 228.

15. Ibid., chap. 3.

16. The intellectual mentor of many of modern Japan's founders, Yoshida Shōin, for example, observed in 1848 that "the Qing should be concerned about their people within, not barbarians from without. . . . Although the Qing are weak, their land is vast and its population is enormous. If they could have unified the hearts of high and low, promoted the righteous and brave, and cut out the nefarious and fawning,

encroachment by foreign barbarians would never have taken place" (Wakabayashi, "Opium, Expulsion, Sovereignty," pp. 19–20).

17. According to Michael Barnhart, "More direct action would be necessary to preserve Japan (and the Emperor) in the face of a Western threat that Satsuma saw as more real than ever" (Barnhardt, *Japan and the World Since 1868*, p. 9).

18. Michael Barnhart has so defined Japan's modern history, beginning with the remarkable assertion that "Japan's twentieth century began in 1853." He explains, "The arrival of four American warships under the command of Matthew G. Perry alarmed the Japanese Government and triggered a debate. . . . The nature of Japan's confrontation with the West would dominate the foreign policy of Japan from 1853 to the present" (ibid., p. 5). In Japanese, the idea of a long-term confrontation with the West appears most prominently in Hayashi Fusao, *Daitōa sensō kōtei ron*.

19. Thomas Huber makes a similar point when he notes that Perry's arrival offered ideal justification for a program of political reform long advocated by the activist samurai from the Chōshū domain, Yoshida Shōin. "Perry's dramatic and menacing appearance," Huber offers, "may have been almost welcome to [Shōin]" (Huber, *The Revolutionary Origins of Modern Japan*, p. 64).

20. Eight of the remaining large *tozama* domains (fiefs that were not traditional vassals of the Tokugawa) either sided with the Tokugawa or remained neutral at Sekigahara, where Tokugawa Ieyasu finally secured military and political hegemony (Albert Craig, *Chōshū in the Meiji Restoration*, p. 20).

21. John Whitney Hall long ago struck the proper balance between domestic and foreign affairs in the 1868 revolution when he noted that "from 1864 through 1866 various groups in Japan were obviously probing for weakness in the *baku-han* system" (Hall, *Japan*, p. 262).

22. Indeed, as George Sansom aptly observed many years ago, the sudden "enlightened" attitudes by leading members of the feudal nobility toward the first U.S. consul-general to Japan, Townsend Harris, after the latter had been received by the shōgun in 1857 indicate that "the anti-foreign movement was to a great extent dictated by hostility to the Bakufu" (Sansom, *The Western World and Japan*, p. 293).

23. *Meiji*, meaning "enlightened rule," was the name given the reign of Emperor Mutsuhito from 1868 to 1912. *Meiji ishin* was later officially translated as the "Meiji restoration," to indicate a return to imperial rule after eight centuries of warrior control. But "restoration" is best expressed by the alternative term *ōsei fukko*. The literal translation of *ishin* is "renovation." The champions of a Meiji, Taishō, and Shōwa *ishin* would all advocate a thorough internal rejuvenation.

24. The most recent description of the event along these lines in English is Calman, *The Nature and Origins of Japanese Imperialism*.

25. Banno Junji, too, has recently stressed the internal political significance of Japan's early imperialist ventures. The enthusiasm of the military and samurai for an

invasion of Korea in 1873, the expedition to Taiwan in 1874, and the Kanghwa incident of 1875, he argues, owed more to the revolutionary (political) slogan of "grounds to attack the shogunate, a basis for renovation" (*tōbaku no kongen, goisshin no moto*) than to foreign policy considerations (Banno, *Kindai Nihon no kokka kōsō*, p. 12). Long before Banno, Robert Pollard perceptively noted that the issue in the *seikan ron* debate "was not so much who should rule Korea as who should rule Japan" (Pollard, "Intangible in Japanese Foreign Policy," p. 406). I am indebted to Bob Kane for bringing this article to my attention.

26. For a groundbreaking analysis of early Japanese overtures toward Korea in the context of Japanese nation-building, see Key-Hiuk Kim, *The Last Phase of the East Asian World Order*, chap. 5.

27. As Ōkuma Shigenobu, then a councilor (*sangi*), later lamented, "Korea had been our subject country for more than two thousand years, although our past regimes neglected to control the country; now Korea became boldly contemptuous, looking down on us as if it were a superior country" (quoted in Duus, *The Abacus and the Sword*, p. 39).

28. Saigō Takamori to Itagaki Taisuke, August 17, 1873; translated in Tsunoda et al., *Sources of Japanese Tradition*, 2: 149–50.

29. A typical example of the mistaken belief in the external strategic origins of the Imperial Japanese Army may be found in a recent study: "The Imperial Army was . . . a child of necessity, of Japan's urgent need to preserve her independence from the nineteenth-century imperialist powers" (Harries and Harries, *Soldiers of the Sun*, p. 493).

30. Crowley, "From Closed Door to Empire," pp. 275–76. For a detailed examination of the domestic political significance of the Meiji conscription system, see Norman, *Soldier and Peasant in Japan*.

31. Irokawa, *Kindai kokka no shuppatsu*, p. 440.

32. Japan never became the object of great power attention that China did. The British had voluntarily abandoned their trade with the archipelago in the seventeenth century after determining that such commerce "could never become an object of importance." And when Perry arrived at Uraga Bay in the 1850s demanding concessions, he sought not commerce but coal. He viewed the archipelago primarily as a coaling station for a new steamship route to China. Japan did come under physical attack by the great powers three times in the 1860s, with the bombardment of shore batteries in the Satsuma and Chōshū domains. But each of these operations was a response to violent provocations by the Japanese, and they marked the first and last physical blows to Japan until fifteen American B-25s dropped their payloads on Japanese cities in April 1942. Before the Second World War, the great powers never physically threatened Japan as they did China. Tokyo was left alone to pursue her imperial interests in East Asia unimpeded. On the British lack of interest in Japan,

see Goodman, *Japan*, p. 12. For a captivating account of the significance of steam power in America's mid-century overture to Japan, see McDougall, *Let the Sea Make a Noise*, pp. 269–76.

33. See Jansen, "Japanese Imperialism," pp. 65–66.

34. Duus, *The Abacus and the Sword*, pp. 16–17.

35. Ibid., pp. 17–18.

36. Roosevelt's comment comes from his most celebrated imperialist tract, "The Strenuous Life" (1899); cited in Hofstader, *Social Darwinism in American Thought*, p. 180. For Ukita, see Jansen, "Japanese Imperialism," p. 73.

37. Quoted in Wakabayashi, "Opium, Expulsion, Sovereignty," p. 20.

38. See Kimitada Miwa, "Fukuzawa Yukichi's 'Departure from Asia.'"

39. From a speech on the adoption of the Meiji constitution; see Tsunoda et al., *Sources of Japanese Tradition*, 2: 164.

40. *Jiji shinpō*, July 29, 1894; cited in Conroy, *The Japanese Seizure of Korea*, p. 255. For the best firsthand account of the Sino-Japanese War as part of a "civilizing" mission, see the autobiography of Japan's foreign minister during the war, Mutsu Munemitsu, in Berger, *Kenkenroku*. According to Mutsu, "it was patently clear to all that the real cause of friction [between China and Japan] would be a collision between the new civilization of the West and the old civilization of East Asia. . . . Now that the Chinese government was rejecting our proposal for a joint reform commission, it fell to Japan alone to carry out the reform of Korea" (Berger, *Kenkenroku*, p. 28).

41. For a succinct discussion of these changes in the larger context of European warfare from the fall of the Roman empire, see Howard, *War in European History*, pp. 97–101.

42. The classic formulation is that of Fairbank, Reischauer, and Craig, who long ago described the domestic achievements of the Meiji leaders as "the national Cinderella-story of modern times" and stressed the "rampant nineteenth-century imperialism" that threatened the same men from abroad (Fairbank et al., *East Asia*, pp. 244–45).

43. Comparisons of leadership in China and Japan follow the vicissitudes of respective national fortunes. In the summer of 1998, when China, with its robust economy and eagerness to accommodate American desires for economic stability in Asia, began to steal American favor away from the economically and politically troubled Japan, Nakamura Ken'ichi, a Japanese foreign affairs expert, noted matter-of-factly that "they [the Chinese] have smarter leaders" (quoted in Watts, "Jilted Japan," p. 16).

44. Fairbank, Reischauer, and Craig note that "the new regime, within a decade of its coming to power, had established a firm grip on the whole nation" (Fairbank et al., *East Asia*, p. 244).

45. For a precise analysis of the legal framework of governance in Imperial Japan, see Takeuchi, *War and Diplomacy in the Japanese Empire*, chaps. 1–8. For a succinct survey of the preeminent political forces in early twentieth-century Japan, see Suetake, *Taishōki no seiji kōzō*, pp. 21–45.

46. The original tax qualification of fifteen yen enfranchised about 450,000 voters, or 1 percent of the population.

47. Carol Gluck, for example, identifies the principal concern of modern Japan's founders as the creation of a "sense of nation" and fashioning of a Japanese "modernity." For Gluck, the new imperial institution of the Meiji years represents no more than Japan's attempt to emulate the modern constitutional monarchies of the West and the moral precepts of the 1890 Imperial Rescript on Education simply a new Japanese "sense of nation" (Gluck, *Japan's Modern Myths*).

48. For a comprehensive survey of the growing importance of German thought and institutions during the Meiji period, see Ōtsuka, *Meiji ishin to doitsu shisō*. In English, see Yanaga, *Japan Since Perry*, chaps. 5–8, 12–14.

49. Akita, *Foundations of Constitutional Government in Modern Japan*, p. 61.

50. Itō had heard lectures by Gneist during his tour of Germany in 1882 and in 1884 had appointed Roessler adviser and consultant to the Japanese Committee for the Drafting of the Constitution.

51. At the turn of the century, advocate of representative government Ukita Kazutami would observe that there were various versions of imperialism to choose from and urge the abandonment of the militarist imperialist model of Germany (Jansen, "Japanese Imperialism," p. 73).

52. See Crowley, "From Closed Door to Empire," pp. 276–77.

53. Takayama Chogyū, "Meiji shisō no hensen" (1897); cited in Gluck, *Japan's Modern Myths*, p. 136.

54. See Scalapino, *Democracy and the Party Movement in Prewar Japan*, p. 88, n131.

55. Fellow Chōshū elder Yamagata Aritomo reacted to this initiative in bewilderment. Why, he asked Itō in June 1898, did he plan such "eccentric projects?" (Hackett, *Yamagata Aritomo and the Rise of Modern Japan, 1838–1922*, p. 182).

56. Stoddard, *Lectures*, 3: 116. Finding in Japan's victory over China evidence of the "genius of Japanese civilization," famed interpreter of things Japanese Lafcadio Hearn also described Japan as "the most extraordinary country in the world" (Hearn, *Kokoro*, p. 9).

57. In 1895, the Diet sanctioned a doubling of the standing army and navy, to thirteen divisions (150,000 soldiers, with a mobilization potential of 600,000) and 278,000 tons, respectively.

58. Takayama Chogyū, "Meiji shisō no hensen" (1897), in Gluck, *Japan's Modern Myths*, p. 136. Observers were delighted, as well, by the economic fruits of the war. "What a surprise!" declared Fukuzawa Yukichi's business paper, the *Jiji shinpō*.

"Contrary to expectations, there is no sign that domestic business or industry is feeling any hardship whatsoever [due to the war]. Foreign trade, in particular, has not only continued despite the war, it appears, they say, to be more successful than last year" (cited in Itō Yukio, "Dai-niji Itō naikakuki no seitō to hanbatsu kanryō," p. 281).

59. In February 1895, the Lower House demonstrated even greater support with a unanimous resolution to approve any amount of appropriations needed to prosecute the war (Takeuchi, *War and Diplomacy in the Japanese Empire*, p. 113).

60. Pollard, "Intangible in Japanese Foreign Policy," p. 406.

61. Tariff autonomy, which took effect in 1911, had actually been negotiated with the British in 1894, at the same time that London agreed to abolish the other main pillar of Japan's "unequal treaties" with the powers, extraterritoriality. Japanese legal jurisdiction over foreign nationals on her soil began in 1899.

62. Katsura Tarō served as prime minister, Yamagata Aritomo as chief of the Army General Staff, and Ōyama Iwao commanded Japanese forces in Manchuria. See Okamoto, *The Japanese Oligarchy and the Russo-Japanese War*, p. 38.

63. John Lewis Gaddis (*We Now Know*) has recently made a similar point about the Soviet Union and the Cold War.

64. Viscount Hayashi Tadasu, at the time Japan's minister to the Court of St. James, described the outburst as proof of "the rudimentary state of the Japanese mind in relation to foreign affairs" (Pooley, *The Secret Memoirs of Count Tadasu Hayashi*, p. 227).

65. For the first time in the history of Japanese politics, no cabinet post except that of the prime minister went to a titled peer. Out of the twelve ministers, only three came from the traditionally dominant Satsuma or Chōshū domains.

66. Tsunoda, *Manshū mondai to kokubō hōshin*, p. 659.

67. Oka, "Generational Conflict After the Russo-Japanese War," p. 216.

68. Shimanuki, "Nichi-Ro sensō igo ni okeru kokubō hōshin," p. 3

69. The 1907 Basic Plan of National Defense marked the first instance in which a plan of national defense was decided without any input from the cabinet (Imai Seiichi, "Taishōki ni okeru gunbu no seijiteki chii," p. 5).

70. This brought the standing army from the prewar level of thirteen divisions to nineteen divisions. The postwar augmentation marked an expansion of ground power in two years equal to the dramatic leap from seven to thirteen divisions after the Sino-Japanese War. See Muroyama, "Nichi-Ro sengo no gunbi kakuchō mondai," for a detailed analysis of Japanese military expansion after the Russo-Japanese War.

71. Wakatsuki, *Meiji, Taishō, Shōwa seikai hisshi*, p. 172.

72. Makino, *Kaisōroku*, 2: 61.

73. To shorten his audiences with the field marshal, for example, the emperor

would present to Yamagata, as if bestowing on him parting gifts, any objects he could find close at hand and usher him to the door (Fujimura, *Yamagata Aritomo*, p. 274). In the fall of 1916, the emperor asked the field marshal when he intended to resign the presidency of the Privy Council. At the same time, the emperor expressed concern to Prime Minister Terauchi that Yamagata "lacked popularity" (Oka, *Yamagata Aritomo*, p. 155).

74. "Meiji jidai no igi," *Tōyō jiji*, September 1912; cited in Ishibashi, *Tanzan kaisō*, p. 188.

75. Yamagata hoped to send one or two divisions to Manchuria, ostensibly to protect against Russian expansion in the region. But members of the Imperial Army hoped to expand the area of operation of Japanese troops even south of the Great Wall. To create an excuse for Japanese military intervention, the army supplied China's revolutionary forces with military aid (Kitaoka, *Nihon rikugun to tairiku seisaku*, pp. 93–96). Kitaoka highlights Army General Staff Second Bureau Chief Utsunomiya Tarō as one of the more active proponents of Japanese military intervention in China at this time; Utsunomiya actually advocated the partition of China. Among the energetic promoters of military aid to China's revolutionaries was War Ministry Military Affairs Bureau Chief Tanaka Giichi. Despite the failure in 1912, Tanaka, as vice chief of the Army General Staff, would again attempt in 1916 to create an excuse for a major expedition of Japanese troops to China. The second experiment would collapse, however, with the death of Chinese president Yuan Shikai. See Chapter 4 herein.

76. In a 1911 memorandum to the cabinet, Terauchi insisted that Japan prevent the creation of a republic in China "by any means of intervention" (cited in Shinobu, *Taishō seijishi*, 2: 349).

77. Specifically, he abolished the active-duty rule that had enabled Yamagata and Uehara to bring down the Saionji cabinet in 1912. If the war minister and vice minister could be chosen from the inactive service ranks, Japan's generals could no longer blackmail the cabinet by refusing to provide candidates. The admiral also proposed expanding cabinet authority over the army's sacred preserve, Manchuria. He abolished the Colonial Bureau and transferred jurisdiction of the South Manchuria Railway and Guandong Government from that body to the Railroad Office and the Foreign Ministry, respectively. Spurred by the Seiyūkai's Hara Takashi, he also replaced the president and vice president of the South Manchuria Railway with Seiyūkai party members. Finally, Yamamoto planned to allow civilian governors general in Korea and Taiwan but was forced out of office by the Siemens scandal before such plans materialized (Kitaoka, *Nihon rikugun to tairiku seisaku*, pp. 117–20; see also Kobayashi Michihiko, *Nihon no tairiku seisaku*, pp. 300–304).

78. Among the positions opened up to nonprofessional bureaucrats were all vice ministerial posts, all counselors appointed by the emperor, the chief of the Legisla-

tive Bureau, the chief of the Security Bureau in the Interior Ministry, and the police superintendent (Imai, *Nihon kindaishi*, p. 97).

79. Itō Masanori, *Katō Takaaki*, 1: 773. Field Marshal Yamagata's allies in the House of Peers belonged to the Good Fortune Club (Saiwai Kurabu), otherwise known as the "bureaucratic clique." Included were such prominent men as Viscount Hirata Tōsuke; Barons Den Kenjirō, Takei Morimasa, and Arichi Shinanojū; and Komatsubara Eitarō, Egi Kazuyuki, and Ichiki Kitokurō. See Ōtsu, *Dai Nihon kenseishi*, 7: 276, for a description of this faction's role in deposing Yamamoto. This marked the first instance in the history of Imperial Japan that a budget was actually defeated in the Diet. Other budgets had failed, but because of a Diet dissolution (Imai, *Nihon kindaishi*, p. 106).

80. In a meeting of March 26 (YDH, pp. 43–44).

81. One should distinguish here between what has so far been described as the international vogue of constitutional government that modern Japan's founders emulated and the specific use of the term "constitutional government" (*kensei*) by opponents of the Meiji regime. In creating the Real Constitutional Government Party in 1898 and then promoting the "movement to protect constitutional government" (*kensei yōgo undō*) in 1912, Japan's rising party politicians pushed for parliamentary politics to replace the unrepresentative "clique rule" (*hanbatsu seiji*) of the elder statesmen.

Chapter 2

1. Shimazaki Tōson, "Senji no Pari kara Furansu dayori," *Tokyo Asahi shinbun*, September 18, 1914; found in Taishō nyūsu jiten hensen iinkai, *Taishō nyūsu jiten*, 1: 274.

2. "Sensō to Karyūkai," *Miyako shinbun*, August 5, 1914; found in Watanabe Katsumasa, *Shinbun shūroku taishōshi*, 2: 291.

3. See Usui, *Nihon to Chūgoku*, pp. 42–45.

4. At the height of the Second World War, for example, a professor of history at the University of Nevada published an analysis of Japan's entrance in the First World War suggesting a direct link between Japan's expansion "at the expense of her British ally" in 1914 and her drive for hegemony in Asia in the 1940s. See Charles Hicks, *Japan's Entry into the War, 1914*. I am indebted to Bob Kane for bringing this pamphlet to my attention. Peter Lowe (*Great Britain and Japan*, chap. 6) describes the decline of the alliance more delicately by saying that the Anglo-Japanese discussions in the summer and fall of 1914 marked a reversal of respective positions of power. For the first time in the history of the alliance, Lowe argues, Britain was more dependent on Japan than vice versa. Ian Nish marks the August tussle as "the first major dispute between the allies. . . . The damage done was not irreparable; but confidence could only be restored by exercising extreme caution" (Nish, *Alliance in Decline*, p. 131).

5. In Beasley, *Japanese Imperialism*, for example, the discussion of Japan's entrance into the First World War is buried under the subtitle, "The Twenty-One Demands" (see Beasley, p. 109).

6. The notable exception to this, of course, has been Japan's Marxist scholars, who have long highlighted the Great War as the beginning of monopoly capitalism in Japan. Many of these scholars begin their analyses of Japanese aggression in the 1930s with World War I. See, for example, Tōyama et al., *Shōwashi*, p. 7.

7. The lack of serious assessment of the Great War in the history of modern Japan has led to some surprising alternative propositions as to the true beginnings of the twentieth century in Japan. Michael Barnhart, for example, declares that "Japan's twentieth century began in 1853" (Barnhart, *Japan and the World Since 1868*, p. 5). Hagihara Nobutoshi ("What Japan Means to the Twentieth Century," p. 20), on the other hand, argues that Japan remained outside of the Great War and thus persisted as a "nineteenth century state" until 1945.

8. Silver, *Esprit de Corps*, p. 26.

9. Bruno Frank, "Stolze Zeit, 1914"; cited in Gordon Craig, *Germany*, p. 339.

10. Queen's Hall speech, September 19, 1914; cited in Ferro, *The Great War*, pp. 20–21.

11. Inoue Kaoru kō denki hensankai, *Segai Inoue kō den*, 5: 367.

12. Yoshino Sakuzō, *Nisshi kōshōron* (Tokyo, 1915), p. 255; cited in Hirono, "Yoshino Sakuzō Chūgoku ron oboegaki," p. 48.

13. Ioki Ryōzō, "Shin kiun o ridō seyo," *Nihon oyobi Nihonjin*, January 1, 1915; cited in Banno, *Taishō seihen*, p. 211.

14. Katō was minister to London, 1894–1900, ambassador, 1908–1912, and foreign minister, October 1900–June 1901, January–March 1906, and January–February 1913.

15. Itō Masanori, *Katō Takaaki*, 1: 173, 800.

16. Ibid., p. 179.

17. Ibid., pp. 12, 14.

18. HN, 4: 27 (diary entry for August 12, 1914).

19. YDH, pp. 61, 65.

20. For Katō's early promotion of the Anglo-Japanese alliance, see Itō Masanori, *Katō Takaaki*, 1: 3, 241–42, 283, 289–90.

21. In July 1907, July 1910, and July 1912. See p. 139 herein.

22. Although the sensitive nature of this enterprise kept it from moving far beyond the planning stage and ensured that it remain a strictly guarded secret (hidden from the gaze of historians as well as contemporaries), abundant circumstantial evidence indicates that it was given serious thought by some of Japan's most influential elites in the military-bureaucratic establishment. The records of four powerful men, in particular, highlight this campaign. First, Gotō Shinpei, whom Kobayashi Michihiko ("Nichi-Ro sengo no Nichi-Doku dōmei ron") identifies as the principal

champion of a German-Japanese alliance, drafted a memorandum soon after the outbreak of the Chinese Revolution describing the turmoil in China as a "golden opportunity" to "approach" Germany, given Britain's increasing "decrepitude." Second, Chōshū elder Katsura Tarō, having recently completed a second term as prime minister, traveled to Moscow in July 1912 (accompanied by Gotō) in an apparent bid to begin talks with Berlin over an alliance. As recounted to Sun Yatsen by Katsura, a German-Japanese pact aimed to "topple British (political and economic) hegemony" in Turkey, India, and China. The plan was to avoid international attention by negotiating with German representatives in Moscow. But Katsura's entourage received word of the Meiji emperor's imminent death as soon as they arrived in Moscow and thus headed for home without beginning discussions (Tai Kitō, *Nihon ron*, p. 98). Third, after having championed a Russo-Japanese alliance in 1906 to divide British possessions in Asia, Yamagata protégé Major General Tanaka Giichi urged a political alliance with Germany on the eve of the Great War to "contain Russia on her Western border" (see Tanaka, "Tai-Man shokan [II]," May, 1914, in Tanaka Giichi kankei monjo, no. 15. Yamaguchi Prefectural Library, Yamaguchi. Although a photocopy of the original document may be found in the National Diet Library in Tokyo, only the original in Yamaguchi prefecture contains the reference to Germany. I am indebted to Kobayashi Michihiko for bringing this to my attention). Finally, like Tanaka, Yamagata, as we shall see, began moving away from the Anglo-Japanese alliance soon after the Russo-Japanese War. And, while he stressed closer Russo-Japanese relations, he urged reinforced ties with Germany at the expense of Britain, as well.

23. Itō Masanori, *Katō Takaaki*, 2: 79. British ambassador to Tokyo Sir Coyningham Greene had only just made a formal request for Japanese assistance earlier that day (August 7). Katō's swiftness owed, in part, to his confidence in a British victory. He informed the cabinet that no matter how long the war, the British would emerge victorious. Even in the worse case scenario, the contest would end in a stalemate (Itō Masanori, p. 73). Given the recent history of sentiment in Tokyo for a German-Japanese alliance, one might also speculate that Katō hoped with a quick declaration of war on Germany to forestall any movement in Japan to join the battle on the side of the Central Powers.

24. At the cabinet meeting of August 7; see Ōkuma kō hachijūgonenshi hensankai, *Ōkuma kō hachijūgonenshi*, 3: 169. Imperial Germany, it will be recalled, had served as the principal model for the Meiji state. And Imperial Japanese Army officers, who regularly traveled to Berlin for training, had a particular affinity for the Reich.

25. See Nagaoka, "Katō Takaaki ron," p. 32.

26. Japan's leases on Port Arthur (Lüshun), Dairen (Dalian), and the Andong-Mukden Railway (which connected the South Manchuria Railway to the Korean

railways) were due to expire in 1923. Her lease on the South Manchuria Railway was up in 1938.

27. Lowe, *Great Britain and Japan*, pp. 226–27. Nagaoka Shinjirō ("Katō Takaaki ron," pp. 34–35) stresses the coincidence of Katō's aims with those of the Imperial Army, and their divergence from those of the more cautious elder statesmen.

28. See Tōyama et al., *Shōwashi*, p. 7. Nomura Otojirō has spoken of the Twenty-One Demands as the "first step of a continuous aggressive war from the Manchurian Incident to the Pacific War" (Nomura, "Tai-Ka nijūikkajō mondai to Katō Takaaki," pt. 1, p. 1).

29. It must be added that Katō never contemplated the unconditional return of Jiaozhou to China. The initial ultimatum to Germany demanded the transfer of the territory to Japan "with a view to the eventual restoration of the same to China." But Katō aimed to exchange Jiaozhou for concessions in Japan's main area of interest on the continent, South Manchuria. See Itō Masanori, *Katō Takaaki*, 2: 83–85. The foreign minister, therefore, resisted British minister to China Sir John Jordan's suggestion to guarantee the return of the territory in a proposed joint Anglo-Japanese declaration to China in August 1914 (see Usui, *Nihon to Chūgoku*, pp. 44–45). And he strongly objected to China's demand during talks in 1915 for the unconditional return of Jiaozhou, on the grounds that Japan had now expended much blood and money to seize the territory from Germany. Reflecting the new situation after the opening of hostilities between Japan and Germany, the final exchange of notes between China and Japan covering the return of Jiaozhou (signed on May 25), then, stipulated compensation not in Manchuria, but in Jiaozhou itself. China would open all of Jiaozhou as a commercial port and allow a Japanese settlement in the territory (see Usui, *Nihon to Chūgoku*, pp. 65–67).

30. This group of elder statesmen was divided evenly between the Chōshū and Satsuma domains. Yamagata and Inoue Kaoru hailed from Chōshū, while Matsukata Masayoshi and Ōyama Iwao came from Satsuma.

31. Yamagata had commanded the First Army against China in 1894 and directed the war with Russia in 1904 as chief of the Army General Staff. He had, as well, been personally entrusted by the Meiji emperor to give advice on "all important military matters" and was the principal architect of the army's continental mission. See Hackett, *Yamagata Aritomo in the Rise of Modern Japan, 1838–1922*, p. 156.

32. See Akita and Itō, "Yamagata Aritomo to 'jinshū kyōsō' ron"; Hackett, *Yamagata Aritomo in the Rise of Modern Japan, 1838–1922*; and Oka, *Yamagata Aritomo*.

33. Akita and Itō, "Yamagata Aritomo to 'jinshū kyōsō' ron," pp. 109–10.

34. Ibid., p. 113.

35. For the clearest expression of this distinction, see Kitaoka, *Nihon rikugun to tairiku seisaku*. See also Banno, "Nihon rikugun no Ōbeikan to Chūgoku seisaku," pp. 441–64.

36. "Evil genius" was the term applied by E. H. Norman (*Soldier and Peasant in Japan*, p. 47); Yamagata's great-grandson once noted his anger at high school history lessons (between 1975 and 1978) that presented the field marshal as the man who "laid the tracks of Japanese militarism" (Akita and Itō, "Yamagata Aritomo to 'jinshū kyōsō' ron," p. 113, *n*4); see also Akita and Itō, pp. 95–97, for a succinct history of the fluctuation of Yamagata's historical reputation.

37. HN, 3: 416 (April 3, 1914); Hara frequently referred to Yamagata's stratagems as "Yamagata's way" (*Yamagata ryū*).

38. In June 1915, for example, both *genrō* were exasperated when, after having been incited by Yamagata to apply pressure on Ōkuma to sack Foreign Minister Katō, the field marshal "changed his opinion midway" (HN, 4: 111 [July 7, 1915]; also see Chapter 3 herein).

39. Fujimura, *Yamagata Aritomo*, p. 271.

40. Ibid.

41. "Yamagata gensui no yuigon, sono ta ni, san," Tanaka Giichi kankei monjo, no. 480, Kensei shiryōshitsu, National Diet Library, Tokyo.

42. "Tai-Shi saigo tsūchō jijō," May 1915, in Futagami Hyōji kankei monjo, no. 6.

43. YDH, p. 61.

44. See pp. 286–87*n*11, herein.

45. See p. 139 herein.

46. Yamagata fought on the two occasions of Western bombardment and invasion of the Chōshū domain in 1863 and 1864. In the latter engagement, he was wounded by enemy fire (Oka, *Yamagata Aritomo*, pp. 8, 11–12).

47. YDH, p. 60. A celebrated recent history of U.S.-Japanese relations implies that racial concerns colored the worldviews of Yamagata and Woodrow Wilson in equal measure (LaFeber, *The Clash*, chap. 4). But granting that both Wilson and Yamagata shared the racial prejudices characteristic of their times, one should make a distinction between simply subscribing to widespread assumptions about race and actually constructing a strategic vision based on such assumptions. Aside from the oft-cited recommendation by Wilson in February 1917 that the United States stay out of the world war "in order to keep the white race or part of it strong to meet the yellow race," there is little evidence that fear of a "yellow peril" shaped Wilson's foreign policy in the manner that hopes for Sino-Japanese "cooperation" in anticipation of a future "race war" defined Yamagata's international outlook.

48. YDH, p. 60.

49. From Yamagata's "Opinion on China Policy," presented soon after the August 15 dispatch of an ultimatum to Germany; see YAI, p. 343.

50. Ibid.

51. YDH, p. 65.

52. See Gaimushō, *Nihon gaikō nenpyō narabi ni shuyō bunsho, 1840–1945,* 1: 231, 252–53.

53. Yamagata's "Basic Plan of National Defense Personal Draft" (Teikoku ko-kubō hōshin shian) of October 1906 read: "From now on, the best means of pro-moting [Japan's] national prosperity and the happiness of the people is a strategy of guarding the north and advancing south [in China] (*hokushu nanshin*)" (YAI, p. 300). Although Tanaka Giichi formulated the initial draft of this "Personal Draft," this line was Yamagata's personal addition. See Tsunoda, *Manshū mondai to kokubō hō-shin,* pp. 686, 699–700.

54. In the same "Basic Plan of National Defense Personal Draft" of October 1906 (YAI, p. 296).

55. Nothing came of the proposed discussions because of Katsura's early depar-ture from Moscow with news of the Meiji emperor's imminent death (Tai Kitō, *Ni-hon ron,* p. 98). See also Takekoshi Yosaburō, *Tōankō* (Tokyo: Sōbungaku, 1930), pp. 274–75; cited in Kobayashi Michihiko, "Nichi-Ro sengo no Nichi-Doku dōmei ron," p. 86.

56. See Tanaka, "Tai-Man shokan (II)," May 1914, Tanaka Giichi kankei monjo, no. 15. Yamaguchi Prefectural Library, Yamaguchi. Although a photocopy of the original document may be found in the National Diet Library in Tokyo, only the original in Yamaguchi prefecture contains the reference to Germany. I am indebted to Kobayashi Michihiko for bringing this to my attention.

57. YDH, p. 59. Yamagata shared this sentiment with his contemporary from the Chōshū domain, Privy Councilor Viscount Miura Gorō. Miura (*Kanju shōgun kaisōroku,* p. 359) himself offered that, unlike other countries, Japan harbored no "old grudges" against Germany.

58. YDH, p. 59.

59. Mochizuki to Inoue, August 19, 1914, in ONS, p. 92.

60. YDH, pp. 59–60.

61. In a *genrō* conference with the prime minister on September 24, 1914 (To-kutomi, *Kōshaku Yamagata Aritomo den,* 3: 917).

62. HN, 4: 113 (July 8, 1915). See p. 141 herein.

63. Ibid.

64. In his February 1915 memorandum advocating a Russo-Japanese alliance (YAI, p. 346).

65. HN, 4: 114 (July 8, 1915), Terauchi monjo 315-37, Tanaka to Terauchi, June 23, 1915. For a brief survey of earlier appeals for stronger ties with both Russia and Germany, see Kobayashi Michihiko, "Nichi-Ro sengo no Nichi-Doku dōmei ron."

66. HN, 4: 156 (January 24, 1916).

67. YDH, p. 60; Mochizuki to Inoue, August 19, 1914, in ONS, p. 91.

68. YDH, p. 61; Mochizuki to Inoue, August 19, 1914, in ONS, p. 91.

69. YDH, p. 61.

70. "Tai-Shi saigo tsūchō jijō," May 1915, Futagami Hyōji kankei monjo, no. 6.

71. Yamagata, "Opinion on China Policy," in YAI, p. 345.

72. Ibid., pp. 344–45.

73. The early Meiji statesman Saigō Takamori dubbed Inoue "the chief manager of Mitsui."

74. In a memorandum presented to Prime Minister Ōkuma and Field Marshal Yamagata on August 10 (Inoue Kaoru kō denki hensankai, Segai Inoue kō den, 5: 367).

75. Ibid.

76. While Inoue also recognized the financial strength of Britain, the United States, and Germany, he found these powers more inclined to circulate their wealth internally. He viewed France, on the other hand, as most likely to invest in foreign markets (see Inoue Kaoru kō denki hensankai, Segai Inoue kō den, 5: 320–21).

77. Ibid., pp. 367–68.

78. Ibid., pp. 368–69.

79. From Inoue discussion with personal secretary Mochizuki Kotarō on August 22, 1914 (ibid., p. 382).

80. From the August 10 memorandum to Prime Minister Ōkuma and Field Marshal Yamagata (ibid., p. 368).

81. "Jikyoku irai no tebikae" (August 9–September 16, 1914), in ONS, p. 72.

82. Inoue Kaoru kō denki hensankai, Segai Inoue kō den, 5: 380–81.

83. William Morton's Tanaka Giichi and Japan's China Policy, the only English-language biography of Tanaka, devotes just one chapter to Tanaka's activities before his ascension to the presidency of the Seiyūkai in 1925.

84. "Miscellaneous Notes" (Zuikan zatsuroku), 1906; cited in Tsunoda, Manshū mondai to kokubō hōshin, p. 699.

85. Tanaka proposed a transfer of all British concessions in China to Japan and her territory in India to Russia; see "Miscellaneous Notes" (Zuikan zatsuroku), 1906; cited in Tsunoda, Manshū mondai to kokubō hōshin, pp. 686-87.

86. It is worth noting, however, that, in contrast to Gotō Shinpei and Katsura Tarō, who earlier advocated an alliance with Germany to counter British power in Asia, Tanaka's plan in May 1914 called for an alliance to "contain Russia on her Western border"; see Tanaka, "Tai-Man shokan (II)," May 1914, Tanaka Giichi kankei monjo, no. 15. Yamaguchi Prefectural Library, Yamaguchi. Although a photocopy of the original document may be found in the National Diet Library in Tokyo, only the original in Yamaguchi prefecture contains the reference to Germany.

87. For a brief reference by Tanaka to the Great War as a "race war," see Oka Ichinosuke monjo 7-1, Tanaka to Oka, August 1914.

88. Terauchi Masatake kankei monjo 315-24, Tanaka to Terauchi, August 12, 1914.

89. Oka Ichinosuke monjo 7-1, Tanaka to Oka, August 1914.

90. In anticipation of a unified system of railways throughout Manchuria and Korea; Oka Ichinosuke monjo 7-3, Tanaka to Oka, August 18, 1914.

91. Tanaka had originally suggested eliminating Yuan to a close friend, Chief of the Guandong Army General Staff Fukuda Masatarō, during his two-month sojourn in Manchuria (Kuroita, *Fukuda taishō den*, pp. 278–79).

92. Terauchi Masatake kankei monjo 315-24, Tanaka to Terauchi, August 12, 1914.

93. Terauchi Masatake kankei monjo 315-25, Tanaka to Terauchi, August 31, 1914.

94. Oka Ichinosuke monjo 7-1, Tanaka to Oka, August 1914.

95. In a book titled *Tsugi no issen* (The next war); for a description, see Hirama, "Dai-ichiji sekai taisen e no sansen to tai-Bei kankei," p. 36.

96. Inoue Kaoru monjo 544, Tanaka to Inoue, September 2, 1914.

97. Both Kitaoka Shin'ichi and Banno Junji stress Yamagata's opposition to the campaign to depose Yuan as representative of a fundamental difference between the elder statesman's desire for Sino-Japanese cooperation (*Nitchū teikei*) and the general staff's attempt at partition in China. See Kitaoka, *Nihon rikugun to tairiku seisaku*, pp. 90–99, for the cooperation versus partition distinction, and p. 190 for Yamagata's specific objection to the anti-Yuan campaign; and Banno, "Nihon rikugun no Ōbeikan to Chūgoku seisaku."

98. Yamagata and Tanaka had initially attempted to create a Terauchi regime after the fall of the second Saionji cabinet in December 1912. At that time, the majority Seiyūkai foiled the initiative.

99. See, in particular, Kitaoka, *Nihon rikugun to tairiku seisaku*; and Banno, "Nihon rikugun no Ōbeikan to Chūgoku seisaku."

100. For the unsuccessful efforts of Tanaka, Akashi, and the commander of the Korea military police, Tachibana Koichirō, to persuade Terauchi in April 1916 to support the campaign against Yuan, see Kitaoka, *Nihon rikugun to tairiku seisaku*, pp. 90–92; and Banno, "Nihon rikugun no Ōbeikan to Chūgoku seisaku," pp. 450–51.

101. Consistent with their image of Terauchi as a cautious elder, both Kitaoka (*Nihon rikugun to tairiku seisaku*, pp. 199–200) and Banno ("Nihon rikugun no Ōbeikan to Chūgoku seisaku," pp. 452–54) describe the general's China policy during his prime ministry as a revision of the overt interference of the Ōkuma cabinet to nonintervention in China's internal affairs.

102. The letters exchanged by these two men between the Russo-Japanese War and Terauchi's death in 1919, in fact, remain an important resource for studying the affairs of the most powerful conservative political force in Taishō Japan, the Yamagata faction.

103. During Hioki's stop in Seoul en route to his new post.

104. Akashi Motojirō monjo 32-11, Terauchi to Akashi, August 22, 1914; in Nihon seiji gaikōshi kenkyūkai, "Akashi Motojirō monjo oyobi kadai," p. 96.

105. Terauchi Masatake kankei monjo 421-3, Terauchi to Sugiyama, 1915.

106. See, for example, Chang and Myers, "Japanese Colonial Development Policy in Taiwan"; Hayase, "The Career of Gotō Shimpei," pp. 40–90; more recently, see Myers and Peattie, *The Japanese Colonial Empire, 1895–1945*, pp. 84–85; 281–82.

107. See Myers, "Japanese Imperialism in Manchuria." Myers speaks of Gotō's aims for "informal empire" and an "open door" for equal economic access for third parties in South Manchuria. For a less charitable image of Gotō's aims, see Fogel, *Life Along the South Manchurian Railway*, pp. 7–15. Gotō is seen here promoting massive Japanese immigration to South Manchuria on the model of similar settlement in Korea to attain Japanese "sovereignty" there. "We have to implement a cultural invasion," Gotō urged (Fogel, pp. 9, 14).

108. See Kitaoka Shin'ichi, "Gaikō shidōsha toshite no Gotō Shinpei."

109. Yoshino Sakuzō (Kosen Gakujin, pseud.), "Shin naishō Gotō dan," p. 89.

110. Ibid.

111. HN, 4: 221 (October 11, 1916).

112. Gotō was by no means alone in this enterprise. The plan for invasion, in fact, initially received the endorsement of the Yamagata cabinet (see Kobayashi Michihiko, *Nihon no tairiku seisaku*, pp. 38–39).

113. Ibid., pp. 195–96.

114. Kobayashi Michihiko, "Nichi-Ro sengo no Nichi-Doku dōmei ron," pp. 82–88.

115. HN, 4: 97 (May 5, 1915).

116. Specifically, he appealed for one million Japanese troops to occupy Russia east of Lake Baikal at a cost of 5 billion yen a year. See Chapter 5 herein.

117. See Chapter 5 herein.

118. Tsurumi, *Gotō Shinpei*, 3: 535.

119. From Gotō's memorandum to Prime Minister Terauchi, "A New China Policy," November 21, 1916; in ibid., p. 645.

120. "China Policy Draft," December 1916; in ibid., 3: 648–49.

121. Peter Duus (*Party Rivalry and Political Change in Taishō Japan*, p. 82), for example, describes Hara Takashi as much better prepared for the "environment of Japanese politics" than Katō.

122. Those statesmen were Kido Takayoshi, Ōkubo Toshimichi, and Itō Hirobumi (Shōda, *Jūshintachi no Shōwashi*, 1: 98).

123. Itō Masanori, *Katō Takaaki*, 1: 803–4.

124. They were Katsura Tarō, Yamagata Aritomo, and Ōyama Iwao, respectively (Okamoto, *The Japanese Oligarchy and the Russo-Japanese War*, p. 38).

125. Itō Masanori, *Katō Takaaki*, 1: 451–54.

126. Ibid., pp. 698–701. Katō's third stint as foreign minister (for Prime Minister Katsura Tarō) lasted only a brief twenty-two days.

127. YDH, p. 65.

128. Itō Masanori, *Katō Takaaki*, 2: 83–85.

129. By contrast, Berlin's ultimatum to Belgium on August 2 and London's ultimatum to Berlin on August 4 allowed only twelve hours. Katō's ultimatum to China on May 7 regarding the Twenty-One Demands granted forty-eight hours.

130. While in hindsight Katō seems naive in his hope that Berlin would capitulate without a fight, it was clear that Germany dreaded the prospect of a Japanese declaration of war. Soon after the outbreak of hostilities in Europe, the German ambassador to Tokyo, Count Rex, sought assurances from Katō that the war would not spread to Asia. The day after the late-night Japanese cabinet meeting to decide on war, Rex paid a visit to the Japanese vice minister of foreign affairs in such a state of agitation that he broke the leg of the chair upon which he was sitting and almost tumbled to the floor. He had arrived with an admonition and left with a sheepish apology. Katō was delighted with this story and, when recounting it to the British ambassador in Tokyo, described it as ample reason to declare war on Germany. Even as Rex and the German delegation were being escorted to Yokohama for evacuation, the German ambassador continued to chastise his Japanese hosts for their action, pausing in his criticism only briefly when overcome by seasickness on the small tug ride out to the ship in the harbor (Matsui, *Matsui Keishirō jijoden*, pp. 78–81). Japan's sudden participation in the war was greeted in Berlin, as well, with great indignation. Restaurants refused to serve Japanese customers, and Japanese civilians were soon interned at a racecourse near the capital converted for the purpose (Gilbert, *The First World War*, p. 46).

131. YDH, pp. 43–44.

132. The "Association for the Protection of the Constitution" consisted of members of the Seiyū Hontō and Kokumintō parties. The Dōshikai also joined the campaign for fiscal reform when it submitted a bill in the Diet in January 1914 to abolish business taxes. But despite its reliance upon the Dōshikai, the new Ōkuma cabinet, in deference to its military supporters, did not include the anti-tax proposal in its official statement of policy in May. For a detailed analysis of this anti-tax movement, see Eguchi, "1914-nen no haizei undō."

133. Inoue Kaoru kō denki hensankai, *Segai Inoue kō den*, 5: 367.

134. Tokutomi, *Kōshaku Yamagata Aritomo den*, 3: 912.

135. This was Yamagata's complaint to fellow elder statesman Matsukata Masayoshi (YDH, p. 61).

136. YDH, p. 59.

137. Mochizuki to Inoue, August 19, 1914, in ONS, p. 91. The Japanese were ap-

proached about a possible alliance on August 4 by the French and on August 10 by the Russians (Takeuchi, *War and Diplomacy in the Japanese Empire*, p. 196).

138. YDH, pp. 63–64; Mochizuki to Inoue, August 19, 1914, in ONS, p. 91; HN, 4: 33 (August 15, 1914).

139. YDH, pp. 65–66; Mochizuki to Inoue, August 19, 1914, cited in ONS, p. 92. In his "Opinion on China Policy," Yamagata argued that a temporary Japanese occupation of the concession would neither prevent another power from occupying the territory nor guarantee concessions from China elsewhere, as Katō anticipated (Tokutomi, *Kōshaku Yamagata Aritomo den*, 3: 924). The ultimatum's reference to the return of Jiaozhou became a focal point of attack for the government's enemies in the Thirty-Fourth (September 4–9, 1914) and Thirty-Fifth (December 7–25, 1914) Diets.

140. Itō Masanori, *Katō Takaaki*, 1: 291.

141. YDH, p. 61.

142. Tsurumi, *Gotō Shinpei*, 3: 530–31.

143. Already on August 15, he approached Seiyūkai president Hara Takashi about building a coalition of Seiyūkai and anti-Katō forces in the House of Peers to destroy the cabinet (HN, 4: 32 [August 15, 1914]).

144. Tsurumi, *Gotō Shinpei*, 3: 542. Yamagata, on the other hand, suggested to Prime Minister Ōkuma that he dispatch the second-in-command in the Yamagata faction, General Terauchi Masatake, to China ("Tai-Shi saigo tsūchō jijō," May 1915, Futagami Hyōji kankei monjo, no. 6).

145. Military ordinance number one of 1907, for example, granted the army the power to make decisions regarding military organization, education, personnel, and rules of engagement without the prime minister's signature or Privy Council deliberation. The elimination in December 1908 of the requirement for war minister approval of changes in defense planning and force levels, moreover, increased general staff autonomy from the Ministry of War (Imai, "Taishōki ni okeru gunbu no seijiteki chii," pt. 1, pp. 5–6).

146. Indeed, as Imai Seiichi ("Taishōki ni okeru gunbu no seijiteki chii," pt. 2, p. 106) once observed, the "China problem" for the Japanese Army was always a means of expanding political power.

147. The latest Japanese biography of Tanaka, in fact, finds the origins of the Siberian Intervention and the China and Pacific Wars in Tanaka's ideas as chief of the Second Infantry Brigade in 1912; see Tazaki, *Hyōden Tanaka Giichi*, 1: 409–10.

148. Jōhō, *Rikugunshō gunmukyoku*, p. 143; Humphreys, *The Way of the Heavenly Sword*, p. 14.

149. Tanaka would declare in 1924 that the Reservists Association had "preserved national stability by supressing socialism" (Kōketsu, "Taisenkanki ni okeru rikugun no kokumin dōin seisaku," pp. 16–20).

150. Terauchi Masatake kankei monjo 315-34, Tanaka to Terauchi, February 3, 1915. For more on the political function of the Reservists Association and national youth corps, see Tazaki, Hyōden Tanaka Giichi, 1: 409–44. For Tanaka's aims for these organizations in the context of preparations for "total war," see Kōketsu, "Taisenkanki ni okeru rikugun no kokumin dōin seisaku," pp. 16–20.

151. Jōhō, Rikigunshō gunmukyoku, p. 145.

152. "Manmō shokan," in Takakura, Tanaka Giichi denki, 1: 547–84.

153. Ibid., pp. 548–49.

154. For details, see Kitaoka, Nihon rikugun to tairiku seisaku, pp. 120–22.

155. Takakura, Tanaka Giichi denki, 1: 549–50. For army objections in the 1930s to the politicization of the South Manchuria Railway, see Harada, Saionji kō to seikyoku, 2: 63.

156. Takakura, Tanaka Giichi denki, 1: 557.

157. Ibid., p. 584.

158. Ibid., pp. 578–79.

159. In deference to navy wishes, the 1923 revision of the Basic Plan of National Defense replaced Russia with the United States as Japan's number-one potential enemy. But even this plan defined the mission of the bulk of Japan's ground forces (aside from the two to three divisions required for an invasion of the U.S. possessions of Luzon Island and Guam) as defense against Russia and China (see Shimanuki, "Dai-ichiji sekai taisen igo no kokubō hōshin," p. 70).

160. In July 1938, Japanese troops challenged the arrival of a new Soviet detachment at Zhangufeng near the Korea-Soviet border and were forced to sue for peace after 1,440 casualties. In 1939, a clash with Soviet troops at Nomonhan near the western border of Manchukuo developed into a full-scale war and the decisive rout of the Guandong Army's Twenty-Third Division. For detailed coverage, see Coox, Nomonhan.

161. See Shimanuki, "Dai-ichiji sekai taisen igo no kokubō hōshin," pp. 72–75.

162. Tanaka recognized the possibility of a Russian defeat by Germany (an eventuality he deemed "undesirable") in a letter to mentor Terauchi Masatake at the end of August; see Terauchi Masatake kankei monjo 315-25, Tanaka to Terauchi, August 31, 1914.

163. Ibid.

164. Gotō Shinpei monjo R-86, Terauchi to Gotō, August 7, 1914.

165. Kobayashi Michihiko, "'Teikoku kokubō hōshin' saikō," pp. 45–46.

166. Ibid., pp. 46, 63.

167. Hatano, "Tai-Doku kaisen to Nihon gaikō," p. 46.

168. Kobayashi Michihiko, "'Teikoku kokubō hōshin' no dōyō," p. 59.

169. Ibid., p. 61.

170. Muroyama, "Nichi-Ro sengo no gunbi kakuchō mondai," p. 1245.

171. Banno et al., *Takarabe Takeshi nikki*, 2: 316 (August 5, 1914); HN, 4: 32 (August 14, 1914).

172. Suzuki Hajime, *Suzuki Kantarō jiden*, p. 193.

173. Kaigun daijin kanbō, *Kaigun gunbi enkaku*, p. 179.

174. Hatano, "Tai-Doku kaisen to Nihon gaikō," p. 46.

175. Hirama, "Dai-ichiji sekai taisen e no sanka to kaigun," p. 30.

176. Ibid.

177. Banno et al., *Takarabe Takeshi nikki*, 2: 319 (August 14, 1914).

178. Hatano, "Tai-Doku kaisen to Nihon gaikō," pp. 63–64.

179. Usui, *Nihon to Chūgoku*, pp. 48–52.

180. Hatano, "Tai-Doku kaisen to Nihon gaikō," p. 67.

181. Ibid.

182. Gaimushō, *Nihon gaikō bunsho*, 1914, 3: 666.

183. For a richly textured and authoritative account of Japanese interests in Micronesia (including the Imperial Navy) from the 1880s until 1945, see Peattie, *Nan'yō*.

184. Takeuchi, *War and Diplomacy in the Japanese Empire*, p. 177.

185. *Yomiuri shinbun*, September 6, 1914, in STH, 1914, 2: 389.

186. *Tokyo Asahi shinbun*, August 19, 1914, in STH, 1914, 2: 317.

187. "Inoue kō e hōkoku yōten" (August 20, 1914), "Inoue, Ōkuma kaikenki" (September 12, 1914), and "Inoue, Ōkuma kaikenki" (September 21, 1914), in ONS, pp. 97, 118–28, 138–48.

188. Mochizuki to Inoue (September 4, 1914), "Inoue, Ōkuma kaikenki" (September 12, 1914), in ONS, pp. 116, 122.

189. Rumor had it that Inoue planned to destroy the cabinet; see Banno et al., *Takarabe Takeshi nikki*, 2: 328 (September 11, 1914).

190. "Inoue, Ōkuma kaikenki" (September 21, 1914), in ONS, p. 145.

191. Tokutomi, *Kōshaku Yamagata Aritomo den*, 3: 912.

192. Ibid., pp. 912–13.

193. Ibid., p. 917.

194. The field marshal had complained at the September 24 meeting that Katō continued to oppose two new divisions; see "Ōkuma shushō to yon genrō kaiken danwa hikki" (September 24, 1914), in ONS, p. 173.

195. "Important Domestic Political Matters," in Tokutomi, *Kōshaku Yamagata Aritomo den*, 3: 918.

196. Ibid., p. 915.

197. Ibid., p. 917.

198. Ibid.

199. "Ōkuma shushō to yon genrō kaiken danwa hikki" (September 24, 1914), in ONS, p. 177.

Chapter 3

1. "Chintō kanraku shukuga chōchin gyōretsu de kyūjō mae wa hi no umi," *Jiji shinpō*, November 9, 1914; in Taishō nyūsu jiten hensan iinkai, *Taishō nyūsu jiten*, 1: 414–15.

2. See Lowe, *Great Britain and Japan*, pp. 226–27, for Katō's connection with belligerent elements. For the Twenty-One Demands as a critical step in Japan's eventual war with China, see Tōyama et al., *Shōwashi*, p. 7; and Nomura, "Tai-Ka nijūikkajō mondai to Katō Takaaki," pt. 1, p. 1.

3. Just as they would mourn May 4, the start of a nationwide wave of protests over the transfer of Shandong province to Japan at the Versailles Peace Conference in 1919, the Chinese designated May 7 and 9, the days on which Japan issued and received a reply, respectively, to an ultimatum over the Twenty-One Demands, as national humiliation days.

4. See Fifield, *Woodrow Wilson and the Far East*, p. 48.

5. Kitaoka Shin'ichi ("Nijūikkajō yōkyū saikō," p. 150) appropriately describes the demands as representative of the "old diplomacy," which did not fit the "new diplomacy" championed by the United States.

6. See Beasley, *Japanese Imperialism*, pp. 69–71; and Lowe, *Great Britain and Japan*, pp. 147–48, for a discussion of spheres of influence and their significance in the diplomacy of Imperial Japan.

7. Technically speaking, the United States did receive a concession in 1898 in the form of an agreement to construct a railway from Hankou to Guangzhou. But U.S. interests did not pursue the enterprise, with the result that the concession was canceled in 1905; see Moon, *Imperialism and World Politics*, p. 367.

8. As the foreign minister informed Hioki, the first three of five articles "do not in any way aim to bring about a new situation" (Itō Masanori, *Katō Takaaki*, 2: 155).

9. See LaFargue, *China and the World War*, chaps. 2 and 3, for a comprehensive treatment of the history of Japanese interests in China as it relates to the Twenty-One Demands. For a full text of the demands, see LaFarge, pp. 241–43. Briefly stated, those demands were as follows:

Group 1

The transfer of all German rights in Shandong to Japan

A Chinese guarantee not to lease or cede any territory in Shandong to another power

Permission to Japan to build a railway linking Jihe or Longkou with the Jiaozhou-Jinan Railway

The opening of important cities in Shandong for foreign residence and commerce

Group 2

A 99-year extension on the Port Arthur and Dairen leases and the South Manchuria and Andong-Mukden Railways, cession of the Jirin-Changchun Railway for 99 years

Permission for Japanese subjects to lease or own land; to travel, reside, and conduct business; and to mine in South Manchuria and Eastern Inner Mongolia

Japanese consent before permitting foreign railway construction or loans in
these areas

Consultation with Japan before engaging political, financial, or military advisers
here

Group 3

The Han-Ye-Ping Company to become a Sino-Japanese joint concern; no mines
in the neighborhood to be worked by anyone else without this company's
consent

Group 4

No cession or lease to another power of any harbor, bay, or island along the
China coast

Group 5

China to engage Japanese political, financial, and military advisers and to grant
Japanese hospitals, temples, and schools in the Chinese interior the right to
own land

Joint Japanese and Chinese administration of police in problem areas

Purchase of Japanese arms or establishment of a Sino-Japanese joint arsenal
with advisers from Japan

Japanese rights to construct railways between Wuchang and the Jiujiang-
Nanchang line, between Nanchang and Hangzhou, and between Nanchang
and Chaozhou

Consultation with Japan before admitting foreign capital for railways, mines,
and harbor works in Fujian

Japanese rights to preach in China

10. The leases on Port Arthur, Dairen, and the Andong-Mukden Railway, which
connected the South Manchuria Railway with the Korean railways were due to expire in 1923, and that upon the South Manchuria Railway in 1938 (Chi, *China Diplomacy*, p. 32).

11. American railway magnate Edward H. Harriman had made a tentative
agreement with Prince Itō Hirobumi and Marquis Katsura Tarō in September 1905
for joint American-Japanese ownership and control of the South Manchuria Railway. In October 1909, Willard Straight, first as U.S. consul-general in Mukden and

later as representative of Harriman and his financial associates, negotiated an agreement with Beijing to construct a line parallel to the South Manchuria Railway to be financed by a group of U.S. banks (J. P. Morgan and Co., Kuhn Loeb and Co., First National Bank, and the National City Bank) and operated by an Anglo-American-Chinese company. In November of the same year, U.S. Secretary of State Philander Knox proposed a "neutralization" plan to Great Britain, whereby all loans to and railway construction in Manchuria be entrusted to a neutral coalition of powers. Finally, a four-power banking consortium (comprising the Deutsch-Asiatische Bank, the Hongkong and Shanghai Banking Corporation, the Banque de l'Indo-chine, and the same syndicate of U.S. banks as above) signed an agreement with Beijing in April 1911 promising to lend fifty million dollars to standardize the Chinese currency and promote industrial enterprises in Manchuria (see Moon, *Imperialism and World Politics*, pp. 366–70).

12. While demanding consultation with Japan on the appointment of all advisers in the region was a new development, Beijing had had a long history of employing foreign help, from the initial appointment of Jesuit missionaries as astronomers at the Qing court in the seventeenth century. Beginning in the latter part of the nineteenth century, the placing of advisers had become one aspect of great power rivalry on the continent.

13. Butow, *Tojo and the Coming of the War*, pp. 103–4.

14. In 1914 the northern border of Zhili extended more than 100 miles to the northwest of Mukden in Manchuria (LaFargue, *China and the World War*, p. 39, n33).

15. See ibid., pp. 39–41; and Usui, *Nihon to Chūgoku*, p. 70.

16. Usui, *Nihon to Chūgoku*, p. 13.

17. Ibid., p. 73; LaFargue, *China and the World War*, p. 44.

18. See Griswold, *The Far Eastern Policy of the United States*, pp. 83–84.

19. LaFargue, *China and the World War*, pp. 41–42.

20. Katō informed the U.S. ambassador to Tokyo, George Guthrie, in March 1915 of his concern over U.S. intentions in Fujian (Fifield, *Woodrow Wilson and the Far East*, p. 39).

21. See Jansen, *The Japanese and Sun Yat-sen*, p. 180. Usui Katsumi (*Nihon to Chūgoku*, pp. 58–60) describes the demands as the product of China adventurer Uchida Ryōhei.

22. Lowe, *Great Britain and Japan*, pp. 226–27.

23. See, for example, the exchange between Peter Lowe and Malcolm Kennedy in ibid., pp. 227–28, n5. Katō's biographer claims that Group 5 was forced on Katō (Itō Masanori, *Katō Takaaki*, 2: 200).

24. Chi, *China Diplomacy*, pp. 44–46.

25. HN, 4: 101 (May 18, 1915); Takahashi Yoshio, *Banshōroku*, 3: 181 (diary entry for May 14, 1915); Takahashi was a tea master and close friend of Yamagata's.

26. Usui, *Nihon to Chūgoku*, p. 75.

27. Before the Sino-Japanese negotiations of 1915, Yuan Shikai had commissioned the services of an impressive roster of foreign help, including Australian journalist George Morrison, French military adviser Lieutenant-Colonel Brissaud des Maillets, American constitutional scholar Frank J. Goodnow, and two prominent Japanese aides who continued to serve the Chinese president, international jurist Ariga Nagao and Japanese Army General Staff Colonel Banzai Rihachirō (Feuerwerker, *The Foreign Establishment in China in the Early Twentieth Century*, pp. 105–7). Regarding landownership for hospitals, temples, and schools, the powers had, by virtue of their own most-favored-nation clauses, already taken advantage of an article of the Sino-French treaty of 1860 permitting the purchase of land and construction of buildings throughout China (Feuerwerker, p. 39).

28. Bryan presumed that, by the most-favored-nation clause, the Japanese were already entitled to the privileges that had been granted to European and American missionaries (Chi, *China Diplomacy*, p. 44).

29. Namely, the eighty-mile Jiujiang-Nanchang line and the Zhaozhoufu-Shantou line.

30. LaFargue, *China and the World War*, pp. 42–43; Usui, *Nihon to Chūgoku*, pp. 75–76.

31. Usui, *Nihon to Chūgoku*, pp. 71–72. The question of Japanese legal jurisdiction over its subjects in South Manchuria had become of increasing concern in Tokyo after the annexation of Korea in 1910. Since the Jiandao Agreement of 1909, Beijing had allowed Korean farmers to live under Chinese jurisdiction in the Jindao region adjacent to the Korean border. But when these farmers became Japanese subjects with the annexation of Korea, Tokyo hoped to exercise greater control over the population.

32. Ironically, one of the staunchest opponents of this bid in 1915 for greater Sino-Japanese military cooperation, Chinese Army Chief of Staff Duan Qirui, would, as prime minister in 1918, negotiate the Sino-Japanese Military Agreement.

33. Yoshino Sakuzō, *Nisshi kōshō ron* (Tokyo: Keiseisha, 1915), pp. 255–56; cited in Mitani, *Taishō demokurashii ron*, p. 190.

34. These were the words of the French ambassador to Tokyo in an article for *Le Temps*. The French minister in Beijing went so far as to advise Yuan Shikai to accept the demands as they stood (Chi, *China Diplomacy*, p. 39). In his memoirs, British foreign secretary Edward Grey (*Twenty-Five Years*, 2: 104–5) described Japanese actions in 1915 as eminently understandable and even demonstrative of great "restraint." For the United States, see note 28.

35. They also reflect the growing power of public opinion in imperialist diplomacy. In protesting to Japan, both Wilson and British foreign secretary Edward

Grey were responding largely to the outburst of criticism in their own country's press and public opinion (see Fifield, *Woodrow Wilson and the Far East*, pp. 40, 45).

36. Kiyosawa Kiyoshi (*Nihon gaikōshi*, 2: 363) also stresses the economic thrust of the Twenty-One Demands. Yoshino Sakuzō, too, a man who would describe Katō's terms as the "bare minimum" necessary, emphasized their economic over their political and territorial value (Usui, *Nihon to Chūgoku*, p. 60).

37. Japanese minister Hioki was not merely making idle threats when he informed Chinese president Yuan Shikai on January 18 that Katō's demands were moderate compared to the radical opinion in Japan that called for support for the Chinese revolutionary party and the overthrow of Yuan. Should a special envoy be sent to Beijing in keeping with the wishes of Japan's most powerful statesmen, Hioki added, the scale of demands would be "considerable" and the consequences "unimaginable" (see Usui, *Nihon to Chūgoku*, p. 62).

38. See Chapter 2 herein for the details of these proposals.

39. Oka Ichinosuke monjo 1-2, Akashi to Oka, August 16, 1914.

40. Inoue Kaoru kō denki hensankai, *Segai Inoue kō den*, 5: 372.

41. Yamagata to Tokutomi Sohō, November 1914, in Itō Takashi et al., *Tokutomi Sohō kankei monjo*, 2: 391.

42. HN, 4: 68 (November 26, 1914).

43. Usui Katsumi, "Nanman, Tōmō jōyaku no seiritsu zengo," in Kurihara, *Tai-Manmō seisakushi no ichimen*, p. 176. For the details of the proposals by Fukushima Yasumasa and successor Nakamura Satoru, see Kurihara, p. 116. Hatano ("Tai-Doku kaisen to Nihon gaikō," p. 65) speculates that Katō arranged for Fukushima's premature retirement from the Guandong governor-generalship.

44. "Inoue shimei, Ōkuma to no kaidan" (October 1, 1914), in ONS, p. 217.

45. Both Yamagata and Satsuma *genrō* Matsukata Masayoshi would claim after the commencement of negotiations that they had learned the details of the talks only after Chinese president Yuan Shikai leaked their substance to the press (see Oka, *Yamagata Aritomo*, p. 141; for Matsukata, see HN, 4: 96 [April 19, 1915]). In reality, however, Katō had explained the details to Yamagata in a December 30 meeting. The elder statesman was angry at that time that the foreign minister had not consulted him prior to the final draft. But his only comment on the substance of the proposal was that Katō should be prepared for "resolute determination" (*ichidai kesshin*) on the items covering Manchuria and Mongolia, which were of the greatest interest to Japan (see "Tai-Shi saigo tsūchō jiken," May 1915, in Futagami Hyōji kankei monjo, no. 6). Yamagata's ex post facto fabrication undoubtedly reflected a new attempt to distance himself from a policy whose substance he had supported but which had exacerbated tensions between Tokyo and Beijing.

46. Instructions of August 27, 1914; in Itō Masanori, *Katō Takaaki*, 2: 154.

47. In a November 6 letter to mentor Terauchi, Tanaka Giichi had complained that two recent meetings between Field Marshal Yamagata and the foreign minister had revealed little "ambition or will" on Katō's part regarding China policy (Terauchi Masatake kankei monjo 315-27, Tanaka to Terauchi, November 6, 1914). The Foreign Ministry's representative in Beijing, Hioki Eki, had recommended a decision on negotiations with China as early as August 26 (see Nagaoka, "Tai-Ka nijūikkajō yōkyū jōkō," p. 74).

48. Gaimushō, *Nihon gaikō bunsho*, 1914, 3: 506.

49. *Tokyo Asahi shinbun*, November 12, 1914, p. 2.

50. See Gaimushō, *Nihon gaikō bunsho*, 1914, 3: 567, for the Japanese text of the instructions.

51. The one conspicuous exception is Nomura, "Tai-Ka nijūikkajō mondai to Katō Takaaki," pt. 1, pp. 9–10. Nomura argues, however, that Katō delayed the talks with China not to avoid army interference in diplomacy but to avoid the adverse effects of difficult diplomatic talks on the army campaign in Shandong. He also hints at Katō's anticipation of the upcoming general election, but without any elaboration.

52. *Tōkyō Asahi shinbun*, December 4, 1914, p. 2.

53. Itō Masanori, *Katō Takaaki*, 2: 34.

54. Ōtsu, *Dai Nihon kenseishi*, 7: 382.

55. Ibid., pp. 389–98.

56. The Military Affairs Council aimed to provide the institutional framework for defense allocations that the Meiji polity had lacked. Not responsible under the Meiji constitution to the civilian cabinet, the Imperial Army and Navy had been plagued from their inception by severe interservice competition for resources. The council brought together the premier, the foreign and finance ministers, the two service ministers, and the chiefs of the two general staffs to rationalize the budgetary process. But the new organization turned out to be as powerless as Japan's civilian cabinets to regulate the competing demands of both services. It could do no more than simply approve the budgetary requests of the army and navy without amendment. See Muroyama, "Nichi-Ro sengo no gunbi kakuchō mondai," pp. 1247–49.

57. HN, 4: 56 (October 9, 1914).

58. This was confirmed by both Tanaka (on November 7) and Marquis Saionji Kinmochi (on November 26) (ibid., pp. 63, 68 [November 7, 26, 1914]).

59. Ibid., p. 69 (November 29, 1914). At the same time, Gotō Shinpei urged Yamagata to prevent a Diet dissolution, which, Gotō argued, was simply a government ploy to remain in power (HN, 4: 65 [November 20, 1914]).

60. The Hara diary entry for December 2, 1914, records Yamagata's complaints regarding Katō and Wakatsuki's opposition to army expansion in the Military Affairs Council and speculation that these two were inciting the Seiyūkai to opposition (ibid., p. 70 [December. 2, 1914]).

61. Ibid., p. 69 (November 29, 1914).

62. Ibid., p. 70 (November 30, 1914).

63. Ibid., pp. 70, 72 (November 30, December 6, 1914).

64. In an address to his party (Itō Masanori, *Katō Takaaki*, 2: 34).

65. HN, 4: 75–76 (December 14, 16, 1914).

66. Ibid., pp. 71–72, 78 (December 4, 5, 19, 1914).

67. Ibid., p. 71 (December 4, 1914).

68. Ibid., p. 78 (December 19, 1914).

69. Ōtsu, *Dai Nihon kenseishi*, 7: 412; Ōkuma kō hachijūgonenshi hensankai, *Ōkuma kō hachijūgonenshi*, 3: 205.

70. HN, 4: 81 (December 22, 1914).

71. Ibid., p. 83 (December 25, 1914).

72. Dōshikai members returning to party headquarters after the 11 P.M. decision to dissolve the Diet danced in jubilation, with shouts of "banzai" and exclamations that "the scheme went entirely as planned" (*Tokyo Asahi shinbun*, December 26, 1914, p. 5). Tanaka Giichi informed Terauchi on January 24, 1915, that Ōkuma, in a meeting with Tanaka that day, had expressed delight that the Seiyūkai had become ensnared in his trap and had given the cabinet an excuse to dissolve the Diet as planned (Terauchi Masatake kankei monjo 315-33, Tanaka to Terauchi, January 24, 1915).

73. See especially Usui, *Nihon to Chūgoku*, pp. 61–85. In English, see LaFargue, *China and the World War*, chap. 3.

74. Among the most resolute advocates of resistance to Japan's demands in 1915 was Chinese Army Chief of Staff Duan Qirui, who, as prime minister in 1917, would become the chief beneficiary of Japanese financial aid (in the form of the "Nishihara loans"). In cabinet deliberations in anticipation of a Japanese ultimatum in early May, Duan urged staunch resistance to avoid a humiliating national collapse (Usui, *Nihon to Chūgoku*, p. 82).

75. HN, 4: 111 (July 7, 1915).

76. Takahashi Yoshio, *Banshōroku*, 3: 255 (July 2, 1915).

77. Ōtsu, *Dai Nihon kenseishi*, 7: 550–51.

78. Terauchi Masatake kankei monjo 315-32, Tanaka to Terauchi, January 20, 1915.

79. Terauchi Masatake kankei monjo 6-42, Akashi to Terauchi, January 22, 1915.

80. Tanaka Giichi kankei monjo, Terauchi to Tanaka, January 27, 1915.

81. Mochizuki to Inoue, February 26, 1915, in ONS, p. 263.

82. HN, 4: 69, 78 (November 29, December 19, 1914).

83. "Tai-Shi saigo tsūchō jiken," May 1915, Futagami Hyōji kankei monjo, no. 6.

84. Untitled Miura memorandum of 1915, in Yamamoto, *Miura Gorō kankei monjo*, p. 17.

85. Akashi Motojirō monjo 41-1, Yamagata to Akashi, January 23, 1915; in Nihon seiji gaikōshi kenkyūkai, "Akashi Motojirō monjo oyobi kadai," p. 100.

86. HN, 4: 32 (August 14, 1914).

87. Ibid., p. 91 (March 10, 1915).

88. Ibid.

89. Katō to Hioki, February 3, 1915, in Gaimushō, Nihon gaikō bunsho, 1915, 3-1: 132.

90. Katō to Hioki, March 24, 1915, in Gaimushō, Nihon gaikō bunsho, 1915, 3-1: 257.

91. Tokyo Asahi shinbun, March 23, 1915, p. 2.

92. Ibid.

93. This was Ōkuma's closing appeal in a speech pressed into record form for distribution during the campaign (Ōkuma kō hachijūgonenshi hensankai, Ōkuma kō hachijūgonenshi, 3: 236).

94. HN, 4: 69 (November 29, 1914).

95. Oka Ichinosuke monjo 7-6, Tanaka to Oka, November 26, 1914.

96. HN, 4: 84 (December 30, 1914).

97. Ibid., p. 81 (December 22, 1914).

98. According to Tanaka, Vice Chief of the Army General Staff Akashi Motojirō made a similar assessment of Oka (Terauchi Masatake kankei monjo 315-29, Tanaka to Terauchi, December 29, 1914).

99. HN, 4: 87 (January 18, 1915). Oka was spared at this point in part because of Terauchi's objection to forcing him out (see Terauchi Masatake kankei monjo 315-34, Tanaka to Terauchi, February 3, 1915).

100. See Uzaki Keijō, "Oka rikushō to Yashiro kaishō," Chūō kōron 29, no. 5 (May 1914): 69.

101. Oka submitted a memorandum to Katō in November delineating army demands (see Nagaoka, "Tai-Ka nijūikkajō yōkyū jōkō," p. 80).

102. Mirroring their reluctance to support Japanese belligerence in August 1914, representatives of the Imperial Navy, like Foreign Minister Katō, hoped to minimize army involvement in negotiations with China in 1915. Navy Minister Yashiro Rokurō agreed to the Twenty-One Demands in January on the condition that force not be used. And on the eve of the May 7 ultimatum to China, Vice Admiral Nawa Matahachirō, commander of the Second Fleet, argued for a naval blockade, rather than the mobilization of troops, to enforce Japan's final terms (Hirama, "Tai-Ka nijūikkajō no yōkyū to kaigun," pp. 30, 32).

103. Tanaka Giichi kankei monjo, Terauchi to Tanaka, January 27, 1915.

104. Terauchi Masatake kankei monjo 315-32, Tanaka to Terauchi, January 20, 1915.

105. Ibid., 6-42, Akashi to Terauchi, January 22, 1915.

106. Ibid., 315-34, Tanaka to Terauchi, February 3, 1915.

107. Akashi Motojirō monjo 41-1, Yamagata to Akashi, January 23, 1915; in Nihon seiji gaikōshi kenkyūkai, "Akashi Motojirō monjo oyobi kadai," p. 100; "Tai-Shi saigo tsūchō jijō," May 1915, in Futagami Hyōji kankei monjo, no. 6. There were others, of course, who appealed for more than merely the application of military force. Japanese Army General Staff officer and adviser to Chinese president Yuan Shikai, Banzai Rihachirō, for example, urged in April 1915 the immediate annexation of China (Banzai to Terauchi, April 19, 1915, Terauchi Masatake kankei monjo 24-10; cited in Banno, "Nihon rikugun no Ōbeikan to Chūgoku seisaku," pp. 449–50).

108. Terauchi Masatake kankei monjo, 315-32, Tanaka to Terauchi, January 20, 1915. While the reason for Yamagata's complaints about Oka are not explicit in this letter from Tanaka to Terauchi, they are described at a time when the use of force had become a topic of discussion. Katō had just informed Yamagata that the cabinet had yet to discuss military operations. And Akashi Motojirō apprised Terauchi on January 29 of Oka's hesitation to use force (Terauchi Masatake kankei monjo, 6-43, Akashi to Terauchi, January 29, 1915).

109. Ibid., 315-34, Tanaka to Terauchi, February 3, 1915.

110. Ibid., 6-44, Akashi to Terauchi, February 3, 1915.

111. Ibid., 6-48, Akashi to Terauchi, February 22, 1915.

112. Gaimushō, Nihon gaikō bunsho, 1915, 3: 171–72.

113. Ōsaka Asahi shinbun, March 1, 1915, in STH, 1915, 1: 366.

114. Gaimushō, Nihon gaikō bunsho, 1915, 3-1: 206–7; Terauchi Masatake kankei monjo 6-50, Akashi to Terauchi, March 8, 1915.

115. Itō Masanori, Katō Takaaki, 1: 60, 2: 165.

116. Gaimushō, Nihon gaikō bunsho, 1915, 3-1: 342.

117. HN, 4: 96 (April 19, 1915).

118. Itō Masanori, Katō Takaaki, 1: 26.

119. This is not to say that Katō did not keep the genrō informed about his talks with China. The foreign minister had met privately with Yamagata on November 1, December 30, and April 21 and had sent Foreign Ministry Secretary Matsui Keishirō to Odawara on March 8 to brief the field marshal on the progress of the discussions. The problem from Yamagata's perspective, however, was that these were meant as briefings, without any intention of soliciting the elder statesman's advice (see "Tai-Shi saigo tsūchō jijō," Futagami Hyōji kankei monjo, no. 6).

120. Hioki to Katō, April 23, 1915, in Gaimushō, Nihon gaikō bunsho, 1915, 3-1: 341. Katō's response in ibid., p. 342.

121. Tōkyō Asahi shinbun, May 4, 1915, p. 2; cited in Takeuchi, War and Diplomacy in the Japanese Empire, p. 188, n26.

122. Itō Masanori, Katō Takaaki, 1: 24; Wakatsuki, Meiji, Taishō, Shōwa seikai hisshi, pp. 205–6; Duus, Party Rivalry and Political Change in Taishō Japan, p. 95. Gotō

Shinpei and his associates argued at this point that Japan would "descend into a dangerous position" if she did not declare war on China (HN, 4: 97 [May 5, 1915]).

123. Nomura, *Kindai Nihon seiji gaikōshi kenkyū*, p. 194.

124. Ibid.

125. HN, 4: 101 (May 18, 1915).

126. Ibid., p. 111 (July 7, 1915).

127. Kitaoka Shin'ichi (*Nihon rikugun to tairiku seisaku*, pp. 176–77), too, rejects the idea that Yamagata objected either to the substance of Group 5 of the demands or to an aggressive Japanese posture. He argues, however, not that the field marshal criticized the clause for political reasons (as asserted here), but that he worried about great power reaction to a strong Japanese stance. In that sense, Kitaoka preserves the image of the elder statesman as a voice of caution.

128. Akashi Motojirō monjo 41-1, Yamagata to Akashi, January 23, 1915; in Nihon seiji gaikōshi kenkyūkai, "Akashi Motojirō monjo oyobi kadai," p. 100; "Tai-Shi saigo tsūchō jijō," May 1915, Futagami Hyōji kankei monjo, no. 6.

129. "Tai-Shi saigo tsūchō no jijō," May 1915, Futagami Hyōji kankei monjo, no. 6.

130. Inoue Kaoru monjo, vol. 30, Yamagata to Inoue, May 4, 1915.

131. In a conversation with Inoue secretary Mochizuki on May 4, Yamagata acknowledged his support in April for the use of force against China. He continued, "looking at the future in such a case, Marquis Inoue's idea of coordinating with Britain, the United States, and Russia is necessary" (Mochizuki to Inoue, May 5, 1915, in ONS, p. 267). The full text of the quotation from Yamagata's May 4, 1915, letter to Inoue reads, "If Foreign Minister Katō personally goes to China to negotiate directly, *even if we do not achieve a peaceful resolution*, we will have expressed the sincerity of the empire and thereby maintain the trust of the powers and gain the sympathy of the people" (emphasis my own; Inoue Kaoru monjo, vol. 30, Yamagata to Inoue, May 4, 1915).

132. Yamagata had solicited the memorandum to marshal Inoue's support in the fight with the cabinet. Inoue was unable to attend the cabinet meeting because of illness (Mochizuki to Inoue, May 5, 1915, in ONS, p. 266).

133. "Genrō, shushō ate Inoue Kaoru iken," May 6, 1915, in ibid., p. 268.

134. Mochizuki to Inoue, May 7, 1915, in ibid., p. 269.

135. Until the late 1980s, Katō's powerful promotion of Foreign Ministry supremacy in foreign-policy decision making was celebrated by a lone bust of the former foreign minister in the front lobby of the Foreign Ministry archives. I am indebted to Baba Akira for bringing this fact to my attention.

136. Takahashi Yoshio, *Banshōroku*, 3: 181 (diary entry for May 14, 1915). Yamagata later boasted that the cabinet had avoided war over the demands by listening to the *genrō*. But Marquis Saionji Kinmochi aptly noted the incongruity of this claim with

the reality of continuing *genrō* antipathy toward the cabinet, marked by a new offensive in June (HN, 4: 111 [July 6, 1915]).

137. HN, 4: 100 (May 18, 1915). From Yamagata's visit and from recent "unprecedented" approaches by Home Minister Ōura, Hara suspected that the elder statesman might be planning to eject Katō and create a new cabinet around Hara and Ōura (ibid., 103 [May 20, 1915]).

138. Ibid., pp. 111 (Matsukata), 112, 114 (Inoue) (July 7, 8, 1915). Yamagata, of course, realized that Katō was reluctant to share diplomatic papers with all of the elder statesmen, not just Inoue (see ibid., p. 101 [May 18, 1915]; and Tokutomi, *Kōshaku Yamagata Aritomo den*, 3: 910).

139. Terauchi Masatake kankei monjo 315-38, Tanaka to Terauchi, July 3, 1915.

140. HN, 4: 112, 114 (July 7, 8, 1915); Terauchi Masatake kankei monjo 315-38, Tanaka to Terauchi, July 3, 1915.

141. HN, 4: 110 (July 7, 1915); Terauchi Masatake kankei monjo 315-38, Tanaka to Terauchi, July 3, 1915.

142. Itō Masanori, *Katō Takaaki*, 2: 48. Indicative of Yamagata's sentiments at this point, he penned the following poem at a June 20 gathering of the Tokiwakai, an informal poetry association, when given the theme of "fan":

> While aware of its end
> With autumn,
> The fluttering fan
> Works through the summer.

Because the poem insinuated the transient nature of the cabinet, Yamagata requested his fellow bards to keep it to themselves (Takahashi Yoshio, *Banshōroku*, 3: 241 [June 21, 1915]). In response to Ōkuma's suggestion at the June 25 meeting that Katō come to explain his policies personally to the *genrō*, Inoue snapped, "That stupid fool knows nothing about diplomacy. If he comes, I'll turn him away at the door!" (Takahashi Yoshio, p. 255 [July 2, 1915]).

143. Hara inferred from this that what he had heard from another party was probably true—namely, that "Yamagata instigated Inoue and company while remaining the innocent and made use of the fact that Inoue and Matsukata would not be appeased" (HN, 4: 111 [July 7, 1915]).

144. Terauchi Masatake kankei monjo 315-38, Tanaka to Terauchi, July 3, 1915.

145. The reference, of course, was to the Taishō political crisis (ibid., 315-39, Tanaka to Terauchi, July 6, 1915). Hara Takashi guessed that Yamagata preferred Ōkuma in power for fear of another debacle like the Yamamoto cabinet, that is, of a Satsuma or Seiyūkai resurgence with a cabinet headed by Matsukata or someone sympathetic to the Seiyūkai (HN, 4: 121 [August 9, 1915]).

146. HN, 4: 121 (August 9, 1915).

147. Takahashi Yoshio, *Banshōroku*, 3: 258 (July 5, 1915).

148. This is how Tanaka described the objective to Terauchi (Terauchi Masatake kankei monjo 315-39, Tanaka to Terauchi, July 6, 1915).

149. HN, 4: 124–25 (August 18, 1915); Terauchi Masatake kankei monjo 315-43, Tanaka to Terauchi, August 10, 1915.

150. Hiranuma would go on to play a pivotal role in the destruction of party government in Japan in his capacity as chairman of the National Foundation Society and vice president of the Privy Council.

151. HN, 4: 122 (August 13, 1915).

152. Both Takahashi Yoshio and Mochizuki Kotarō speculated that this was Katō's aim (see Takahashi Yoshio, *Banshōroku*, 3: 298 [August 7, 1915]; and Mochizuki to Inoue, August 3, 1915, in ONS, p. 286). Ōkuma informed Yamagata on August 4 of Katō's determination to break with a failing cabinet to run for the prime ministry (YDH, p. 72).

153. Mochizuki to Inoue, August 7, 1915, in ONS, p. 291.

Chapter 4

1. Harries and Harries, *Soldiers of the Sun*, pp. 110–11. For an in-depth study of German POWs in Japan during the First World War, see Hayashi Keisuke, *Bandō horyo shūyōjo*. In English, see Burdick and Moessner, *German Prisoners-of-War in Japan*.

2. Terauchi Masatake kankei monjo 315-38, Tanaka to Terauchi, July 3, 1915.

3. HN, 4: 156 (January 24, 1916).

4. Yoshino, "Kyokutan naru Doitsu sanbironsha o imashimu," pp. 73–76.

5. Yoshino, "Kensei no hongi o toite."

6. Mochizuki to Inoue, August 7, 1915, in ONS, p. 290.

7. Shidehara and Katō were related through their wives, who were sisters and daughters of the head of the Mitsubishi conglomerate, Iwasaki Yatarō. In 1915, Yamagata worried that Katō would use these family ties with Shidehara to maintain his hold on the Foreign Ministry (HN, 4: 141 [October 30, 1915]).

8. Ōkuma Shigenobu kankei monjo, Yamagata to Ōkuma, August 18, 1915.

9. Germany had approached Japan about a separate peace several times since January 1915, but Katō had communicated these overtures to the Allies (Iklé, "Japanese-German Peace Negotiations During World War I," pp. 63–65).

10. Yoshimura, *Nihon to Roshia*, p. 215. This would not be the last of Allied concerns regarding pro-German sentiment in Tokyo. A commander I. V. Gillis, who was sent by the U.S. State Department to Japan in May 1916 to report on Japanese attitudes, noted the following February that Japan was taking no active measures against the kaiser. Rather, everyone "seemed to be of the opinion that Japan was actively preparing for war against the United States" (Chi, *China Diplomacy*, p. 104).

Even during the Paris Peace Conference, some of Woodrow Wilson's advisers were convinced that the Japanese were negotiating behind the scenes with the Germans (Fifield, *Woodrow Wilson and the Far East*, p. 221, n6).

11. Itō Masanori, *Katō Takaaki*, 2: 49.

12. Ōkuma to Ishii, August 26, 1915, in Gaimushō, *Nihon gaikō bunsho*, 1915, 3-1: 31.

13. Ibid.

14. Yamagata Aritomo monjo, vol. 26, Akashi to Yamagata, September 25, 1915. Ishii himself was initially not adverse to the idea of an alliance with Russia. He wired Ōkuma on August 22 that including Russia in the Anglo-Japanese alliance "would not pose a great obstacle" (Ishii to Ōkuma, August 22, 1915, in Gaimushō, *Nihon gaikō bunsho*, 1915, 3-1: 30).

15. Terauchi Masatake kankei monjo 360-10, Yamagata to Terauchi, September 20, 1915.

16. Inoue to Ōkuma, August 31, 1915, in Gaimushō, *Nihon gaikō bunsho*, 1915, 3-1: 33.

17. Takeuchi, *War and Diplomacy in the Japanese Empire*, pp. 198–99.

18. Cited in Chi, *China Diplomacy*, p. 65.

19. Foreign Ministry text of the warning to Yuan, in Gaimushō, *Nihon gaikō bunsho*, 1915, 2: 99–100.

20. HN, 4: 136 (October 14, 1915).

21. Hamaomote Matasuke monjo, no. 4, Banzai to Hamaomote, December 10, 1914, in HMM, pp. 212–14.

22. "Teikoku seifu no Chūgoku seifu ni taisuru teisei enki kankoku ni kanshi kōhyō no ken," October 29, 1915, in Gaimushō, *Nihon gaikō bunsho*, 1915, 2: 100.

23. Katō to Hioki, July 29, 1915; cited in Usui, "Nanman, Tōmō jōyaku no seiritsu zengo," p. 126.

24. Ibid.

25. *Tokyo Asahi shinbun*, October 8, 1915, p. 4.

26. Usui, "Nanman, Tōmō jōyaku no seiritsu zengo," p. 127.

27. Negishi had served as field director for the Tōa Dōbun Shoin in Shanghai and would become a renowned China economist at Hitotsubashi University.

28. HN, 4: 141 (October 29, 1915).

29. Ibid., p. 136 (October 14, 1915).

30. Kitaoka Shin'ichi (*Nihon rikugun to tairiku seisaku*, pp. 181–93), too, analyzes the Ōkuma cabinet's "anti-Yuan" policy in terms of a shift of power from Katō Takaaki to the Army General Staff. But he stresses, as well, the increased importance of the China *rōnin* with the influx of former Kokumintō politicians in the reshuffled cabinet in August and sees all three Ōkuma cabinet decisions on China from October 1915 to March 1916 as the handiwork of these anti-Katō forces. He explains the policy shift between November 1915 and March 1916, then, not in terms of a shift

from Katō to the Army General Staff but in terms of a policy change within the anti-Katō camp. In English, see Kitaoka, "China Experts in the Army," pp. 352–60.

31. Chief of the Army General Staff Hasegawa Yoshimichi's lack of favor with Yamagata also contributed to Tanaka's political success.

32. Terauchi Masatake kankei monjo 315-46, Tanaka to Terauchi, October 13, 1915.

33. Ibid.

34. HN, 4: 140 (October 29, 1915).

35. Ibid., pp. 135, 141 (October 14, November 2, 1915). Further evidence that the October cabinet decision was not the product of anti-Katō forces, as Kitaoka Shin'ichi suggests, is found in the Hara diary. Negishi Tadashi informed Hara Takashi at the end of the month that Foreign Ministry Political Affairs Bureau Chief Koike Chōzō had consulted with Katō in drafting the policy (HN, 4: 140–41 [October 29, 1915]). For Kitaoka's argument, see Kitaoka, Nihon rikugun to tairiku seisaku, pp. 186–87; and Kitaoka, "China Experts in the Army," pp. 352–54.

36. Tokyo Asahi shinbun, October 29, 1915, p. 2.

37. Chi, China Diplomacy, p. 70.

38. In an extraordinary cabinet session called on November 3 to discuss Yuan's intransigence (HN, 4: 142 [November 6, 1915]).

39. Chi, China Diplomacy, pp. 70–71.

40. The plan was to pave the way for a national unity cabinet under Yamagata's rule (HN, 4: 142 [November 6, 1915]).

41. In a meeting of November 3, 1915 (Chi, China Diplomacy, p. 71).

42. HN, 4: 142 (November 6, 1915).

43. "Kakugi kettei" (November 18, 1915), in Gaimushō, Nihon gaikō bunsho, 1915, 2: 139–40.

44. Chi, China Diplomacy, p. 75.

45. Hamaomote Matasuke monjo, no. 6, Tanaka to Banzai, December 18, 1915, in HMM, p. 215.

46. Ishii soon instructed Hioki to schedule the visit of a Chinese envoy for around January 20, 1916 (Hamaomote Matasuke monjo, no. 7, Ishii to Tanaka, December 21, 1915, in HMM, p. 215).

47. Terauchi Masatake kankei monjo 315-46, Tanaka to Terauchi, October 13, 1915.

48. Hamaomote Matasuke monjo, no. 6, Tanaka to Banzai, December 18, 1915, in HMM, p. 215.

49. Takakura, Tanaka Giichi denki, 1: 629.

50. Zai was a former governor of Yunnan (Chi, China Diplomacy, p. 78).

51. Ibid., p. 80.

52. Hamaomote Matasuke monjo, no. 9, Tanaka to Banzai, December 1915, in HMM, p. 216.

53. Banzai to Tanaka, January 3, 1916, in Yamamoto, *Banzai Rihachirō shokan hōkokushū*, p. 33.

54. In the mid-December telegram to Banzai cited in note 52, Tanaka expressed great interest in Yuan's reaction to recent disturbances in southern China. "There have been frequent urgent reports about disturbances in Yunnan, Guizhou, and Sichuan," he informed Banzai. "And it seems that the northern armies are being sent south. You are to check and report how Yuan judges the situation" (Hamaomote Matasuke monjo, no. 9, Tanaka to Banzai, December 1915, in HMM, p. 216).

55. Banzai to Tanaka, January 14, 1916, in Yamamoto, *Banzai Rihachirō shokan hōkokushū*, p. 35.

56. Banzai to Tanaka, January 3, 1916, in ibid., p. 32.

57. Chi, *China Diplomacy*, p. 76.

58. Banzai to Tanaka, January 3, 1916, in Yamamoto, *Banzai Rihachirō shokan hōkokushū*, p. 32.

59. Chi, *China Diplomacy*, p. 78.

60. Hamaomote Matasuke monjo, no. 15, Tanaka to Banzai, January 17, 1916, in HMM, pp. 221–22.

61. Ibid. Kitaoka Shin'ichi ("China Experts in the Army," p. 355) presents a considerably milder version of Tanaka's aims by arguing that Army General Staff policy changed because of the anti-Yuan sentiment of staff officers in the field and as a response to growing animosity in Japanese public opinion toward the Chinese president. As we shall see, however, even Hara Takashi found such sentiment to be a fabrication by the general staff. In his earlier work, Kitaoka (*Nihon rikugun to tairiku seisaku*, p. 187) stresses, as noted here, the general staff's frustration with Yuan's unwillingness to build a cooperative relationship with Japan.

62. While this memorandum became the basis for the January 19 cabinet decision, this last clause was deleted, in accordance with navy wishes, before being presented to the cabinet (Hamaomote Matasuke monjo, no. 14, "Tai-Shi ikensho gen'an," January 15, 1916, in HMM, p. 221). Despite Field Marshal Yamagata's objection to the subsequent decision to cancel the visit of a special Chinese envoy to Tokyo, he was not averse to postponing the Chinese president's enthronement. On January 12 he queried Foreign Minister Ishii, "Since we have already sent a warning to China and, as we predicted, a rebel army has arisen in Yunnan and we have an unstable situation in various other areas, is it not impossible from the standpoint of the State's prestige to immediately recognize an imperial system [in China] at this time?" (YDH, p. 78).

63. "Banzai taisa ga En Segai ni taishi Nihon wa Chūgoku teisei ni kyōkō hantai naru o anji shitaru ken," in Gaimushō, *Nihon gaikō bunsho*, 1916, 2: 22.

64. Hamaomote Matasuke monjo, no. 23, Tanaka to Banzai, January 1916, in HMM, p. 227.

65. See *Tōkyō Asahi shinbun*, January 30, p. 4; February 1, p. 2; February 3, p. 4; February 4, p. 4; February 5, 1916, p. 4. On January 31, the Army General Staff ordered a study of China policy to be completed by February 15 (Hatano, "Chūgoku daisan kakumei to Nihon gaikō," p. 82).

66. Hamaomote Matasuke monjo, no. 31, Army General Staff to Aoki, February 1916, in HMM, p. 233.

67. Hamaomote Matasuke monjo, no. 27, Teranishi to Fukuda, February 1, 1916, in ibid., p. 230.

68. Specifically, he proposed supplying Yuan's enemies with machine guns (Hamaomote Matasuke monjo, no. 32, Teranishi to Uehara, February 7, 1916, in ibid., p. 233).

69. Terauchi Masatake kankei monjo 315-49, Tanaka to Terauchi, February 13, 1916.

70. Ibid.

71. Oka Ichinosuke monjo 7-10, Tanaka to Oka, February 21, 1916.

72. Hamaomote Matasuke monjo, no. 38, Teranishi to Uehara, February 19, 1916, in HMM, p. 237.

73. Oka Ichinosuke monjo 7-14, Tanaka to Oka, February 28, 1916.

74. Ibid., 7-13, Tanaka to Oka, March 1, 1916.

75. Ibid.

76. Terauchi Masatake kankei monjo 315-52, Tanaka to Terauchi, May 5, 1916.

77. HN, 4: 161 (March 3, 1916).

78. See, for example, Kitaoka, *Nihon rikugun to tairiku seisaku*, p. 190. Also see Banno, "Nihon rikugun no Ōbeikan to Chūgoku seisaku," p. 50.

79. Oka Ichinosuke monjo 7-13, Tanaka to Oka, March 1, 1916. The perception of the first Chinese revolution as a missed opportunity and the fear of missing another were prevalent sentiments among the army leadership at the time. Teranishi had argued in early February for machine guns to the south because "the main reason for Hanyang's defeat during the first revolution was the fact that the government army had forty machine guns while the revolutionary army did not possess even one" (Hamaomote Matasuke monjo, no. 32, Teranishi to Uehara, February 7, 1916, in HMM, p. 233). Tanaka could sympathize with this position because, as chief of the Military Affairs Bureau in the Army General Staff in December 1911, he had invested considerable energy in an army plan to send arms to the southern revolutionaries to increase the empire's influence in the area, only to be thwarted by a Japanese cabinet decision for neutrality and Yuan Shikai's abrogation of power. Tanaka's involvement in this plan is hinted at in Honjō Yasutarō to Uehara, December 15, 1911, in UKM, p. 454. Field Marshal Yamagata, too, had expressed great disap-

pointment when the cabinet killed his plan to send two divisions to Manchuria in response to the first revolution (Terauchi Masatake kankei monjo 360-90, Yamagata to Terauchi, February 13, 1912). It comes as no surprise, then, that Yamagata supported Tanaka in March 1916.

80. "Kakugi kettei" (March 7, 1916), in Gaimushō, Nihon gaikō bunsho, 1916, 2: 45–46. Financial aid for operations in Manchuria would eventually come from the Ōkura group, which had extensive mining, coal, and steel interests in the region. Kuhara Fusanosuke and Yasukawa Keiichirō would fund operations in Shandong and southern China (Kawada, Hara Takashi, tenkanki no kōsō, p. 66).

81. "Kakugi kettei" (March 7, 1916), in Gaimushō, Nihon gaikō bunsho, 1916, 2: 46.

82. Such a conference within the Foreign Ministry was highly irregular (Hatano, "Chūgoku daisan kakumei to Nihon gaikō," p. 90).

83. HN, 4: 163 (March 16, 1916).

84. Kurihara Ken, "Dai-ichiji dai-niji Manmō dokuritsu undō," p. 150.

85. On March 16, the Foreign Ministry helped negotiate a 500,000 yen loan from Kuhara Mining to Sun Yatsen and the southern revolutionaries. It also obtained British, French, and Russian approval in mid-April to withdraw payment of the surplus Chinese salt revenue to Beijing (see Hatano, "Chūgoku daisan kakumei to Nihon gaikō," pp. 93–94; see also Chi, China Diplomacy, pp. 82–83).

86. Hamaomote Matasuke monjo, no. 41, Tanaka to Banzai, March 1916, in HMM, p. 239.

87. Ibid.

88. Hamaomote Matasuke monjo, no. 61, Tanaka to Morioka, May 1916, in ibid., p. 253.

89. Ibid.

90. Hamaomote Matasuke monjo, no. 64, Tanaka to Aoki, May 20, 1916, in ibid., p. 255.

91. Kuroita, Fukuda taishō den, p. 274. Whether or not inspired by this first participation in a "plot," Koiso was to help plan the March Incident of 1931, which aimed to replace the civilian cabinet of Hamaguchi Osachi with a military government in anticipation of an army takeover in Manchuria (see Karita, Shōwa shoki seiji gaikōshi kenkyū, pp. 99–105).

92. The previous commander, Duan Zhigui, had fled to Beijing on hearing of Japanese designs (Kurihara, "Dai-ichiji dai-niji Manmō dokuritsu undō," p. 151). On April 19, the day of Zhang's inauguration, Chief of Staff Tamura of the Japanese forces at Port Arthur ordered a postponement of the Manchurian independence plan (Takakura, Tanaka Giichi denki, 1: 635). Tanaka wrote Terauchi in the beginning of May 1916 that Japan should "save the problem of the Zongshedang, etc., for another day" (the Zongshedang was the party supporting Manchurian independence; Terauchi Masatake kankei monjo 315-52). But Tanaka had not completely

given up on Manchuria. An uprising in the three eastern provinces was simply given a secondary place in his overall plan. As he explained to Aoki in mid-May, "We should take decisive action on a Manchurian uprising when the north and south take up arms and the spirit of the south wanes. Because this area is completely within our sphere of influence, if we take action and are, for example, pressured by Zhang, it would impinge on our prestige. In that event, we would have to pursue our objective even by a public display of arms. This, in other words, is the time to force Yuan's abdication." Tanaka attempted to salvage the situation, in other words, by viewing Zhang's ascension to power and possible opposition to Japan as further justification for the eventual plan to take up arms (see Hamaomote Matasuke monjo, no. 64, Tanaka to Aoki, May 1916, in HMM, pp. 255–56). For more on the Manchuria independence movement, see Kurihara, "Dai-ichiji dai-niji Manmō dokuritsu undō." In English, see Kitaoka, "China Experts in the Army," pp. 352–60.

93. Hamaomote Matasuke monjo, no. 64, Tanaka to Aoki, May 1916, in HMM, p. 255.

94. Hamaomote Matasuke monjo, no. 68, Tanaka to Itogawa, June 3, 1916, in ibid., p. 259.

95. Hamaomote Matasuke monjo, no. 61, Tanaka to Morioka, May 1916, in ibid., p. 253.

96. Usui, Nihon to Chūgoku, p. 99.

97. Hamaomote Matasuke monjo, no. 68, Tanaka to Itogawa, June 3, 1916, in HMM, p. 259.

98. Hamaomote Matasuke monjo, no. 70, "Tai-Shi iken gen'an," June 7, 1916, in ibid., p. 260.

99. Ibid.

100. Fukuda, it will be recalled, had coordinated Tanaka's scheme as chief of the Army General Staff's Second Bureau (Kuroita, Fukuda taishō den, p. 270).

101. Hioki to Ishii, June 10, 1916, in Gaimushō, Nihon gaikō bunsho, 1916, 2: 160.

102. Nara Takeji nikki, June 13, 1916; courtesy of the Nara Takeji monjo kenkyūkai.

103 Ibid., June 12, 1916.

104. Ishii to Hioki, June 11, 1916, in Gaimushō, Nihon gaikō bunsho, 1916, 2: 163.

105. Tokyo Asahi shinbun, January 13, 1916, in STH, 1916, 1: 80.

106. Kitaoka Shin'ichi (Nihon rikugun to tairiku seisaku, p. 215) argues that relations with Russia were at the center of Yamagata's policy of cooperation with the great powers.

107. For texts of the Russo-Japanese treaties, see Price, The Russo-Japanese Treaties of 1907–1916. In Japanese, see Gaimushō, Nihon gaikō nenpyō narabi ni shuyō bunsho, vol. 1. For a succinct summary of the four treaties, see Kawada, Hara Takashi, tenkanki no kōso, pp. 69–70.

108. In compensation, in other words, for Japanese arms aid to Russia (Terauchi Masatake kankei monjo 178-2, Motono to Terauchi, December 27, 1915; cited in Yoshimura, *Nihon to Roshia*, p. 281).

109. "Nichi-Ro shin kyōyaku teiketsu mondai ni kanshi 'Kozakofu' kyokutō kyokuchō Terauchi Chōsen sōtoku to kaidan no ken," January 11, 1916, in Gaimushō, *Nihon gaikō bunsho*, 1916, 1: 109. Kozakov neither confirmed nor denied the possibility of an agreement covering all of the Changchun-Harbin Railway.

110. YDH, p. 86.

111. He also intimated that Japan might be forced to obtain this privilege by means other than a treaty: "We may be unable to avoid taking means other than a draft proposal [to accomplish this goal]" (Terauchi Masatake kankei monjo 422-2, Terauchi to Tanaka, April 1915; see also Tanaka Giichi monjo, Terauchi to Tanaka, March 9, 1916; and Yamagata monjo, vol. 26, Terauchi to Yamagata, April 4, 1916).

112. YDH, p. 89.

113. Ibid., p. 85.

114. Hamaomote Matasuke monjo, no. 34, "Kokubō hōshin gen'an," February 12, 1916, in HMM, p. 234.

115. YDH, p. 85.

116. In the 1907 Basic Plan of National Defense. See Chapter 2 herein.

117. Tokutomi, *Kōshaku Yamagata Aritomo den*, 3: 917.

118. The *Ōsaka Mainichi shinbun* (January 18, 1912; cited in Nish, *Alliance in Decline*, p. 82) accused Britain of betraying the principle of territorial integrity in China by dealing with the revolutionary forces and branded the alliance a dead letter.

119. The Japanese press played up rumors in November 1915 that Britain was attempting to negotiate an alliance with China (Nish, *Alliance in Decline*, pp. 166–70.) Beginning in late January 1916 more reports circulated concerning a British attempt to mediate between Yuan and the southern revolutionaries.

120. As he relayed Inoue's observations to Hara Takashi (HN, 4: 113 [July 8, 1915]). Inoue's father, elder statesman Inoue Kaoru, it will be recalled, had already lamented at the outbreak of war the coolness of British attitudes toward the Anglo-Japanese alliance (Inoue Kaoru kō denki hensankai, *Segai Inoue kō den*, 5: 367–68). See pp. 49–50 herein.

121. Namely, the Taft-Katsura agreement of July 1905 and the Root-Takahira agreement of November 1908.

122. As Yamagata put it in 1918, "Before our wounds from the war with Russia had healed . . . we sedulously concluded three agreements with the tsar to counter the establishment of American power [in Asia]" ("Kokubō hōshin kaitei ikensho," in YAI, pp. 374–75).

123. Nish, *Alliance in Decline*, p. 78.

124. "Tai-Ro keikai ron," in YAI, p. 336.

125. See Chapter 2 herein.

126. Gotō Shinpei monjo R-86, Terauchi to Gotō, August 7, 1914.

127. See Chapter 2 herein.

128. Shimanuki, "Nichi-Ro sensō igo ni okeru kokubō hōshin," p. 16.

129. Emphasis my own; Hamaomote Matasuke monjo, no. 34, "Kokubō hōshin gen'an," February 12, 1916, in HMM, p. 234.

130. YAI, p. 347.

131. Gaimushō, *Nihon gaikō nenpyō narabi ni shuyō bunsho*, 1: 420.

132. HN, 4: 156 (January 24, 1916).

133. See Ishii's memoirs, *Gaikō yoroku*, p. 130. Sazonov assured the U.S. ambassador to Russia in July 1916 that Germany was the target of the agreement; see U.S. Department of State, *Papers Relating to the Foreign Relations of the United States, 1916*, p. 436.

134. In Japanese, see Yoshimura, *Nihon to Roshia*, pp. 313–15. For the strongest denial in English of the anti-American thrust of the pact, see Peter Berton, "The Secret Russo-Japanese Alliance of 1916."

135. Terauchi Masatake kankei monjo 178-2, Motono to Terauchi, December 27, 1915, outlines the ostensible reasons for the visit; Nakajima to Foreign Ministry, December 13, 1915, stresses Russia's desire for more arms; both cited in Yoshimura, *Nihon to Roshia*, p. 281. See also "Rokoku gaishō no Nichi-Ro kyōyaku teiketsu no kibō ni kanshi 'Kozakofu' kyokutō kyokuchō danwa no ken," January 10, 1916, in Gaimushō, *Nihon gaikō bunsho*, 1916, 1: 107.

136. Iklé, "Japanese-German Peace Negotiations During World War I," p. 65.

137. Yoshimura, *Nihon to Roshia*, p. 215.

138. Nish, *Alliance in Decline*, p. 164.

139. Motono to Katō, July 27, 1915, in Gaimushō, *Nihon gaikō bunsho*, 1915, 3-1: 13–15.

140. "Rokoku gaishō no Nichi-Ro kyōyaku teiketsu no kibō ni kanshi 'Kozakofu' kyokutō kyokuchō danwa no ken," January 10, 1916, in Gaimushō, *Nihon gaikō bunsho*, 1916, 1: 107–8. The Anglo-Japanese alliance, which had enabled Japan to fight and defeat Russia, was, Wilhelm had told Sazonov, a "great sin against the solidarity of the white races," and it had suddenly shifted the center of gravity in the Far East to Japan.

141. "Rokoku gaishō no Nichi-Ro kyōyaku teiketsu no kibō ni kanshi 'Kozakofu' kyokutō kyokuchō danwa no ken," January 10, 1916, in Gaimushō, *Nihon gaikō bunsho*, 1916, 1: 107–8.

142. "Nichi-Ro no kessoku ni kanshi 'Sazanofu' gaishō no ikō Nihon seifu ni dentatsu no ken" (January 14, 1916, in ibid., pp. 111–12).

143. YDH, p. 85.

144. Ibid., pp. 86–87.

145. Ibid., p. 90.

146. Ishii instructed that "both signatories consider China's falling under the political hold of a third country possessing an aggressive tendency toward one or both signatories a threat to all pressing interests of the signatories" (Ishii to Motono, February 15, 1916, in Gaimushō, *Nihon gaikō bunsho*, 1916, 1: 123).

147. Motono to Ishii, February 19, 1916, in ibid., p. 124.

148. Motono to Ishii, February 21, 1916, in ibid., p. 125.

149. Ishii to Motono, February 23, 1916, in ibid., p. 127.

150. Motono to Ishii, March 23, 1916, in ibid., p. 135.

151. Ishii to Motono, April 18, 1916, in ibid., p. 138. Sazonov's proposal for mutual consultation before one party signed an "international agreement" concerning its special interests in China is described in Motono to Ishii, March 23, 1916, in ibid., p. 135.

152. Ishii to Motono, May 10, 1916, in ibid., p. 145.

153. The Russians finally acquiesced to Ishii's simple verbal agreement after the tsar's intervention (Motono to Ishii, June 12, 1916, in ibid., p. 152).

154. Technically speaking, Sazonov had precluded the possibility of coming to Japan's aid in the event of a U.S. challenge in China by making mutual military assistance contingent upon a guarantee of assistance to Japan and Russia by their respective allies (in article 4 of the secret convention; Gaimushō, *Nihon gaikō nenpyō narabi ni shuyō bunsho*, 1: 420). Since Britain had gone on record refusing to fight against the United States, this significantly diluted the Russian obligation of support in such an event. But, as we have seen, Washington had not ratified the arbitration treaty that would have legally excused London from her obligation to defend Japanese interests against an American challenge. The abrogation of the Anglo-Japanese alliance, moreover, would immediately eliminate the legal obstacle to Russian support in the event of an American challenge. By making Russian aid contingent on the action of Japan's ally Britain, Sazonov had intended to eliminate the possibility of going to war against the United States. What he may have actually done, however, was to increase the incentive in Tokyo to abandon the Anglo-Japanese alliance.

155. "Ichigatsu hatsuka kanchū ni oite Ishii gaimu daijin yori san genrō e kyōgi no Rokoku gaishō naiteigi ni taisuru kaitōan ni kansuru ken," January 20, 1916, in ibid., p. 117.

156. Ishii to Motono, January 20, 1916, in ibid., p. 116.

157. YDH, p. 89.

158. Ibid.

159. "Ichigatsu hatsuka Ishii gaishō 'Kozakofu' kaidan yōryō," January 20, 1916, in Gaimushō, *Nihon gaikō bunsho*, 1916, 1: 114–15.

160. YDH, p. 91.

161. Tanaka Giichi monjo, Terauchi to Tanaka, February 2, 1916.

162. Ibid. The actual scope of these assurances remains obscure.

163. Terauchi Masatake kankei monjo 315-48, Tanaka to Terauchi, February 7, 1916.

164. "Kakugi kettei" (February 14, 1916), in Gaimushō, Nihon gaikō bunsho, 1916, 1: 118–19; see Terauchi Masatake kankei monjo 315-49, Tanaka to Terauchi, February 13, 1916, for the link between the cabinet decision and Oka's incapacity due to illness.

165. Berton, "The Secret Russo-Japanese Alliance of 1916," p. 155.

166. Terauchi Masatake kankei monjo 315-49, Tanaka to Terauchi, February 13, 1916.

167. Tokutomi, Kōshaku Yamagata Aritomo den, 3: 952–53.

Chapter 5

1. Gilbert, The First World War, p. 303.

2. Suehiro, "Nichi-Beikan ni yokotawaru sandai mondai," p. 79.

3. Ōyama Ikuo, "Amerikanizumu to pan-Amerikanizumu," p. 77.

4. Suehiro, "Nichi-Beikan ni yokotawaru sandai mondai," p. 79.

5. Satō, "Beikoku kaigun no shōrai," pp. 80–84; anonymous army officer, "Beikoku rikugun no dai kakuchō," Chūō kōron 31, no. 13 (December 1916): 85–87.

6. Yoshino, "Beikoku no tai-Tōyō seisaku," p. 90.

7. YDH, p. 125.

8. Terauchi had been the Yamagata faction's hope for a revitalization of its power since 1912, when the faction had deposed Prime Minister Saionji. Yamagata and his colleagues had seen Saionji as favoring the Seiyūkai Party and the navy and hoped to replace him with Terauchi.

9. It would go on to do so on October 10.

10. In a meeting with Ōkuma on August 6. Terauchi Masatake kankei monjo 441-1, "Taishō gonen kōshō tenmatsu nikki," in TNS, 1: 112.

11. YDH, p. 121.

12. Ōsaka Mainichi shinbun, October 6, 1916; cited in TNS, 1: 441.

13. Tokyo Mainichi shinbun, October 6, 1916; Yorozu chōhō, October 6, 1916; both cited in TNS, 1: 440.

14. Yoshino, "Terauchi naikaku no shutsugen ni taisuru gensei hihan to tairiku seisaku," p. 86.

15. Kitaoka, Nihon rikugun to tairiku seisaku, pp. 199, 204.

16. HN, 4: 103 (May 20, 1915).

17. Oka, Taishō demokurashiiki no seiji, p. 13 (diary entry for July 19, 1916); see also Duus, Party Rivalry and Political Change in Taishō Japan, p. 98.

18. Despite his trouble with Katō during the Ōkuma regime, Yamagata recognized the importance of accommodating the current majority party in the Diet.

While refusing to entertain Ōkuma's suggestions for Katō's appointment as prime minister, then, the field marshal hoped to include Katō in the cabinet in some capacity (Terauchi Masatake kankei monjo 441-1, "Taishō gonen kōshō tenmatsu nikki," in TNS, 1: 109).

19. See Chapter 2 herein.

20. Tsurumi, *Gotō Shinpei*, 3: 615.

21. HN, 4: 221 (October 11, 1916).

22. Ibid.

23. Mizuno Rentarō, "Hansei no omoide o kataru," cited in Kitaoka, *Nihon rikugun to tairiku seisaku*, p. 195, n52. Inoue, it will be recalled, had proposed Gotō in the fall 1914 as a high-profile emissary to negotiate a comprehensive agreement with Beijing. See Chapter 2 herein.

24. HN, 4: 256 (January 15, 1917).

25. Recognizing Japan's financial weakness, elder statesman Inoue Kaoru had proven receptive to American railway magnate E. H. Harriman's idea of joint American-Japanese operation of Manchurian railways. Finance Minister Sone Arasuke and representatives of the Mitsui and Mitsubishi companies persuaded Prime Minister Katsura to come to a provisional agreement with Harriman in October 1905. But Foreign Minister Komura Jutarō, feeling partnership with the United States too high a price to pay for financial support, wrecked the scheme (see Kobayashi Michihiko, *Nihon no tairiku seisaku*, pp. 114–19; Beasley, *Japanese Imperialism*, p. 93).

26. Tanaka, it will be recalled, was advocating here a preemptive strike against the United States.

27. Following a balance of payments deficit in 1914 of 13.5 million yen, Japan recorded a surplus of 219.6 million yen in 1915. The enormous surpluses were to continue through 1919 (see table A31 in Ohkawa and Shinohara, *Patterns of Japanese Economic Development*, p. 334).

28. The decision also included the threat that if Beijing continued to doubt the intentions of the empire, Japan would be compelled to "think of another policy suited to the occasion" (Gaimushō, *Nihon gaikō nenpyō narabi ni shuyō bunsho*, 1: 424–27).

29. From Gotō's "China Policy Draft" of December 1916; in Tsurumi, *Gotō Shinpei*, 3: 649.

30. From Gotō's memorandum to the prime minister, "A New China Policy," November 21, 1916, in ibid., pp. 643–46.

31. Shōda would serve as finance minister in the Terauchi cabinet (see Kitamura, *Yume no shichijūyonen*).

32. Ibid., p. 75.

33. Ibid., pp. 83–86.

34. Terauchi Masatake kankei monjo 208-11, Nishihara to Terauchi, October 2, 1916, in TNS, 1: 101–2.

35. Terauchi Masatake kankei monjo 448-23, Nishihara Kamezō, "Kibō," October 11, 1916, in ibid., p. 185.

36. Memorandum of November 22, 1916. Terauchi monjo 448-25, Nishihara Kamezō, "Mōgon," in ibid, p. 282.

37. Without divulging his earlier call for the annexation of all of China, Nishihara assured Cao that if Japan wanted to take Manchuria, she could do so in a matter of days. "But show me someone who can say with confidence that eternal peace in the Far East could be preserved by so doing" (Kitamura, *Yume no shichijūyonen*, p. 137).

38. Ibid., pp. 87–88.

39. Terauchi Masatake kankei monjo 27-50, Gotō to Terauchi, October 3, 1916.

40. HN, 4: 224 (October 12, 1916).

41. Ibid., p. 229 (November 5, 1916). Miura also informed Terauchi of a consensus among party leaders Hara and Inukai Tsuyoshi (Kokumintō), and Itō Miyoji on the need to remove Tanaka (Terauchi Masatake kankei monjo 441-6, "Miura shishaku danwa yōryō," October 12, 1916, in TNS, 1: 187). Den and Hirata agreed in a discussion in November on the advisability of dismissing the vice chief of staff (Den Kenjirō nikki, November 17, 1916, in TNS, 1: 146).

42. HN, 4: 223 (October 11, 1916).

43. Ibid., p. 229 (November 5, 1916).

44. Yamamoto, *Nishihara Kamezō nikki*, pp. 152–53 (October 26, November 1, 1916).

45. Lieutenant General Aoki Nobuzumi had originally been ordered by the Army General Staff in December 1915 to inflame opposition to Yuan in southern China; Major General Saitō Suejirō had commanded Japanese occupation forces in Shandong and was now military attaché in Beijing; and Kawashima Naniwa had worked closely with Colonel Doi Ichinoshin and Major Koiso Kuniaki on an uprising in Manchuria.

46. Terauchi Masatake kankei monjo 208-13, Nishihara to Terauchi, December 12, 1916, in TNS, 1: 155–56. Later, he orchestrated the Japanese government's refusal to receive Xiang Xiling, a man with little power in Duan's regime, in Cao's stead (Terauchi Masatake kankei monjo 208-14, Nishihara to Terauchi, December 18, 1916, in ibid., p. 157; Yamamoto, *Nishihara Kamezō nikki*, p. 159 [December 11, 1916]).

47. Terauchi Masatake kankei monjo 208-15, 16, 17, Nishihara to Terauchi, December 24, 26, 29, 1916, in TNS, 1: 160–66, 169–71.

48. Terauchi Masatake kankei monjo 208-15, 17, Nishihara to Terauchi, December 24, 29, 1916, in ibid., pp. 162, 170.

49. HN, 4: 231 (November 9, 1916).

50. The prime minister informed the army and navy chiefs and vice chiefs of staff about the new policy only that evening, after the event (Yamamoto, *Terauchi Masatake nikki*, p. 726 [diary entry for January 9, 1917]; Nara Takeji nikki, January 9, 1917 [courtesy of Nara Takeji monjo kenkyūkai]).

51. HN, 4: 242 (December 1, 1916).

52. In fact, because Katō refused to meet with the other party heads, Prime Minister Terauchi saw him separately in the morning. Katō later declined to join the Advisory Council on Foreign Affairs (ibid., p. 256 [January 15, 1917]).

53. See Nishihara's objections in Terauchi Masatake kankei monjo 208-14, 15, Nishihara to Terauchi, December 15, 24, 1916, in TNS, 1: 157–58, 161–62. For Tanaka's appointment of Taga, see Tanaka to Taga, January 18, 1917, in Takakura, *Tanaka Giichi denki*, 1: 664.

54. Hamaomote Matasuke monjo, no. 53, Tanaka to Aoki, April 1916, in HMM, pp. 246–47.

55. Hamaomote Matasuke monjo, no. 69, Tanaka Giichi, "Tai-Shi iken sōkō," June 7, 1916, in ibid., pp. 259–60.

56. Terauchi Masatake kankei monjo 315-60, Tanaka to Terauchi, June 24, 1917, in HMM, 1: 712.

57. Terauchi Masatake kankei monjo 336-33, Uehara to Terauchi, May 15, 1917.

58. Takakura, *Tanaka Giichi denki*, 1: 653–58; emphasis Tanaka's.

59. Although Tanaka argued against a restoration attempt, his encouragement of Zhang's participation in the reordering of the political map in Beijing certainly did not dissuade the general from proceeding with his plans. Some of Zhang's supporters would later claim that Tanaka had agreed to their mentor's scheme (see ibid., pp. 661–62, 671, for Tanaka's subsequent effort to keep Zhang from marching on Beijing). Feng Guozhang informed Lieutenant Colonel Taga in early June about Zhang's supporters' claims (Takakura, 1: 671).

60. Ibid., p. 658. Duan had agreed to retain Li, provided that Li would not interfere with the administration of government (Chi, *China Diplomacy*, p. 121).

61. Tanaka had also met with Tang and Cen in Shanghai (Tanaka to Taga, May 28, 1917, in Takakura, *Tanaka Giichi denki*, 1: 660, 667).

62. Tanaka to Taga, June 7, 1917, in ibid., p. 668.

63. Taga to Tanaka, June 8, 1917, in ibid., p. 669.

64. Tanaka to Taga, June 13, 1917, in ibid., p. 673.

65. Taga to Terauchi, June 14, 1917, in ibid.

66. Nishihara to Shōda, June 26, 1917, in Gaimushō, *Nihon gaikō bunsho*, 1917, 2: 681.

67. Nishihara to Shōda, June 10, 1917, docs. 665, 666, in ibid., pp. 665–68.

68. Terauchi Masatake kankei monjo 315-60, Tanaka to Terauchi, June 24, 1917, in TNS, 1: 712–13.

69. The legal means entailed replacing the old constitution with one that would grant the president the power to make cabinet appointments (Kitamura, *Yume no shichijūyonen*, p. 159). Financially, Nishihara promised 5 million yen in aid to provinces refusing to recognize the new prime minister, Li Jiangxi (Yamamoto, *Nishihara Kamezō nikki*, p. 209 [June 27, 1917]).

70. Takakura, *Tanaka Giichi denki*, 1: 41.

71. Yamamoto, *Nishihara Kamezō nikki*, p. 210 (July 2, 1917).

72. Gaimushō, *Nihon gaikō nenpyō narabi ni shuyō bunsho*, 1: 437–38.

73. Akashi Motojirō monjo 30-2, Tanaka to Akashi, July 28, 1917; in Nihon seiji gaikōshi kenkyūkai, "Akashi Motojirō monjo oyobi kadai," p. 94.

74. Tanaka, "Tai-Shi keiei shiken," in Takakura, *Tanaka Giichi denki*, 1: 676–712.

75. Ibid., p. 702.

76. Yamamoto, *Nishihara Kamezō nikki*, pp. 220–21 (August 30, September 2, 1917). The idea of Japanese control in the Dutch East Indies had already become a topic of public discussion by the time of Nishihara's proposal. Seiyūkai politician Takekoshi Yosaburō, for example, had suggested in a popular Japanese journal soon after the fall of Qingdao that the preoccupation of the great powers in Europe offered an opportune moment to seize the islands. See A. Morgan Young, *Japan Under Taisho Tenno*, pp. 95–96.

77. See, for example, the classic study of U.S.-Japanese relations in the early twentieth century, Griswold, *The Far Eastern Policy of the United States*, which devotes an entire chapter to immigration and race.

78. Where the United States entrance into the war does play into a discussion of rising U.S.-Japanese tensions, it does so in terms of the issue of race. "Wilson's decision for war," notes Walter LaFeber, "rested in part on his evaluation of how best to protect the interest of 'white races' against Japanese power" (LaFeber, *The Clash*, p. 114).

79. *Tokyo Asahi shinbun*, February 12, 1917; cited in Yoshino (Kosen Gokujin, pseud.), "Kuru beki kōwa," p. 109.

80. Yoshino, "Kuru beki kōwa," p. 112.

81. Yamamoto, *Nishihara Kamezō nikki*, p. 163 (December 27, 1916).

82. Kitamura, *Yume no shichijūyonen*, p. 141; Yamamoto, *Nishihara Kamezō nikki*, p. 183 (February 10, 1917).

83. Interestingly, Wilson rival Theodore Roosevelt expressed the same sentiment when he insisted that "the United States did not go to war to make democracy safe, but to make the world safe for the U.S. against Germany" (Mayer, *Wilson Vs. Lenin*, p. 344).

84. Terauchi Masatake kankei monjo 441-10, "Ōshū taisen to kokumin no kaku-go," April 1917, in TNS, 1: 886–89.

85. Yoshino, "Beikoku sansen no bunmeiteki igi," p. 95.

86. Thus, there is a monograph devoted to the impact of the Russian revolution in Japan; see Hosoya, *Roshia kakumei to Nihon*. Even before this, the two classic studies of the Siberian Intervention explicitly sought lessons for the emerging Cold War in the first allied response to revolution in Russia; see Hosoya, *Shiberia shuppei no shiteki kenkyū*; and Morley, *The Japanese Thrust into Siberia*. As Morley put it, his analysis of the Japanese intervention in Siberia aimed to foster greater mutual understanding among the "free nations" in the present to "contribute to the cause of freedom" (p. ix). A decade later, Seki Hiroharu titled his study of Japan's response to the Russian revolution "Birth of the Present International Environment in East Asia" (Seki, *Gendai higashi Ajia kokusai kankyō no tanjō*).

87. Terauchi Masatake kankei monjo 441-10, "Ōshū taisen to kokumin no kaku-go," April 1917, in TNS, 1: 887–89.

88. Yamagata, "Kazoku kyōiku ni kansuru iken," presented to Prince Tokugawa Iesato on June 25; in YAI, pp. 348–52.

89. See, again, the items by Hosoya, Morley, and Seki cited in note 86 in this chapter.

90. The most recent study in this vein is Hara Teruyuki's *Shiberia shuppei*, revealingly subtitled "Revolution and intervention, 1917–1922" (*Kakumei to kanshō*).

91. "China must not err," Nishihara warned, "in measures taken in concert with this." Specifically, he suggested that Beijing should be prepared to mobilize the Heilongjiang Regular Army (Yamamoto, *Nishihara Kamezō nikki*, p. 231 [November 25, 1917]). Terauchi had responded to Nishihara's proposal for bold action with the tacit encouragement: "In diplomacy, nothing can be accomplished by offering one's name card at the door" (Yamamoto, *Nishihara Kamezō nikki*, p. 229 [November 15, 1917]).

92. Ibid., p. 231 (December 4, 1917). Two days earlier, French field marshal Ferdinand Foch had suggested at the Inter-Allied Conference at Paris that U.S. and Japanese troops "take possession of the Trans-Siberian Railroad" to prevent German penetration across Russia and Siberia (Morley, *The Japanese Thrust into Siberia*, pp. 32–33).

93. Yamamoto, *Nishihara Kamezō nikki*, pp. 232–34 (December 6–23, 1917).

94. Ibid., pp. 232–34 (December 12, 16, 26, 1917); Nishihara, "Jigon," December 1917, in TNS, 2: 425–28.

95. Nishihara, "Jigon," December 1917, in TNS, 2: 426.

96. Morley, *The Japanese Thrust into Siberia*, pp. 50–51, 329–331. At the same time, the Japanese Navy began planning for ferrying these troops to North Manchuria and the Russian Maritimes (Usui, *Nihon to Chūgoku*, p. 121). The navy had made

preparations in early November to send ships to Vladivostok, but they were restrained by the posture of the British (Morley, *The Japanese Thrust into Siberia*, p. 39).

97. See, for example, Banno, "Nihon rikugun no Ōbeikan to Chūgoku seisaku," pp. 457–58. By contrast, Kitaoka Shin'ichi (*Nihon rikugun to tairiku seisaku*, p. 219) appropriately describes the agreement in terms of facilitating the army's expansionary aims in Siberia.

98. Hara Takashi confirmed after a conversation with Yamagata on March 30 that the field marshal seemed to place emphasis upon military options in China. HN, 4: 376 (March 30, 1918).

99. Yamagata, "Tai-Shi iken," January 1918, in YAI, pp. 353–54.

100. Ibid., p. 353.

101. Nara Takeji nikki, December 22, 1917. Courtesy of Nara Takeji monjo kenkyūkai.

102. Morley, *The Japanese Thrust into Siberia*, p. 113.

103. Ibid., p. 115; Usui, *Nihon to Chūgoku*, p. 128.

104. Morley, *The Japanese Thrust into Siberia*, pp. 162–65.

105. Gaimushō, *Nihon gaikō nenpyō narabi ni shuyō bunsho*, 1: 441–43; for an English translation, see Morley, *The Japanese Thrust into Siberia*, pp. 363–65.

106. Morley, *The Japanese Thrust into Siberia*, pp. 201–2.

107. Terauchi Masatake kankei monjo 315-68, Tanaka to Terauchi, April 27, 1918, in TNS, 2: 185.

108. Terauchi Masatake kankei monjo 40-6, Hayashi to Terauchi, May 1, 1918, in ibid., p. 187; Morley, *The Japanese Thrust into Siberia*, pp. 190–91.

109. The adjunct was signed on September 6, 1918 (Gaimushō, *Nihon gaikō nenpyō narabi ni shuyō bunsho*, 1: 443–44).

110. Nara Takeji nikki, June 6, 1918. Terauchi also approved the decision by Tanaka and War Minister Ōshima to send the Fortieth Infantry Brigade and the Seventh Division to North Manchuria to support the Third Division and patrol the Chinese Eastern Railway (Morley, *The Japanese Thrust into Siberia*, p. 292).

111. Yamamoto, *Nishihara Kamezō nikki*, p. 234 (December 23, 1917).

112. Morley, *The Japanese Thrust into Siberia*, p. 68.

113. Ibid., pp. 68–69.

114. Usui, *Nihon to Chūgoku*, p. 128; Morley, *The Japanese Thrust into Siberia*, p. 102.

115. Both Kitaoka Shin'ichi (*Nihon rikugun to tairiku seisaku*, pp. 215–16) and Takahashi Hidenao ("Sōryokusen seisaku to Terauchi naikaku," p. 13), for example, note the concern of Field Marshal Yamagata and General Terauchi with the spread of German power east. Kitaoka (*Nihon rikugun to tairiku seisaku*, p. 217) also highlights Hara Takashi's appeal in December 1917 for political unity in China "to prevent China from being abandoned to Germany."

116. Takakura, *Tanaka Giichi denki*, 2: 141–42.

117. Shinobu, *Taishō seijishi*, 2: 536.

118. Terauchi Masatake kankei monjo 360-118, Yamagata to Terauchi, February 3, 1918, in TNS, 2: 55.

119. In a memorandum circulated to Terauchi, Foreign Minister Motono, and Home Minister Gotō (Yamagata, "Jikyoku iken," March 15, 1918, in YAI, p. 360).

120. Ibid.

121. Terauchi Masatake kankei monjo 360-118, Yamagata to Terauchi, in TNS, 2: 55.

122. Yamagata, "Jikyoku iken," March 15, 1918, in YAI, pp. 357, 359. Nishihara Kamezō shared this sentiment, as indicated by his disappointment in January 1918 at learning of the possibility of U.S. and British involvement in an expedition. "I hear a report that both America and Britain are looking favorably upon an expedition of troops to Siberia," he recorded in his diary that month. "I have reason to believe that this has come from Foreign Minister Motono's lack of discipline. As a momentous event for the State, it is of unbearably great regret" (Yamamoto, Nishihara Kamezō nikki, p. 238 [January 8, 1918]).

123. In a series of memoranda drafted with the aid of secretaries Matsushima Hajime and Matsuoka Yōsuke between November 1917 and the Treaty of Brest-Litovsk in March 1918 (Morley, The Japanese Thrust into Siberia, pp. 53–55).

124. In a February 23 meeting with the ambassador (Shinobu, Taishō seijishi, 2: 434).

125. Tsurumi, Gotō Shinpei, 3: 886–88; Shinobu, Taishō seijishi, 2: 422–24.

126. HN, 4: 435, 439 (September 1, 5, 1918); Takahashi Hidenao, "Hara naikaku no seiritsu to sōryokusen seisaku," p. 27. It should come as no surprise that the mercurial Gotō, who pushed so aggressively in 1918 for a gargantuan expedition to Siberia, had by 1923 metamorphosed into a friend of the Bolsheviks and negotiated, in his capacity as home minister, a normalization of relations with Soviet Russia.

127. Yamamoto, Nishihara Kamezō nikki, pp. 159–60 (December 14, 1916). In January 1918, Terauchi authorized the dispatch of reconnaissance missions to Siberia (HN, 4: 351, 365 [January 1, February 28, 1918]). To Hara's warning in mid-March that the government not get involved in an independence movement in Siberia, Terauchi replied that if the great powers provided support for such movements, Japan could not help but do the same (HN, 4: 373 [March 13, 1918]).

128. For studies that highlight army efforts to construct the bases of general mobilization during the First World War, see Kisaka, "Gunbu to demokurashii"; Kōketsu, "Taisenkanki ni okeru rikugun no kokumin dōin seisaku"; and Yamaguchi, "Kokka sōdōin kenkyū josetsu." For an analysis that connects army concerns for general mobilization during the First World War to Japan's subsequent war with the United States, see Barnhart, Japan Prepares for Total War. Finally, for specific references to the Siberian Intervention as an opportune means to strengthen the bases of general mobilization, see Takahashi Hidenao, "Sōryokusen seisaku to Terauchi

naikaku"; and Takahashi Hidenao, "Hara naikaku no seiritsu to sōryokusen seisaku."

129. Kisaka, "Gunbu to demokurashii," similarly stresses the political motives of the army's general mobilization policy.

130. See Chapter 2 herein.

131. Tanaka, "Kokubō tōitsu ni kansuru gi," in Shimanuki, "Nichi-Ro sensō igo ni okeru kokubō hōshin," pp. 15–16. The exact date of this memorandum remains unclear, but it is most likely that Tanaka drafted it immediately prior to his promotion to lieutenant general and appointment as vice chief of the Army General Staff in October 1915.

132. Terauchi Masatake kankei monjo 315-59, Tanaka to Terauchi April 30, 1917, in TNS, 1: 573.

133. Kitaoka, Nihon rikugun to tairiku seisaku, p. 326; HN, 4: 378 (March 30, 1918).

134. See Kitaoka, Nihon rikugun to tairiku seisaku, pp. 320–22; Dingman, Power in the Pacific, pp. 58–59.

135. HN, 4: 353 (January 15, 1918); Kitaoka, Nihon rikugun to tairiku seisaku, pp. 320–21.

136. Kitaoka, Nihon rikugun to tairiku seisaku, pp. 321–22.

137. HN, 4: 341, 377 (December 6, 1917; March 30, 1918).

138. Tsunoda, Ugaki Kazushige nikki, 1: 145.

139. Yamagata, "Kokubō hōshin kaitei iensho," June 1918, in YAI, p. 373.

140. Yamagata, "Kazoku kyōiku ni kansuru iken," presented to Prince Tokugawa Iesato on June 25, in YAI, pp. 348–52.

141. "Shuppei keikaku ni kanrenshi junbi moshiku wa jikkō seru jikō," in Rikugun sanbō honbu, Shiberia shuppeishi, 1: 36–38; for an English translation, see Morley, The Japanese Thrust into Siberia, pp. 336–37.

142. Yamagata, "Kokubō hōshin kaitei iensho," June 1918, in YAI, p. 375.

143. Ibid., p. 375. I am indebted to Kobayashi Michihiko for bringing this reference to Singapore to my attention.

144. If we consider all cities over 100,000 inhabitants (Naikaku tōkeikyoku, Nihon teikoku tōkei nenkan, 38: 28).

145. "Kidaore no Kyōto fujin," Yomiuri shinbun, May 22, 1917; cited in Nakajima et al., Shinbun shūroku Taishōshi, 5: 174; Seidensticker, Low City, High City, pp. 269–71. The publication of twenty-four of these nudes was banned by the police ("Taihei yōgakai ni genmei kudaru," Jiji, May 4, 1917; cited in Nakajima et al., 5: 154).

146. Garon, The State and Labor in Modern Japan, p. 249.

147. Ioki, "Shin kiun o ridō seyo"; cited in Banno, Taishō seihen, p. 209.

148. Tsurumi, Gotō Shinpei, 3: 643–46.

149. HN, 4: 353 (Jan. 15, 1918); Kitaoka, Nihon rikugun to tairiku seisaku, pp. 320–21.

150. Ōtsu, Dai Nihon kenseishi, 7: 163–64.

151. Kuroda, Gensui Terauchi hakushaku den, p. 878.

152. Oka, *Tenkanki no Taishō*, p. 89.

153. Terauchi Masatake kankei monjo 297-20, Shōda to Terauchi, January 30, 1918, in TNSm 2: 45.

154. HN, 4: 421 (July 26, 1918).

155. "Gotō naimu daijin no ikensho," in Kobayashi Tatsuo, *Suiusō nikki*, p. 809. Thomas W. Burkman ("Japan, the League of Nations, and the New World Order, 1918–1920," p. 78) dates this memorandum March 1918.

156. Kobayashi Tatsuo, *Suiusō nikki*, pp. 809–11.

157. See, for example, Hosoya, *Shiberia shuppei no shiteki kenkyū*; Suetake Yoshiya, "Dai-ichiji sekai taisenki no shoseitō no dōkō"; Takahashi Hidenao, "Sōryokusen seisaku to Terauchi naikaku." In English, see Morley, *The Japanese Thrust into Siberia.*

158. HN, 4: 416 (July 16, 1918).

159. Ibid., p. 328 (October 22, 1917).

160. Ibid., p. 342 (December 10, 1917).

161. Yamagata lamented such a loss particularly in the aftermath of the rice riots. Tokutomi monjo 40-42, Yamagata to Tokutomi, September 5, 1918, in Itō Takashi et al., *Tokutomi Sohō kankei monjo*, 2: 395.

162. Yamagata, "Jikyoku iken," March 15, 1918, in YAI, p. 360.

163. HN, 4: 376 (March 30, 1918).

164. Yamagata, "Kokubō hōshin kaitei ikensho," June 1918, in YAI, p. 373.

165. HN, 4: 430 (August 15, 1918).

166. Morley, *The Japanese Thrust into Siberia*, p. 309.

167. War Minister Tanaka Giichi informed the Advisory Council on Foreign Affairs in a December 8 meeting that Japanese troops in Siberia stood at around 52,000 to 53,000 men (Kobayashi Tatsuo, *Suiusō nikki*, p. 343).

168. Kitaoka, *Nihon rikugun to tairiku seisaku*, p. 327.

169. Matsuo, "Kome sōdō chin'atsu no shuppei kibo," p. 181. For an in-depth study of the rice riots and their enormous social and political repercussions, see Lewis, *Rioters and Citizens.*

170. Tokutomi monjo 40-42, Yamagata to Tokutomi, September 5, 1918, in Itō Takashi et al., *Tokutomi Sohō kankei monjo*, 2: 395.

171. Uehara monjo 102-19, Machida to Uehara, August 28, 1918, in UKM, p. 484.

172. Tokutomi monjo 40-42, Yamagata to Tokutomi, September 5, 1918, in Itō Takashi et al., *Tokutomi Sohō kankei monjo*, p. 395.

Chapter 6

1. Becker, *The Great War and the French People*, p. 320; Marwick, *The Deluge*, p. 260.

2. Nagai, *Danchōtei nichijō*, 1: 19.

3. Japan's delegates initially asked not for "racial equality" but for the "abolition of racial discrimination," and their proposed ammendment to the Covenant of the

League of Nations, worked out with Woodrow Wilson's special adviser, Colonel Edward House, referred to the "equality of nations" and called for "equal treatments and rights in law" of aliens in the territories of the contracting parties. As Naoko Shimazu (Japan, Race and Equality) perceptively notes, none of the three powers locked into the racial discrimination debate at Versailles—Japan, Britain, or the United States—recognized racial equality as a universal principle. In promoting the clause, Japan intended principally to eliminate legal discrimination against her nationals abroad.

4. Terasaki, Shōwa tennō dokuhakuroku, p. 20.

5. For the most exhaustive treatment of the debate in Tokyo surrounding "racial equality," see Burkman, "Japan, the League of Nations and the New World Order, 1918–1920, " pp. 172–80. In Japanese, see Nomura Otojirō, "Pari heiwa kaigi to chōken bunran jiken," pp. 108–9.

6. See Curry, Woodrow Wilson and Far Eastern Policy, 1913–1921; Fifield, Woodrow Wilson and the Far East; Griswold, The Far Eastern Policy of the United States; and Burkman, "'Sairento paatonaa' hatsugen su," p. 103.

7. Indeed, the one book-length study of the Shandong problem at Versailles was authored by a specialist of American diplomacy; see Fifield, Woodrow Wilson and the Far East.

8. By contrast, surveys of American–East Asian relations, typically written by specialists of American foreign policy familiar with the historiographical importance of the Great War, do highlight the war and Versailles; see, for example, Griswold, The Far Eastern Policy of the United States; LaFeber, The Clash; and McDougall, Let the Sea Make a Noise.

9. HN, 4: 236 (November 11, 1916); in Suetake, "Dai-ichiji sekai taisenki," p. 5.

10. In meetings of November 19 and December 2 (Kobayashi Tatsuo, Suiusō nikki, pp. 307, 321).

11. In meetings of November 19 and December 2 (HN, 5: 39 [November 19, 1918]; Kobayashi Tatsuo, Suiusō nikki, pp. 307, 322).

12. In the council meeting of December 2 (Kobayashi Tatsuo, Suiusō nikki, pp. 322–23).

13. Ibid., p. 325.

14. Ibid., pp. 347–48; Gaimushō, Nihon gaikō bunsho, 1918, 3: 666.

15. Usui, Nihon to Chūgoku, p. 139.

16. Fifield, Woodrow Wilson and the Far East, p. 250; Kobayashi Tatsuo, Suiusō nikki, p. 468.

17. Kobayashi Tatsuo, Suiusō nikki, p. 380.

18. Ibid., pp. 380–81.

19. Terauchi Masatake kankei monjo 441–10, "Ōshū taisen to kokumin no kakugo," April 1917, in TNS, 1: 886–89. See p. 178 herein.

20. Yoshino, "Gurei kyō no 'kokusai dōmei ron' o yomu," pp. 56–62.

21. In a meeting of the council on December 2 (Kobayashi Tatsuo, *Suiusō nikki*, p. 326).

22. Ibid., p. 337.

23. This was after many years of Marxist orthodoxy, which considered "Taishō democracy" nothing but "bourgeois" democracy betraying the interests of the people and Hara the symbol of political party complicity with the state. In his most compromised form, Hara became not the leader of Japan's first party cabinet but one of "the most sinister figures in Japanese public life," as a police informer and then as home minister. For this sinister side of Hara, see E. H. Norman in Dower, *Origins of the Modern Japanese State*, pp. 331, 461. Hara's name was originally rehabilitated by Mitani Taichirō, in *Nihon seitō seiji no keisei*. Mitani's work was disseminated to English-speaking audiences by one of his first American disciples, Tetsuo Najita, in *Hara Kei in the Politics of Compromise*.

24. With the exception of the foreign minister and the two service ministers. Career bureaucrat Uchida Yasuya assumed the helm at Kasumigaseki, and the Army and Navy Ministries went to Yamagata protégé Tanaka Giichi and the incumbent navy minister Katō Tomosaburō, respectively.

25. Mitani Taichirō (*Kindai Nihon no sensō to seiji*, pp. 55–56) speaks of the Hara regime in similar terms. By contrast, Banno Junji (*Taishō seihen*, pp. 12–13) describes the Hara cabinet as a conservative product of the war. The new wartime prosperity, he argues, enabled the Seiyūkai to use its traditional emphasis on pork-barrel spending to capture the prime ministry.

26. The classic study of political shifts in European capitals during the Great War is Mayer, *Wilson Vs. Lenin*.

27. Editors, "Hara naikaku o mukau," *Chūō kōron* 33, no. 10 (October 1918): 1; Yoshino, "Hara naikaku ni taisuru yōbō," pp. 81–107. In addition to Fukuda Tokuzō, the forum included Yoshino Sakuzō, Maida Minoru, Ōyama Ikuo, Miyake Setsurei, Matsuyama Chūjirō, Nakano Seigō, Sawayanagi Masatarō, and Ukita Kazutami.

28. Fukuda, "Hara naikaku ni yōbō-su," p. 71.

29. Again, the classic study in this regard is Mitani, *Nihon seitō seiji no keisei*. Among recent publications, see Itō Yukio, *Taishō demokurashii to seitō seiji*; Itō Yukio, "Dai-ichiji taisen to sengo Nihon no keisei"; Kawada, *Hara Takashi, tenkanki no kōsō*; Kawada, *Hara Takashi to Yamagata Aritomo*; and Seki Shizuo, "Hara Takashi no gaikō shidō."

30. Yoshino, "Hara naikaku ni taisuru yōbō," p. 82.

31. Koizumi to Hara, August 9, 1918, in HKM, 1: 556. Terauchi Masatake kankei monjo 315-71, Tanaka to Terauchi, August 31, 1918, in TNS, 2: 237.

32. Tanaka had already developed a cordial working relationship with the Seiyū-kai president in 1914, when he had mediated a Hara-Yamagata compromise on the two-division expansion bill. And with the Seiyūkai's adoption of the "perfection of national defense" as party policy after the April 1915 electoral defeat and, more recently, Hara's hints that he shared the concern for more Imperial Army funding, Tanaka and other officers determined that he was an attractive alternative to Tera-uchi. Hara had offered his wishes for greater army funding in meetings with Field Marshal Yamagata throughout the Terauchi cabinet (HN, 4: 215, 227, 314, 350, 412 [October 5, November 4, 1916; December 6, 28, 1917; July 14, 1918]). In mid-August 1918, the Seiyūkai's Fukui Saburō informed the party president that the army viewed him as "vastly superior to Terauchi" in terms of his likely ability to direct the most immediate project of national defense, the Siberian expedition. Japan's generals, he added, intended to persuade a reluctant Yamagata of the same (Fukui to Hara, August 20, 1918, in HKM, 3: 134). Army dissatisfaction with Terauchi in August 1918 focused mainly on the prime minister's Siberian expedition, which had been marred by the rice riots (see Uehara monjo 102-19, Machida Keiu to Terauchi, August 28, 1918, in UKM, p. 484).

33. HN, 5: 20 (October 7, 1918).

34. These included Lieutenant General Aoki Nobuzumi, Major Generals Saitō Suejirō and Banzai Rihachirō, and Lieutenant Colonel Taga Muneyuki.

35. Yoshizawa to Uchida, October 10, 1918, in Gaimushō, *Nihon gaikō bunsho*, 1918, 2-1: 44; HN, 5: 36 (November 13, 1918).

36. "Tai-Ka shakkan mondai kaigi giji," November 11, 1918, in Gaimushō, *Nihon gaikō nenpyō narabi ni shuyō bunsho*, 1: 472–75; HN, 5: 36 (November 13, 1918). The appeal for unity was, in part, aimed at Nishihara Kamezō's usurpation of Foreign Ministry prerogative.

37. Takakura, *Tanaka Giichi denki*, 2: 142.

38. HN, 5: 24 (October 11, 1918).

39. Ibid., p. 29 (October 18, 1918).

40. Ibid., p. 51 (December 18, 1918).

41. See Kitaoka, *Nihon rikugun to tairiku seisaku*, p. 230.

42. Takakura, *Tanaka Giichi denki*, 2: 194.

43. Editors, "Hara naikaku o mukau," *Chūō kōron* 33, no. 10 (October 1918): 1.

44. Tanaka Giichi monjo, no. 460, Fukui Saburō, "Hara naikaku to Tanaka ri-kushō," April 15, 1930.

45. Hara's principal party rival, Katō Takaaki, called his pragmatism "white paperism" (*hakushi shugi*). Conservative intellectual and longtime Yamagata friend Tokutomi Sohō described it as "todayism" (*kyō shugi*) (Mitani, *Nihon seitō seiji no keisei*, pp. 20–21).

46. Hara's abolition of the active military service requirement for Japanese governors-general would particularly enrage Yamagata. The field marshal's private sec-

retary Matsumoto Gōkichi later recalled that he had "exploded" when apprised of Hara's plans to subsume the Guandong Army under civilian rule in South Manchuria (HN, 5: 87 [April 23, 1919]).

47. Ibid., 4: 236 (November 11, 1916).

48. Hara Takashi, "Naikaku kōtetsu ni tsuki" (October 15, 1916), Seiyū, no. 199 (November 5, 1916), in Bunken shiryō kankōkai, Seiyū, 19: 3546.

49. HN, 4: 236 (November 11, 1916).

50. See Chapter 5 herein.

51. HN, 4: 316 (September 13, 1917).

52. Ibid., p. 325 (October 20, 1917).

53. Ibid., p. 328 (October 22, 1917).

54. Ibid., p. 378 (March 30, 1918).

55. Takahashi Korekiyo, "Naigai kokusaku shiken" (September 1920), in Oka et al., Ogawa Heikichi kankei monjo, 2: 137.

56. Yoshino, "Hara naikaku ni taisuru yōbō," p. 83.

57. Ōtsu, Dai Nihon kenseishi, 8: 371.

58. Yoshino, "Hara naikaku ni taisuru yōbō," p. 83; Ōtsu, Dai Nihon kenseishi, 8: 371.

59. In a conversation with Prime Minister Terauchi (HN, 4: 287 [May 26, 1917]).

60. Bryan's remarks were directed at the Twenty-One Demands (Fifield, Woodrow Wilson and the Far East, p. 38).

61. HN, 4: 393 (April 27, 1918).

62. Ibid., p. 319 (September 29, 1917).

63. Ibid., p. 320 (October 3, 1917).

64. Ibid., p. 366 (March 2, 1918).

65. Ibid., p. 413 (July 14, 1918). See Hosoya, Shiberia shuppei no shiteki kenkyū, for the classic contention that Hara's principal aim with the Siberian expedition was U.S.-Japanese cooperation.

66. Ibid., p. 321 (October 3, 1917). Ishii's discussion, of course, would produce a brief and controversial accommodation between the United States and Japan known as the Lansing-Ishii agreement. Although this episode often plays a prominent role in discussions of U.S.-Japanese relations during the Great War, the present study implies that the principal foreign policy actors of the Terauchi cabinet paid little attention to the initiative relative to the more pressing matters of the Nishihara loans, the Sino-Japanese Military Agreement, and the Siberian Intervention. For more on the agreement, see the classic studies of U.S.-Japanese relations, Griswold, The Far Eastern Policy of the United States; and Curry, Woodrow Wilson and Far Eastern Policy, 1913–1921.

67. HN, p. 390 (April 22, 1918).

68. Ibid., p. 307 (July 31, 1917).

69. Ibid., p. 390 (April 22, 1918).

70. *Hōchi shinbun*, October 11, 1918, in STH, 1918, 2: 303.

71. HN, 5: 27 (October 16, 1918).

72. Ibid., p. 34 (November 3, 1918).

73. *Ōsaka Asahi shinbun*, November 15, 1918, in STH, 1918, 2: 550.

74. Kobayashi Tatsuo, *Suiusō nikki*, p. 322. Compare this idea that Hara's attitude toward the new diplomacy was conservative from the start with Nomura Otojirō's ("Pari heiwa kaigi to chōken bunran jiken," pp. 105–6) argument that the prime minister was forced to alter his fundamentally pro-American stance in order to appease conservative domestic forces such as Itō Miyoji.

75. Kobayashi Tatsuo, *Suiusō nikki*, pp. 326–28. Makino's remarks were based on a November 30, 1918, memorandum drafted by Foreign Ministry Political Affairs Bureau chief Komura Kin'ichi and presented to the baron just prior to the council session (Gaimushō hyakunenshi hensan iinkai, *Gaimushō no hyakunen*, 1: 709–10).

76. Meeting of December 8, 1918 (Kobayashi Tatsuo, *Suiusō nikki*, p. 334).

77. Ibid., pp. 339–40.

78. Yoshino, "Gurei kyō no 'kokusai dōmei ron' o yomu," pp. 56–62.

79. Kobayashi Tatsuo, *Suiusō nikki*, p. 310.

80. In a meeting of December 8 (ibid., p. 342).

81. Kobayashi Tatsuo, *Suiusō nikki*, p. 308; Gaimushō, *Nihon gaikō bunsho*, 1918, 3: 538; instructions dated December 26, 1918. Nomura Otojirō ("Pari heiwa kaigi to chōken bunran jiken," p. 106) similarly stresses the substantive problems that the Hara cabinet had with the idea of a League of Nations. Compare with Thomas W. Burkman's ("'Sairento paatonaa' hatsugen su," p. 103) notion that the instructions to postpone a concrete agreement at Paris on a League of Nations reflected principally a lack of time for proper consideration of the problem.

82. Remark made at a November 13, 1918, meeting of the Advisory Council (Kobayashi Tatsuo, *Suiusō nikki*, p. 293).

83. *Ōsaka Asahi shinbun*, November 24, 1918, in STH, 1918, 2: 621–22.

84. Roger Dingman ("Nihon to Uirusonteki sekai chitsujo," pp. 102–3), too, stresses Hara's concern with the domestic political effects of peace.

85. Makino, *Kaisōroku*, 2: 172–73.

86. Gaimushō hyakunenshi hensan iinkai, *Gaimushō no hyakunen*, 1: 708; HN, 5: 41 (November 22, 1918).

87. *Ōsaka Asahi shinbun*, November 24, 1918, in STH, 1918, 2: 621–22.

88. *Yorozu chōhō*, November 17, 1918, in Nakajima et al., *Shinbun shūroku Taishōshi*, 6: 413.

89. Hara Takashi, "Kōwa to shin shisō," *Seiyū*, no. 224 (November 25, 1918), in Bunken shiryō kankōkai, *Seiyū*, 21: 5177–79. Hara's Home Ministry had just com-

pleted a study titled "Democratic Thought in Our Country," which argued that American pronouncements to protect democracy intended not only to establish international equality but to democratize the political systems of all countries (Mitani, *Taishō demokurashii ron*, p. 25).

90. Den Kenjirō nikki, December 1, 1918, Kensei shiryōshitsu, National Diet Library, Tokyo.

91. Ibid., December 10, 1918. Those present at the meeting included Hirata Tōsuke, Kiyoura Keigo, Den Kenjirō, Gotō Shinpei, Kubota Yuzuru, Tanaka Giichi, Komatsubara Eitarō, Ichiki Kitokurō, Yasuhiro Ban'ichirō, Hirayama Narinobu, Arimatsu Hideyoshi, Kamiyama Mitsunoshin, Inoue Tomoichi, and Irie Kan'ichi.

92. Oka, *Tenkanki no Taishō*, p. 129, n1.

93. Itō Yukio, *Taishō demokurashii to seitō seiji*, p. 18.

94. See Den Kenjirō nikki, August 7, 1919; cited in Itō Yukio, "Seitō seiji no teichaku," p. 263.

95. Katō's remarks were made at a party rally on November 10 (Itō Masanori, *Katō Takaaki*, 2: 297–301).

96. Hamaguchi Osachi, "Tōrai no sandai mondai," *Tōkyō Nichinichi shinbun*, January 5, 1919; cited in Mitani Taichirō, "Taishō demokurashiiki no kenryoku to chishikijin," 2: 69.

97. Itō Masanori, *Katō Takaaki*, 2: 302–4; Ōtsu, *Dai Nihon kenseishi*, 8: 378–80.

98. Itō Masanori, *Katō Takaaki*, 2: 302–4; Ōtsu, *Dai Nihon kenseishi*, 8: 378–80, 397–98; Shūgiin and Sangiin, *Gikai seido hyakunenshi*, 1: 728. In April, Katō Takaaki criticized Hara's investment in the transportation network as aimed at expanding the Seiyūkai's base of support (Itō Masanori, *Katō Takaaki*, 2: 305–6).

99. HN, 5: 80 (March 26, 1919).

100. Imai Yoshiyuki, "Ganmeisharyū yori mitaru futsū senkyo," in Tanaka Kōji, *Reimei kōenshū*, 1: 65–66.

101. *Tōyō keizai shinpō*, March 15, 1919; cited in Oka, *Tenkanki no Taishō*, pp. 120–22.

102. Garon, *The State and Labor in Modern Japan*, p. 33.

103. The Public Peace Police Law had been used by the government to battle unionization (Oka, *Tenkanki no Taishō*, pp. 122–23).

104. HN, 5: 74 (March 2, 1919).

105. Takakura, *Tanaka Giichi denki*, 2: 158.

106. Ibid.

107. Usui, *Nihon to Chūgoku*, p. 146.

108. Ibid.

109. Yoshino, "Chōsen bōdō zengosaku," p. 122; Yoshino, "Pekin gakuseidan no kōdō o manba suru nakare," p. 1.

110. Maeda, *Tokonami Takejirō den*, pp. 513–14.

111. HN, 5: 82 (April 2, 1919).

112. Ibid.

113. Mitani, "Taishō demokurashiiki no kenryoku to chishikijin," p. 77.

114. HN, 5: 110 (May 24, 1919).

115. Maeda, *Tokonami Takejirō den*, pp. 515–17; HN, 5: 101, 108 (May 30, June 17, 1919).

116. HN. 5: 94 (May 15, 1919).

117. Ibid., pp. 84, 105 (April 9, June 10, 1919).

118. Fifield, *Woodrow Wilson and the Far East*, p. 250; Kobayashi Tatsuo, *Suiusō nikki*, p. 468.

119. The consortium materialized in May 1920, after the signatories agreed to exempt Manchuria from its provisions (Mitani, *Nihon seitō seiji no keisei*, p. 295).

120. HN, 5: 139 (September 9, 1919); Gaimushō, *Nihon gaikō nenpyō narabi ni shuyō bunsho*, 1: 503–6.

121. Den Kenjirō nikki, June 30, 1919.

122. Utsunomiya to Uehara Yūsaku, June 14, 1919, in UKM, p. 110.

123. Tanaka Giichi, "Tai-Shi seisaku ni kansuru iken," September 19, 1919, in Kobayashi Tatsuo, *Suiusō nikki*, p. 812.

124. Den Kenjirō nikki, June 17, 1919.

125. Yoshino, "Kyōran seru Shina yōchō ron," p. 1.

126. Yoshino, "Sekai no dai shuchō to sono junnōsaku oyobi taiōsaku," p. 143.

Conclusion

1. Benedict, *The Chrysanthemum and the Sword*, pp. 1–2.

2. The most conspicuous attempt to equate Japanese aims with the worst sins of Nazi Germany is, of course, the *New York Times* bestseller by Iris Chang, *The Rape of Nanking*, provocatively subtitled "The Forgotten Holocaust of World War II."

3. The classic, and arguably most valuable, survey of American images of Japan and vice versa in the modern era is Iriye, *Mutual Images*.

4. Even today, "the yellowness of the Yellow Peril is never far below the surface" of Western criticism of Japan, warns Ian Littlewood (*The Idea of Japan*, p. 209).

5. Griswold, *The Far Eastern Policy of the United States*, p. 405.

6. LaFeber, *The Clash*, pp. 396 - 97.

7. Commenting on the dearth of traditional research themes in paper proposals for a recent conference on Taishō Japan, Dower observed, "Apparently the state has been finished off, and the capitalists too (almost), along with all those bourgeois chameleons in the Diet, not to mention the bureaucracy and military" (Minichiello, *Japan's Competing Modernities*, p. xii).

8. For a brief analysis of agency in Japanese foreign policy during the Great War, particularly, the political motivations of Japan's principal foreign policy actors, see Dickinson, "Japan's Asia in the Politics of a New World Order, 1914–19."

9. Hobsbawm and Ranger, *Invention of Tradition*; Anderson, *Imagined Communities*.

10. See, in particular, Hobsbawm, "Mass-Producing Traditions."

11. For a convenient overview of this literature and the questions that drive it, see Hobsbawm, *Nations and Nationalism Since 1780*. For a survey of the issues that have attracted Japan scholars, see the two important collections of essays: Minichiello, *Japan's Competing Modernities*; and Vlastos, *Mirror of Modernity*. The closest the reader will come in these volumes to analyses of foreign policy are studies of "inventions" in Japanese colonial policy. Similar analyses of the "constructions" involved in empire-building have, of course, had a central role in driving the latest wave of international scholarship on nations and nationalism.

12. Yoshino, "Terauchi naikaku no shutsugen" p. 67.

13. The classic studies in each of these categories are Gluck, *Japan's Modern Myths*; Kitaoka, *Nihon rikugun to tairiku seisaku*; and Garon, *Molding Japanese Minds*.

14. For the most eloquent formulation of this new perspective on "modernity," see Garon, "Rethinking Modernization and Modernity in Japanese History."

15. Myers and Peattie, *The Japanese Colonial Empire*, p. 13. The other two volumes in this valuable series are Duus et al., *The Japanese Informal Empire in China*; and Duus et al., *The Japanese Wartime Empire*.

16. This was the foreign policy ramification of what Benedict (*The Chrysanthemum and the Sword*, p. 316) described as the "situational ethics" of the Japanese people.

17. Duus et al., *The Japanese Wartime Empire*, p. xxi.

18. See Beasley, *Japanese Imperialism*, p. 175.

19. Duus et al., *The Japanese Wartime Empire*, p. xvii.

20. The classic treatment in English of Japan's road to war in the 1930s as an opportunity eagerly embraced for long-term nationalist aims rather than as a defensive response to immediate external events is found in three ground-breaking articles by James B. Crowley: "Intellectuals as Visionaries of the New Asian Order"; "A New Asian Order: Some Notes on Prewar Japanese Nationalism"; and "A New Deal for Japan and Asia: One Road to Pearl Harbor."

21. As Y. Tak Matsusaka ("Managing Occupied Manchuria, 1931–1934" p. 102n15) appropriately points out, there is a growing body of Japanese literature that strongly suggests that most Japanese policymakers did not consider Chinese nationalism in Manchuria to be as serious a threat as their public rhetoric indicated. Matsusaka refers, in particular, to the work of Ogata Yōichi and Yoshii Ken'ichi.

22. Tsunoda, *Ugaki Kazushige nikki*, 1: 784 (January 29, 1931).

23. Ibid. (January 1, 29, 1931).

24. John Dewey, "Japan and America," *Dial* 66 (1919), pp. 501–3; reprinted in Boydston, *Essays on China, Japan, and the War*, 11: 151.

25. For a clear and cogent analysis of the differences between the two principal political parties on such important social issues as urban labor and rural tenants' rights, see Garon, *The State and Labor in Modern Japan*.

26. Tsunoda, *Ugaki Kazushige nikki*, 1: 767 (August 27, 1930).

27. Ōuchi, *Fashizumu e no michi*, p. 297; for an English translation, see Hane, *Modern Japan*, p. 248.

28. Mitani, *Kindai Nihon no sensō to seiji*, pp. 113–17.

29. Hearn, *Kokoro*, p. 90.

30. Mitani, *Kindai Nihon no sensō to seiji*, p. 355.

31. Ibid., pp. 355–56.

32. For a comprehensive survey of the national enthusiasm surrounding the Manchurian Incident and the creation of Manchukuo, see Louise Young, *Japan's Total Empire*.

Epilogue

1. It was in this context that political commentator Tawara Sōichirō made the remarks cited above (Fukuda Kazuya, "Rūru o tsukuru no wa Nihon da," p. 79).

2. Indeed, some of Japan's most active champions of domestic political reform became vocal proponents of a weakening of the bilateral alliance; see, for example, Hosokawa Morohiro's call for a withdrawal of American troops from Japan in "Are U.S. Troops in Japan Needed?"

Bibliography

Unpublished Sources in Japanese

Akashi Motojirō monjo (Papers of Akashi Motojirō). Kensei shiryōshitsu, National Diet Library, Tokyo.

Den Kenjirō nikki (Den Kenjirō diary). Kensei shiryōshitsu, National Diet Library, Tokyo.

Futagami Hyōji kankei monjo (Papers relating to Futagami Hyōji). Kensei shiryōshitsu, National Diet Library, Tokyo.

Gotō Shinpei monjo (Papers of Gotō Shinpei). Kensei shiryōshitsu, National Diet Library, Tokyo.

Inoue Kaoru monjo (Papers of Inoue Kaoru). Kensei shiryōshitsu, National Diet Library, Tokyo.

Nara Takeji nikki (Diary of Nara Takeji). Courtesy of Nara Takeji monjo kenkyū-kai, Tokyo.

Oka Ichinosuke monjo (Papers of Oka Ichinosuke). Kensei shiryōshitsu, National Diet Library, Tokyo.

Ōkuma Shigenobu kankei monjo (Papers relating to Ōkuma Shigenobu). Kensei shiryōshitsu, National Diet Library, Tokyo.

Takeshita Isamu nikki (Diary of Takeshita Isamu). Courtesy of Nihon seiji gaikō-shi kenkyūkai.

Tanaka Giichi kankei monjo (Papers relating to Tanaka Giichi). Kensei shiryōshitsu, National Diet Library, Tokyo. Also, Yamaguchi Prefectural Library, Yamaguchi.

Terauchi Masatake kankei monjo (Papers relating to Terauchi Masatake). Kensei shiryōshitsu, National Diet Library, Tokyo.

Yamagata Aritomo monjo (Papers of Yamagata Aritomo). Kensei shiryōshitsu, National Diet Library, Tokyo.

Periodicals, Newspapers

Aka
Chūō kōron
Jiji shinpō
Ōsaka puck
Tokyo Asahi shinbun
Tokyo Puck

Published Sources in Japanese

Akita, George, and Itō Takashi. "Yamagata Aritomo to 'jinshū kyōsō' ron" (Yamagata Aritomo's theory of racial conflict). In Kindai Nihon kenkyūkai, ed., *Nihon gaikō no kiki ninshiki*, pp. 95–118. Tokyo: Yamakawa shuppansha, 1985.

Araki Sadao, ed. *Gensui Uehara Yūsaku den* (Biography of Field Marshal Uehara Yūsaku). 2 vols. Tokyo: Gensui Uehara Yūsaku denki kankōkai, 1937.

Banno Junji. *Kindai Nihon no kokka kōsō* (The conception of the state in modern Japan). Tokyo: Iwanami shoten, 1996.

———. "Nihon rikugun no Ōbeikan to Chūgoku seisaku" (The Japanese army's view of the West and their China policy). In Hosoya Chihiro and Saitō Makoto, eds., *Washinton taisei to Nichi-Bei kankei*, pp. 441–64. Tokyo: Tokyo daigaku shuppankai, 1978.

———. *Taishō seihen: 1900-nen taisei no hōkai* (The Taishō political crisis: collapse of the 1900 system). Tokyo: Mineruba shobō, 1994.

Banno Junji et al., eds. *Takarabe Takeshi nikki* (Diary of Takarabe Takeshi). 2 vols. Tokyo: Yamakawa shuppansha, 1983.

Bunken shiryō kankōkai, ed. *Seiyū* (Seiyūkai party magazine). 44 vols. Tokyo: Kashiwa shobō, 1980.

Burkman, Thomas W. "'Sairento paatonaa' hatsugen su" (The "silent partner" speaks). *Kokusai seiji*, no. 56 (1976): 102–16.

Dickinson, Frederick R. "Daiyon no 'kaikoku' wa jitsugen suru ka: futatsu no kokkazō ni yureru Nihon" (Will a fourth "opening of the country" materialize?: Japan between two conceptions of state). *AΣTEION*, no. 36 (Spring 1995): 149–60.

Dingman, Roger. "Nihon to Uirusonteki sekai chitsujo" (The Wilsonian world order and Japan). In Satō Seizaburō and Roger Dingman, eds., *Kindai Nihon no taigai taido*. Tokyo: Tokyo daigaku shuppankai, 1974.

Eguchi Keiichi. "1914-nen no haizei undō: Taishō demokurashii to kyū chūkansō" (The anti-tax movement of 1914: Taishō democracy and the old middle class). In Inoue Kiyoshi, ed., *Taishōki no seiji to shakai*, pp. 53–115. Tokyo: Iwanami shoten, 1969.

Fujimura Michio. *Yamagata Aritomo*. Tokyo: Yoshikawa kōbunkan, 1961.

Fukuda Kazuya. "Rūru o tsukuru no wa Nihon da" (It is Japan that will make the rules). *Chūō kōron* 113, no. 10 (September 1998): 70–79.

Fukuda Tokuzō et al. "Hara naikaku ni yōbō-su" (Wishes for the Hara cabinet). *Chūō kōron* 33, no. 10 (October 1918): 71–107.

Gaimushō, ed. *Nihon gaikō bunsho: Taishō jidai* (Documents on Japanese diplomacy: Taishō period). 36 vols. Tokyo: Gaimushō, 1964–87.

———. *Nihon gaikō nenpyō narabi ni shuyō bunsho, 1840–1945* (Japan diplomatic chronicle and principal documents). 2 vols. Tokyo: Hara shobō, 1965.

Gaimushō hyakunenshi hensan iinkai, ed. *Gaimushō no hyakunen* (One hundred years of the Foreign Ministry). 2 vols. Tokyo: Hara shobō, 1969.

Hara Keiichirō, ed. *Hara Takashi nikki* (Diary of Hara Takashi). 6 vols. Tokyo: Fukumura shuppan, 1981.

Hara Takashi monjo kenkyūkai, ed. *Hara Takashi kankei monjo* (Papers relating to Hara Takashi). 11 vols. Tokyo: Nihon hōsō shuppan kyōkai, 1984–89.

Hara Teruyuki. "Nihon no Kyokutō Roshia gunji kanshō no shomondai" (Various problems relating to Japan's military intervention in the Russian Far East). *Rekishigaku kenkyū*, no. 478 (March 1980): 1–14.

———. *Shiberia shuppei: kakumei to kanshō, 1917–1922* (Siberian expedition: revolution and intervention, 1917–1922). Tokyo: Chikuma shobō, 1989.

Harada Kumao, ed. *Saionji kō to seikyoku* (Prince Saionji and the political situation). 9 vols. Tokyo: Iwanami shoten, 1950.

Haraguchi Takejirō. "Beikokuteki seishin" (The American spirit). *Chūō kōron* 31, no. 10 (October 1916): 84–92.

Hatano Masaru. "Chūgoku daisan kakumei to Nihon gaikō" (The third Chinese revolution and Japanese diplomacy). *Ajia kenkyū* 36, no. 4 (September 1990): 77–113.

———. "Kaigun taishō Takeshita Isamu kankei monjo" (Papers relating to naval admiral Takeshita Isamu). *Gunji shigaku* 17, no. 2 (September 1981): 73–81.

———. "Tai-Doku kaisen to Nihon gaikō" (Japanese diplomacy and the outbreak of war with Germany). *Keiō daigaku hōgaku kenkyū* 61, no. 8 (August 1988): 44–75.

Hayashi Fusao. *Daitōa sensō kōtei ron* (Affirming the Greater East Asia War). Tokyo: Banchō shobō, 1975.

Hayashi Keisuke. *Bandō horyo shūyōjo: dai kyū kōkyōkyoku no rūtsu* (Bandō prisoner-of-war camp: roots of the ninth symphony). Tokyo: Nankai bukusu, 1978.

Hirama Yōichi. "Dai-ichiji sekai taisen e no sanka to kaigun" (Participation in the First World War and the navy). *Gunji shigaku* 22, no. 1 (June 1986): 27–37.

———. "Dai-ichiji sekai taisen e no sansen to tai-Bei kankei" (Participation in the First World War and relations with America). *Seiji keizai shigaku*, no. 246 (October 1986): 32–43.

————. "Dai-ichiji taisenchū no Yōroppa hahei mondai to kaigun no taiō" (The navy's response to the problem of sending troops to Europe in World War I). *Shin bōei ronshū* 16, no. 3 (December 1988): 91–110.

————. "Tai-Ka nijūikkajō no yōkyū to kaigun" (The Twenty-One Demands and the navy). *Gunji shigaku* 23, no. 1 (June 1987): 30–42.

Hirono Yoshihiko. "Yoshino Sakuzō Chūgoku ron oboegaki" (The China memoranda of Yoshino Sakuzō). *Kyōto daigaku hōgaku ronsō* 121, no. 6 (1987): 48–81.

Hosoya Chihiro. *Roshia kakumei to Nihon* (The Russian revolution and Japan). Tokyo: Hara shobō, 1972.

————. *Shiberia shuppei no shiteki kenkyū* (Historical analysis of the Siberian expedition). Tokyo: Yūhikaku, 1955.

Imai Seiichi. *Nihon kindaishi* (Part II) (History of modern Japan). Tokyo: Iwanami shoten, 1977.

————. "Taishōki ni okeru gunbu no seijiteki chii" (The political position of the military in the Taishō period). 2 pts. *Shisō*, no. 399 (September 1957): 3–21; no. 402 (December 1957): 106–22.

Inoue Kaoru kō denki hensankai. *Segai Inoue kō den* (Biography of the late Lord Inoue). 5 vols. Tokyo: Hara shobō, 1968.

Irokawa Daikichi. *Kindai kokka no shuppatsu* (Beginnings of a modern nation). Tokyo: Chūō kōronsha, 1966.

Ishibashi Tanzan. *Tanzan kaisō* (Tanzan's reminiscences). Tokyo: Iwanami shoten, 1985.

Ishii Kikujirō. *Gaikō yoroku* (Various jottings on diplomacy). Tokyo: Iwanami shoten, 1933.

Itō Masanori. *Katō Takaaki* (Biography of Katō Takaaki). 2 vols. Tokyo: Katō haku denki hensan iinkai, 1929.

Itō Takashi, ed. *Taishō shoki Yamagata Aritomo danwa hikki* (Record of Yamagata Aritomo's conversations in early Taishō). Tokyo: Yamakawa shuppansha, 1981.

Itō Takashi et al., eds. *Tokutomi Sohō kankei monjo* (Papers relating to Tokutomi Sohō). 3 vols. Tokyo: Yamakawa shuppansha, 1985.

Itō Yukio. "Dai-ichiji taisen to sengo Nihon no keisei" (The First World War and the formation of postwar Japan). *Hōgaku ronsō* (Kyōto University) 140, no. 3/4 (January 1997): 155–211.

————. "Dai-niji Itō naikakuki no seitō to hanbatsu kanryō" (Political parties and the bureaucratic clique during the period of the second Itō cabinet). *Nagoya daigaku bungakubu kenkyū ronshū*, no. 113 (March 1992): 271–99.

————. "Seitō seiji no teichaku" (Stabilization of party politics). In Banno Junji and Miyaji Masato, eds., *Nihon kindaishi ni okeru tenkanki no kenkyū*, pp. 257–348. Tokyo: Yamakawa shuppansha, 1985.

————. *Taishō demokurashii to seitō seiji* (Taishō democracy and party politics). Tokyo: Yamakawa shuppansha, 1987.

Jōhō Yoshio. *Rikugunshō gunmukyoku* (Military Affairs Bureau of the Ministry of War). Tokyo: Fuyō shobō, 1979.

Kaigun daijin kanbō, ed. *Kaigun gunbi enkaku* (Development of naval armaments). Tokyo: Gannandō shoten, 1934.

Karita Tōru. *Shōwa shoki seiji gaikōshi kenkyū* (Study of politics and diplomacy in the early Shōwa period). Tokyo: Sōbunsha, 1978.

Kawada Minoru. *Hara Takashi, tenkanki no kōsō: kokka shakai to Nihon* (Hara Takashi's conception at the watershed: Japan and the international community). Tokyo: Miraisha, 1995.

————. *Hara Takashi to Yamagata Aritomo: kokka kōsō o meguru gaikō to naisei* (Hara Takashi and Yamagata Aritomo: domestic politics, foreign policy, and the conception of the state). Tokyo: Chūō kōronsha, 1998.

Kisaka Jun'ichirō. "Gunbu to demokurashii" (The military and democracy). *Kokusai seiji*, no. 38 (1967): 1–39.

————. "Taishōki minponshugisha no kokusai ninshiki" (The international outlook of Taishō era democrats). *Kokusai seiji*, no. 51 (1974): 59–108.

Kitamura Hironao, ed. *Yume no shichijūyonen: Nishihara Kamezō jiden* (Seventy some odd years' dream: autobiography of Nishihara Kamezō). Tokyo: Heibonsha, 1965.

Kitaoka Shin'ichi. "Gaikō shidōsha toshite no Gotō Shinpei" (Gotō Shinpei as foreign policy leader). In Kindai Nihon kenkyūkai, ed., *Kindai Nihon to Higashi Ajia*, pp. 55–95. Tokyo: Yamakawa shuppansha, 1980.

————. *Nihon rikugun to tairiku seisaku* (The Japanese army and continental policy). Tokyo: Tokyo daigaku shuppankai, 1978.

————. "Nijuikkajō yōkyū saikō" (Reevaluation of the Twenty-One Demands). In Kindai Nihon kenkyūkai, ed., *Nihon gaikō no kiki ninshiki*, pp. 119–50. Tokyo: Yamakawa shuppansha, 1985.

Kiyosawa Kiyoshi. *Nihon gaikōshi* (History of Japanese diplomacy). 2 vols. Tokyo: Tōyō keizai shinpōsha, 1942.

Kobayashi Michihiko. "Nichi-Ro sengo no Nichi-Doku dōmei-ron" (Post-Russo-Japanese War discussion of a German-Japanese alliance). *Nihon rekishi*, no. 532 (September 1992): 82–88.

————. *Nihon no tairiku seisaku, 1895–1914* (Japan's continental policy, 1895–1914). Tokyo: Nansōsha, 1996.

————. "'Teikoku kokubō hōshin' no dōyō" (Tremors in the "Basic Plan of National Defense"). *Nihon rekishi*, no. 507 (August 1990): 57–73.

————. "'Teikoku kokubō hōshin' saikō: Nichi-Ro sengo ni okeru riku-kaigun no kyōchō" (A reconsideration of the "Basic Plan of National Defense": army-navy cooperation after the Russo-Japanese War). *Shigaku zasshi* 98, no. 4 (April 1989): 36–71.

Kobayashi Tatsuo. *Suiusō nikki: Itō ke monjo* (Green rain diary: Itō family papers). Tokyo: Hara shobō, 1966.

Koiso Kuniaki. *Koiso Kuniaki jiden* (Autobiography of Koiso Kuniaki). Tokyo: Marunouchi shuppan, 1968.

Kōketsu Atsushi. *Kindai Nihon no seigun kankei: gunjin Tanaka Giichi no kiseki* (Civil-military relations in modern Japan: Legacy of Tanaka Giichi the soldier). Tokyo: Ōfusha, 1987.

———. "Taisenkanki ni okeru rikugun no kokumin dōin seisaku" (The army's national mobilization policy between the wars). *Gunji shigaku* 17, no. 4 (March 1982): 13–25.

Kurihara Ken. "Dai-ichiji dai-niji Manmō dokuritsu undō to Koike gaimushō seimukyokuchō no jishoku" (The First and Second Manchuria-Mongolia independence movements and the resignation of Foreign Ministry Political Affairs Bureau chief Koike). In Kurihara Ken, ed., *Tai-Manmō seisakushi no ichimen*, pp. 139–61. Tokyo: Hara shobō, 1966.

Kurihara Ken, ed. *Tai-Manmō seisakushi no ichimen* (One aspect of the history of Japan's Manchuria and Mongolia policy). Tokyo: Hara shobō, 1966.

Kuroda Kōshirō. *Gensui Terauchi hakushaku den* (Biography of Field Marshal Count Terauchi). Tokyo: Gensui Terauchi hakushaku denki hensansho, 1920.

Kuroita Katsumi. *Fukuda taishō den* (Biography of General Fukuda). Tokyo: Fukuda taishō den kankōkai, 1937.

Kurosawa Fumitaka. "Nihon rikugun no sōryokusen kōsō" (The Japanese army's conception of total war). *Jōchi shigaku*, no. 27 (1982): 65–87.

———. "Nihon rikugun no tai-Bei ninshiki" (The Japanese army's perception of America). *Kokusai seiji*, no. 91 (May 1989): 19–38.

Maeda Renzan. *Hara Takashi* (Biography of Hara Takashi). Tokyo: Jiji tsūshinsha, 1958.

Maeda Renzan, ed. *Tokonami Takejirō den* (Biography of Tokonami Takejirō). Tokyo: Tokonami Takejirō denki kankōkai, 1939.

Makino Nobuaki. *Kaisōroku* (Memoirs). 2 vols. Tokyo: Chūō kōronsha, 1978.

Masumi Junnosuke. *Nihon seitōshi ron* (Discourse on Japanese political history). 4 vols. Tokyo: Tōkyō daigaku shuppankai, 1968.

Matsui Keishirō. *Matsui Keishirō jijoden* (Autobiography of Matsui Keishirō). Tokyo: Kankōsha, 1983.

Matsuo Takayoshi. "Kome sōdō chin'atsu no shuppei kibo" (The scale of the rice riot suppression). *Shirin* 71, no. 1 (January 1988): 175–83.

———. *Taishō demokurashii no kenkyū* (Study of Taishō democracy). Tokyo: Aoki shoten, 1966.

Meiji Taishō Shōwa shinbun kenkyūkai, ed. *Shinbun shūsei Taishō hennenshi* (Newspaper compilation: chronicles of Taishō). 43 vols. Tokyo: Meiji Taishō Shōwa shinbun kenkyūkai, 1969–81.

Mitani Taichirō. *Kindai Nihon no sensō to seiji* (Politics and war in modern Japan). Tokyo: Iwanami shoten, 1997.

————. *Nihon seitō seiji no keisei* (Formation of Japanese party politics). Tokyo: Tōkyō daigaku shuppankai, 1967.

————. "Taishō demokurashiiki no kenryoku to chishikijin" (Power and intellectuals during the Taishō democracy period). In Kokka gakkai hyakunen kinen, ed., *Kokka to shimin*. 3 vols. Tokyo: Yūhikaku, 1987.

————. *Taishō demokurashii ron: Yoshino Sakuzō no jidai to sono go* (Discourse on Taishō democracy: the age of Yoshino Sakuzō and after). Tokyo: Chūō kōronsha, 1974.

Miura Gorō. *Kanju shōgun kaisōroku* (Memoirs of General Kanju). Tokyo: Chūō kōronsha, 1988.

Miyake Masaki. "Dai-ichiji sekai taisen ni okeru Nichi-Doku kankei to Nichi-Ro kankei" (Japanese-German relations and Japanese-Russian relations during the First World War). *Kokusai seiji*, no. 38 (1967): 105–33.

Muroyama Yoshimasa. "Nichi-Ro sengo no gunbi kakuchō mondai" (The problem of military expansion after the Russo-Japanese War). In Inoue Mitsusada et al., *Nihon rekishi taikei*, 4: 1217–53. Tokyo: Yamakawa shuppansha, 1987.

Nagai Kafū. *Danchōtei nichijō* (House of grief—Nagai Kafū's diary). 2 vols. Tokyo: Iwanami shoten, 1990.

Nagaoka Shinjirō. "Katō Takaaki ron" (Discourse on Katō Takaaki). *Kokusai seiji*, no. 33 (1966): 27–40.

————. "Tai-Ka nijūikkajō yōkyū jōkō no kettei to sono haikei" (The decision on the articles of the Twenty-One Demands and its background). *Nihon rekishi*, no. 144 (June 1960): 66–80.

Naikaku tōkeikyoku, ed. *Nihon teikoku tōkei nenkan* (Statistical yearbook of the Japanese empire). 59 vols. Tokyo: Tōkyō ripurinto shuppansha, 1962–67.

Nakajima Kenzō et al., comps. *Shinbun shūroku Taishōshi* (Taishō history through the newspapers). 15 vols. Tokyo: Taishō shuppan, 1978.

Nihon kokusai seiji gakkai, ed. *Nihon gaikōshi kenkyū: Taishō jidai* (Study of Japanese diplomatic history: the Taishō period). Tokyo: Yushindo, 1958.

Nihon seiji gaikōshi kenkyūkai, ed. "Akashi Motojirō monjo oyobi kadai" (Papers of Akashi Motojirō and issues outstanding). *Keiō daigaku hōgaku kenkyū* 58, no. 9 (September 1985): 75–103.

Nomura Otojirō. *Kindai Nihon seiji gaikōshi kenkyū* (Study of the politics and diplomacy of modern Japan). Tokyo: Tōsui shobō, 1982.

————. "Pari heiwa kaigi to chōken bunran jiken" (The Paris Peace Conference and the constitutional disturbance). *Seiji keizai shigaku*, no. 250 (February 1987): 101–11.

————. "Tai-Ka nijūikkajō mondai to Katō Takaaki" (The Twenty-One Demands and Katō Takaaki). 2 pts. *Seiji keizai shigaku*, no. 131 (April 1977): 1–10; no. 132 (May 1977): 16–25.

Oka Yoshitake. *Tenkanki no Taishō* (The turning point of Taishō). Tokyo: Tōkyō daigaku shuppankai, 1969.

————. *Yamagata Aritomo: Meiji Nihon no shōchō* (Yamagata Aritomo: symbol of Meiji Japan). Tokyo: Iwanami shoten, 1958.

Oka Yoshitake, ed. *Taishō demokurashiiki no seiji: Matsumoto Gōkichi seiji nisshi* (Politics during the era of Taishō democracy: political diary of Matsumoto Gōkichi). Tokyo: Iwanami shoten, 1957.

Oka Yoshitake et al., eds. *Ogawa Heikichi kankei monjo* (Papers relating to Ogawa Heikichi). 2 vols. Tokyo: Misuzu shobō, 1973.

Ōkuma kō hachijūgonenshi hensankai, ed. *Ōkuma kō hachijūgonenshi* (The eighty-five-year history of Marquis Ōkuma). 3 vols. Tokyo: Hara shobō, 1970.

Ōtsu Jun'ichirō. *Dai Nihon kenseishi* (Constitutional history of Greater Japan). 10 vols. Tokyo: Hara shobō, 1970.

Ōtsuka Minao. *Meiji ishin to doitsu shisō* (The Meiji Restoration and German thought). Tokyo: Nagasaki shuppan, 1977.

Ōuchi Tsutomu. *Fashizumu e no michi* (Road to fascism). Tokyo: Chūō kōronsha, 1967.

Ōyama Azusa, comp. *Yamagata Aritomo ikensho* (Written opinions of Yamagata Aritomo). Tokyo: Hara shobō, 1966.

Ōyama Ikuo. "Amerikanizumu to pan-Amerikanizumu" (Americanism and pan-Americanism). *Chūō kōron* 31, no. 10 (October 1916): 69–77.

Rikugun sanbō honbu, ed. *Shiberia shuppeishi* (History of the Siberian expedition). 3 vols. Tokyo: Shin jidaisha, 1972.

Saitō Seiji. "Nishihara Kamezō no tai-Chūgoku kōsō" (Nishihara Kamezō's conception of China). *Kokusai seiji*, no. 71 (August 1982): 54–71.

————. "Terauchi naikaku ni okeru en Dan seisaku kakuritsu no keii" (Formulating the policy of aid to Duan Qirui during the Terauchi cabinet). *Kokusai seiji*, no. 83 (October 1986): 143–61.

————. "Terauchi naikaku to Nishihara Kamezō" (The Terauchi cabinet and Nishihara Kamezō). *Kokusai seiji*, no. 75 (October 1983): 12–71.

Satō Kentarō. "Beikoku kaigun no shōrai" (The future of the U.S. navy). *Chūō kōron* 31, no. 12 (December 1916): 80–84.

Seki Hiroharu. *Gendai higashi Ajia kokusai kankyō no tōjō* (Emergence of the international environment in contemporary East Asia). Tokyo: Fukumura shuppan, 1966.

Seki Shizuo. "Hara Takashi no gaikō shidō" (Hara Takashi's foreign policy leadership). *Tezukayama daigaku kiyō* 37 (March 1994): 56–76.

Shimanuki Takeji. "Dai-ichiji sekai taisen igo no kokubō hōshin, shoyō heiryoku, yōhei kōryō no hensen" (Post–World War I changes in the Basic Plan of National Defense, required armaments, and the outline of necessary troops). *Gunji shigaku* 9, no. 1 (June 1973): 65–75.

————. "Nichi-Ro sensō igo ni okeru kokubō hōshin, shoyō heiryoku, yōhei kōryō no hensen" (Post-Russo-Japanese War changes in the Basic Plan of National Defense, required armaments, and the outline of necessary troops). *Gunji shigaku* 8, no. 4 (March 1973): 2–16.

Shinobu Seizaburō. *Taishō seijishi* (Taishō political history). 4 vols. Tokyo: Kawade shobō, 1951.

Shōda Tatsuo. *Jūshintachi no Shōwa-shi* (A Shōwa history of the statesmen). 2 vols. Tokyo: Bungei shunju, 1981.

Shūgiin and Sangiin, eds. *Gikai seido hyakunenshi* (Hundred years' history of the parliamentary system). 12 vols. Tokyo: Ōkurashō, 1990.

Somura Yasunobu. "En Segai teisei mondai to Nihon no gaikō" (Japanese diplomacy and the problem of imperial government under Yuan Shikai). *Kokusaihō gaikō zasshi* 56, no. 2 (May 1957): 1–34.

Suehiro Shigeo. "Nichi-Beikan ni yokotawaru sandai mondai" (Three problems between Japan and the United States). *Chūō kōron* 31, no. 10 (October 1916): 77–84.

Suetake Yoshiya. "Dai-ichiji sekai taisenki no shoseitō no dōkō" (Trends of the various parties during World War I). In Kindai Nihon kenkyūkai, ed., *Seitō naikaku no seiritsu to hōkai*, pp. 1–28. Tokyo: Yamakawa shuppansha, 1984.

————. "Dai-niji Ōkuma naikaku ni okeru seitō to genrō" (Political parties and elder statesmen during the second Ōkuma cabinet). *Shigaku zasshi* 91, no. 6 (June 1982): 47–78.

————. "Taishō gonen no Ōkuma kōkei naikaku mondai" (The problem of a successor cabinet to Ōkuma in 1916). *Nihon rekishi*, no. 413 (October 1982): 59–76.

————. "Taishōki ni okeru Gotō Shinpei o meguru seiji jōkyō" (Politics surrounding Gotō Shinpei during the Taishō era). *Shigaku zasshi* 96, no. 6 (June 1987): 1–31.

————. *Taishōki no seiji kōzō* (The structure of politics in the Taishō period). Tokyo: Yoshikawa kōbunkan, 1998.

Suzuki Hajime, ed. *Suzuki Kantarō jiden* (Autobiography of Suzuki Kantarō). Tokyo: Ogikukai shuppan, 1949.

Suzuki Takeo, ed. *Nishihara shakkan shiryō kenkyū* (Study of documents relating to the Nishihara loans). Tokyo: Tokyo daigaku shuppankai, 1972.

Tai Kitō (Dai Zhidao). *Nihon ron* (Discourse on Japan). Translated by Ichikawa Hiroshi. Tokyo: Shakai shisōsha, 1972.

Taishō nyūsu jiten hensan iinkai, ed. *Taishō nyūsu jiten* (Dictionary of Taishō news). 8 vols. Tokyo: Mainichi Communications, 1986.

Takahashi Hidenao. "Hara naikaku no seiritsu to sōryokusen seisaku" (Formation of the Hara cabinet and total war policy). *Shirin* 68, no. 3 (May 1985): 1–34.

————. "Sōryokusen seisaku to Terauchi naikaku" (Total war policy and the Terauchi cabinet). *Rekishigaku kenkyū*, no. 552 (March 1986): 1–16.

————. "Terauchi naikakuki no seiji taisei" (The political system during the Terauchi cabinet). *Shirin* 67, no. 4 (July 1984): 39–74.

————. "Terauchi naikaku seiritsuki no seiji jōkyō" (The political situation surrounding the formation of the Terauchi cabinet). *Nihon rekishi*, no. 434 (July 1984): 58–74.

Takahashi Yoshio. *Banshōroku: Takahashi sōan nikki* (Comprehensive record: diary of the Takahashi hermitage). 8 vols. Tokyo: Shibunkaku shuppan, 1986–87.

Takakura Tetsuichi, *Tanaka Giichi denki* (Biography of Tanaka Giichi). 2 vols. Tokyo: Tanaka Giichi denki kankōkai, 1958.

Takekoshi Yosaburō. *Tōankō* (Prince Tōan). Tokyo: Sōbungaku, 1930.

Tanaka Kōji, ed. *Reimei kōenshū* (Compilation of the Dawn Society speeches), vol. 1. Tokyo: Daitōkaku, 1919.

Tanaka Tomokichi, ed. *Hara Takashi zenshū* (Complete works of Hara Takashi). 2 vols. Tokyo: Hara Takashi zenshū kankōkai, 1929.

Taya Kiyoshi. *Hara Takashi Taishō hachinen* (Hara Takashi in the eighth year of Taishō). Tokyo: Nihon hyōronsha, 1987.

Tazaki Suematsu, *Hyōden Tanaka Giichi* (Critical biography of Tanaka Giichi). 2 vols. Tokyo: Heiwa senryaku sōgō kenkyūsho, 1981.

Terasaki Hidenari. *Shōwa tennō dokuhakuroku: Terasaki Hidenari goyōgakari nikki* (The Shōwa emperor's monologue: diary of Imperial Household official Terasaki Hidenari). Tokyo: Bungei shunjū, 1991.

Tokito Hideto. "Inukai Tsuyoshi to dai-ichiji taisen" (Inukai Tsuyoshi and the First World War). *Gunji shigaku* 19, no. 4 (March 1984): 24–35.

Tokutomi Iichirō, ed. *Kōshaku Matsukata Masayoshi den* (Biography of Prince Matsukata Masayoshi). 3 vols. Tokyo: Meiji bunken, 1976.

————. *Kōshaku Yamagata Aritomo den* (Biography of Prince Yamagata Aritomo). 3 vols. Tokyo: Hara shobō, 1969.

Tōyama Shigeki, Imai Seiichi, and Fujiwara Akira. *Shōwashi* (History of Shōwa). Tokyo: Iwanami shinsho, 1959.

Tsunoda Jun. *Manshū mondai to kokubō hōshin* (The Manchuria problem and the Basic Plan of National Defense). Tokyo: Hara shobō, 1967.

Tsunoda Jun, comp. *Ugaki Kazushige nikki* (Diary of Ugaki Kazushige). 3 vols. Tokyo: Misuzu shobō, 1968.

Tsurumi Yūsuke. *Gotō Shinpei* (Biography of Gotō Shinpei). 4 vols. Tokyo: Keisō shobō, 1965–67.

Uehara Yūsaku kankei monjo kenkyūkai, ed. *Uehara Yūsaku kankei monjo* (Papers relating to Uehara Yūsaku). Tokyo: Tōkyō daigaku shuppankai, 1976.

Usui Katsumi. "Nanman, Tōmō jōyaku no seiritsu zengo" (Around the conclusion of the South Manchuria and Eastern Inner Mongolia Treaties). In Kurihara Ken, ed., *Tai-Manmō seisakushi no ichimen*, pp. 115–37. Tokyo: Hara shobō, 1966.

———. *Nihon to Chūgoku: Taishō jidai* (Japan and China: the Taisho era). Tokyo: Hara shobō, 1972.

Wakatsuki Reijirō. *Meiji, Taishō, Shōwa seikai hisshi: kofūan kaikoroku* (Secret history of Meiji, Taishō, Shōwa: memoirs of Wakatsuki Reijirō). Tokyo: Kodansha, 1990.

Washio Yoshitsugu et al., eds. *Inukai Bokudō den* (Biography of Inukai Tsuyoshi). 3 vols. Tokyo: Tōyō keizai shinpōsha, 1938–39.

Watanabe Ikujirō. *Monjo yori mitaru Ōkuma Shigenobu kō* (Archival look at Marquis Ōkuma Shigenobu). Tokyo: Nisshin, 1932.

Watanabe Katsumasa, comp. *Shinbun shiroku Taishōshi* (Collected newspapers of the Taishō era). 15 vols. Tokyo: Taishō shuppan, 1978.

Yamaguchi Toshiaki. "Kokka sōdōin kenkyū josetsu" (Introduction to the study of national mobilization). *Kokka gakkai zasshi* 93, no. 4 (April 1979): 105–21.

Yamaguchi Toshiaki, comp. "Hamaomote Matasuke monjo" (Papers relating to Hamaomote Matasuke). In Kindai Nihon kenkyūkai, ed., *Kindai Nihon to higashi Ajia*, pp. 205–70. Tokyo: Yamakawa shuppansha, 1980.

Yamamoto Shirō. "Terauchi naikaku jidai no Nitchū kankei no ichimen: Nishihara Kamezō to Banzai Rihachirō" (One aspect of Sino-Japanese relations during the Terauchi cabinet: Nishihara Kamezō and Banzai Rihachirō). *Shirin* 64, no. 1. (January 1981): 1–36.

Yamamoto Shirō, ed. *Banzai Rihachirō shokan hōkokushū* (Letters and reports of Banzai Rihachirō). Tokyo: Tōsui shobō, 1989.

———. *Dai-niji Ōkuma naikaku kankei shiryō* (Documents relating to the second Ōkuma cabinet). Kyōto: Kyōto joshi daigaku, 1979.

———. *Miura Gorō kankei monjo* (Papers relating to Miura Gorō). Tokyo: Meiji shiryō kenkyū renrakukai, 1960.

———. *Nishihara Kamezō nikki* (Diary of Nishihara Kamezō). Kyōto: Kyōto joshi daigaku, 1983.

———. *Terauchi Masatake kankei bunsho: shushō izen* (Papers relating to Terauchi Masatake: before his prime ministry). Kyōto: Kyōto joshi daigaku, 1984.

————. *Terauchi Masatake naikaku kankei shiryō* (Documents relating to the Terauchi Masatake cabinet). 2 vols. Kyōto: Kyōto joshi daigaku, 1985.

————. *Terauchi Masatake nikki* (Diary of Terauchi Masatake). Kyōto: Kyōto joshi daigaku, 1980.

Yoshida Yutaka. "Nihon teikokushugi no Shiberia kanshō sensō" (Japanese imperialism's war of intervention in Siberia). *Rekishigaku kenkyū*, no. 490 (March 1981): 1–14.

Yoshimura Michio. *Nihon to Roshia* (Japan and Russia). Tokyo: Hara shobō, 1968.

Yoshino Sakuzō. "Beikoku no tai-Tōyō seisaku" (America's East Asia policy). *Chūō kōron* 31, no. 12 (December 1916): 90–92.

———— (Kosen Gakujin, pseud.). "Beikoku sansen no bunmeiteki igi" (The significance for civilization of American participation in the war). *Chūō kōron* 32, no. 5 (May 1917): 92–95.

————. "Chōsen bōdō zengosaku" (Solution for the Korean uprising). *Chūō kōron* 34, no. 4 (April 1919): 121–23.

————. "Gurei kyō no 'kokusai dōmei ron' o yomu" (Reading Lord Grey's "discourse on an international alliance"). *Chūō kōron* 33, no. 7 (July 1918): 56–62.

————. "Hara naikaku ni taisuru yōbō" (Wishes for the Hara cabinet). *Chūō kōron* 33, no. 10 (October 1918): 80–84.

————. "Kensei no hongi o toite sono yūshū no bi o sumasu no michi o ronzu" (Preaching the essentials of constitutional government and discussing the road to its fulfillment). *Chūō kōron* 31, no. 1 (January 1916): 17–114.

———— (Kosen Gakujin, pseud.). "Kuru beki kōwa to Kōshūwan oyobi Nan'yō shotō no shobun" (The coming peace and the disposal of Jiaozhou Bay and the South Pacific islands). *Chūō kōron* 32, no. 3 (March 1917): 109–12.

————. "Kyokutan naru Doitsu sanbironsha o imashimu" (Admonishing the extreme German admirers). *Chūō kōron* 30, no. 8 (August 1915): 73–76.

————. "Kyōran seru Shina yōchō ron" (The frenzied calls for chastisement of China). *Chūō kōron* 34, no. 7 (July 1919): 1.

————. "Pekin gakuseidan no kōdō o manba suru nakare" (Do not revile the actions of the Beijing students). *Chūō kōron* 34, no. 6 (June 1919): 1.

————. "Rikugun kakuchō ni hantai-su" (Against army expansion). *Chūō kōron* 33, no. 11 (November 1918): 48–51.

————. "Sekai no dai shuchō to sono junnōsaku oyobi taiōsaku" (Great world trends and policies of adaptation and response). *Chūō kōron* 34, no. 1 (January 1919): 142–46.

———— (Kosen Gakujin, pseud.). "Shin naishō Gotō dan" (The new home minister, Baron Gotō). *Chūō kōron* 31, no. 11 (November 1916): 89–91.

————. "Tai-Shi gaikō no gensei hihan" (A stern criticism of our China diplomacy). *Chūō kōron* 30, no. 6 (June 1915): 51–80.

————. "Terauchi naikaku no shutsugen ni taisuru gensei hihan" (A stern criticism of the emergence of the Terauchi cabinet). *Chūō kōron* 30, no. 11 (November 1916): 66–86.

Published Sources in English

Akita, George. *Foundations of Constitutional Government in Modern Japan, 1868–1900.* Cambridge, Mass.: Harvard University Press, 1967.

Altman, Albert. "Sun Yat-sen and the Japanese, 1914–16." *Modern Asian Studies* 6, no. 4 (1972): 385–400.

Anderson, Benedict. *Imagined Communities.* London: Verso, 1983.

Barnhart, Michael. *Japan and the World Since 1868.* London: Arnold, 1995.

————. *Japan Prepares for Total War: The Search for Economic Security, 1919–1941.* Ithaca: Cornell University Press, 1987.

Beasley, W. G. *Japanese Imperialism, 1894–1945.* Oxford: Clarendon Press, 1987.

Becker, Jean-Jacques. *The Great War and the French People.* Translated by Arnold Pomerans. Oxford: Berg Publishers, 1990.

Benedict, Ruth. *The Chrysanthemum and the Sword: Patterns of Japanese Culture.* Boston: Houghton Mifflin, 1946.

Berger, Gordon, ed. and trans. *Kenkenroku: A Diplomatic Record of the Sino-Japanese War, 1894–1895.* Princeton: Princeton University Press, 1982.

Borton, Hugh. *Japan's Modern Century.* New York: Ronald Press, 1973.

Boydston, Jo Ann, ed. *Essays on China, Japan, and the War, 1918–1919: The Middle Works of John Dewey, 1899–1924*, vol. 11. Carbondale: Southern Illinois University Press, 1988.

Burdick, C., and U. Moessner. *The German Prisoners-of-War in Japan, 1914–20.* Landham, Md.: University Press of America, 1984.

Butow, Robert. *Tojo and the Coming of the War.* Stanford: Stanford University Press, 1961.

Calman, Donald. *The Nature and Origins of Japanese Imperialism: A Re-interpretation of the Great Crisis of 1873.* London: Routledge, 1992.

Chang, Han-yu, and Ramon Myers. "Japanese Colonial Development Policy in Taiwan, 1895–1906: A Case of Bureaucratic Entrepreneurship." *Journal of Asian Studies* 22, no. 3 (August 1963): 433–49.

Chang, Iris. *The Rape of Nanking: The Forgotten Holocaust of World War II.* New York: Basic Books, 1997.

Chi, Madeleine. *China Diplomacy, 1914–1918.* Cambridge, Mass.: Harvard University Press, 1970.

————. "Ts'ao Ju-lin (1876–1966): His Japanese Connections." In Akira Iriye, ed., *The Chinese and the Japanese*, pp. 140–60. Princeton: Princeton University Press, 1980.

Conroy, Hilary. *The Japanese Seizure of Korea, 1868–1910: A Study of Realism and Idealism in International Relations.* Philadelphia: University of Pennsylvania Press, 1960.

Coox, Alvin. *Nomonhan: Japan Against Russia, 1939.* 2 vols. Stanford: Stanford University Press, 1985.

Craig, Albert. *Chōshū in the Meiji Restoration.* Cambridge, Mass.: Harvard University Press, 1961.

Craig, Gordon. *Germany, 1866–1945.* New York: Oxford University Press, 1978.

Crowley, James B. "From Closed Door to Empire: The Formation of the Meiji Military Establishment." In Bernard S. Silberman and Harry Harootunian, eds., *Modern Japanese Leadership: Transition and Change,* pp. 261–87. Tucson: University of Arizona Press, 1966.

——. "Intellectuals as Visionaries of the New Asian Order." In James Morley, ed., *Dilemmas of Growth in Prewar Japan,* pp. 319–73. Princeton: Princeton University Press, 1971.

——. "A New Asian Order: Some Notes on Prewar Japanese Nationalism." In Bernard Silberman and H. Harootunian, eds., *Japan in Crisis,* pp. 270–98. Princeton: Princeton University Press, 1974.

——. "A New Deal for Japan and Asia: One Road to Pearl Harbor." In James B. Crowley, ed., *Modern East Asia: Essays in Interpretation,* pp. 235–64. New York: Harcourt, Brace & World, 1970.

Curry, Roy Watson. *Woodrow Wilson and Far Eastern Policy, 1913–1921.* New York: Octagon Books, 1968.

Daniels, Roger. *The Politics of Prejudice: The Anti-Japanese Movement in California and the Struggle for Japanese Exclusion.* New York: Atheneum, 1969.

Dickinson, Fred. "Japan's Asia in the Politics of a New World Order, 1914–19." In Harald Fuess, ed., *The Japanese Empire in East Asia and Its Postwar Legacy,* pp. 27–48. Munich: Iudicium-Verl, 1998.

Dingman, Roger. *Power in the Pacific: The Origins of Naval Arms Limitation, 1914–1922.* Chicago: University of Chicago Press, 1976.

Dos Passos, John. *1919.* New York : Harcourt, Brace, 1932.

Dower, John, ed. *Origins of the Modern Japanese State: Selected Writings of E. H. Norman.* New York: Pantheon Books, 1975.

Dull, Paul S. "Count Katō Kōmei and the Twenty-One Demands." *Pacific Historical Review* 19, no. 2 (May 1950): 151–61.

Duus, Peter. *The Abacus and the Sword: The Japanese Penetration of Korea, 1895–1910.* Berkeley: University of California Press, 1995.

——. *Party Rivalry and Political Change in Taishō Japan.* Cambridge, Mass.: Harvard University Press, 1968.

Duus, Peter; Ramon H. Myers; and Mark R. Peattie, eds. *The Japanese Informal Empire in China, 1895–1937.* Princeton: Princeton University Press, 1989.

————. *The Japanese Wartime Empire, 1931–1945.* Princeton: Princeton University Press, 1996.

Fairbank, John K., ed. *The Chinese World Order: Traditional China's Foreign Relations.* Cambridge, Mass.: Harvard University Press, 1968.

Fairbank, John K.; Edwin O. Reischauer; and Albert M. Craig. *East Asia: The Modern Transformation.* Boston: Houghton Mifflin, 1965.

Ferro, Marc. *The Great War, 1914–1918.* London: Routledge, 1973.

Feuerwerker, Albert. *The Foreign Establishment in China in the Early Twentieth Century.* Ann Arbor: Center for Chinese Studies, University of Michigan, 1976.

Fifield, Russell H. *Woodrow Wilson and the Far East.* Hamden: Archon Books, 1965.

Fogel, Joshua A. *Life Along the South Manchurian Railway: The Memoirs of Itō Takeo.* New York: M. E. Sharpe, 1988.

Fujitani, Takashi. *Splendid Monarchy: Power and Pageantry in Modern Japan.* Berkeley: University of California Press, 1996.

Fussell, Paul, ed. *The Norton Book of Modern War.* New York: Norton, 1991.

Gaddis, John Lewis. *We Now Know: Rethinking Cold War History.* Oxford: Oxford University Press, 1997.

Garon, Sheldon. *Molding Japanese Minds: The State in Everyday Life.* Princeton: Princeton University Press, 1997.

————. "Rethinking Modernization and Modernity in Japanese History: A Focus on State-Society Relations." *Journal of Asian Studies* 53, no. 2 (1994): 346–66.

————. *The State and Labor in Modern Japan.* Berkeley: University of California Press, 1987.

Gay, Peter. *Weimar Culture: The Outsider as Insider.* New York: Harper & Row, 1968.

Gilbert, Martin. *The First World War: A Complete History.* New York: Henry Holt, 1994.

Gluck, Carol. *Japan's Modern Myths: Ideology in the Late Meiji Period.* Princeton: Princeton University Press, 1985.

Goodman, Grant. *Japan: The Dutch Experience.* London: Athlone Press, 1986.

Grey, K. G., Viscount of Fallodon. *Twenty-Five Years, 1892–1916.* 2 vols. New York: Frederick A. Stokes, 1925.

Griswold, A. Whitney. *The Far Eastern Policy of the United States.* New York: Harcourt, Brace, 1938.

Hackett, Roger. *Yamagata Aritomo in the Rise of Modern Japan, 1838–1922.* Cambridge, Mass.: Harvard University Press, 1971.

Hagihara, Nobutoshi. "What Japan Means to the Twentieth Century." In Nobutoshi Hagihara, Akira Iriye, Georges Nivat, and Philip Windsor, eds., *Experiencing the Twentieth Century,* pp. 15–29. Tokyo: University of Tokyo Press, 1985.

Hall, John Whitney. *Japan: From Prehistory to Modern Times.* Tokyo: Charles E. Tuttle, 1971.

Hane, Mikiso. *Modern Japan*. Boulder: Westview Press, 1992.

Harries, Meiron, and Susie Harries. *Soldiers of the Sun: The Rise and Fall of the Imperial Japanese Army*. New York: Random House, 1991.

Harris, Sheldon H. *Factories of Death: Japanese Biological Warfare, 1932–45, and the American Cover-up*. London: Routledge, 1994.

Hearn, Lafcadio. *Kokoro: Hints and Echoes of Japanese Inner Life*. Boston: Houghton, Mifflin, 1896.

Hicks, Charles. *Japan's Entry into the War, 1914*. Nevada: University of Nevada Press, 1944.

Hicks, George. *The Comfort Women: Japan's Brutal Regime of Enforced Prostitution in the Second World War*. New York: W. W. Norton, 1994.

Hobsbawm, Eric. "Mass-Producing Traditions: Europe, 1870–1914." In Eric Hobsbawm and Terence Ranger, eds., *The Invention of Tradition*, pp. 263–307. Cambridge, Eng.: Cambridge University Press, 1983.

————. *Nations and Nationalism Since 1780: Programme, Myth, Reality*. Cambridge, Eng.: Cambridge University Press, 1990.

Hobsbawm, Eric, and Terence Ranger, eds. *The Invention of Tradition*. Cambridge, Eng.: Cambridge University Press, 1983.

Hofstader, Richard. *Social Darwinism in American Thought*. Boston: Beacon Press, 1992.

Hosokawa, Morihiro. "Are U.S. Troops in Japan Needed?" *Foreign Affairs* 77, no. 4 (July/August 1998): 2–5.

Howard, Michael. *War in European History*. Oxford: Oxford University Press, 1976.

Huber, Thomas M. *The Revolutionary Origins of Modern Japan*. Stanford: Stanford University Press, 1981.

Humphreys, Leonard A. *The Way of the Heavenly Sword: The Japanese Army in the 1920's*. Stanford: Stanford University Press, 1995.

Ikei, Masaru. "Ugaki Kazushige's View of China and His China Policy, 1915–1930." In Akira Iriye, ed., *The Chinese and the Japanese*, pp. 199–219. Princeton: Princeton University Press, 1980.

Iklé, Frank. "Japanese-German Peace Negotiations During World War I." *American History Review*, no. 71 (October 1965): 62–76.

Iriye, Akira. *Pacific Estrangement: Japanese and American Expansion, 1897–1911*. Cambridge, Mass.: Harvard University Press, 1972.

Iriye, Akira, ed. *Mutual Images: Essays in American-Japanese Relations*. Cambridge, Mass.: Harvard University Press, 1975.

Jansen, Marius B. *The Japanese and Sun Yat-sen*. Cambridge, Mass.: Harvard University Press, 1954.

———. "Japanese Imperialism: Late Meiji Perspectives." In Ramon H. Myers and Mark M. Peattie, eds., *The Japanese Colonial Empire, 1895–1945*, pp. 61–79. Princeton: Princeton University Press, 1984.

———. "Yawata, Hanyehping, and the Twenty-One Demands." *Pacific Historical Review* 23, no. 1 (February 1959): 31–48.

Kennedy, Malcolm. *The Military Side of Japanese Life*. London: Constable, 1924.

Kennedy, Paul M. *The Samoan Tangle: A Study in Anglo-German-American Relations, 1878–1900*. New York: Harper & Row, 1974.

Kim, Key-Hiuk. *The Last Phase of the East Asian World Order: Korea, Japan and the Chinese Empire, 1860-1882*. Berkeley: University of California Press, 1980.

Kitaoka, Shin'ichi. "China Experts in the Army." In Peter Duus, Ramon H. Myers, and Mark R. Peattie, eds., *The Japanese Informal Empire in China, 1895–1937*, pp. 330–68. Princeton: Princeton University Press, 1989.

LaFargue, Thomas E. *China and the World War*. Stanford: Stanford University Press, 1937.

LaFeber, Walter. *The Clash: U.S.-Japanese Relations Throughout History*. New York: W. W. Norton, 1997.

Langdon, Frank C. "Japan's Failure to Establish Friendly Relations with China in 1917–1918." *Pacific Historical Review* 26, no. 3 (August 1957): 245–79.

Leitch, Richard D., Jr.; Akira Kato; and Martin E. Weinstein. *Japan's Role in the Post–Cold War World*. Westport, Conn.: Greenwood Press, 1995.

Lewis, Michael. *Rioters and Citizens: Mass Protest in Imperial Japan*. Berkeley: University of California Press, 1990.

Littlewood, Ian. *The Idea of Japan: Western Images, Western Myths*. Chicago: Ivan R. Dee, 1996.

Lowe, Peter. *Great Britain and Japan, 1911–15*. London: Macmillan, 1969.

McDougall, Walter. *Let the Sea Make a Noise: A History of the North Pacific from Magellan to MacArthur*. New York: Basic Books, 1993.

Marwick, Arthur. *The Deluge: British Society and the First World War*. London: Macmillan, 1965.

Matsusaka, Y. Tak. "Managing Occupied Manchuria, 1931–1934." In Peter Duus, Ramon H. Myers, and Mark R. Peattie, eds., *The Japanese Wartime Empire, 1931–1945*, pp. 97–135. Princeton: Princeton University Press, 1996.

May, Ernest R. "American Policy and Japan's Entrance into World War I." *Mississippi Valley Historical Review* 40, no. 2 (1953): 279–90.

Mayer, Arno J. *Wilson Vs. Lenin: Political Origins of the New Diplomacy, 1917–1918*. Cleveland: World Publishing, 1964.

Minichiello, Sharon A., ed. *Japan's Competing Modernities: Issues in Culture and Democracy, 1900–1930*. Honolulu: University of Hawai'i Press, 1998.

Miwa, Kimitada. "Fukuzawa Yukichi's 'Departure from Asia': A Prelude to the Sino-Japanese War." In Edmund Skrzypczak, ed., *Japan's Modern Century*, pp. 1–26. Tokyo: Charles E. Tuttle, 1968.

———. "Japanese Opinions on Woodrow Wilson in War and Peace." *Monumenta Nipponica* 22, no. 3–4 (1967): 368–89.

Moon, Parker T. *Imperialism and World Politics*. New York: Macmillan, 1926.

Morley, James W. *The Japanese Thrust into Siberia*. New York: Columbia University Press, 1957.

Morton, William F. *Tanaka Giichi and Japan's China Policy*. New York: St. Martin's Press, 1980.

Myers, Ramon H. "Japanese Imperialism in Manchuria: The South Manchuria Railway Company, 1906–1933." In Peter Duus, Ramon H. Myers, and Mark R. Peattie, eds., *The Japanese Informal Empire in China, 1895–1937*, pp. 101–32. Princeton: Princeton University Press, 1989.

Myers, Ramon H., and Mark. R. Peattie, eds. *The Japanese Colonial Empire, 1895–1945*. Princeton: Princeton University Press, 1984.

Najita, Tetsuo. *Hara Kei in the Politics of Compromise, 1905–1915*. Cambridge, Mass.: Harvard University Press, 1967.

Neumann, William. *America Encounters Japan: From Perry to MacArthur*. Baltimore: The Johns Hopkins Press, 1963.

Nish, Ian. *Alliance in Decline*. London: Athlone Press, 1972.

Norman, E. Herbert. *Soldier and Peasant in Japan: The Origins of Conscription*. New York: Institute of Pacific Relations, 1943.

Ohkawa, Kazushi, and Miyohei Shinohara, eds. *Patterns of Japanese Economic Development: A Quantitative Appraisal*. New Haven: Yale University Press, 1979.

Oka, Yoshitake. "Generational Conflict After the Russo-Japanese War." In Tetsuo Najita and J. Victor Koschmann, eds., *Conflict in Modern Japanese History: The Neglected Tradition*, pp. 197–225. Princeton: Princeton University Press, 1982.

Okamoto, Shumpei. "Ishibashi Tanzan and the Twenty-One Demands." In Akira Iriye, ed., *The Chinese and the Japanese*, pp. 184–98. Princeton: Princeton University Press, 1980.

———. *The Japanese Oligarchy and the Russo-Japanese War*. New York: Columbia University Press, 1970.

Peattie, Mark. *Nan'yō: The Rise and Fall of the Japanese in Micronesia, 1885–1945*. Honolulu: University of Hawai'i Press, 1988.

Pollard, Robert T. "Intangible in Japanese Foreign Policy" *Amerasia* 1, no. 9 (November 1937): 405–9.

Pooley, A. M. *The Secret Memoirs of Count Tadasu Hayashi*. London: Eveleigh Nash, 1915.

Price, Ernest B. *The Russo-Japanese Treaties of 1907–1916 Concerning Manchuria and Mongolia.* Baltimore: The Johns Hopkins University, 1933.

Sansom, G. B. *The Western World and Japan: A Study in the Interaction of European and Asiatic Cultures.* London: Barrie & Jenkins, 1950.

Scalapino, Robert A. *Democracy and the Party Movement in Prewar Japan.* Berkeley: University of California Press, 1953.

Seidensticker, Edward. *Low City, High City.* New York: Knopf, 1983.

Seki Hiroharu. "The Manchurian Incident, 1931." In James William Morley, ed., *Japan Erupts: The London Naval Conference and the Manchurian Incident, 1928–1932,* pp. 139–230. New York: Columbia University Press, 1984.

Shao, Hsi-Ping. "From the Twenty-One Demands to the Sino-Japanese Military Agreement, 1915–1918: Ambivalent Relations." In Alvin Coox and Hilary Conroy, eds., *China and Japan,* pp. 37–57. Santa Barbara, Calif.: Clio Press, 1978.

Shimazu, Naoko. *Japan, Race and Equality: The Racial Equality Proposal of 1919.* London: Routledge, 1998.

Silver, Kenneth. *Esprit de Corps: The Art of the Parisian Avant-Gard and the First World War, 1914–1925.* Princeton: Princeton University Press, 1989.

Stoddard, John L. *John L. Stoddard's Lectures,* 10 vols. Chicago: Geo. L. Shuman, 1897.

Takeuchi, Tatsuji. *War and Diplomacy in the Japanese Empire.* New York: Doubleday, Doran, 1935.

Tanaka, Stephan. *Japan's Orient: Rendering Pasts into History.* Berkeley: University of California Press, 1993.

Tanaka, Yuki. *Hidden Horrors: Japanese War Crimes in World War II.* Boulder, Colo.: Westview Press, 1996.

Toby, Ronald. *State and Diplomacy in Early Modern Japan: Asia in the Development of the Tokugawa Bakufu.* Princeton: Princeton University Press, 1984.

Tsunoda, Ryusaku; Wm. Theodore de Bary; and Donald Keene, comps. *Sources of Japanese Tradition.* 2 vols. New York: Columbia University Press, 1958.

U. S. Department of State, *Papers Relating to the Foreign Relations of the United States, 1916.* Washington, D.C.: Government Printing Office, 1929.

Vlastos, Stephen, ed. *Mirror of Modernity: Invented Traditions of Modern Japan.* Berkeley: University of California Press, 1998.

Wakabayashi, Bob Tadashi. "Opium, Expulsion, Sovereignty: China's Lessons for Bakumatsu Japan." *Monumenta Nipponica* 47, no. 1 (Spring 1992): 1–25.

Watts, Jonathan. "Jilted Japan Looks Sourly at Clinton's Beijing Love-in." *The Guardian,* July 3, 1998: 16.

Yanaga, Chitoshi. *Japan Since Perry.* Hamden: Archon Books, 1966.

Yim, Kwanha. "Yuan Shih-k'ai and the Japanese." *Journal of Asian Studies* 24, no. 1 (November 1964): 63–73.

Young, A. Morgan. *Japan Under Taisho Tenno, 1912–1926.* London: George Allen & Unwin, 1928.

Young, Louise. *Japan's Total Empire: Manchuria and the Culture of Wartime Imperialism.* Berkeley: University of California Press, 1997.

Yuan, Tsing. "The Japanese Intervention in Shantung During World War I." In Alvin Coox and Hilary Conroy, eds., *China and Japan*, pp. 21–33. Santa Barbara, Calif.: Clio Press, 1978.

Unpublished Sources in English

Berton, Peter. "The Secret Russo-Japanese Alliance of 1916." Ph.D. dissertation, Columbia University, 1957.

Burkman, Thomas W. "Japan, the League of Nations, and the New World Order, 1918–1920." Ph.D. dissertation, University of Michigan, 1975.

Hayase, Yukiko. "The Career of Gotō Shimpei: Japan's Statesman of Research, 1857–1929." Ph.D. dissertation, Florida State University, 1974.

Index

active-duty rule, 67, 74, 271n77
Adachi Mineichirō, 139
Advisory Council on Foreign Affairs
    (Gaikō chōsakai), 168, 198, 199, 208–
    11, 224–25
Akashi Motojirō, 41, 55, 92, 101, 105, 106,
    279n100, 292n98
Allied occupation of Japan, xvi–xvii
Amoy, 57
Amur River Society (Kokuryūkai), 89,
    91
Anderson, Benedict, 241
Andreev (Russian agent), 187
Anglo-Japanese alliance, 8, 147,
    304n140; and outbreak of war in
    Europe, 33–34, 75; centerpiece of
    Japanese diplomacy, 37–38, 121–22;
    declining Japanese enthusiasm for,
    37–38, 42–48, 49–50, 79–80, 81, 120,
    139, 141–45, 148, 152, 251, 303n118
Aoki Nobuzumi, 129, 131, 132, 136, 167,
    170, 308n45, 318n34
Arc de Triomphe, 257–58
Arichi Shinanojū, 272n79
Ariga Nagao, 288n27
Arimatsu Hideyoshi, 321n91
arms reductions, 209–10, 253, 254
army, see Imperial Army
Asakusa opera, 195

Asian development bank, 58, 66, 161
Asian Monroe Doctrine, 55–56, 183,
    189

Banno Junji, 266–67n25, 275n35,
    279n97, 279n101, 312n97, 317n25
Banzai Rihachirō, 124, 129, 131, 135,
    137, 288n27, 293n107, 318n34
Barnhart, Michael, 265n4, 266nn17–
    18, 273n7, 313n128
Basic Plan of National Defense
    (1907), 67, 71, 73–74, 209; as ex-
    pression of Yamagata Aritomo's
    conception of the state, 27–28, 51;
    revision, 140, 143–44, 192, 194, 199,
    283n159
Beasley, W. G., 264–65n4, 273n5
Beiyang clique, 170, 171, 172
Benedict, Ruth, 239, 248
Berton, Peter, 304n134
Bethlehem Steel Corporation, 89
Bismarck, Otto von, 22
Boxer Uprising (1900), 43
Brissaud des Maillets, Lieutenant
    Colonel, 288n27
Britain, 8, 10, 35, 91, 156–57, 147, 193,
    216, 234, 258, 272n4; joint military
    operations with Japan, 2, 45, 46;
    and war in Europe, 2, 3, 47, 54, 84,

117, 122, 154–55, 200, 204; declining
Japanese enthusiasm for, 22, 42–43,
45–46, 49–50, 52, 57, 141, 144; British parliamentarism, 23, 31, 61, 62; as
obstacle to Japanese expansion, 30,
33–34, 37–38, 44, 45, 47, 80, 110, 131–
32, 141–42, 189–90, 234, 251, 303n119,
312n96; Katō Takaaki in Britain, 36–
37, 38–39, 60; centerpiece of Japanese
diplomacy, 37–38, 121–22; interests in
Yangzi valley, 38, 39, 86, 90, 141; as
model for Katō Takaaki, 61, 62, 86,
92, 228; and imperialist diplomacy,
77, 87, 177, 208, 224; recognizes
Japanese wartime gains, 177, 208. See
also Anglo-Japanese alliance; Grey,
Edward

Bryan, William Jennings, 90, 221,
288n28

Burkman, Thomas W., 315n155, 320n81

Calman, Donald, 266n24

Cao Rulin, 164, 166, 167, 173, 174

Cen Chunxuan, 137, 171

Chang, Iris, 322n2

Chen Duxiu, 231

Chen Shufan, 172

Cherry Blossom Society (Sakurakai),
255

Chiang Kaishek, 124

China: Japanese aims for annexation, 2,
163, 164, 293n107; Japanese opinion
of, 4, 84–85, 95, 127, 132, 133, 299n61;
great power imperialism in, 8, 15, 38,
85–87, 250; Qing dynasty, 10–12, 18,
30; Japanese plans to wage war
against, 16, 105, 109, 110, 293–94n122;
threat of U.S. influence in, 30, 47–
48, 50, 54, 80, 81, 88, 89, 142–45, 152,
155, 177, 221–23, 224–25, 231, 234–35,

237, 248–49; advent of a republic,
30, 210; Anglo-Japanese conflict
in, 37–38, 44, 45, 47, 80, 131–32,
234, 251; Japanese calls for comprehensive settlement with, 39–
40, 44, 50, 52–53, 55–56, 66, 71–
72; Japanese aims for "intimate"
Sino-Japanese ties (Asian Monroe
Doctrine), 43–44, 47, 50, 55–56,
81, 92, 161, 183, 234–35, 247, 249,
250; Japanese aims for a protectorate, 44, 89; Japanese plans for
invasion of, 53, 92, 106, 135–36, 163;
Japanese aims to depose Yuan
Shikai, 53, 120, 132–35, 152, 170;
Japanese aims for economic hegemony in, 58, 162, 163–64, 173–
74, 201; likened to Turkey, 70,
146, 234; defies Japan, 90, 100, 102,
124–32 passim, 136–37, 143, 224;
Japanese desire to control events
in, 123–34 passim, 170–73; Japan
promotes civil war in, 129–37, 248,
300n68; under Japanese security
umbrella, 140, 144, 194–95, 234–
35; severs relations with Germany,
169, 221; Japanese proposals to
withdraw troops from, 225, 253;
May Fourth Movement, 231, 237.
See also Chinese nationalism; Chinese Revolution; Nishihara loans;
Sino-Japanese Military Agreement; Sino-Japanese War;
Twenty-One Demands; Yuan
Shikai

Chinese nationalism, 86, 123, 231, 237;
connection to Japanese aggression
in 1930s, 248, 253–54

Chinese Revolution (1911), 30, 35, 39,
49, 53, 57, 123, 141, 179

Chūseikai (Association for Impartiality), 157
Civilization and Enlightenment Movement (nineteenth century), 22, 207
Clemenceau, Georges, 156
Cold War, xvi, xvii, 179, 180, 181, 227, 259, 260, 270n63
Colonial Bureau, 271n77
colonies, 8; civilian rule in, 30, 212, 231, 245–46, 271n77, 318–19n46; supression of uprisings in, 231, 233
Committee for the Development of the National Destiny, 182, 183
consortium, international banking, 58, 233, 287n11, 322n119
"constitutional government," see movement to protect constitutional government
constitutional monarchy, 15, 21, 23, 25, 30; in China, 123
Counter Russia Association (Tai-Ro dōshikai), 162

Dairen (Dalian), 39, 91, 274–75n26, 286nn9–10
Daniels, Roger, 265n9
Dawn Society (Reimeikai), 229
Daye (Tayeh) mines, 89
democratic reform, 3–4, 29; effect of war on in Japan, 178–79, 195–97, 204, 210, 226–37, 321n89; importance relative to "Bolshevism," 227; as greatest threat to military-bureaucratic power, 256
Den Kenjirō, 166, 174, 197, 227, 234, 272n79, 321n91
Dewey, John, 254, 255
Diet, see Imperial Diet
Dingman, Roger, 320n84
Doi Ichinoshin, 308n45

Dōshikai (Constitutional Association of Friends), 36, 57, 66, 102, 114, 115, 157, 291n72
Dos Passos, John Roderigo, 1
Dower, John, 240, 322n7
dreadnought, 28, 74
Duan Qirui, 158, 164, 167, 169–73, 186, 214, 288n32, 291n74, 309n60
Duan Zhigui, 172, 301n92
Dutch East Indies, 174, 310n76
Duus, Peter, 252, 265n4

Eastern Inner Mongolia, see Mongolia
Egi Kazuyuki, 272n79
emperor, 19–20, 70; modern creation of imperial symbol, 4, 243; as ruler of Asia, 56, 72, 92; "unparalleled" in the world, 178, 179

Fashoda Crisis, 10
Fairbank, John King, 10, 268n42, 268n44
Feng Guozhang, 170, 171, 172, 214
Fifield, Russell, 316n7
financial diplomacy, 160–61. See also Nishihara loans
Fitzpatrick, Ernest Hugh, 264n5
Foch, Ferdinand, 194, 311n92
Fogel, Joshua, 280n107
Four power alliance (Britain, France, Russia, Japan), 77–78, 79
foreign policy, domestic sources of, 4–5, 241–43, 251–56; Tokugawa, 10–13; Meiji, 14–17, 19; study of, 240–41
Foreign Ministry (Kasumigaseki), 105; Katō Takaaki's promotion of, 60–63, 82, 93–107, 111, 115, 120–21,

246, 294n135; distress over declining
authority, 125, 135, 137–38, 214–15,
318n36; and policy to depose Yuan
Shikai, 134–35, 167, 301n85. *See also*
Katō Takaaki
France, 17, 23, 35, 49, 143–44, 147, 156–
57; imperialist diplomacy, 8, 10;
Franco-Prussian War, 17, 22, 23, 33;
French liberalism, 23, 228; and An-
glo-Japanese alliance, 43, 49; and war
in Europe, 54, 84, 117, 122, 154–55,
200, 204; interests in China, 86, 87;
recognizes Japanese wartime gains,
177, 208; and Siberian Intervention,
189–90, 216; proposal for Franco-
Japanese alliance, 281–82n137
France, Anatole, 34
Franco-Japanese Bank, 49
Franco-Prussian War, 17, 22, 23, 33
Frank, Bruno, 34
Franz Ferdinand, Archduke, 33
Freedom and Peoples' Rights Move-
ment (nineteenth century), 14, 19
Fujian province, 57, 76, 87, 89, 90, 160
Fukuda Masatarō, 132, 137, 214,
302n100
Fukuda Tokuzō, 213, 218
Fukui Saburō, 218, 318n32
Fukushima Yasumasa, 289n43
Fukuzawa Yukichi, 16, 269n58
Fundamentals of National Policy
(1936), 250

Gaddis, John Lewis, 270n63
Gaikō chōsakai, *see* Advisory Council
on Foreign Affairs
Garon, Sheldon, 323n14
general mobilization, 190–91
General Staff College, 23
General Staff system, 17, 21, 23

genrō (elder statesmen), 20; declining
political power, 64, 113; excluded
by Katō Takaaki from decision
making, 61–63, 65, 82, 95, 108, 112,
113, 115, 156. *See also* Inoue Kaoru;
Matsukata Masayoshi; Ōyama
Iwao; Yamagata Aritomo
genrō-cabinet conferences: Aug. 8,
1914, 41–45 *passim*, 49, 63, 75; Aug.
14, 1914, 44; May 4, 1915, 108–10
genrō-Ōkuma conferences: Sept. 24,
1914, 78–80; June 25, 1915, 111–12
Gentlemen's Agreement (1911), 175
Georgii Mikhailovich, Grand Duke,
138
German Micronesia (Marshall,
Mariana, Caroline Islands), 2, 73,
76–77, 82–83, 176, 206, 208, 224–
25, 233, 235
Germany, 10, 43, 86, 143–44, 169, 202;
Japanese operations against, 2, 75–
77, 84, 145; threat of separate
peace with Japan, 2, 121, 145, 152,
296n9; symbol of modern progress, 3, 17, 21–23; principal model
for Meiji Japan, 3, 17, 21–25, 118,
210, 242, 274n24; symbol of bankrupt militarism and authoritarianism, 3, 157, 177–79, 269n51; and
war in Europe, 3, 38, 54, 84, 117,
154–55, 204, 251; Franco-Prussian
War, 17, 22, 23, 33; Nazi Germany,
22, 239, 251; Japanese declaration
of war on, 38, 45, 63, 76, 80, 93, 95;
pro-German sympathy in Japan,
38, 45–46, 85, 117–19, 145, 211, 245,
246, 274n24, 277n57, 296–97n10;
Japanese plans for alliance with,
38, 45, 57, 251, 273–74n22; Russian
attempt to counter influence of in

Japan, 144–48, 152, 304n133. *See also* German Micronesia; Jiaozhou; Qingdao; Shandong

Gilbert, Martin, 264n4

Gillis, I. V., 296n10

Gluck, Carol, 269n47

Gneist, Rudolf, 23, 269n50

Good Fortune Club (Saiwai kurabu), 272n79

Goodnow, Frank J., 288n27

Gotō Shinpei, 56–58, 67, 72, 280n107, 313n126, 321n91; and aggressive foreign policy posture, 57, 190, 197, 273–74n22, 293–94n122; and financial diplomacy, 58, 161–62, 196, 201, 248; conflict with Katō Takaaki, 66, 82, 282n143, 290n59; architect of Terauchi China policy, 159–62, 165; and racial conception of Sino-Japanese relations, 161–62, 196; and threat of U.S., 197, 222, 248

Greater East Asia Co-prosperity Sphere, 249, 250

Greater Japan General Federation of Labor and the Friendly Society (Dai Nihon Rōdō Sōdōmei-Yūaikai), 230

Great War, see World War I

Greene, Sir Coyningham, 61, 274n23

Grey, Sir Edward, 39, 88, 121, 122, 141, 145, 149, 288n34

Griswold, A. Whitney, 240, 310n77, 316n8

Gropius, Walter, 1

Guandong (Kwantung), 52, 88, 88, 139

Guandong Army, 106, 199, 255, 318–19n46

Guomindang, 167, 169

Guthrie, George, 287n20

Hagihara Nobutoshi, 273n7

Hall, John Whitney, 266n21

Hamaguchi Osachi, 228, 301n91

Han-Ye-Ping Company, 89, 286n9

Hara Takashi, 168, 318n45; reviles Yamagata Aritomo, 41–42, 112, 276n37; symbol of liberal reform, 59, 62, 212–17, 214, 236, 244, 245–46, 318–19n46; compared with Katō Takaaki, 60–61, 245–46; accommodation with Yamagata Aritomo, 97, 99, 212, 218–20, 223, 236, 318n32; conflict with Ōkuma cabinet, 98–99, 101–3; aggressive proponent of Japanese rights in China, 102, 223, 224, 225, 233, 237; conservative response to democratic reform, 114, 204, 217–28 passim, 232, 236, 237; counsels caution in China, 133, 222, 223; and Siberian Intervention, 198, 202, 222; concern over American power, 219, 221, 223; resistance to new world order, 225–26, 230–33, 236–37. *See also* Seiyūkai

Hara Teruyuki, 311n90

Harbin, 139, 140, 185

Harries, Meiron, 267n29

Harriman, Edward H., 286–87n11, 307n25

Harris, Townsend, 8

Hasegawa Yoshimichi, 106, 298n31

Hatano Masaru, 289n43

Hay, John, 221

Hayashi Fusao, 265n4, 266n18

Hayashi Gonsuke, 177

Hayashi Tadasu, 270n64

Hearn, Lafcadio, 257, 269n56

Hearst, William Randolph, 264n5

Hegel, Georg Friedrich, 22

Hibiya Park, 84, 204, 229, 230, 237

Hicks, Charles, 272n4

Hindenburg, Paul von Beneckendorff und, 154

Hioki Eki, 91, 94, 100, 106, 108, 111, 128, 289n37, 290n47

Hiranuma Kiichirō, 113, 296n150

Hirata Tōsuke, 159, 226, 272n79, 321n91

Hirayama Narinobu, 321n91

Hiroshima, 239, 240, 264n4

Hirota Kōki, 250

Hobsbawm, Eric, 241

Hongō Fusatarō, 214

Horvath, Dmitry Leonidovich, 186, 187

Hosokawa Morohiro, 324n2

Hosoya Chihiro, 311n86, 319n65

House, Edward M., 316n3

Huber, Thomas, 266n19

Ichiki Kitokurō, 127, 272n79, 321n91

Imai Seiichi, 282n146

Imai Yoshiyuki, 229

Immigration Act of 1924 (U.S.), 9, 175, 248

Imperial Army, 30, 31, 32; origins, 14, 17, 27, 40–41; autonomy from civilian rule, 21, 24, 67, 282n145; as first line of national defense, 23, 28, 29, 193; sympathy for Imperial Germany, 23, 197, 274n24; competition with navy, 24, 27, 29, 67, 70, 76–77, 83, 191–93, 210, 290n56; and Chinese Revolution, 53, 182, 271n75, 300n79; plans for operations against U.S., 53–54, 143, 318n32; post–Russo-Japanese War strength, 62, 67, 73; restrained by Katō Takaaki, 63, 95–96, 105–7; declining political authority, 67, 69–72, 105, 202, 254–55; and opportunity of European war, 68, 82–83;

spiritual emphasis of, 68–69; battles parliamentary politics, 69, 70, 72–73, 99, 191–92, 253; political importance of continental expansion for, 69–70, 193–94, 202, 282n146; and Russian "threat," 71–72, 192, 202; proposed operations on the continent, 72, 76, 106, 182, 186; operations during World War I, 76, 82–83, 199; and plans for civil war in China, 129–37, 167, 300n68; opposition to new world order, 233, 237. See also Tanaka Giichi; Terauchi Masatake; Yamagata Aritomo

Imperial Diet, 21–26 passim; resists military expansion, 27, 28, 67, 74, 209; unanimous approval of war budget, 26, 77

—Seventh (Oct. 18–22, 1894), 26

—Twenty-Fourth (Dec. 28, 1907– Mar. 26, 1908), 74

—Thirty-First (Dec. 26, 1913–Mar. 23, 1914), 64

—Thirty-Third (June 22–28, 1914), 64

—Thirty-Fourth (Sept. 4–9, 1914), 77, 282n139

—Thirty-Fifth (Dec. 7–25, 1914), 96, 282n139

—Thirty-Sixth (May 20–June 9, 1915), 100

—Forty-First (Dec. 27, 1918–Mar. 26, 1919), 228, 237

imperialism: alleged "reactive" nature of Japanese imperialism, 7–8, 247–48; late nineteenth-century imperialism, 8, 15–17, 29, 85–87; proactive Japanese imperialism, 16–17, 248–52, 255–57, 269n51;

Katō Takaaki's free trade imperialism, 38–40, 80–81, 245, 246
Imperial Military Reservists Association, 68–69, 282n149
Imperial Navy, 9, 73–77, 127, 194, 299n62,311n96; operations during World War I, 2, 76, 82–83; competition with army, 27, 29, 70, 74–77, 83, 191–93, 210, 290n56, 292n102; granted budget priority, 28, 30, 67, 191, 192; genrō attempt to supress, 31, 78, 79
Imperial Rule Assistance Association (1940), 249
Ijūin Hikokichi, 111
Indochina, 47
Inoue Kaoru, 42, 48–51, 63–65, 66, 307n23; views war as "divine aid," 35, 48–49, 64, 239, 243; disenchantment with Anglo-Japanese alliance, 49–50; on a race war, 50, 248; on threat of U.S., 50; plans for Japanese hegemony in China, 50, 92; conflict with Katō Takaaki, 63, 77, 82, 100, 111–12, 295n142; distaste for parliamentary politics, 64–65, 249; and Twenty-One Demands, 101, 110
Inoue Katsunosuke, 111, 141
Inoue Tomoichi, 321n91
International Labor Conference, 233, 237
International Labor Organization, 230
International Military Tribunal for the Far East, 7, 51
Inukai Tsuyoshi, 168, 176, 211, 225
Ioki Ryōzō, 35, 196
Iriye Kan'ichi, 321n91
Ishibashi Tanzan, 29, 243
Ishii Kikujirō, 120, 122, 165; and Yuan Shikai's proposed enthronement, 128–34 passim, 298n46; political

weakness, 128–29, 135, 137–38, 152; and 1916 Russo-Japanese Convention, 139, 144, 146–51, 244, 297n14
Ishiwara Kanji, 7, 256
Italy, 47, 177, 208
Itō Hirobumi, 15, 16, 23–27 passim, 41, 42, 49, 62, 162, 269n50, 280n122
Itō Masanori, 287n23
Itō Miyoji, 208, 225, 320n74
Itō Yukio, 263n3, 317n29
Itogawa Tatsuzō, 136, 137
Iwasaki Yatarō, 296n7

Japan: operations against Germany, 2, 45, 75–77, 84; threat of separate peace with Germany, 2, 121, 145, 152, 296n9; prospect of war with U.S., 2, 53, 54, 142–43, 296–97n10; as progressive international force, 3, 17, 25, 205, 257, 268n40, 269n56; favorable diplomatic circumstances, 3, 8–9, 25–26, 36, 84, 205, 267n32; economic effects of war in, 3, 33, 161, 195–96, 212, 219, 236, 249, 307n27; affinity for Germany, 3, 17, 21–25, 38, 45–46, 85, 117–19, 121, 145, 211, 242, 245, 246, 274n24, 277n57, 296–97n10; associated with bankrupt militarism and authoritarianism, 3–4, 178–79, 196, 210, 239; opinion of China, 4, 84–85, 95, 127, 132, 133, 299n61; as land besieged by the powers, 7–8, 9–10, 234, 239; compared to Qing China, 10–12, 18; pattern of political instability, 18–19, 24–30, 32, 59, 240–42; declining enthusiasm for Britain, 22, 42–43, 45–46, 49–50, 52, 57, 141, 144; conflict with

Britain in China, 37–38, 44, 45, 47, 80, 131–32, 234, 251
Japan-China Association, 173
Jiandao, 125, 288n31
Jiaozhou (Kiaochow), 39; plans for eventual restoration of, 40, 63, 275n29; criticism of proposed restoration, 77, 96, 176, 282n139. *See also* Qingdao; Shandong
Jilin Regular Army, 185
Jin Yunpeng, 182–83
Joint Committee on Military Affairs, 187, 194, 215
Jordan, Sir John N., 132

Kaishintō (Reform Party), 31, 57
Kamei Rokurō, 167
Kamiyama Mitsunoshin, 321n91
Kanghwa Island, 8, 265n5
Kasumigaseki, *see* Foreign Ministry
Katō Takaaki, 34, 36–40, 45, 50, 64, 94, 113, 168, 229, 243, 296n7, 298n35, 309n52; Japan's foremost Anglophile, 36–37, 61, 81, 92, 151, 228, 245, 246, 247; champion of Anglo-Japanese alliance, 37–38, 40, 81, 112, 121–22, 151; consummate practitioner of imperialist diplomacy, 38–39, 82, 86, 92, 246, 250; expansionist goals as comparatively modest, 40, 42, 43, 48, 53, 58, 63, 80–81, 92, 107, 114–15, 120–22, 126, 139, 148, 161, 165, 174, 184, 201, 208, 246, 250, 289n37; conflict with Yamagata Aritomo, 45, 63, 65–66, 77–79, 82, 85, 107–13, 284n194, 293n119; champion of parliamentary politics, 59–63, 82, 83, 93–107, 151, 157, 245–46, 254; promotes Foreign Ministry, 60, 62, 63, 82, 93–107, 111, 115, 120–21, 246, 294n135; compared

with Hara Takashi, 60–61, 245–46, 318n45; excludes *genrō* from decision making, 61, 63, 65, 82, 95, 108, 112, 115, 156; attempts to restrain army, 63, 76, 94, 95–96, 98, 105–7, 115; conflict with Inoue Kaoru, 63, 77–79, 82, 100; conflict with Gotō Shinpei, 66, 82, 159; conflict with Tanaka Giichi, 72, 97–99, 290n47; conflict with Seiyūkai, 101–3; accommodation with Oka Ichinosuke, 103–5, 244; rejects stronger ties with Russia, 113, 120–22, 151; rejects sympathy for Germany, 228, 274n23, 281n130. *See also* Twenty-One Demands
Katō Tomosaburō, 75, 133, 208, 317n24
Katsura Tarō, 27, 29, 39, 45, 57, 64, 66, 270n62, 274n22
Kawada Minoru, 263n3, 317n29
Kawashima Naniwa, 167, 308n45
Kennedy, Malcolm, 287n23
Kensei Hontō (Real Constitutional Government Party), 27, 31, 162
Kenseikai (Association for Constitutional Government), 228, 237, 253, 254–55
Kerensky, Aleksandr Fyodorovich, 182
Kido Takayoshi, 7, 280n122
Kingly Way (ōdōshugi), 163, 201
Kitaoka Shin'ichi, 275n35, 279n97, 279n101, 285n5, 294n127, 297–98n30, 298n35, 299n61, 302n106, 312n97, 312n115
Kiyosawa Kiyoshi, 289n36
Kiyoura Keigo, 75, 321n91
Knox, Philander C., 265n8, 287n11
Kobayashi Michihiko, 273–74n22

Kodama Gentarō, 57
Kodama Hideo, 166
Koike Chōzō, 91, 94, 108, 134–35, 137, 165, 298n35
Koiso Kuniaki, 136, 301n91, 308n45
Kokuhonsha (National Foundation Society), 296n150
Kokumintō (Constitutional Peoples' Party), 99, 297n30
Kokuryūkai (Amur River Society), 89, 91
Komatsubara Eitarō, 272n79, 321n91
Kōmuchi Tomotsune, 162
Komura Jutarō, 62, 307n25
Komura Kin'ichi, 320n75
Konoe Fumimaro, 47, 249
Korea, 11, 13, 15, 55, 163, 271n77; incorporated into Japanese empire, 8, 13, 17, 23, 25, 44; Sino-Japanese competition over, 26, 125, 288n31; Japanese plans to expand influence in, 27–28, 70–71, 164, 233. See also March First Movement
Kōyū Club (Friends' Club), 157
Kozakov, Grigorii, 139, 145–50
Kubota Yuzuru, 321n91
Kuhara Fusanosuke, 301n80

labor strife, 195–96, 230, 232–33, 254–55
LaFeber, Walter, 240, 265n11, 276n47, 310n78, 316n8
Lansing-Ishii agreement, 222–23, 319n66
Lea, Homer, 264n5
League of Nations, 9, 175, 206, 211, 225, 234, 236, 252
Lenin (Ulyanov), Vladimir Ilych, 180
Li Yuanhong, 137, 169–73
Liang Qichao, 129
Liaodong peninsula, 9, 206
Liberal Democratic Party, 260

List, Friedrich, 22
Liu Fuman, 185
Lloyd George, David, 34, 154, 156, 209
London Declaration (1914), 122, 151
London Naval Treaty (1930), 253, 255
Lowe, Peter, 272n4, 285n2, 287n23
Lower House, 21, 30. See also Imperial Diet
Lu Zhengxiang, 100
Lu Zongyu, 128, 130
Ludendorff, Erich, 154
Luzon Island, 143

Machida Keiu, 200
Maida Minoru, 317n27
Makino Nobuaki, 29, 211, 224–25, 226
Malevski-Malevich, Nicholas, 145, 150
Manchukuo, 163, 250, 256
Manchu restoration, 30, 170–73
Manchuria, Japanese aims for expansion in, 2, 27–28, 52–53, 55, 69–70, 71–72, 80, 94–95, 105, 139–40, 160, 164, 184, 185, 190; Japanese interests in, 8, 26, 38, 87, 88, 206; Anglo-American interest in, 9, 43, 47, 87, 88, 142, 251; and Russo-Japanese conventions, 37, 43, 52, 182; Imperial Army presence in, 67, 106, 271n77; and Twenty-One Demands, 87, 88, 90–91, 286n9; Japanese plans for annexation, 92, 164; erosion of Japanese rights in, 124–25; plot for Manchurian independence, 136, 301n92; plans for joint U.S.-Japanese exploitation of, 160, 307n25. See also Manchukuo; Manchurian Incident; North Manchuria
Manchurian Incident, 70, 92, 239, 252, 255–56, 258

Mann, Thomas, 154
Marchand, Captain, 10
March First Movement (1919), 230–31, 237
March Incident (1931), 301n91
Marxist scholarship, xvi, 8, 252, 273n6
Masuda Takashi, 113
Matsui Keishirō, 108, 121, 122, 293n119
Matsukata Masayoshi, 42, 66, 77, 78, 108, 111, 112, 149, 289n45, 295n145
Matsuoka Yōsuke, 47, 251, 313n123
Matsusaka, Y. Tak, 323n21
Matsushima Hajime, 313n123
Matsuyama Chūjirō, 317n27
Mauclair, Camille, 1
May Fourth Movement (1919), 231, 237
McDougall, Walter, 316n8
Meckel, Jacob, 23
Meiji constitution, 15, 20, 27
Meiji emperor, 28–29, 31, 35, 42, 78, 242, 243
Meiji Japan (1868–1912), fortuitous diplomacy, 8–9, 16–17; turbulent politics, 17–19, 24–25, 26–28, 59, 243; "national Cinderella-story," 268n42
Meiji Renovation, xvi, 12, 18, 20, 25, 31, 78, 252, 255–56
Mexico, 163
Military Affairs Council, 76, 97, 290n56
military expansion, 25–28, 32, 67, 71–77 passim, 97, 192–93, 270n70; two-division expansion, 98, 99, 103, 104
Mill, John Stuart, 22
minponshugi, 119, 227
Minseitō (Constitutional Democratic Party), 253, 254–55, 256
Mitani Taichirō, 256, 317n23, 317n25, 317n29
Mitsui Company, 89

Miura Gorō, 166, 168, 219, 277n57
Miyake Setsurei, 317n27
Mizuno Hironori, 53
Mizuno Rentarō, 99, 103
Mochizuki Kotarō, 50, 78, 101, 296n152
Mongolia, 37, 43, 52–53, 69–70, 80, 88, 139, 160, 286n9
Mori Ōgai, 154, 227
Morioka Morishige, 135, 136
Morrison, George, 288n27
Morley, James W., 311n86
Morton, William, 278n83
Motono Ichirō, 111, 120, 139, 145–47, 183, 190
movement to protect constitutional government, 29–30, 31–32, 59, 64, 81, 102, 116, 119, 155, 272n81. See also Taishō political crisis
Mukden (Shenyang), 125, 136, 257
Mutsu Munemitsu, 268n40
Myers, Ramon, 280n107

Nagai Kafū, 204
Nagaoka Shinjirō, 275n27
Najita, Tetsuo, 317n23
Nakajima Masatake, 187
Nakamura Ken'ichi, 268n43
Nakamura Satoru, 165, 289n43
Nakano Jirō, 183, 187
Nakano Seigō, 317n27
Nakashōji Ren, 159
Nana, 33
Nanjing massacre, 240
Nara Takeji, 185, 187
National Foundation Society (Kokuhonsha), 296n150
national renovation, 5, 17, 118, 218, 245, 252, 255–56; calls for, 12, 31, 78, 207, 219, 232, 254. See also Meiji

Renovation; Shōwa Renovation;
  Taishō Renovation
navy, *see* Imperial Navy
Nawa Matahachirō, 292*n*102
Negishi Tadashi, 125, 297*n*27
Neo-Confucianism, 11, 163
Neutrality Pact (1941), 47
New Order in Asia, 249
Ni Shichong, 172
Nicholas II, Tsar, 146. *See also* Nicholas
  Alexandrovich
Nicholas Alexandrovich, Tsarevich, 138.
  See also Nicholas II
Nish, Ian, 272*n*4
Nishihara Kamezō: plan for Japanese
  hegemony in China, 161, 162–64, 183,
  201, 308*n*37; architect of Terauchi
  cabinet financial diplomacy, 162–64,
  310*n*69, 318*n*36; conflict with Tanaka
  Giichi, 166–74, 199, 214; negotiates
  Chinese participation in the war,
  169, 176–77, 221; plan to seize Dutch
  East Indies, 174; and Siberian Inter-
  vention, 182–83, 190, 311*n*91, 313*n*122.
  See also Nishihara loans
Nishihara loans, 161, 164–73, 244. *See
  also* Nishihara Kamezō
Nivelle, Robert, 154
Nomura Otojirō, 275*n*28, 285*n*2, 290*n*51,
  320*n*74, 320*n*81
Norman, E. H., 276*n*36, 317*n*23
North Manchuria, 71, 182–90 *passim*.
  See also Manchukuo; Manchuria;
  Manchurian Incident
Nomonhan Incident, 71, 283*n*160

Obata Yukichi, 76, 166, 214
ōdōshugi (Kingly Way), 163, 201
Ogawa Heikichi, 96, 100
Ōi Shigemoto, 188

Oka Ichinosuke, 52, 53, 72, 98, 104,
  107; accommodation with Ōkuma
  cabinet, 103–6, 149, 244; conflict
  with Tanaka Giichi, 103–4, 106,
  127, 133, 134; promotes civilian
  function of minister of war, 104–5,
  215; political effect of illness, 134,
  150, 152, 306*n*164
Oka Yoshitake, 257–58
Ōkubo Toshimichi, 280*n*122
Okuda Yoshito, 159–60
Ōkuma Shigenobu, 38, 66, 123–26,
  158, 165, 177, 267*n*27; symbol of
  "constitutional government," 23,
  31, 157; charged with destroying
  genrō enemies, 31, 36, 60, 83; conflict with *genrō*, 77, 78–80, 95, 97,
  98, 107–8, 112–13, 121–22, 127, 149,
  150–51; conflict with Seiyūkai, 98,
  99, 291*n*72; conflict with army, 137,
  191
Ōkura group, 301*n*80
Ōoka Ikuzō, 77
"open door," 86, 87, 90, 221
Opium War, 12, 86
Ōshima Ken'ichi, 99, 105, 121, 137, 149,
  185, 214
Ōtani Masao, 182
Ōura Kanetake, 98–99, 102, 113,
  295*n*137
Ōyama Ikuo, 155, 317*n*27
Ōyama Iwao, 78, 108, 143, 149, 191,
  270*n*62
Ozaki Yukio, 128, 196

Pacific War, *see* World War II
Pacific Western Painting Exhibition
  (1917), 195
Pan-Asianism, 250. *See also* "plan for
  Japanese hegemony in China"

under Nishihara Kamezō; "advocates Japanese hegemony in China" *under* Tanaka Giichi; "advocates Asian Monroe Doctrine" *under* Terauchi Masatake; "promotes 'inseparable' Sino-Japanese ties" *under* Yamagata Aritomo; "desire for Asian regional hegemony" *under* Yamagata faction

Patria (1917 U.S. film), 264n5

peasant rebellion, 14, 19

peerage, 20, 22

Perry, Matthew Gailbraith, 7, 8, 12, 16, 48, 176, 178, 179, 207

Pescadores Islands, 8, 25, 206

Philippines, 9, 16, 143

political parties: growing power of, 24–32 *passim*, 35, 59, 64, 70, 253–55; viewed as threat, 31, 64–65, 70, 253–56. *See also* Hara Takashi; Katō Takaaki

Pollard, Robert, 26, 267n25

Port Arthur (Lüshun), 39, 136, 274–75n26, 286n10

Portsmouth Peace Conference (1905), 9, 10, 27, 205, 206

Princip, Gavrilo, 33

Privy Council, 20, 41, 122, 253

Puyi (P'u-i), 171

Qingdao: Japanese siege, 39, 73, 117, 257; German surrender, 84, 93–94; calls for restoration to China, 76, 176, 231; Japanese calls for perpetual occupation of, 208. *See also* Jiaozhou; Shandong

"race war" and racial conflict, 43–44, 47, 50, 52, 54, 56, 58, 81, 162, 176, 250, 276n47

racial nondiscrimination clause, 9, 175, 206, 236, 248, 257, 315–16n3

Railways, 49, 57; Andong-Mukden Railway, 39, 274–75n26, 286n9; Shandong Railway, 39, 40, 76, 136, 208; South Manchuria Railway, 39, 56, 66, 70, 139, 140, 174, 256, 271n77, 274–75n26, 283n155, 286nn9–10, 286–87n11; Manchurian and Mongolian railways, 53, 71, 139; Jinan-Pukou Railway, 136; Changchun-Harbin Railway, 139, 150, 182, 185, 303n109; Chinese Eastern Railway, 185, 186, 187, 312n110; Korean railways, 286n10; Jiujiang-Nanchang Railway, 286n9, 288n29; Zhaozhoufu-Shantou Railway, 288n27; Jiaozhou-Jinan Railway, 285n9

Reimeikai (Dawn Society), 229

Reischauer, Edwin O., 10

republican government, Japanese rejection of, 30, 123, 178, 210, 271n76

Rex, Count, 281n130

rice riots, 200, 203, 212, 229

Roessler, Herman, 23, 269n50

Rokumeikan, 48

Roosevelt, Theodore, 9, 16, 142, 310n83

Root-Takahira agreement, 142, 265n7

Russia, 86, 87, 132, 143–44, 147, 177; Japanese proposals for a Russo-Japanese alliance, 38, 49, 52, 79–80, 120, 281–82n137, 297n14; as counterweight to American threat in China, 43, 47–48, 50, 142, 144, 145, 152; Soviet Union, 47, 56, 71, 179, 180–81, 248, 270n63; and war in Europe, 54, 84, 122; as principal raison d'être of Imperial Army, 71,

74, 202; Japanese resistance to a
Russo-Japanese alliance, 107–8, 113,
120–22, 148–49, 151; Japanese arms
aid to, 121, 145, 149. *See also* Russian
Revolution; Russo-Japanese Convention (1916); Russo-Japanese conventions (1907–12); Russo-Japanese
War

Russian Revolution, 71, 144, 179, 180,
182, 227, 251

Russo-Japanese Convention (1916), 138–
51; counterweight to American
threat in China, 47–48, 120, 144, 145,
152; and expansion of Japanese interests in Manchuria, 120, 182; substitute for Anglo-Japanese alliance, 120,
148, 305*n*154; "third country" clause,
144, 146, 147–48; counterweight to
German influence in Japan, 144–48;
as classic imperialist treaty, 178, 181

Russo-Japanese conventions (1907–12),
37, 43, 49, 52, 88, 139, 142, 152, 251

Russo-Japanese War (1904–5), and
Japanese international status, 8, 84,
205; and Japanese territorial gains, 8,
26, 32, 39, 49; as opportunity, 12, 80;
shaped military-bureaucratic cast of
Meiji Japan, 14–15, 26, 28, 51, 64, 73,
259; followed by military-
bureaucratic decline, 35, 62, 67, 82;
and Anglo-Japanese alliance, 42–43,
45, 49; and quest for unlimited
Japanese power, 43, 257; and U.S.,
142, 264*n*5; and Japanese domestic
unity, 197, 200, 203, 209, 242–43.
See also Portsmouth Peace Conference

Ryūkyūs, 11, 14

Saigō Takamori, 14, 278*n*73

Saionji, Kinmochi, 29, 60, 67, 74, 89,
123, 226, 294–95*n*136

Saitō Makoto, 74

Saitō Suejirō, 137, 163, 167, 173,
308*n*45, 318*n*34

Sakhalin Island, 8, 9, 206

Sakabe Toshio, 187

Sakurakai (Cherry Blossom Society),
255

samurai rebellions (nineteenth century), 14, 19

Sansom, George B., 266*n*22

Satō Tetsutarō, 74

Satsuma faction, *genrō* attempt to
contain, 31, 83, 112

Satsuma Rebellion (1877), 14

Sawara Tokuzō, 167

Sawayanagi Masatarō, 317*n*27

Sazonov, Sergei, 121, 144–48, 304*n*133

seikan ron, 13

Seiyūkai (Constitutional Association
of Political Friends), 24–25, 27, 57,
66, 75; and liberal reform, 30, 67,
70, 236, 271*n*77, 279*n*98; *genro* attempt to destroy, 31, 36, 83, 98; as
conservative political force, 64,
102, 217–19, 220–21, 228, 237, 253,
255; conflict with Ōkuma cabinet,
96–99, 101–3, 113; accommodation
with Yamagata faction, 97, 99,
220, 318*n*32; electoral defeat, 102–3,
220; political use of China policy,
102–3. *See also* Hara Takashi

Seki Hiroharu, 311*n*86

Seki Shizuo, 317*n*29

Sekigahara, 12

Semyonov, Grigory Mikhailovich,
186, 187

Shandong, 86, 160, 253; army operations in, 2, 76, 82, 95–96, 106, 191,

224; at the Versailles Conference, 9,
206–8, 211, 233, 235; plans for resto-
ration to China, 63, 91, 208, 231; and
Twenty-One Demands, 87–88; and
plan for civil war in China, 136, 167;
Japanese calls for perpetual occupa-
tion of, 208. *See also* Jiaozhou; Qing-
dao
Shibusawa Eiichi, 99
Shidehara Kijūrō, 120–21, 165, 296n7
Shimamura Hayao, 76
Shimazaki Tōson, 33
Shimazu, Naoko, 316n3
Shimonoseki Peace Conference (1895),
9, 205, 206
Shōda Kazue, 162, 166, 172, 197, 307n31
shōgun, 8, 11
Shōwa Emperor, 206
Shōwa Renovation, 254
Shuntian shibao, 167
Siberia, 2, 33, 57, 140, 183, 186, 187, 190.
See also Siberian Intervention
Siberian Intervention, 39, 140; as means
of confronting American challenge,
48, 202; and Cold War, 180–81,
311n86; as golden opportunity, 181–
82, 187–88, 189, 194; as continental expansion, 182–83, 185, 189, 190, 202; as
chance to buttress military-
bureaucratic power, 188, 190–95,
197–200, 202–3, 255; as justification
for increased army funding, 191, 194,
199, 255; as opportunity to repair
strained U.S.-Japanese relations, 198,
202; as act of national creation, 255–
56. *See also* Siberia
Siemens scandal, 31, 271n77
Singapore, plans to seize, 2, 195
Sino-Japanese Military Agreement
(1918), 48, 183–87

Sino-Japanese War (1894–95), 25,
26–27, 257; and Japanese international status, 8, 16–17, 25, 84, 205;
and Japanese territorial gains, 8,
25, 32, 39; as opportunity, 12, 80;
shaped military-bureaucratic cast
of Meiji Japan, 25, 64, 259; and
Japanese domestic unity, 25–26,
197, 200, 203, 209, 242–43; and
great power imperialism, 38, 40,
86. *See also* Shimonoseki Peace
Conference
Smith, Adam, 22
Social Darwinism, 15–16
Society for Planning Peace, 123
Sone Arasuke, 307n25
sonnō jōi, 12
South America, 163
South Asia, 28
South Manchuria, *see* Manchuria
South Pacific, 174. *See also* German
Micronesia
Spanish-American War, 9, 142
Stoddard, John, 25
Straight, Willard, 286–87n11
Suehiro Shigeo, 155
Sugiyama Shigemaru, 56
Sun Yatsen, 89, 169, 171, 301n85
Sungari River, 139, 150, 182, 185
Suzuki Kantarō, 75

Tachibana Koichirō, 279n100
Taft, William Howard, 9, 142
Taft-Katsura agreement, 142, 265n7
Taga Muneyuki, 170, 171, 172,
318n34
Tai-Ro dōshikai (Counter Russia
Association), 162
"Taishō democracy," 59, 119
Taishō Emperor, 29, 78, 270–71n73

Taishō political crisis, 29–30, 31, 35, 59, 64–69 *passim*, 82, 97, 98, 118, 210

Taishō Renovation, 31, 78

Taiwan, 8, 13–14, 25, 56, 57, 66, 206, 271n77

Taiwan Straits, plans to blockade, 195

Takahashi Hidenao, 312n115, 313–14n128

Takahashi Korekiyo, 220

Takahashi Yoshio, 90, 287n25, 296n152

Takei Morimasa, 272n79

Takekoshi Yosaburō, 310n76

Tanaka Giichi: as symbol of aggressive, "clandestine" China policy, 41, 54, 55, 133, 165–66, 213, 214–15, 244, 300n79, 308n41; sympathy for Germany, 45, 52, 118, 151, 274n22, 278n86; as prime minister, 51, 124, 215; contrasted with "cautious" army elders, 52–55, 158, 161, 244; devalues Anglo-Japanese alliance, 52, 216, 234, 278n85; views war as opportunity, 52–53, 54; advocates Japanese hegemony in China, 52–54, 140, 173–74, 234; advocates preemptive strike against U.S., 53–54, 81, 83, 92, 248–49, 307n26; plan to depose Yuan Shikai, 53, 54, 55, 124, 132–35, 214, 244; plan for Japanese invasion of China, 53, 182, 271n75; conflict with Terauchi Masatake, 55, 133, 165–66, 170, 201–2, 213–14, 244, 279n100; harbinger of 1930s, 68, 69, 70, 282n147; promotes political authority of army, 68–72, 104, 126, 215; decries party politics, 70, 118, 119, 191–92, 232; conflict with Katō Takaaki, 72, 97–99, 290n47; accommodation with Seiyūkai, 97, 99, 214, 218, 223, 236, 318n32; conflict with Oka Ichinosuke, 103–4, 106, 127, 133, 134; promotes army expansion, 104, 192, 213, 215; promotes resort to arms, 105, 106, 160–61, 209–10; promotes civilian function of minister of war, 105, 215, 216–17, 244; seizes foreign policy initiative, 119–20, 126–27, 128–29, 131, 135, 148, 152, 199, 201–2, 216; plot for civil war in China, 129–37, 248, 299n54; and Manchurian independence, 136, 301–2n92, 309n59; and revision of Basic Plan of National Defense, 140, 143–44, 191–92, 213; conflict with Nishihara Kamezō, 167, 169–73, 199, 214; and Sino-Japanese Military Agreement, 183–87; and Siberian Intervention, 187–89, 215–17; resistance to new world order, 208, 225, 232, 321n91

Tang Shaoyi, 171, 222, 224

Tawara Sōichirō, 259

Tazaki Suematsu, 282n147

Teranishi Hidetaka, 132, 300n79

Terauchi Masatake, 30, 42, 57, 101, 192; on threat of the U.S., 1, 4, 143, 178, 210; advocates Asian Monroe Doctrine, 55–56, 92, 249; contrasted with belligerent Tanaka, 55, 158, 161; conflict with Tanaka Giichi, 55, 133, 165–74, 199, 201–2, 244, 292n99; concern over social, political dissipation, 72–73, 196–97; advocates resort to arms, 105, 271n76, 303n111; as Yamagata faction candidate for return to military-bureaucratic rule, 114, 118, 119, 151, 152–53, 155, 178, 306n8; and Russo-Japanese Convention, 138, 140, 149–50; cabinet as "triumph of militarism," 157–58, 196;

Terauchi cabinet China policy, 158, 160–64, 168, 279n101; conflict with Yamagata Aritomo, 158–59, 193, 244; and Siberian Intervention, 182–83, 190, 311n91, 312n110, 313n127; likened to Konoe Fumimaro, 249. *See also* Nishihara loans

Tōa Dōbun Shoin, 297n27

Toby, Ronald, 11

Tōjō Hideki, 88, 239

Tokonami Takejirō, 232–33

Tokugawa Ieyasu, 11, 12, 13

Tokugawa Japan (1600–1867), 8, 10–12, 18–19, 25

Tokutomi Sohō, 318n45

Tokyo Imperial University, 20, 22

total war, 191, 248

Tōyama Shigeki, 273n6, 285n2

Transportation Bank, 163, 164, 166, 168

Treaty port imperialism, 8, 86

Tripartite Pact (1940), 47, 251

Triple Intervention, 8, 10, 206, 257

Truman, Harry S., 264n4

Twenty-One Demands, 57, 85–116, 264n5, 285–86n9; large historiographical presence, 34, 119, 164; and Japanese aggression in 1930s, 39, 85, 246, 275n28, 285n2; and Katō Takaaki, 53, 80, 87–116; political watershed, 93–107, 115; unexceptional product of nineteenth-century imperialism, 80–81, 85–92, 114, 120, 184; economic character of, 92, 246, 289n36; symbol of Katō Takaaki's conception of the national essence, 86, 246. *See also* Katō Takaaki

Uchida Ryōhei, 287n21

Uchida Yasuya, 235, 317n24

Uehara Yūsaku, 29, 67, 98, 104, 132, 215, 217

Ugaki Kazushige, 117, 193, 254–55

Ukita Kazutami, 16, 269n51, 317n27

"unequal treaties," 8, 19, 26

United States, 10, 14, 22, 47, 216, 248, 260; prospect of war with Japan, 2, 53, 54, 142–43, 155, 156, 264n5, 296–97n10; symbol of new world order, 3, 155–56, 177–79, 203, 204, 211, 235, 236, 247; ideological threat to Japan, 3–4, 23, 57, 178–79, 197, 211; military threat to Japan, 7, 71, 143–44, 155, 192–93; budding Asian empire, 9, 47, 142, 285n7; restricts Japanese immigration, 9, 175–76, 206, 248, 264n5; threat to Japanese interests in Asia, 30, 47, 48, 50, 54, 80, 81, 120, 123, 142–43, 152, 155, 163, 176–77, 189–90, 200–201, 205, 221, 223, 234, 248, 249, 251; interest in South Manchuria, 43, 88, 307n25; Japanese policy of confrontation toward, 47–48, 53–54, 81, 83, 92, 120, 144, 145, 152, 163, 197, 202, 248–49, 251, 307n26; and "open door" in China, 86, 90, 221; interest in Fujian, 87, 89, 287n20; and Twenty-One Demands, 90, 91, 264n5, 288n28; joins war against Germany, 175–79, 180, 196

universal manhood suffrage, 227, 229–30, 237, 253, 254

Upper House (House of Peers), 20, 21, 31, 253. *See also* Imperial Diet

Usui Katsumi, 287n21

Utsunomiya Tarō, 234, 271n75

Versailles Peace Conference, 9, 85–86, 175, 177, 180, 205–7, 217, 233, 236–37
Vladivostok, 187, 191, 199

Wakatsuki Reijirō, 29, 102, 113, 290n60
Wang Shizhen, 185, 186
War College, 23
Weixian, 40, 76, 136
Welch, Herbert, 233
Wilhelm I, Kaiser, 3, 22
Wilhelm II, Kaiser, 146, 304n140
Wilson, Woodrow, 3, 4, 9, 86, 221, 260; at Versailles Peace Conference, 9, 175, 206–7, 211; champion of new world order, 156, 177–78, 179, 180, 203, 209, 217, 222, 236, 247; effect in Japan of appeal to internationalism, 176–79, 198–99, 207–9, 211, 224–25, 230–34 *passim*, 252; effect in Japan of calls for democracy, 178–79, 196–99, 207, 210, 219, 226–36 *passim*, 321n89; effect in Japan of appeal to arms reductions, 209–10; effect in Asia of calls for self-determination, 230–31
World War I: twentieth century watershed, xv, xvii, 2–3, 32, 34, 179; parallels with post–Cold War era, xvi–xvii, 259–60; war in Asia, 2, 45, 75–77, 84, 199, 204; war in Europe, 2, 3, 84, 117, 122, 154–55, 200, 204; war to make world "safe for democracy," 3, 178, 210, 219; opportunity for Japan, 3, 12, 35, 39, 48, 52, 53, 56, 62, 64, 67–68, 80, 81, 82, 87, 132, 171, 184, 205, 243; economic effects of, in Japan, 3, 33, 161, 195–96, 212, 219, 236, 249, 307n27; in national memory, 3, 258;

as Japanese struggle for national identity, 4, 34, 176, 247, 252; war to punish German "militarism," 38, 178, 210; link to Japanese aggression in 1930s, 40, 247–56
World War II ("Fifteen Years' War"), xvi, 2, 206, 239, 247–56, 258, 259, 263n2

Xiang Xiling, 308n46
Xu Shichang, 171, 172, 173, 233
Xuzhou Conference, 171

Yamagata Aritomo, 23, 28–29, 30, 49, 50, 57, 75, 93–94, 270n62, 270–71n73, 276n46, 282n139, 299n62, 306–7n18; military-bureaucratic conception of the national essence, 27–28, 32, 78–80, 112, 157, 247; attempt to suppress navy, 28, 31, 74, 78, 79, 193; on closer ties with Russia, 37, 43, 251; conflict with Katō Takaaki, 37, 45, 63, 65–66, 77–79, 82, 85, 92, 95, 97–99, 100, 107–13, 118, 121, 284n194, 293n119; purported voice of caution in Japanese foreign affairs, 41, 42, 46–47, 54, 55, 107, 109, 134, 139, 188–89, 249, 279n97, 294n127, 294–95n136; political schemer, 41, 111, 276n38, 295n138. 295n143, 295n145; and Anglo-Japanese alliance, 42–43, 44–45, 49, 79–80, 116, 120, 141; disenchantment with British, 42–48, 118, 139, 141–45, 148; promotes "inseparable" Sino-Japanese ties, 43–44, 47, 80, 184–85, 250; on a "race war," 43–44, 47, 54, 250, 276n47; desires foreign policy autonomy, 45, 47–48, 189–90, 234–35; affinity for Germany, 45–46, 85, 118, 146, 246, 247, 274n22; promotes Russo-Japanese alliance, 46, 47–48, 79, 107, 112, 113, 120, 121–22, 138, 139–51; harbinger of 1930s, 47–48, 68; on threat of U.S., 47–48, 80, 142–45, 219, 234, 303n122; contrasted with Tanaka Giichi, 52–55, 244; distaste for parliamentary politics, 64–65, 112, 217–18, 269n55, 318–19n46; attempt to restore genrō power, 65–66, 78–80, 107–13, 116; and Twenty-One Demands, 90, 100, 101, 105, 109, 110, 289n45, 293n119; accommodation with Seiyūkai, 97, 99, 111, 212, 218–20, 236; conflict with Ōkuma cabinet, 103, 106, 127, 295n142; appeal for military action in China, 105, 106, 109–10, 184–85, 271n75, 294n131, 300–301n79, 312n98; includes China under Japanese security umbrella, 140, 146, 194–95, 234–35, 277n53; includes Siberia under Japanese security umbrella, 140, 146, 248; promotes "national unity" cabinet, 151, 157, 158–59, 178, 279n98, 298n40; conflict with Terauchi Masatake, 158–59, 193, 244; and Siberian Intervention, 188–90, 255; champions arms and militarism, 193–94, 198–99, 220, 235, 255; resistance to new world order, 198–99, 219–20, 227, 234–35, 236, 255. See also genrō; genrō-cabinet conferences; genrō-Ōkuma conferences; Yamagata faction

Yamagata faction, 27, 28, 30, 55, 56, 152–53, 243; bid for political supremacy, 27, 28, 31, 41, 157; on political defen-sive, 30, 82, 93, 157; recovers political authority, 119–20, 150, 181, 199, 201–2; military-bureacratic conception of the state, 32, 152–53, 157; desire for Asian regional hegemony, 155, 188, 201, 202, 247, 249, 251; exaltation of Imperial Germany, 245, 246. See also Tanaka Giichi; Terauchi Masatake; Yamagata Aritomo

Yamagata Hatsuo, 129

Yamamoto Gonnohyōe, 64; assault on army prerogative, 30–31, 67, 70, 74, 104, 271n77

Yangzi valley: Japanese interest in, 44–45, 87, 90, 141, 163; great power interest in, 86, 87, 90; and Twenty-One Demands, 88–89. See also Han-Ye-Ping Company

Yashiro Rokurō, 75, 76, 108, 113, 292n102

Yasuhiro Ban'ichirō, 321n91

Yasukawa Keiichirō, 301n80

Yasukuni Shrine, 258

Yellow Peril, 146, 276n47

Yokohama Specie Bank, 89

Yokota Sennosuke, 197

Yoshida Shōin, 16, 265–66n16, 266n19

Yoshino Sakuzō, 35, 57; and Twenty-One Demands, 91, 289n36; sympathy for Britain, 118–19; reviles proponents of militarism and authoritarian rule, 118–19, 151, 158, 235, 242–43; champion of democracy in Japan, 119, 220–21; concern over consequences of peace, 155, 176, 200–201; hails Wilson's new world order, 179, 204, 211, 225, 231, 235, 237; decries Japanese back-

wardness, 211, 225; suspicion of Tanaka Giichi, 213, 215, 218
Yoshizawa Kenkichi, 214
youth corps, 68–69
Yūaikai (Friendly Society), 230, 237
Yuan Shikai, 30; proposals for Yuan "reliance" on Japan, 44, 50, 56; and plan for Japanese invasion of China, 53, 120, 152; Japanese attempt to depose, 53–54, 120, 124, 132–35, 152, 170, 244; and Twenty-One Demands, 85, 89, 100, 123; confounds Japanese attempts at control, 102, 127–28, 136–37, 182; Japanese warning against enthronement of, 123–31, 151–52; weakness of revolutionary movements against, 124, 132; Tanaka plan to recognize enthronement of, 127, 129–31; and Japanese plans for civil war in China, 129–37, 167. See also China; Twenty-One Demands
Yunnan province, 132–33, 136

Zai Ao, 129, 298n50
Zhang Shizhao, 223
Zhang Xun, 170–73, 174, 309n59
Zhang Zongxiang, 167
Zhang Zuolin, 51, 136, 301–2n92
Zhangufeng, 283n160
Zola, Emile, 33
Zongshedang, 167, 301–2n92

Harvard East Asian Monographs
(* out-of-print)

*1. Liang Fang-chung, *The Single-Whip Method of Taxation in China*

*2. Harold C. Hinton, *The Grain Tribute System of China, 1845–1911*

3. Ellsworth C. Carlson, *The Kaiping Mines, 1877–1912*

*4. Chao Kuo-chün, *Agrarian Policies of Mainland China: A Documentary Study, 1949–1956*

*5. Edgar Snow, *Random Notes on Red China, 1936–1945*

*6. Edwin George Beal, Jr., *The Origin of Likin, 1835–1864*

7. Chao Kuo-chün, *Economic Planning and Organization in Mainland China: A Documentary Study, 1949–1957*

*8. John K. Fairbank, *Ching Documents: An Introductory Syllabus*

*9. Helen Yin and Yi-chang Yin, *Economic Statistics of Mainland China, 1949–1957*

*10. Wolfgang Franke, *The Reform and Abolition of the Traditional Chinese Examination System*

11. Albert Feuerwerker and S. Cheng, *Chinese Communist Studies of Modern Chinese History*

12. C. John Stanley, *Late Ching Finance: Hu Kuang-yung as an Innovator*

13. S. M. Meng, *The Tsungli Yamen: Its Organization and Functions*

*14. Ssu-yü Teng, *Historiography of the Taiping Rebellion*

15. Chun-Jo Liu, *Controversies in Modern Chinese Intellectual History: An Analytic Bibliography of Periodical Articles, Mainly of the May Fourth and Post–May Fourth Era*

*16. Edward J. M. Rhoads, *The Chinese Red Army, 1927–1963: An Annotated Bibliography*

17. Andrew J. Nathan, *A History of the China International Famine Relief Commission*

*18. Frank H. H. King (ed.) and Prescott Clarke, *A Research Guide to China-Coast Newspapers, 1822–1911*

19. Ellis Joffe, *Party and Army: Professionalism and Political Control in the Chinese Officer Corps, 1949–1964*

*20. Toshio G. Tsukahira, *Feudal Control in Tokugawa Japan: The Sankin Kōtai System*

21. Kwang-Ching Liu, ed., *American Missionaries in China: Papers from Harvard Seminars*

22. George Moseley, *A Sino-Soviet Cultural Frontier: The Ili Kazakh Autonomous Chou*

23. Carl F. Nathan, *Plague Prevention and Politics in Manchuria, 1910–1931*

*24. Adrian Arthur Bennett, *John Fryer: The Introduction of Western Science and Technology into Nineteenth-Century China*

25. Donald J. Friedman, *The Road from Isolation: The Campaign of the American Committee for Non-Participation in Japanese Aggression, 1938–1941*

26. Edward LeFevour, *Western Enterprise in Late Ching China: A Selective Survey of Jardine, Matheson and Company's Operations, 1842–1895*

27. Charles Neuhauser, *Third World Politics: China and the Afro-Asian People's Solidarity Organization, 1957–1967*

28. Kungtu C. Sun, assisted by Ralph W. Huenemann, *The Economic Development of Manchuria in the First Half of the Twentieth Century*

*29. Shahid Javed Burki, *A Study of Chinese Communes, 1965*

30. John Carter Vincent, *The Extraterritorial System in China: Final Phase*

31. Madeleine Chi, *China Diplomacy, 1914–1918*

*32. Clifton Jackson Phillips, *Protestant America and the Pagan World: The First Half Century of the American Board of Commissioners for Foreign Missions, 1810–1860*

33. James Pusey, *Wu Han: Attacking the Present through the Past*

34. Ying-wan Cheng, *Postal Communication in China and Its Modernization, 1860–1896*

35. Tuvia Blumenthal, *Saving in Postwar Japan*

36. Peter Frost, *The Bakumatsu Currency Crisis*

37. Stephen C. Lockwood, *Augustine Heard and Company, 1858–1862*

38. Robert R. Campbell, *James Duncan Campbell: A Memoir by His Son*

39. Jerome Alan Cohen, ed., *The Dynamics of China's Foreign Relations*

40. V. V. Vishnyakova-Akimova, *Two Years in Revolutionary China, 1925–1927*, tr. Steven L. Levine

*41. Meron Medzini, *French Policy in Japan during the Closing Years of the Tokugawa Regime*

42. Ezra Vogel, Margie Sargent, Vivienne B. Shue, Thomas Jay Mathews, and Deborah S. Davis, *The Cultural Revolution in the Provinces*

*43. Sidney A. Forsythe, *An American Missionary Community in China, 1895–1905*

*44. Benjamin I. Schwartz, ed., *Reflections on the May Fourth Movement.: A Symposium*

*45. Ching Young Choe, *The Rule of the Taewŏngun, 1864–1873: Restoration in Yi Korea*

46. W. P. J. Hall, *A Bibliographical Guide to Japanese Research on the Chinese Economy, 1958–1970*

47. Jack J. Gerson, *Horatio Nelson Lay and Sino-British Relations, 1854–1864*

48. Paul Richard Bohr, *Famine and the Missionary: Timothy Richard as Relief Administrator and Advocate of National Reform*

49. Endymion Wilkinson, *The History of Imperial China: A Research Guide*

50. Britten Dean, *China and Great Britain: The Diplomacy of Commercial Relations, 1860–1864*

51. Ellsworth C. Carlson, *The Foochow Missionaries, 1847–1880*

52. Yeh-chien Wang, *An Estimate of the Land-Tax Collection in China, 1753 and 1908*

53. Richard M. Pfeffer, *Understanding Business Contracts in China, 1949–1963*

54. Han-sheng Chuan and Richard Kraus, *Mid-Ching Rice Markets and Trade: An Essay in Price History*

55. Ranbir Vohra, *Lao She and the Chinese Revolution*

56. Liang-lin Hsiao, *China's Foreign Trade Statistics, 1864–1949*

*57. Lee-hsia Hsu Ting, *Government Control of the Press in Modern China, 1900–1949*

58. Edward W. Wagner, *The Literati Purges: Political Conflict in Early Yi Korea*

*59. Joungwon A. Kim, *Divided Korea: The Politics of Development, 1945–1972*

*60. Noriko Kamachi, John K. Fairbank, and Chūzō Ichiko, *Japanese Studies of Modern China Since 1953: A Bibliographical Guide to Historical and Social-Science Research on the Nineteenth and Twentieth Centuries, Supplementary Volume for 1953–1969*

61. Donald A. Gibbs and Yun-chen Li, *A Bibliography of Studies and Translations of Modern Chinese Literature, 1918–1942*

62. Robert H. Silin, *Leadership and Values: The Organization of Large-Scale Taiwanese Enterprises*

63. David Pong, *A Critical Guide to the Kwangtung Provincial Archives Deposited at the Public Record Office of London*

*64. Fred W. Drake, *China Charts the World: Hsu Chi-yü and His Geography of 1848*

*65. William A. Brown and Urgrunge Onon, translators and annotators, *History of the Mongolian People's Republic*

66. Edward L. Farmer, *Early Ming Government: The Evolution of Dual Capitals*

*67. Ralph C. Croizier, *Koxinga and Chinese Nationalism: History, Myth, and the Hero*

*68. William J. Tyler, tr., *The Psychological World of Natsume Sōseki*, by Doi Takeo

69. Eric Widmer, *The Russian Ecclesiastical Mission in Peking during the Eighteenth Century*

*70. Charlton M. Lewis, *Prologue to the Chinese Revolution: The Transformation of Ideas and Institutions in Hunan Province, 1891–1907*

71. Preston Torbert, *The Ching Imperial Household Department: A Study of Its Organization and Principal Functions, 1662–1796*

72. Paul A. Cohen and John E. Schrecker, eds., *Reform in Nineteenth-Century China*

73. Jon Sigurdson, *Rural Industrialism in China*

74. Kang Chao, *The Development of Cotton Textile Production in China*

75. Valentin Rabe, *The Home Base of American China Missions, 1880–1920*

*76. Sarasin Viraphol, *Tribute and Profit: Sino-Siamese Trade, 1652–1853*

77. Ch'i-ch'ing Hsiao, *The Military Establishment of the Yuan Dynasty*

78. Meishi Tsai, *Contemporary Chinese Novels and Short Stories, 1949–1974: An Annotated Bibliography*

*79. Wellington K. K. Chan, *Merchants, Mandarins and Modern Enterprise in Late Ching China*

80. Endymion Wilkinson, *Landlord and Labor in Late Imperial China: Case Studies from Shandong by Jing Su and Luo Lun*

*81. Barry Keenan, *The Dewey Experiment in China: Educational Reform and Political Power in the Early Republic*

*82. George A. Hayden, *Crime and Punishment in Medieval Chinese Drama: Three Judge Pao Plays*

*83. Sang-Chul Suh, *Growth and Structural Changes in the Korean Economy, 1910–1940*

84. J. W. Dower, *Empire and Aftermath: Yoshida Shigeru and the Japanese Experience, 1878–1954*

85. Martin Collcutt, *Five Mountains: The Rinzai Zen Monastic Institution in Medieval Japan*

86. Kwang Suk Kim and Michael Roemer, *Growth and Structural Transformation*

87. Anne O. Krueger, *The Developmental Role of the Foreign Sector and Aid*

*88. Edwin S. Mills and Byung-Nak Song, *Urbanization and Urban Problems*

 89. Sung Hwan Ban, Pal Yong Moon, and Dwight H. Perkins, *Rural Development*

*90. Noel F. McGinn, Donald R. Snodgrass, Yung Bong Kim, Shin-Bok Kim, and Quee-Young Kim, *Education and Development in Korea*

 91. Leroy P. Jones and Il SaKong, *Government, Business, and Entrepreneurship in Economic Development: The Korean Case*

 92. Edward S. Mason, Dwight H. Perkins, Kwang Suk Kim, David C. Cole, Mahn Je Kim et al., *The Economic and Social Modernization of the Republic of Korea*

 93. Robert Repetto, Tai Hwan Kwon, Son-Ung Kim, Dae Young Kim, John E. Sloboda, and Peter J. Donaldson, *Economic Development, Population Policy, and Demographic Transition in the Republic of Korea*

 94. Parks M. Coble, Jr., *The Shanghai Capitalists and the Nationalist Government, 1927–1937*

 95. Noriko Kamachi, *Reform in China: Huang Tsun-hsien and the Japanese Model*

 96. Richard Wich, *Sino-Soviet Crisis Politics: A Study of Political Change and Communication*

 97. Lillian M. Li, *China's Silk Trade: Traditional Industry in the Modern World, 1842–1937*

 98. R. David Arkush, *Fei Xiaotong and Sociology in Revolutionary China*

*99. Kenneth Alan Grossberg, *Japan's Renaissance: The Politics of the Muromachi Bakufu*

100. James Reeve Pusey, *China and Charles Darwin*

101. Hoyt Cleveland Tillman, *Utilitarian Confucianism: Chen Liang's Challenge to Chu Hsi*

102. Thomas A. Stanley, *Ōsugi Sakae, Anarchist in Taishō Japan: The Creativity of the Ego*

103. Jonathan K. Ocko, *Bureaucratic Reform in Provincial China: Ting Jih-ch'ang in Restoration Kiangsu, 1867–1870*

104. James Reed, *The Missionary Mind and American East Asia Policy, 1911–1915*

105. Neil L. Waters, *Japan's Local Pragmatists: The Transition from Bakumatsu to Meiji in the Kawasaki Region*

106. David C. Cole and Yung Chul Park, *Financial Development in Korea, 1945–1978*

107. Roy Bahl, Chuk Kyo Kim, and Chong Kee Park, *Public Finances during the Korean Modernization Process*

108. William D. Wray, *Mitsubishi and the N.Y.K, 1870–1914: Business Strategy in the Japanese Shipping Industry*

109. Ralph William Huenemann, *The Dragon and the Iron Horse: The Economics of Railroads in China, 1876–1937*

110. Benjamin A. Elman, *From Philosophy to Philology: Intellectual and Social Aspects of Change in Late Imperial China*

111. Jane Kate Leonard, *Wei Yüan and China's Rediscovery of the Maritime World*

112. Luke S. K. Kwong, *A Mosaic of the Hundred Days:. Personalities, Politics, and Ideas of 1898*

113. John E. Wills, Jr., *Embassies and Illusions: Dutch and Portuguese Envoys to K'ang-hsi, 1666–1687*

114. Joshua A. Fogel, *Politics and Sinology: The Case of Naitō Konan (1866–1934)*

*115. Jeffrey C. Kinkley, ed., *After Mao: Chinese Literature and Society, 1978–* 1981

116. C. Andrew Gerstle, *Circles of Fantasy: Convention in the Plays of Chikamatsu*

117. Andrew Gordon, *The Evolution of Labor Relations in Japan: Heavy Industry, 1853–1955*

*118. Daniel K. Gardner, *Chu Hsi and the "Ta Hsueh": Neo-Confucian Reflection on the Confucian Canon*

119. Christine Guth Kanda, *Shinzō: Hachiman Imagery and Its Development*

*120. Robert Borgen, *Sugawara no Michizane and the Early Heian Court*

121. Chang-tai Hung, *Going to the People: Chinese Intellectual and Folk Literature, 1918–1937*

*122. Michael A. Cusumano, *The Japanese Automobile Industry: Technology and Management at Nissan and Toyota*

123. Richard von Glahn, *The Country of Streams and Grottoes: Expansion, Settlement, and the Civilizing of the Sichuan Frontier in Song Times*

124. Steven D. Carter, *The Road to Komatsubara: A Classical Reading of the Renga Hyakuin*

125. Katherine F. Bruner, John K. Fairbank, and Richard T. Smith, *Entering China's Service: Robert Hart's Journals, 1854–1863*

126. Bob Tadashi Wakabayashi, *Anti-Foreignism and Western Learning in Early-Modern Japan: The "New Theses" of 1825*

127. Atsuko Hirai, *Individualism and Socialism: The Life and Thought of Kawai Eijirō (1891–1944)*

128. Ellen Widmer, *The Margins of Utopia: "Shui-hu hou-chuan" and the Literature of Ming Loyalism*

129. R. Kent Guy, *The Emperor's Four Treasuries: Scholars and the State in the Late Chien-lung Era*

130. Peter C. Perdue, *Exhausting the Earth: State and Peasant in Hunan, 1500–1850*

131. Susan Chan Egan, *A Latterday Confucian: Reminiscences of William Hung (1893–1980)*

132. James T. C. Liu, *China Turning Inward: Intellectual-Political Changes in the Early Twelfth Century*

133. Paul A. Cohen, *Between Tradition and Modernity: Wang T'ao and Reform in Late Ching China*

134. Kate Wildman Nakai, *Shogunal Politics: Arai Hakuseki and the Premises of Tokugawa Rule*

135. Parks M. Coble, *Facing Japan: Chinese Politics and Japanese Imperialism, 1931–1937*

136. Jon L. Saari, *Legacies of Childhood: Growing Up Chinese in a Time of Crisis, 1890–1920*

137. Susan Downing Videen, *Tales of Heichū*

138. Heinz Morioka and Miyoko Sasaki, *Rakugo: The Popular Narrative Art of Japan*

139. Joshua A. Fogel, *Nakae Ushikichi in China: The Mourning of Spirit*

140. Alexander Barton Woodside, *Vietnam and the Chinese Model.: A Comparative Study of Vietnamese and Chinese Government in the First Half of the Nineteenth Century*

141. George Elision, *Deus Destroyed: The Image of Christianity in Early Modern Japan*

142. William D. Wray, ed., *Managing Industrial Enterprise: Cases from Japan's Prewar Experience*

143. T'ung-tsu Ch'ü, *Local Government in China under the Ching*

144. Marie Anchordoguy, *Computers, Inc.: Japan's Challenge to IBM*

145. Barbara Molony, *Technology and Investment: The Prewar Japanese Chemical Industry*

146. Mary Elizabeth Berry, *Hideyoshi*

147. Laura E. Hein, *Fueling Growth: The Energy Revolution and Economic Policy in Postwar Japan*

148. Wen-hsin Yeh, *The Alienated Academy: Culture and Politics in Republican China, 1919–1937*

149. Dru C. Gladney, *Muslim Chinese: Ethnic Nationalism in the People's Republic*

150. Merle Goldman and Paul A. Cohen, eds., *Ideas Across Cultures: Essays on Chinese Thought in Honor of Benjamin L Schwartz*

151. James Polachek, *The Inner Opium War*

152. Gail Lee Bernstein, *Japanese Marxist: A Portrait of Kawakami Hajime, 1879–1946*

153. Lloyd E. Eastman, *The Abortive Revolution: China under Nationalist Rule, 1927–1937*

154. Mark Mason, *American Multinationals and Japan: The Political Economy of Japanese Capital Controls, 1899–1980*

155. Richard J. Smith, John K. Fairbank, and Katherine F. Bruner, *Robert Hart and China's Early Modernization: His Journals, 1863–1866*

156. George J. Tanabe, Jr., *Myōe the Dreamkeeper: Fantasy and Knowledge in Kamakura Buddhism*

157. William Wayne Farris, *Heavenly Warriors: The Evolution of Japan's Military, 500–1300*

158. Yu-ming Shaw, *An American Missionary in China: John Leighton Stuart and Chinese-American Relations*

159. James B. Palais, *Politics and Policy in Traditional Korea*

160. Douglas Reynolds, *China, 1898–1912: The Xinzheng Revolution and Japan*

161. Roger Thompson, *China's Local Councils in the Age of Constitutional Reform*

162. William Johnston, *The Modern Epidemic: History of Tuberculosis in Japan*

163. Constantine Nomikos Vaporis, *Breaking Barriers: Travel and the State in Early Modern Japan*

164. Irmela Hijiya-Kirschnereit, *Rituals of Self-Revelation: Shishōsetsu as Literary Genre and Socio-Cultural Phenomenon*

165. James C. Baxter, *The Meiji Unification through the Lens of Ishikawa Prefecture*

166. Thomas R. H. Havens, *Architects of Affluence: The Tsutsumi Family and the Seibu-Saison Enterprises in Twentieth-Century Japan*

167. Anthony Hood Chambers, *The Secret Window: Ideal Worlds in Tanizaki's Fiction*

168. Steven J. Ericson, *The Sound of the Whistle: Railroads and the State in Meiji Japan*

169. Andrew Edmund Goble, *Kenmu: Go-Daigo's Revolution*

170. Denise Potrzeba Lett, *In Pursuit of Status: The Making of South Korea's "New" Urban Middle Class*

171. Mimi Hall Yiengpruksawan, *Hiraizumi: Buddhist Art and Regional Politics in Twelfth-Century Japan*

172. Charles Shiro Inouye, *The Similitude of Blossoms: A Critical Biography of Izumi Kyōka (1873–1939), Japanese Novelist and Playwright*

173. Aviad E. Raz, *Riding the Black Ship: Japan and Tokyo Disneyland*

174. Deborah J. Milly, *Poverty of the Japanese State: Knowledge and the Pursuit of Accommodations*

175. See Heng Teow, *Japan's Cultural Policy Toward China, 1918–1931: A Comparative Perspective*

176. Michael A. Fuller, *An Introduction to Literary Chinese*

177. Frederick R. Dickinson, *War and National Reinvention: Japan in the Great War, 1914–1919*

178. John Solt, *Shredding the Tapestry of Meaning: The Poetry and Poetics of Kitasono Katue (1902–1978)*

179. Edward Pratt, *Japan's Protoindustrial Elite: The Economic Foundations of the Gōnō*

180. Atsuko Sakaki, *Recontextualizing Texts: Modern Japanese Fiction as Speech Act*

181. Soon-Won Park, *Colonial Industrialization and Labor in Korea: The Onoda Cement Factory*

182. JaHyun Kim Haboush and Martina Deuchler, *Culture and the State in Late Chosŏn Korea*

183. John W. Chaffee, *Branches of Heaven: A History of the Imperial Clan of Sung China*

184. Gi-Wook Shin and Michael Robinson, eds., *Colonial Modernity in Korea*